A LAFCADIO HEARN COMPANION

A LAFCADIO HEARN COMPANION

Robert L. Gale

GREENWOOD PRESS
Westport, Connecticut · London

Library of Congress Cataloging-in-Publication Data

Gale, Robert L., 1919–
    A Lafcadio Hearn companion / Robert L. Gale.
        p.   cm.
    Includes bibliographical references and index.
    ISBN 0–313–31737–2 (alk. paper)
    1. Hearn, Lafcadio, 1850–1904—Encyclopedias.   2. Authors, American—19th
century—Biography—Encyclopedias.   3. Americans—Japan—History—19th
century—Encyclopedias.   4. Journalists—United States—Biography—Encyclopedias.   I.
Title.
PS1917.A3G35   2002
813'.4—dc21   2001019999
    [B]

British Library Cataloguing in Publication Data is available.

Library of Congress Catalog Card Number: 2001019999
ISBN: 0–313–31737–2

First published in 2002

Greenwood Press, 88 Post Road West, Westport, CT 06881
An imprint of Greenwood Publishing Group, Inc.
www.greenwood.com

Printed in the United States of America

The paper used in this book complies with the
Permanent Paper Standard issued by the National
Information Standards Organization (Z39.48–1984).

10 9 8 7 6 5 4 3 2 1

To
Al Britton Jr., Ed Chalfant, Dick Ensor,
Alex Fanelli, Jim Robinson, and Bob Searles;
fellow Dartmouth '42 classmates, roommates,
and World War II veterans

Contents

Preface

Lafcadio Hearn is a unique figure in literary history. He was born in one country (Greece) and educated in three others (Ireland, France, and England). Thereafter he was a resident in three more countries (the United States; Martinique, French West Indies; and Japan). Everywhere he went, he absorbed aspects of the culture, with a substantial beginning in the United States (Cincinnati and New Orleans). He lived for prolonged periods, virtually as a native, in two distinct cultures, both non-English-speaking—that of the French West Indies and that of Japan. He wrote beautifully about his life—and that of residents all around him—in Martinique for two years, and in Japan for fourteen. Born on a Greek island to parents of Catholic persuasion, he died in Japan; and though a convert to neither Shintō nor Buddhism, he wrote favorably of both and was accorded Buddhist cremation and burial rites.

Hearn was also an eclectic writer of great versatility. His main genre was nonfictional prose, which took the form of essays, long and short, some of which he pieced together into books, and also assiduous newspaper columns—reportorial, polemical, and even horrific. He also wrote fiction, his forte in this genre being the long short story, more appropriately called the novella. He also freely redacted stories from several bodies of literature, as far from Anglo-American as Chinese, Finnish, and Indian; one subgenre includes his renditions of Japanese children's stories. He was also a translator and a reviewer. Most of his lectures, delivered in Japanese schools, have been published. Moreover, he was a voluminous and verbose writer of hundreds of letters to friends and to friends turned inimical. Hearn's was an irascible personality.

The man was prolific almost beyond belief. The first 12 volumes of the only American selected edition of his works, *The Writings of Lafcadio Hearn* (16 vols., 1922), total 4,696 pages; the last four volumes of the edition comprise a generous, but by no means complete, assembly of his letters. *The Writings of Lafcadio Hearn* contains perhaps 90 percent of his finest works. Many later collections of his efforts, notably newspaper work, critical essays, and special-ized letters, augment the mass. When his Japanese friends published an enor-mous, yet not complete, edition of his works (18 vols., 1926–1932), their labor of love totaled 11,622 pages. American editors, notably Albert Mordell, have gathered fugitive pieces into books. Other editors, American and Japanese, have published specialized books of Hearn's letters; many other letters, although quoted by biographers, have not been put into book form. A complete edition of Hearn's works, I venture to predict, will never be published.

A Lafcadio Hearn Companion contains separate entries on just over 450 works, long or short, by Hearn. Nevertheless this "companion" is not complete. Exigencies of space, to say nothing of editorial energy and longevity, prevent anything approaching the "definitive" in this regard. But what I present here surely represents 98 percent of the best of Lafcadio Hearn. Some pieces simply would have been too hard to track down. A few items that I did locate and include are preserved simply as trophies of an arduous hunt. An easy way to sample many early minor pieces by Hearn would be to read *Lafcadio Hearn's American Days* by Edward Larocque Tinker (New York: Dodd, Mead, 1924), which includes generous quotations from Hearn's newspaper items and his let-ters; it also reproduces as illustrations several of his most raucous editorials, some with his own cartoons. I include birth and death dates of many individuals about whom Hearn wrote. I do this for two reasons: (1) to show the surprising range of his reading and general knowledge, and (2) to show how eager he was to keep up with writers, many of whom are now obscure, and with events of his own era. (Cross-references to these individuals are indicated by asterisks.)

More important than anything said above is a consideration of who Hearn was. His father, Charles Bush Hearn,* was Anglo-Irish. His mother, Rosa An-tonia Cassimati Hearn,* was Greek. Lafcadio was born on a Greek island and was named after it. The lad was abandoned in Dublin by his father, who also abandoned his wife, married a young widow, and in due time died at sea. Hearn was given up by his mother, who was illiterate, married again, and died insane in Greece. His paternal grandmother, Elizabeth Holmes Hearn,* tried to brain-wash him in Dublin to accept her Catholic faith. His paternal great-aunt, Sarah Brenane,* took over and sent him from educational pillar to post, in France and England. Subsequently the young Hearn was blinded in one eye in a schoolyard accident. When his great-aunt lost her fortune, part of which was promised to him, he was sent with a bit of cash from London to Cincinnati. He was short at 5' 3", strong at 137 lbs., shy and shabby. It is almost miraculous that he soon developed into a competent journalist—and much more. He took professional advantage of friendships enabling him to explore Cincinnati and then New Or-leans, and to travel to and reside in the French West Indies. He was always restless. He found it easy to leave his first wife, Alethea Foley,* in Cincinnati and settle in New Orleans. Even when married to Setsu Koizumi* in Japan, he periodically longed, and tried, to get away.

Hearn's first five books—*Stray Leaves from Strange Literature* (1884), *Some*

Chinese Ghosts (1887), *Chita* (1889), *Two Years in the French West Indies* (1890), and *Youma* (1890)—established a considerable renown and made possible his trip to Japan. He expected his stay there to be short, but he remained for the rest of his life. In Japan he was teacher, husband, father, correspondent, citizen, and author of a dozen books attempting to explain Japanese culture. In that country, many aspects of which are still a mystery to most Americans, he is now revered as the first and finest author in English ever to write about his adopted land.

Hearn remains an enigma. He had great curiosity, sympathy, and passions both admirable and otherwise, and he was stylish. I believe that he will continue to be admired, and puzzled over, for five main reasons. First, he will always be cited as the "American" writer who first created a cultural "open-door" policy with respect to Japan. For American and British readers, he was the first to attempt to analyze the Japanese people—their appearance, lifestyles, customs, sundry ways—and also to depict their landscape. Second, he will always be lauded for his unparalleled skill as a journalist. Third, he will be revered by the discerning as a consummate master of English prose style—precise, limpid, painterly, bitter, impressionistic. Fourth, he will be noted for trying, valiantly but not very successfully, to combine the spiritual-evolution theories of Herbert Spencer with aspects of Shintō and Buddhist thought. Fifth, as I have said, he will be reckoned as unique in literary annals. In addition to being the master of two adopted cultures, he was a dreamer, a wild man, a nice and generous but also unstable and cruel associate, a quasi-believer in ghosts and a kind of transmigration of souls, and the husband first of a mulatto and then of a samurai's daughter. His defective vision made it painful for him to read and write; yet he evidently was an uncanny observer of nature and witness of human beauty and depravity.

Hearn was a great stylist. He would, however, have been the first to agree that careful though he was with his pen—and gorgeous, I may add, as his startling, calligraphic penmanship was—he was not perfect. In fact, he often admitted his failings. Although he could have found more errors in my writing, I have found some striking little ones in his. Here are samples to prove he, too, was human: "while journeying on foot . . . the nose is continually assailed" ("Balm of Gilead"); "not unselfish tears" ("Kimiko," in *Kokoro*); "known to daily grovel" ("Opium and Morphia"); "he was only driven to act a part in the frightful assassination through fear of his fiendish father" ("The Furnace Fiends"); "I was not less impressed by . . . than by . . ." ("The Literature of the Dead," in *Exotics*); and "It were a hopeless effort to enumerate" ("Bits of Poetry," in *Ghostly Japan*).

While preparing *A Lafcadio Hearn Companion*, I was urged to keep it to no more than 120,000 words. So I concentrated on treating the contents of the 12-volume edition of his works. (Incidentally, the set is now a collector's item and deserves to be reprinted.) Then I turned to the best of his journalism, as reprinted in *Editorials by Lafcadio Hearn*, edited by Charles Woodward Hutson* (1926), and *Period of the Gruesome . . .*, edited by Jon Christopher Hughes (1990). After that, I began to compress my treatment of the remaining items; and finally, as hinted above, to set aside the unimportant residue. Any difficulties the reader may experience in seeking coverage of specific items by Hearn should be eased by reference to the Index and also to two main although early bibliographies: that of Laura Stedman, published with George Milbry Gould,* *Concerning Lafcadio Hearn* (London: T. Fisher Unwin, 1908), and that of P. D. and Ione Perkins, *Lafcadio Hearn: A Bibliography of His Writings* (1934; reprint New York: Burt Franklin, 1968). Readers may also consult bibliographies in several recent critical and biographical studies of Hearn. The best biographical study is by Paul Murray. The finest to treat Hearn and Japan are by Carl Dawson and Elizabeth Stevenson. Arthur Kunst's is critically the most severe. Jonathan Cott's work has the most generous quotations from Hearn. It must be emphasized, however, that fascinating though Hearn continues to be, he is still a puzzling and somewhat neglected figure, especially, now, in the United States.

What I take from a year's reading devoted to Hearn is a combination of upsets and admirations. His chronic, ultimately predictable downgrading of Christianity is offputting to me. His repetitive praise of almost everything Japanese, together with his extension of his versions of Shintō and Buddhism into aspects of Herbert Spencer's writings, grows tedious. But most admirable are his dazzling prose style and his bravely unantiseptic embrace of the downtrodden and meek everywhere.

I have never been to Japan. Nor have I ever studied comparative religion. Therefore, my better-traveled and more accomplished readers will have to be tolerant of parts of this book. It has been an adventure to prepare it; my hope is that it will enlighten and inspire young and old in many ways. Incidentally, many websites are abuzz with questions and answers concerning Lafcadio Hearn, attesting to his continuing appeal.

While working on *A Companion to Lafcadio Hearn*, I have incurred many gentle debts. For kindness and encouragement, I offer grateful thanks to four colleagues at the University of Pittsburgh: Bruce Dobler, H. David Brumble III, Bruce Janoff, and David O. Mills. To my friends in Pitt's Hillman Library, including Charles E. Aston Jr., Laurie Cohen, Patricia Duff, Arif Jamal, Bentley C. Jensen, Lois Kepes, Annette M. Krupper, Wendy Mann-Eliot, Marie Mazzocco, Ann Mcleod, Vicki Redcay, Lawrence Tomikel, Thomas M. Twiss, Thomas B. Wall, and others at the reference desks and the interlibrary loan terminals, I offer my gratitude as well. And special thanks to Hearn-scholar Sylvia Verdun Metzinger, manager of the Rare Books and Special Collections Department of the Public Library of Cincinnati and Hamilton County, for her helpful suggestions. I could not have completed this work without the ever-genial, unfailing cooperation of editors Dr. George F. Butler and Betty C. Pessagno at Greenwood Press, and the exquisite skill of copyeditor Alice Vigliani. Finally, love to my wife, Maureen, and to our family—John, Jim, Christine, and Bill.

Chronology

1818   Hearn's father, Charles Bush Hearn* (1818–1866), is born.

1823   Hearn's mother, Rosa Antonia Cassimati Hearn (1823–1882), is born on Cerigo, an island off the coast of southern Greece.

1849   Charles Hearn and Rosa Cassimati marry on Leucadia, an island off the coast of western Greece; George Robert Hearn* (1849–1850), Hearn's older brother, is born there.

1850   Charles Hearn is transferred to Dominica and Grenada, British West Indies; Lafcadio Hearn (1850–1904) is born on June 27 on Leucadia.

1852   Rosa and Lafcadio go to Dublin, Ireland, to live with Elizabeth Holmes Hearn,* Charles Hearn's mother.

1853   Charles Hearn, on long sick leave in Dublin, is reunited with Rosa, who is ill, and sees Lafcadio for the first time; Rosa and Lafcadio begin living with Sarah Holmes Brenane,* Charles's mother's younger sister; Rosa suffers a nervous breakdown.

1854   Charles is assigned to Crimea; Rosa returns alone to Greece and gives birth to James Daniel Hearn* (1854–1935), Hearn's younger brother, in Cephalonia, on the way to Cerigo.

1856   Charles returns to Dublin and annuls his marriage to Rosa; Rosa marries Giovanni Cavallini in Greece (they have two sons, two daughters).

1857	Charles marries Alicia Crawford and takes her to his military assignment at Secunderabad, India (they have three daughters: Elizabeth Sarah Maude Hearn [1858–?], Minnie Charlotte Hearn Atkinson* [1859–?], Posey Gertrude Hearn [1860–?]).
1861	Alicia Hearn dies in India.
1862–1863	Lafcadio Hearn may have been sent to the Institution Ecclésiastique near Yvetot, France.
1863–1867	Hearn attends St. Cuthbert's College (Catholic seminary) at Ushaw in County Durham, England; at age 16 he is blinded in the left eye during schoolyard play with a knotted rope.
1866	Charles dies in the Gulf of Suez.
1867–1869	Hearn lives in London with Mrs. Brenane's former maid, Catherine Ronane Delaney, and her husband, a dockworker.
1869–1877	Hearn lives in poverty in Cincinnati; he writes for the *Enquirer* (1872–1875) and *Commercial* (1875–1877).
1874	Hearn illegally "marries" Alethea Foley in Cincinnati. (They separate in 1875.)
1877–1878	Hearn lives in poverty in New Orleans; he writes for the *Item* (1878–1881), *Democrat* (1880–1881), and *Times-Democrat* (1882–1887).
1879	Hearn opens a restaurant, which fails within weeks (partner disappears with all the cash).
1882	Hearn publishes his translation of *One of Cleopatra's Nights* by Théophile Gautier; Rosa dies on Corfu, an island off the coast of northern Greece.
1884	Hearn publishes *Stray Leaves from Strange Literature*.
1887	*Some Chinese Ghosts*; Hearn visits New York and West Indies.
1887–1889	Hearn lives in Martinique, French West Indies.
1889	*Chita*; Hearn lives in Philadelphia.
1890	*Two Years in the French West Indies* and *Youma*; Hearn's translation of Anatole France's *La Crime de Sylvestre Bonnard* is published; Hearn travels from New York through Canada to Japan.
1890–1891	Teaches English at Shimane Prefectural Common Middle School and Normal School, in Matsue, Japan; marries Setsu Koizumi* (they have four children: Kazuo Koizumi,* Iwao Koizumi,* Kiyoshi Koizumi,* Suzuko Koizumi*).

1891–1894	Teaches English at the Fifth Higher Middle School, Kumamoto.
1894–1895	Edits the English-language *Kobe Chronicle*, Kōbe.
1894	*Glimpses of Unfamiliar Japan*
1895	*Out of the East*
1896	Hearn is naturalized as a Japanese citizen, is adopted into the Koizumi family, and changes his name to Yakumo Koizumi; *Kokoro* is published.
1896–1903	Hearn occupies Chair of English Language and Literature, Imperial University of Tokyo.
1897	*Gleanings in Buddha-Fields*
1898	*Exotics and Retrospectives*
1899	*In Ghostly Japan*
1900	*Shadowings*
1901	*A Japanese Miscellany*
1902	*Kottō*
1903	Hearn resigns from Imperial University.
1904	Lectures at Waseda University, Tokyo; *Kwaidan*; Hearn dies of heart failure on September 26 in Okubo, Japan, and is cremated, with his ashes placed in Zoshigaya Cemetery, Tokyo; *Japan: An Attempt at Interpretation* (published posthumously).
1922	*The Writings of Lafcadio Hearn* (16 vols.)
1926–1928	*Koizumi Yakumo Zenshū* (The Complete Works of Koizumi Yakumo, 18 vols.)
1950	Hearn Centenary Celebration is held in Matsue.
1991	Semiannual *Lafcadio Hearn Journal* is founded in Cincinnati by the Lafcadio Hearn Society/U.S.A. (publication ceases in 1995).
1993	Lafcadio Hearn Society of Kumamoto is founded.
1990	Hearn Centennial Festival is held in Matsu.
2000	Lefkada Cultural Association, Island of Lefkada, Greece, marks 150th anniversary of Hearn's birth with a seminar, the featured speaker being Hearn's grandson Akio Inagaki.

Abbreviations

Bisland   Elizabeth Bisland. *The Life and Letters of Lafcadio Hearn*, 2 vols. Boston and New York: Houghton Mifflin, 1906.

Cott   Jonathan Cott. *Wandering Ghost: The Odyssey of Lafcadio Hearn*. New York: Alfred A. Knopf, 1991.

Dawson   Carl Dawson. *Lafcadio Hearn and the Vision of Japan*. Baltimore and London: Johns Hopkins University Press, 1992.

Espey   John J. Espey. "The Two Japans of Lafcadio Hearn," *Pacific Spectator* 4 (1950): 342–351.

Gould   George M. Gould. *Concerning Lafcadio Hearn* with a Bibliography by Laura Stedman London: T. Fisher Unwin, 1908.

Hirakawa   Sukehiro Hirakawa. "Rediscovering Lafcadio Hearn." In *Rediscovering Lafcadio Hearn: Japanese Legends, Life & Culture*, ed. Sukehiro Hirakawa, pp. 1–57. Folkestone, Kent, UK: Global Oriental, 1997.

Kennard   Nina H. Kennard. *Lafcadio Hearn* [1912]. Port Washington, N.Y.: Kennikat Press, 1967.

Kunst   Arthur E. Kunst. *Lafcadio Hearn*. New York: Twayne, 1969.

Miner   Earl Miner. *The Japanese Tradition in English and American Literature*. Princeton, N.J.: Princeton University Press, 1958.

Murray   Paul Murray. *A Fantastic Journey: The Life and Literature of Lafcadio Hearn*. Ann Arbor: University of Michigan Press, 1993.

Stevenson   Elizabeth Stevenson. *Lafcadio Hearn.* New York: Macmillan, 1961. Rev. ed., *The Grass Lark: A Study of Lafcadio Hearn.* New Brunswick, N.J., and London: Transaction, 1999.

Tinker   Edward Larocque Tinker. *Lafcadio Hearn's American Days.* New York: Dodd, Mead, 1924.

A

"AÏDA" (1881). Sketch. Hearn carefully summarizes the plot of Giuseppe Verdi's 1871 opera *Aïda*. Hearn stresses the seeming indifference of Osiris, the stone-eyed Egyptian god.

ALDEN, HENRY MILLS (1836–1919). Editor and author. He was born in Mount Tabor, Vermont; was a bobbin boy in a cotton mill in Hoosick, New York; studied at Ball Seminary, graduated in 1852, and earned a degree at Williams College (1853–1857). His mother wanted him to be a clergyman, so he attended Andover Theological Seminary (1857–1860). Success in placing some essays in the *Atlantic Monthly* prompted him to turn to a literary career instead of being ordained. A heart condition kept him from Civil War service. In 1861 Alden married Susan Frye Foster; they subsequently had four children. He wrote a guidebook on the Central Railroad of New Jersey, published in 1862 by Harper & Brothers. This firm made him a member of its editorial staff in 1863. He was managing editor of *Harper's Weekly* (1863–1869) and editor of *Harper's Magazine* (with variant titles, 1869–1919). He believed in the Darwinian theory of an evolutionary universe but also retained his Christian faith. He was conservative in his literary standards but, along with his friend William Dean Howells, promoted decent realistic fiction that reflected the complexities of life in the late nineteenth century. Alden wrote *God in His World: An Interpretation* (1890), *A Study of Death* (1895), and—most important—*Magazine Writing and the New Literature* (1908). He co-authored several works with Howells. Five years after his wife Susan died in 1895, Alden married Ada Foster Murray; they had no children. Alden was tactful, and hence successful, in handling important authors such as Mary E. Wilkins Freeman, Howells, Henry James, Thomas Hardy, Owen Wister, and Hearn.

In 1886 Hearn sent his manuscript of *Chita* to Alden, who accepted it, paid

$350 in 1887 for its serial version (*Harper's Monthly*, April 1888), and then published it in book form (1889). In between, Hearn went to New York City in 1887 and was encouraged by their mutual friend Henry Edward Krehbiel,* a music critic, to go and meet Alden, which Hearn did in June. Alden invited him to spend a few days at his home in Metuchen, New Jersey. The two initially hit it off well, and Hearn especially responded to Alden's daughter, Annie Alden, to whom he often wrote later. Upon his return in September 1887 from his first trip to Martinique, he sold "A Midsummer Trip to the Tropics" to Alden for $700. In December 1887, back in Martinique, Hearn sent Alden the first version of "Lys," which Alden bluntly rejected and specified why—Alden thought it lacked moral fiber. Hearn took the bad news humbly, replied apologetically, destroyed the draft, later wrote "Lys" in the quite different form in which it appears in *Two Years in the French West Indies* (1890), but later fumed at Alden. Meanwhile, in *Harper's* appeared "A Midsummer Trip to the Tropics" (July, August, September 1888), as well as four more essays (between October 1888 and July 1889) that became part of *Two Years in the French West Indies*. In 1888, from Martinique, Hearn wrote to his friend Rudolph Matas*in New Orleans to ask him to send his 2,000 or so books to Alden, presumably for the possible pleasure of Alden and his family. Agreeing, Alden asked for a document giving him the books "in extreme circumstances." This library caused trouble and expense when Hearn later wanted Alden to send it on to another friend, George Milbry Gould.*

William H. Patten, *Harper's* art director, told Hearn he should visit Japan and write about it. Hearn sent Pattern—obviously for Alden's consideration too—a letter (November 28, 1889) carefully outlining what a book by him on Japan should encompass. Alden responded with a memo specifying what he wanted, but he offered neither a contract nor an advance. Patten took a train to Montreal; conferred with Sir William Cornelius Van Horne,* president of the Canadian Pacific Railroad Company and Steamship Lines; and persuaded him to provide transportation to Japan for Hearn and Charles Dater Weldon,* a *Harper's* illustrator who was to accompany Hearn.

In January 1890, Alden took Hearn to a sumptuous dinner party at the Union League Club, given by Harper & Brothers to honor the painter Edwin Austin Abbey (1852–1911). While there, Hearn met Howells, who was delighted and helped Hearn overcome his panicky feelings at being in such glittering company. Also attending were William Merritt Chase (1849–1916), the painter; A. B. Frost (1851–1928), the illustrator and cartoonist; Frederic Remington (1861–1909), the artist and author; Francis Hopkinson Smith (1838–1915), the engineer-turned-author; and Stanford White (1853–1906), the architect later murdered by Harry K. Thaw. In February, Hearn wrote to Alden indicating that he needed money. Alden assigned Hearn some minor editorial jobs and also the task of translating Anatole France's *La Crime de Sylvestre Bonnard*, which Hearn did in two weeks for $115, counting $15 for an introduction. Alden paid Hearn

$2,000 for the 1890 serial publication of *Youma*, which Hearn had written mostly in Martinique.

Alden was happy to see that Hearn got off to Japan, but the two had no formal contract for writing to be done there. Alden was free to accept or reject whatever Hearn sent back. Ultimately Hearn sent him "A Winter Journey to Japan." Hearn learned that Alden's artist, Charles Dater Weldon, who had been sent to Japan with Hearn, was getting more money per page than he was. Long distressed at editorial changes that Alden and others made in his prose, Hearn asked Alden to send his library to Gould, fretted over (probably imagined) pay owed for earlier work, was annoyed by Alden's theological-academic rejoinders, and in an undated 1890 blast revealed his dark side: "Please to understand that your resentment had for me less than the value of a bottled fart, and your bank-account less consequence than a wooden shithouse struck by lightning." (Other parts of the letter are worse.) Alden remained calm, paid Hearn $150 for "A Winter Journey to Japan," published it (*Harper's*, November 1890), and sent him $402.06 for sales (March–September 1890) of *Chita, Two Years in the French West Indies*, and *Youma*. Their relationship then came to an end.

Bibliography: Bisland; Cott; Frank Luther Mott, *A History of American Magazines, 1885–1905* (Cambridge, Mass.: Belknap Press of Harvard University Press, 1957); Murray; Stevenson; Tinker.

"THE ALEXANDRIAN LIBRARY" (1882). Editorial. A recent detractor says "traditions" regarding the lost Alexandrian library are exaggerated. Not so, when one considers that volumes in ancient times were huge compared to modern books. In addition, the Alexandrian library had statues, mosaics, and paintings. At its peak the library contained 400,000 volumes and its so-called Daughter library contained another 300,000, all studied by some 14,000 students. What was not destroyed during Julius Caesar's siege of Alexandria and later by Theodosius, a Christian emperor, was finally finished off by Arabs under Khalif Omar.

"ALL IN WHITE" (1879). Sketch. In sepulchre-white Havana, the narrator's narrator peers through a window, sees a beautiful young woman—dead, all in white—and steps back as a thousand swarthy, glint-eyed soldiers march past him.

Bibliography: Kunst.

"AMERICAN ART TASTES" (1881). Editorial. Not long ago, Americans were puritanical with regard to nude statues and bowdlerized their translations of much foreign literature. Recently, however, American artists, especially when trained in Europe, and wealthy American art patrons are remedying matters.

Within 50 years, New York "will . . . become . . . the art center of the Western world."

AMERICAN LITERATURE, HEARN ON. While in New Orleans, Hearn wrote hundreds of editorials for the *Item* (June 1878–December 1881) and the *Times-Democrat* (December 1881–June 1887). Upwards of 50 pieces concern American authors. Though partly a product of his times, Hearn was often ahead of better-known critics. Many of his critical judgments, including those concerning neglected "minor" writers, deserve respect; and they, in turn, deserve renewed admiration. Hearn extolled the work of several New Orleans writers but deplored the puffing of mere regionalists. His reviews were springboards for personal digressions, for example, on miscegenation and Oriental literature. His critical pieces are notable for sound judgment and stylistic verve, and they reveal an astonishing range of reading.

Alice Morris Buckner, a New Orleans writer, anonymously published *Towards the Gulf: A Romance of Louisiana* (1887), a novel about miscegenation, a subject Hearn calls "difficult to manage at once delicately and chastely." Having married Alethea Foley,* a mulatto, in 1874, Hearn was attracted to Buckner's tragic novel, which he calls "the most powerful story that any Southern writer . . . has yet produced." In his review, Hearn oddly betrays prejudice when he says that the octoroon heroine's child might reveal "a taint of the blood of slaves" through some "moral rather than a physical atavism."

Hearn reviewed *Mr. Isaacs, a Tale of Modern India* (1882), a popular novel by Francis Marion Crawford (1854–1909); though disliking it, he used it as an excuse to digress on Western literature's debt to Oriental literature, which he adored.

Bret Harte (1836–1902) demonstrated early in his career, Hearn opined, evidence of admirable imagination and spirited romanticism; but Hearn foresaw Harte's decline earlier than his editors and public did.

Hearn regarded George Washington Cable*as the best southern novelist. He also recognized the merits of John Pendleton Kennedy (1795–1870) and William Gilmore Simms (1806–1870) but deplored their having been first popularized in the North, the publishing center he hated.

The style of Ralph Waldo Emerson (1803–1882) was needlessly obscure, in Hearn's view. But he found congenial several aspects of the sage's philosophy, namely, his Transcendental concepts of the union of one's being, the oversoul, and the divine.

Charles Étienne Arthur Gayarré (1805–1895), a New Orleans man of letters, understandably delighted Hearn, who admired the panoramic narratives, vivid descriptive talent, analytical ability, and use of primary documents in his *History of Louisiana* (4 vols., 1851–1866).

Hearn regarded William Dean Howells (1837–1920) as crampingly motivated by neo-Puritanism; therefore, his philosophy Hearn deemed puerile, his moral intentions those of a Sunday-school teacher, and his characters vapid. Hearn unfairly charged Howells with "suppressing in his own work all emotion, all enthusiasm, all veritably natural feeling," but he astutely predicted that "a true realism . . . will be revealed in the literature of the future."

As for Henry James (1843–1916), Hearn briefly noted that he "is as talented a writer of realistic fiction as the English century has produced." In a letter to the U.S. Navy man Mitchell McDonald (April 1898), Hearn said, "James is too fine and delicate a writer—a psychological analogist of the most complex society—ever to become popular."

Hearn greatly admired the poetry of Henry Wadsworth Longfellow (1807–1882). He praised Longfellow's descriptions of nature, his use of symbolism, and his redaction of European and especially Oriental literary material.

Hearn inordinately extolled *Norodam, King of Cambodia: A Romance of the East* (1882), an Oriental novel by New Orleans judge Frank McGloin (1846–1921).

Alfred Mercier (1816–1894), New Orleans physician, wrote a historical romance titled *L'Habitation Saint Ybars* (1881), which attracted Hearn's attention. It dramatizes antebellum Creole life, Civil War devastation, and the suicide of miscegenated lovers. Because of Hearn's marriage to Alethea Foley, Hearn was sensitive to depictions of sexual relations of whites and mulattoes.

When Joaquin Miller (1841?–1913) was ridiculed and lampooned, Hearn tried to defend him as a unique primitive, more formless than thoughtless, and, possibly, America's finest poet.

John Lothrop Motley (1814–1877) struck Hearn as a graphic narrative historian, and one who vivified costumes, manners, and combat actions with brilliant painterly enthusiasm.

Hearn never espoused the theory that Sir Francis Bacon had written William Shakspeare's plays. But when William D. O'Connor (1832–1889) defended the notion in his *Hamlet's Notebook* (1886), Hearn, who corresponded with O'Connor, generously called his speculations "no[t] . . . unreasonable" but confined himself to displaying his own extensive knowledge of the controversy.

When the body of John Howard Payne (1791–1852), author of "Home, Sweet Home" (1823), was brought from Tunis to Washington, D.C., in 1883 for reburial, Hearn used the occasion to summarize Payne's troubled career.

Hearn praised Elizabeth Stuart Phelps (1844–1911) for her efforts in two novels—*The Silent Partner* (1871) and *Dr. Zay* (1882)—to bring "light out of the darkness of the woman-suffrage question." In truth, however, Hearn's sarcastic remarks indicate neither very much understanding of nor any great sympathy for the "question."

Adrien Emmanuel Rouquette* was a New Orleans friend whose novel *La nouvelle Atala* (1879) Hearn admired.

In Hearn's sound opinion, Bayard Taylor (1825–1878) would have been a more significant writer if he had refused his numerous journalistic assignments.

Hearn called Taylor's *Lars: A Pastoral of Norway* (1873) "probably . . . his greatest poem."

Life on the Mississippi (1883) by Mark Twain (1835–1910) combined, according to Hearn, material of "large historical value" and "reminiscences of the old-time river life" in ways only a genius could manage.

The subject of *Parrhasius; or, Thriftless Ambition* (1879), a dramatic poem by Espy Williams (1852–1908) of New Orleans, intrigued Hearn. In it, a Greek artist tortures a slave so as to paint his agony realistically. Hearn mainly showed off his erudition by pointing out errors in a work he nevertheless said has "real poetical strength."

Walt Whitman (1819–1892) was mostly anathema to Hearn, who, though frank himself found Whitman's poetry vulgar, coarse, and "lubricous." Whitman's "I Sing the Body Electric" (1860) "alternately" suggested "a dissecting room and a butcher's shop" to Hearn—oddly, too, because in other newspaper columns Hearn reveled in describing not only dissections but also slaughterhouse gore. Over the years, Hearn modified his opinions concerning Whitman, and wrote both William D. O'Connor (August 1883) and George Milbry Gould* (August 1888) to that effect.

In John Greenleaf Whittier (1807–1892), Hearn found a "gift of melody," a "rhythmic flow," the purity and strength of which "seems to mellow with years like good wine," and "a . . . chord of tenderness." Given his respect for insects, Hearn unduly praised Whittier's unimportant "King Solomon and the Ants" (1878).

Bibliography: Bisland; Lafcadio Hearn, *Essays on American Literature*, ed. Sanki Ichikawa, with introduction by Albert Mordell (Tokyo: Hokuseido Press, 1929); Tinker.

"AMERICAN MAGAZINES" (1879). Editorial. Walt Whitman rightly said that "old fogies like [Josiah Gilbert] Holland [1819–1881] or fops like [William Dean] Howells [1837–1920]" control American magazines, which are also too few in number and too restricted as to contents. The *Atlantic Monthly* used to be fine. *Harper's Magazine* is popular because it is "largely instructive and historical" rather than "purely literary." If such magazines paid less for contributions, they would encourage innovation and not institutionalize a clique of established conservatives.

"AMONG THE SPIRITS" (1874). Cincinnati news article. Hearn, "the reporter," writes about attending a seance and describes details—tying the medium, whose name is Mary, to her chair, nailing her dress to the floor, locking the room door, sitting with others, and watching a tin trumpet move. He felt fingers and hands on his thigh, knee, and foot. Suddenly the medium announced that a spirit wanted to speak with him. In a hoarse whisper, a voice identifying itself as that of his father, Charles Bush H, and calling him P asked for forgiveness of a wrong. Hearn denied any need to do so. The seance, lasting two hours, was suddenly interrupted. Hearn does not believe that anyone in this country could have known such details and reports only that the person who spoke to him lived much of his life in Hindustan and was buried in 1866 in the Mediterranean Sea. *See* Hearn, Charles Bush.

Bibliography: Murray.

"L'AMOUR APRÈS LA MORT" (1884). Sketch. The dead man was made too anguished by the memory of an unnamed beloved to be able to rest even in his tomb. Through a crevice he jealously sees, hears, and smells life outside. Years later, "*She*" chances to walk near his "nameless" tomb. He recognizes "the whisper of her raiment," but she perceives nothing and moves on forever. "L'Amour après la Mort" is a less effective revision of Hearn's 1880 "A Dead Love." *See* Bisland, Elizabeth.

Bibliography: Cott; Kunst.

"APHRODITE AND THE KING'S PRISONER" (1880). Sketch. On a black marble pedestal in the king's beautiful palace stands a statue of Aphrodite, voluptuously nude before the time of "the Christian anachronism of shame." The king will die for love if he once looks at this matchless Pygmalion. A solitary prisoner, struck by her beauty, pours sacrificial dove blood at her feet, bloodies his lips by kissing her, wets her feet with tears, but remains frustrated by her merciless gaze. One night he stabs himself to death before her, but she remains motionless. The king, still averting his gaze, orders the statue broken up; but no servants raise their hands against this ever-smiling "Medusa of beauty." Almost unacceptably erotic when this sketch was published, its enticing prose seems pale in today's freer glare.

APPEARANCE, HEARN'S. At age 16 Hearn was blinded in the left eye at St. Cuthbert's College at Ushaw, near Durham, England, when the knotted end of a rope hit him during a schoolyard game. Surgery failed to help, and his right eye gradually protruded. He became sensitive about his appearance, hid his left eye with his hand when with others, often stood or sat facing away from viewers, and avoided having photographs taken showing his left side. Friends, however, remarked on his animated looks and his fine right-side profile. When mature, he had straight dark hair and olive skin. He was 5' 3" in height and weighed 137 lbs. He fancied that his appearance rendered him physically unattractive, especially to women. He was graceful and light in his movements. Under normal circumstances, he spoke fluently and easily. His voice was soft, musical, usually gentle, and often almost inaudible, and it retained a touch of an Irish brogue. When amused, he usually chuckled but on occasion could bellow like a madman. His manners struck many as eccentric. Compactly built, with a big chest and broad shoulders, he prided himself on his superb swimming ability, especially in deep water. He dressed inexpensively and indifferently; but he was usually clean and neat, and his movements had a feline appearance. His private rooms have been described as plain and neat, like a soldier's. In Japan, Hearn appeared prematurely aged, often haggard and wan.

Bibliography: Bisland; Cott; Kennard; Murray; Stevenson; Tinker.

"ARABIAN WOMEN" (1911). Arabesque. Aesthetic awareness is found in early Oriental literature and architecture, especially that of Arabians—from desert poems to Saracen buildings. The subjects of ante-Islamic verse include animals, hunting, war—and beautiful women. Poems about them are "supple, ardent as the desert itself and as sun-colored." Similes are rife: hair like trelliswork, bow-like brows, arrowy gaze, ostrich-egg complexion, elegant palm-like stature, mare-like flank. Anatomical features are precisely named; degrees of beauty and mere prettiness are ranked. Women of different tribes have separate unique features, including foot, waist, mouth. Caliphs had harem beauties properly called God's masterpieces. Men, seeing such, "died of love." Hearn quotes upwards of a dozen passages of coolly erotic verse written in various Arabian epochs. Sadly, extravagant voluptuousness results in "national enervation," and worse. In his conclusion, Hearn has it both ways. He laments the moral loss of those who succumb to sexual temptation, and he sympathizes with those who resist.

"ARCHAEOLOGY IN CAMBODIA" (1885). Editorial. Early Chinese and Portuguese explorers visited Cambodia, but a French naturalist discovered Angkor-Vat (Angkor Wat) in 1861 and spurred further analysis. Features of the colossal structures are Brahmanic as well as Buddhistic. Hearn names a half dozen scientists but specifically praises the 1880s work of Étienne François Aymonier (1844–1929) and Henri Mouhot (1826–1861?).

"L'ARLÉSIENNE" (1885). Editorial. To satisfy the possible curiosity of American theatergoers, Hearn offers the history of the composition of *L'Arlésienne*. Its plot comes from a story in *Lettres de mon Moulin* (1869) by Alphonse Daudet (1840–1897), who turned it into a lyrical drama, for which Georges Bizet (1838–1875) provided incidental music. Delicate and passionate, it plays "variations upon quaint Provençal themes." However, opening night in Paris, 1875, was a failure because the audience was still in mourning after the recent Franco-Prussian War. Not until 1885 was the work staged again, this time triumphantly. But Daudet, in the audience, mourned the dead Bizet.

ARNOLD, SIR EDWIN (1832–1904). Poet and journalist. Born in Gravesend, England, Arnold was educated at King's School, Rochester, King's College, London, and University College, Oxford (B.A., 1854; M.A., 1856). In 1853 he published his first book of poetry. In 1856 he became the principal of Deccan College, Poona, India, and soon was a Bombay University fellow. He studied Sanskrit, Indian, Persian, and Turkish languages. In England again in 1861, Arnold wrote for the *Daily Telegraph* and later was one of its chief editors (1873–1888). In 1879 he published *The Light of Asia; or, The Great Renunciation*, a phenomenally popular epic poem in blank verse, presenting Buddhist doctrines and legends. The sequel, *The Light of the World* (1891), about Christianity, was written at Queen Victoria's request and was a dismal failure. Knighted in 1888, Arnold became his paper's traveling commissioner and went to East Asia, notably Japan, which he praised in travel essays assembled in *Japonica* (1892). He admired its culture and the conservatism of Japanese women but was apprehensive about its commercial and military advances. He published a melodrama titled *Adzuma: or the Japanese Wife* (1893). In failing health by 1895, he published *Tenth Muse and Other Poems* . . . , which included his renderings of much Japanese verse. He expected, without avail, to become poet laurate of England following Alfred, Lord Tennyson's death in 1892. Married three times, Arnold was survived by his third wife, Tama Kurokawa of Sendai, Japan.

From New Orleans in 1883, Hearn wrote to William Douglas O'Connor, his casual friend and Walt Whitman's late-life sponsor, to praise *The Light of Asia*, saying "[i]t perfumed my mind as with the incense of a strangely new and beautiful worship." He continued: "Buddhism in some esoteric form may prove the religion of the future." In another letter to O'Connor (March 1884) he suggested that Edwin Arnold is "far the nobler man and writer" than (unrelated) Matthew Arnold. From New Orleans, Hearn wrote to his friend Henry Edward Krehbiel* (January 1885) that he was "cheeky" enough to consider writing Arnold for comments, quotable in nature, praising his *Stray Leaves from Strange Literature* (1884), because much of it derived from Oriental works. Evidently Arnold was kind and helpful to Hearn, who dedicated *Kottō* to "Sir Edwin Arnold in grateful remembrance of kind words."

Bibliography: Bisland; Dawson; Miner.

"ARTISTIC VALUE OF MYOPIA" (1887). Editorial. The statement by Philip Gilbert Hamerton (1834–1894), author of *Landscape* (1885), that good eyesight hinders those who are inspired by nature's sublimity may startle some, but it is true. Perceiving details in massive mountains, forests, and swamps spoils the effect. The keensighted pick out leaves in deep woods, whereas "the myope" finds the total scene more suggestive. Andrew Lang (1844–1912) poetized that to the nearsighted most girls are pretty, whereas Charles Baudelaire (1821–1867) opined that the best painters work in hazy environments. Still, the nearsighted have troubles in the practical world.

"AS IF PAINTED BY LIGHTNING" (1881). Editorial. Instantaneous photography captures evanescent moments of rapidly moving animals, circular saws, dancers, and skaters. Imagine such pictures of athletes and, "more fantastic," a prisoner half-guillotined. Fancy depicting the quickly changing facial expressions of children, opera audiences, and criminals. Note Hearn's leaning toward the gruesome.

"THE ASIATIC HORIZON" (1878). Editorial. The proposal of Aleksandr Mikhailovich Gortchakoff (1798–1883) that European nations should not make "the science of modern warfare" available to "the Asiatics" is dangerous and will fail. History shows that every "secret" weapon soon falls into the hands of enemies. Hearn mentions China but not Japan.

"ASSASSINATION" (1874). Cincinnati news article. In gory detail, Hearn reports the murder of a "colored girl" (on Monday, December 28, 1874). She staggered to her fiancé's front door and bled to death, her throat horribly cut. The young man and his mother were arrested, as were not only a white woman living with them but also three other men. In this confusing, incomplete report, Hearn names 14 persons in all, including Joe Brooks, who was "supposed to be the real murderer." *See* "The Monday Night Murder."

"AT THE CEMETERY" (1880). Sketch. In a cemetery, beyond wealthy people's lavish tombs is a tiny flower garden beside a nameless slab. The imprint in its sand of a child's hand inspires the narrator to imagine that the dead person is a sailor remembered by his loving little daughter. The softness of this piece is strengthened by some nice scannable prose, including:

> But when the sea gave up its dead,
> [T]hey bore him to his native city,
> [A]nd laid him in this humble grave . . .

Hearn also brilliantly likens the thick-piled, numbered shelves of the walled dead to "those documents which none may destroy but which few care to read— the Archives of our Necropolis."

ATKINSON, MINNIE CHARLOTTE HEARN (1859–?). Hearn's half-sister. She was born in Secunderabad, India, the daughter of Charles Bush Hearn* and Alicia Goslin Crawford Hearn. Minnie's older sister was Elizabeth Sarah Maude Hearn; her younger sister was Posey Gertrude Hearn. Minnie married Buckby

Atkinson, a lawyer in Portadown, Northern Ireland. They had a son, Carleton Atkinson, and two daughters, Marjory Atkinson and Dorothy Atkinson. Dorothy married Dr. John Holmes; they had three children, including a daughter named Ethne Holmes. She married Basil Hearn (no relation); they had two children, including a daughter named Claudia. She married and became Claudia Wilcox. When Lafcadio Hearn lived in Japan, he and his half-sister Minnie corresponded for a while, beginning in 1892. Tenderly solicitous, he inquired about her children, Carleton and Dorothy. But in 1896, with no explanation, the envelopes of Minnie Atkinson's letters, with their contents removed, were returned to her. Setsu Koizumi,* Hearn's Japanese wife, may have intercepted the letters, returned their envelopes, and by this act of devious diplomacy signaled a desire for the correspondence to cease. In 1909, five years after Hearn's death, Minnie, her daughter, and their friend Nina H. Kennard, Hearn's biographer-to-be, visited Japan. Minnie's successful aim was to interview Setsu, to gain additional knowledge concerning Hearn's personality. She also wanted to do what she could to further the education of Hearn's oldest son, Kazuo Koizumi,* as she had promised Hearn. In this, she was unsuccessful.

Bibliography: Kennard; Murray.

"ATTENTION! AZIM!" (1880). Essay. Azim asks the New Orleans *Item* editor for a gombo recipe. Hearn lists ingredients for *gombo févi* and *gombo filé*, then laments the disappearance of Creole lore concerning both cooking and herbal medicine. A book on both would be welcome. Some secret cures are "heirlooms" from Africa via San Domingo and Martinique. *See La Cuisine Créole.*

B

"BAKAWALI" (1884). Tale. Tajúl-Mulk, a Hindustani rajah's girlishly hand-some son, falls in love with the gloriously beautiful Bakawali, who forgets that she is immortal, abandons her home with Indra in his immortal city of Amar-anagar, and returns Tajúl-Mulk's love. Indra turns "wroth." Commanded to his presence, Bakawali smells of mortal love and is purified by fire but emerges from her white ashes more willowy and beautiful than ever. She returns nightly to love Tajúl-Mulk; when he is asleep again, she is charioted back to Indra and burned again. One night Tajúl-Mulk clings to the chariot, sees the beauties of divine Amaranagar, returns, and later tells Bakawali. Their love will be ruined with Indra's forgiveness. They appear before Indra, and she dances uniquely well before him. Charmed, he promises her anything. She asks only to live with Tajúl-Mulk until he dies. Frowning, Indra must agree but adds that from the waist down Bakawali will be marble for twelve years. For 11 years Bakawali sits mute in a pagoda while Tajúl-Mulk ministers devotedly to her. Peculiar ruination falls upon the land. A fair-limbed tree emerges from the dust, grows, and bears blossoms and rosy fruit. After the twelfth year, one fruit splits open and out comes lovely, immortal Bakawali for her faithful lover.

BAKER, PAGE M. (1840–1910). Journalist. He was born in Pensacola, Flor-ida; was a talented traveling salesman for a New Orleans commercial house; served in the Confederate Army; and in 1868 became a reporter on the New Orleans *Picayune*. For the next decade he edited the *Herald* and then the *Bulletin* and worked for the Louisiana White League, which in 1874 replaced the ap-pointed government with an elected one. In 1879 Baker became a reporter for the New Orleans *Democrat*, and a year later he was named its editor-in-chief and manager. In 1881 it became the *Times-Democrat*, which Baker managed. It evolved into a progressive paper with literary supplements, telegraphic service to Latin America, Spanish supplements, and interstate news.

Hearn began to write for Baker and the *Times-Democrat* in 1881, at $30 a week. In 1880 Hearn had published some translations of French writers in the *Democrat*. Baker tried valiantly to understand Hearn's peculiar personality, appreciated his splendid writing, ordered his unique style never to be copyedited, saw his pieces improve the circulation of the paper, and encouraged him professionally and socially. Hearn admired and respected Baker's wife, Marion Baker. Page Baker also introduced Hearn to his sister-in-law, Jane Wetherall, who liked his writings but regarded him as a depressing companion. Sunday supplements carried Hearn's eclectic translations under "The Foreign Press"; they included bits, sometimes dangerously racy, from Alphonse Daudet, Guy de Maupassant, and Pierre Loti. Baker recommended to J. R. Osgood, the Boston publisher, the manuscript of what became Hearn's *Stray Leaves from Strange Literature* (1884), which Hearn gratefully dedicated to Baker. In 1883 William D. O'Connor, man of letters and Walt Whitman's friend, wrote to Baker praising an anonymously published essay on Gustave Doré. Baker handed the letter to Hearn, the author, thus starting a fruitful correspondence between the two. In 1884 Baker ordered Hearn to take a vacation and persuaded him to try Grand Isle, off the Louisiana coast. Hearn wrote back long descriptive letters about the delightful island. In 1887 Hearn quit his formal relationship with the *Times-Democrat*. A little later, Baker tactlessly showed Elizabeth Bisland,* their mutual friend, a letter from Hearn to him critical of her; the two men had an argument that ended only when Hearn suddenly wrote him a sweet letter from Japan in 1891. In 1892 and 1894 Baker, still editing the *Times-Democrat*, generously published some pieces about Japan by Hearn and even managed to syndicate them widely. When Hearn was uncertain of employment in Japan in 1896, Baker, who had sent him some money, offered him a job, which did not materialize. After Hearn's death, Baker defined his mercurial friend as a genius, extraordinary but impossible to get along with.

Bibliography: Cott; Murray; Stevenson; Tinker.

"BALM OF GILEAD" (1875). Cincinnati news article. Hearn, "the writer," visits a factory manufacturing various products by boiling dead animals. The place emits stinking smells, "like a violated cemetery in a plague-smitten city." Ironically, it is located near the Gilead railroad station outside Cincinnati. Herds of hogs penned nearby are fed on garbage and offal, and then they are slaughtered for human consumption. Dead horses, cattle, hogs, goats, dogs, and cats are boiled to make soap; their bones, blood, and hair are processed for fertilizer. Hearn observes sausage casings made out of hog and cattle intestines, is nonplussed by the nonchalance of workers having lunch near "putrifying entrails," and is shown samples of products including grease, lard, oil, soap, and tallow.

Bibliography: Cott.

"THE BIRD AND THE GIRL" (1881). Sketch. Hearing a mockingbird calling its mate, a fetching, dark-eyed Creole girl named Hortense presents her mouth for a kiss from a gentleman from the West, where, he tells her, men cage singing birds. He says he wishes she were a mockingbird to be taken away with him tomorrow. After they kiss, he departs for the mine fields of the West. She writes him perfumed letters delivered by an amiable U.S. mail-courier to "Cap." Then the letters cease. On the night of August 24 Cap and some friends hear the heart-rending melody of a mockingbird. Weeks later, a letter comes to Cap announcing Hortense's sudden death on August 24 and requesting his immediate return home.

"THE BIRD WIFE" (1884). Tale. Far in the North is a land the gods forgot to finish, where ice walls have faces, dogs howl at the moon, and there is a fountain of fire. And frightening, dangerous monsters, including the Iliseetsut. They are warlocks and wizards, living amid scattered bones, which they shove, together with sea creatures' hearts and brains, into a whale skin. The result is a frightful creation they call the Tupilek. One day a brave ivory hunter sees a flock of birds, well known as shapeshifters; he catches one and holds on as it turns into a slender girl. Her eyes, dark and soft, weep. He takes her into his snow hut, clothes her in furs, feeds her a fish heart, and makes her his loving wife. They have two children. Hunting together, they kill some birds. She gathers feathers and puts them on her children's arms and shoulders, and on hers. Calling them all birds, she flies with them in spirals far over the weeping hunter. Hearn's practice in *Stray Leaves from Strange Literature*, of which this legend is a part, was to combine disparate elements.

BISLAND, ELIZABETH (1861–1929). Journalist, author, and editor. She was born in Camp Bisland, Fairfax Plantation, Teche County, Louisiana. Her family lost its property in the Civil War. While a teenager, she supported herself and her family by writing under the pen name B.L.R. Dane. She admired Hearn's "A Dead Love," published in the New Orleans *Item* (1880); so when he moved in 1881 to the New Orleans *Times-Democrat*, edited by Page M. Baker,* she submitted some poems to it. Partly because he admired her verse, it was published; they met in 1882, and she began to write about women's activities for the *Times-Democrat* "Bric-a-Brac" column. Slow, even fearful, to respond to her beauty and energy, Hearn at first regarded Bisland as dangerously cunning and unfeeling, though attractive and gifted. But early in their friendship, when she had yellow fever, he hung around her hotel and saw to it that she was fed and nursed back to health. In 1884 the two vacationed on Grand Isle at the same time. He kept his distance but drew sketches of her while she was on the beach or swimming.

Bisland became literary editor of the *Times-Democrat* but in 1887 moved to New York City to work on newspapers and periodicals there. Once she was away, Hearn confided in her in numerous letters, at first from New Orleans, later elsewhere. When he resided briefly in New York in 1889 he occasionally visited her rooms at 475 Fourth Avenue and was captivated by her beauty, ability, and bewitching personality. Through Bisland, Hearn met two new friends: Ellwood Hendrick,* who regarded her as the most beautiful woman he had ever seen, and Alice Wellington Rollins,* a well-traveled writer. In an 1889 letter to their mutual friend George Milbry Gould,* Hearn described Bisland as fiercely energetic and her influence on him like hasheesh. Her pro-feminist stance is indicated by her short story "The Coming Subjugation of Man" (*Bedford's Magazine*, October 1889). In it, a scientist, using a powerful microphone, learns the language of bees (Hearn loved bees) and is told that female bees have evolved in such as way as to dominate male bees. Drones know this but can't help their plight. The narrator recognizes that the same fate may befall humankind.

When Bisland was literary editor of *Cosmopolitan Magazine*, she gained notoriety by competing in a trip around the world with Nellie Bly, who was financed by the *New York World*. Bly's 72 days beat Bisland's 76 days, both ending in January 1890.

Hearn missed bidding Bisland farewell in New York when he departed for Japan because she was already on her way around the world. He closed a tender farewell letter by calling her "my dear, sweet, ghostly sister" (March 7–8, 1890). She had given him a letter of introduction to Mitchell McDonald, a U.S. Navy man in Japan whom she had met there and who became one of Hearn's closest friends. She disliked his short story "Karma," both in draft and in print (1890), because in it a man demeans himself before a woman. She did accept two of his essays on the West Indies for *Cosmopolitan* (1890).

Bisland went to Europe and dispatched popular letters from London and Paris to *Cosmopolitan*. She published *A Flying Trip around the World: An Account of a Trip Performed in 76 Days* (1891). She married Charles W. Wetmore, a successful businessman, in October 1891; they resided in Washington, D.C. She wrote a novel titled *A Widower Indeed* (with Rhoda Broughton, 1892). Hearn feared that her marriage would end their friendship. In 1897 he thought of dedicating *Exotics and Retrospectives* to her but did not, out of fear she might find some of its contents shocking. She began writing him again around 1900, and a delightful correspondence ensued. In one letter, addressed to Mrs. Wetmore from Tokyo in 1900, he told her he had a picture of her on a wall of his home. He dedicated *A Japanese Miscellany* (1901) to her.

In 1902 he wrote to her asking whether she could find a lectureship for him in the United States because he wanted his oldest son, Kazuo Koizumi,* to study in America. She asked around and was responsible for his aborted appointment to lecture at Cornell University. He was thrilled at the possibility of seeing her again, but never did. Their attempts through 1903 to secure lecturing engagements for him in other American universities also fell through.

Bisland wrote *The Secret Life* (1907), among other works. She also wrote and edited *The Life and Letters of Lafcadio Hearn* (2 vols., 1906), which she unprofessionally sanitized; the substantial royalties she donated to Hearn's widow, Setsu Koizumi, * and their children. Bisland also published *The Japanese Letters of Lafcadio Hearn* (1910). Squabbles involving Gould and Nina H. Kennard, two correspondents of Hearn and also his future biographers, caused Bisland difficulties in composing these volumes. Later, she and McDonald helped finance Kazuo's education at Waseda University in Tokyo. After McDonald died in the 1923 earthquake in Tokyo, Hearn's family asked Bisland to handle matters involving his publishers. To Hearn, Bisland was alternately "Bessie," "Queen Elizabeth," and "Queen of the Fairies." Bisland's biography of Hearn and her editions of his letters were reprinted as volumes 13, 14, 15, and 16 in *The Writings of Lafcadio Hearn* (16 vols., 1922).

Bibliography: Everett F. Bleiler, *Science Fiction: The Early Years . . .* (Kent, Ohio: Kent State University Press, 1990); Cott; Kennard; Mary S. Logan, *The Part Taken by Women in American History* [1912] (New York: Arno Press, 1972); Murray; Ishbel Ross, *Ladies of the Press: The Story of Women in Journalism by an Insider* (New York and London: Harper & Brothers, 1936); Stevenson; Tinker.

"THE BLACK CUPID" (1880). Sketch. The narrator is fascinated by a painting in his room. It is of a voluptuous young woman—with bare shoulder, bosom partly revealed, beautiful arm, and an earring showing a black Cupid suspending himself by his bow. Does he "preside . . . over unlawful loves"? The woman palpitates, glistens, leans forward to be kissed. In the morning the narrator's landlord explains that the artist, now dead, painted the picture in a madhouse. Five years later in Mexico City, the narrator sees an identical pair of black-Cupid earrings. The shopkeeper says an artist ordered them for a lady named Josefita, whom he killed out of jealousy. The shopkeeper bought them back and will sell them cheap.

"BLACK VARIETIES" (1876). Cincinnati news article. Hearn attends a minstrel show with some other white people, led in by policemen. The moonlit theater has a ballroom, bar, and modest stage. Three-fourths of the audience are white girls—some good, some evil—and dark-skinned ones, of various physiques; their lovers and husbands are roustabouts and stevedores. The show begins with music from six talented performers, five of whom have "negro features." It continues with minstrel jokes, including patter about spelling "blind pig" thus: "pg," leaving out the eye. The conclusion includes a comical scene acted by two men, one dressed as a woman. Much drinking follows, until everyone rushes out to see a steamboat arrive. "Black Varieties" is notable for Hearn's captivating descriptions of the black women's hair, colorful dresses, complexions, arms, hands, and jewelry.

"THE BLUES" (1872). Cincinnati news article. Winter is coming. The cold will cause suffering among the rich as well as the poor. It will also bring disease and other miseries.

"THE BOARDER'S REPLY" (1879). Sketch. A visiting salesman rents a room, is disturbed by the noisy pets of a Creole woman, pays in advance, and loans her piastres and even "two dollaire." The furniture is seized by the owner of the house. Another Creole servant cleans inefficiently and welcomes "strange mens of color" into his room. The salesman rents elsewhere, always unsatisfactorily. He gives an advance to a Frenchwoman of "de face beautiful" who then dies of "mort subite." "Not again do I . . . in advance to pay." This sketch follows "Complaint of Creole Boarding-House-Keeper."

"THE BOOK OF THOTH" (1884). Tale. According to the Egyptian author Thoth, whoever recites the first part of his book will be omnipotent; whoever recites the second, immortal. The magician Noferkephtah finds and uses the book, but his wife, Ahouri, and their son die and when restored are changed, and he lives on although buried with them at Coptos. Generations later, Prince Satni, son of Pharaoh Ousirmari, hears about the book, goes to Coptos, and wrests it from Noferkephtah, who grows menacing. Satni sees beautiful, sensual Thoutboui, demands her love, and is calmly invited to her lavish home. First, she demands his goods. He agrees. Then the execution of his children. Done. Drunk with lust, he asks for a kiss. When she opens her mouth, it is a city of death into which he falls unconscious. Awakening, he is told by Ousirmari that it was all a spell cast by the buried Noferkephtah, to whom Satni returns the book. He agrees to bury Noferkephtah's wife and son with Noferkephtah, and does so at a place now unknown.

"BOUTIMAR, THE DOVE" (1884). Tale. Out of a perfumed cloud, mighty Solomon is offered a cup containing a drink according eternal youth and life. Free to accept or reject it, he asks the advice of genii, peris, wise men, beasts, and birds. Though encouraged to drink, he asks whether anyone under his dominion is absent who might advise. Yes, Boutimar, the wild, uniquely loving dove. When fetched and learning that the drink is for him alone, she asks whether he would want immortality in a world of death and decay. Solomon declines the cup but then weeps diamond-like tears into the gold dust sprinkled in his beard.

"THE BRAHMAN AND HIS BRAHMANI" (1884). Tale. His farseeing Deva follows the Brahman who abandons his family to go with his beloved Brahmani, poisonous to all though she has been. When she dies in the forest, a voice offers him her life again for half of his own. He agrees, she revives, and they proceed.

While the Brahman is off seeking fruits and water for her, an attractive youth appears and persuades her to love him. The three travel together. When the Brahman falls asleep, the Brahmani pushes him into a well, carries the weak youth to a king's city, and introduces him as her husband. Meanwhile, his Deva saves the Brahman; but when he rushes to the king, his Brahmani denies him. The Brahman persuades the king to demand that she return to him what he gave her. It is her life, which she thus loses and falls dead. The moral: Men should not put faith in women.

BRENANE, SARAH HOLMES (1792–1871). Hearn's great-aunt. She was the younger sister of Elizabeth Holmes Hearn,* who was the mother of Hearn's father, Charles Bush Hearn.* Sarah abandoned the Hearn family's Anglican faith in 1823 when she converted to Roman Catholicism and married Captain Justin Brenane, a wealthy Catholic landowner in County Wexford. Widowed in 1846, the childless Mrs. Brenane leased her land and lived with Elizabeth Hearn and her son Richard Hearn,* a painter, in Dublin. In 1849 she moved to a house in Donnybrook, south of Dublin center. In 1851 she moved to Rathmines, a Dublin suburb. In 1854 she accepted the responsibility of welcoming into her home Lafcadio Hearn and his mother, Rosa Antonia Cassimati Hearn.* Elizabeth Hearn had tried to make room for the pair in the home of her daughter, Jane Hearn Stevens, married to a Dublin solicitor named Henry Cloclough Stevens. That arrangement had been difficult from the start. Mrs. Brenane was set in her ways but tried to do her best, according to her beliefs. She used to enjoy rides in her four-wheeled carriage with Rosa and Lafcadio, who called her "Auntie" and whom she called "the Child." She promised Rosa to make Lafcadio one of her heirs. When Rosa returned to Greece in 1854, Lafcadio remained in Dublin with the redoubtable Mrs. Brenane.

In 1856 Charles Hearn revisited Dublin after a tour of duty in the Crimea, annulled his marriage to Rosa, and relinquished Lafcadio to Sarah Brenane's permanent care in her home in Rathmines. Charles's love affair with the wid-owed Alicia Goslin Crawford caused Mrs. Brenane to denounce and disinherit him and take Rosa's side in the matter. In 1857 Charles married Alicia, left for military service in India in 1857, and took her and her two young daughters along. He visited Dublin briefly in 1862, saw Mrs. Brenane again but not Laf-cadio, soon returned to India, and died abroad in 1866.

Mrs. Brenane tried to help Lafcadio Hearn but often in unsuccessful ways. She housed, fed, and dressed him opulently, and sent him to good schools; but when he expressed fear of the dark, she locked him in a dark room for long periods in an effort to cure him. They vacationed, with servants, in the coastal town of Tramore, near Waterford, where Hearn developed his lifelong love of the sea. He went with "Kate" (probably Catherine Ronane, later Mrs. Delaney), the family maid, to Bangor, Wales, and she entertained him with fairy tales. He disliked being schooled in Roman Catholicism by a live-in tutor, but he delighted in Mrs. Brenane's library, where he read for hours. Her hopes that he would become a priest grew dim, especially when she discovered he had located certain books concerning Greek mythology and illustrated with depictions of partially nude figures. The books disappeared briefly, and when he had access to them again he discovered that illustrations of breasts and private parts had been cut out or inked out.

Mrs. Brenane had a distant relative named Henry Hearn Molyneux (1840–1906), a bright, polylingual, commercially educated Roman Catholic. She turned to him in her final years for advice. Molyneux not only got himself financed by Mrs. Brenane in a London business importing goods from the Orient but also suggested that she send Lafcadio, by then rebellious against religious training, to the Institution Ecclésiastique in Yvetot, near Rouen, France. He was probably there in 1862 and 1863. He disliked the school but developed a superb knowledge of French there—and, perhaps, briefly as well at a boarding school in Normandy. By 1863 Mrs. Brenane was living in Redhill, Surrey, England, in the home of Molyneux and his wife, Agnes. Molyneux advised Mrs. Brenane to send Lafcadio to St. Cuthbert's College, a Catholic seminary at Ushaw, about three miles west of Durham City, England. He was a rebellious student there beginning in September 1863. Some of his summers during this period he did not spend at Redhill. By now Molyneux had begun to control Mrs. Brenane, her money, and her emotions. She signed over to one of Agnes Molyneux's relatives a County Wexford estate formerly reserved for Lafcadio. In 1865 she started legal proceedings to force Charles Hearn to repay her for unpaid loans. He died in 1866, during which year Molyneux bungled his way into bankruptcy, Mrs. Brenane's lands were forfeited, and she suffered both impoverishment and mental deterioration. At age 16 Lafcadio was blinded in his left eye during a game with ropes in the playground at Ushaw. Medical treatment, though careful, was of no help. Molyneux, his wife, and Mrs. Brenane, now feeble, moved to Tramore, withdrew Hearn from St. Cuthbert's in October 1867, and sent him to London to live with Catherine Delaney, now long married to a dockworker. Molyneux supplied money now and then for Lafcadio's food. Hearn later reminisced bitterly that Molyneux persuaded Mrs. Brenane to cut him out of an annuity that was probably in the amount of £500. After much misery in London, in 1869 Hearn received a small sum of money from Molyneux, a one-way boat ticket to New York City, and advice to go to Cincinnati and seek out Frances Anne Molyneux Cullinan, Molyneux's sister, and her husband, Thomas Cullinan, for a start in the New World. Hearn left in the spring of 1869, never to see any part of Europe again. In the spring of 1871 Molyneux wrote to Hearn that Mrs. Brenane had died on January 13 of that year.

Bibliography: Louis Allen, "Lafcadio Hearn and Ushaw College," in Hirakawa, pp. 130–157; Cott; Murray; Stevenson.

"THE BURNING OF THE DEAD" (1884). Editorial. Cremation is gaining favor as "superstitions" against it diminish, population everywhere increases, and with it comes more death—until "the earth is overfed with corpses until she can no longer digest them." Cremation is quick, and the vapors thereof are "pure and luminous elements," whereas decomposition is horrible, which exhumation proves. Even Parsee vultures are better. Best is fire. Slow burning was terrible, but modern retorts are swift. Perhaps instantaneous electrical combustion may be invented one day.

C

CABLE, GEORGE WASHINGTON (1844–1925). Author. Cable was born in New Orleans. In 1859 he quit school, worked as a warehouse and then a grocery clerk, and supported his widowed mother and his sisters. He was a Confederate cavalryman, wounded twice, during part of the Civil War (1863–1865). He worked intermittently for cotton merchants (1869–1881) and as a journalist (from 1869). He published sketches in the New Orleans *Picayune* and also the first local-color short stories to feature life in the antebellum South; he assembled a collection titled *Old Creole Days* (1879). *The Grandissimes: A Story of Creole Life* (1880; rev., 1883) powerfully dramatizes slavery and voodooism, animosities toward mixed-bloods, and a feud involving aristocratic families in the early nineteenth century. This novel, together with *The Creoles of Louisiana* (1884, illustrated by Joseph Pennell), was so controversial that Cable moved to Connecticut (1884) and then to Massachusetts (1885) to avoid being socially ostracized in the South. He and his friend Mark Twain went on a 20-week lecture tour together (1884). Cable's essays espousing the cause of African Americans continued to make him unpopular with conservative Southerners. *The Negro Question* (1890) collects six such pieces. Cable's book *John March, Southerner* (1894) concerns Reconstruction problems; *Strange True Stories of Louisiana* (1899) is based on old diaries, letters, and legal documents; *The Cavalier* (1901) was a popular Civil War historical novel. Of Cable's voluminous writings, only *Old Creole Days, The Grandissimes*, and *The Negro Question* are of enduring value.

Cable was married three times. He and Louise Stewart Bartlett had eight children, and Louise died in 1904. He married Eva Colgate Stevenson in 1906. In 1923, after Eva died, he married Hanna Cowing.

Hearn read "Jean-ah Poquelin" (*Scribner's Magazine*, May 1875), Cable's fine short story. Its treatment of the Creole-American conflict, use of Creole dialect, and Gothic elements appealed to Hearn. So when he arrived in New

Orleans he called upon Cable, and the two became friends. Cable entertained Hearn at his home. An amateur musician, Cable notated the melodies of African-Creole street songs while Hearn jotted down the words. Hearn praised *The Grandissimes* (*Item*, September 27, 1880; and elsewhere). He called *Dr. Sevier* a "fine artistic work" and especially admired the "picturesque exquisiteness" he found in it (*Times-Democrat*, October 5, 1884). Cable helped Hearn get published in the *Century* and *Harper's Weekly*, whose editors he knew. Hearn discontinued his friendly relationship with Adrien Emmanuel Rouquette,* a local priest, after Rouquette blasted Cable in *Critical Dialogue between Aboo and Caboo on a New Book; or, A Grandissime Ascension* (1880) by calling him a "witling . . . High-Priest of Negro-Voudouism" and falsely hinting that he had sired half-breed children. In "The Scenes of Cable's Romances" (*Century*, November 1883), Hearn carefully discusses local landmarks featured by Cable. At an 1883 dinner in Cable's home for Pennell, Cable happened to discuss hurricanes that often hit the Louisiana coasts and nearby islands. One such storm in 1856 destroyed virtually everything on Île Dernière (Last Island). A little girl, however, was saved by a fisherman who took her home to his wife. Years later she was returned to Creole life in New Orleans; never happy there, she subsequently went back to her beloved coastal region. Hearn was inspired by this poignant tale to write *Chita: A Memory of Last Island* (1889).

After Cable returned from touring with Twain, Hearn began to feel slighted, while Cable in turn suspected Hearn of rudeness. Cable's puritanical Presbyterianism grated on Hearn's dislike of any formal religion. Moreover, he was jealous of Cable's earlier work on Creole songs. Hearn shared a Creole song in an 1885 letter to the music critic Henry Edward Krehbiel* but asked him not to reveal it to Cable. However, Cable had worked with Krehbiel since 1878 and published "Creole Slave Songs" (*Century*, April 1886) with Krehbiel's help and with illustrations by E. W. Kemble, who was famous for his earlier illustrations of Twain's *Adventures of Huckleberry Finn* (1884). The story of the later estrangement of Hearn and Cable is one of the saddest in American literary annals. It exemplifies Hearn's lifelong inability to retain the friendship of good people.

Bibliography: Bisland; John Cleman, *George Washington Cable Revisited* (New York: Twayne Publishers, 1996); Cott; Stevenson; Tinker; Arlin Turner, *George W. Cable: A Biography* (Durham, N.C.: Duke University Press, 1956).

"CANADA VS BERNHARDT" (1880). Editorial. Ministers in puritanical churches in Canada have warned "their sheep" not to patronize the allegedly sinful actress Sarah Bernhardt (1844–1923). They seemingly cannot separate the woman from her theatrical performances, much appreciated in England. Being critical of a book as immoral will only increase its financial success elsewhere, the same being true for Sarah.

"CENTENNIAL SUICIDES" (1877). Cincinnati news article. Suicide is a phenomenon of civilization, not of savage times. The act is usually courageous, not cowardly. Causes include fear of old age, bad luck, remorse, despair, jealousy, and desire for notoriety. Something is wrong in the families of children who kill themselves. Would-be lovers who are deserted or seduced "suicide" themselves. Some are insane, at least temporarily.

Many seek attention by means of self-destruction. Idle, dissipated, frustrated, and wearily rich people commit suicide, as do the poverty-stricken and unemployed. Those with vicious or worthless spouses do too. Many philosophical types—pessimist, doubter, stoic, social critic—kill themselves. Bad weather can start self-killing epidemics. The tendency toward suicide is sometimes inherited.

Hearn's title derives from two suicides on July 4, 1876. But Hearn, while concentrating on the year 1876, describes suicides that range over many centuries, cites literary sources, names no fewer than 22 suicides, and provides gruesome details of many. Most noteworthy were the man who hanged, drowned, poisoned, burned, shot, bled, and knifed himself; and the man who fashioned, and used, his own guillotine. Hearn also delights in ornate phrasings. Self-killers "go to their long home," "make way with" themselves, "hurr[y] . . . up to enter the golden gate," do "the fatal deed." He concludes with several columns of statistics.

"THE CENTURY'S CRIME" (1874). Cincinnati news article. Hearn describes how a pregnant woman and a physician, both from Indiana, took separate rooms in a hotel. The doctor performed an abortion but aroused an undertaker's suspicions when he asked him to handle "a miscarriage." The coroner and the police were alerted and discovered incriminating correspondence, causing the arrest of all concerned, including the woman's lover.

CHAMBERLAIN, BASIL HALL (1850–1935). Educator and linguist. He was born in Portsmouth, England. His maternal grandfather, a captain in the British navy, went to Korea early in the nineteenth century; his father was a vice admiral in the navy. After living in France and then working in a bank, Chamberlain was advised to travel. He went to Australia, Shanghai, and finally Japan, where he lived for many years, beginning in 1873. While teaching English and mathematics, he mastered both the Japanese language and Japanese calligraphy, translated the *Kojiki* (i.e., *Records of Ancient Matters*) in 1882, and was professor of Japanese and philology at the Imperial University of Tokyo (1886–1890). He lectured on linguistics, introduced principles of comparative grammar and philology, and advanced the study of Japanese morphology through romanizing without the usual restrictions of native syllabary. He joined the Asiatic Society in 1874, became its president (1891–1894), and read 27 papers before it. He published books on the Japanese language, Japanese poetry, Japanese folklore, and travel in Japan. By far his most popular work was *Japanese Things: Being Notes on Various Subjects Connected with Japan* (1890), which went, as *Things Japanese . . .*, through five later editions, often revised (1891, 1898, 1902, 1905,

1939). In the early seventeenth century a Jesuit priest named João Rodriguez (1558–1633, also called Juan Rodrigues) was in Japan, studied Japanese, romanized it, and wrote two books on Japanese grammar: *Arte da Lingoa de Iapam* (Nagasaki, 1604–1608) and *Arte Breue da Lingoa Iapoa* (Macao, 1620). Thus Rodriguez preceded Chamberlain, who has been wrongly credited for too much pioneering linguistic work, as he himself implicitly acknowledged in two pieces he published in 1889 in *Transactions of the Asiatic Society of Japan.*

When Hearn went to Japan in 1890, he took with him a letter of introduction to Chamberlain. It had been provided by William H. Patten, an associate of Henry Mills Alden* of Harper & Brothers. Hearn had read publications by Chamberlain, who in turn had read and admired Hearn's *Some Chinese Ghosts* (1887). Chamberlain helped Hearn obtain teaching positions at secondary schools in Matsue (1890–1891) and then in Kumamoto (1891–1894). Hearn contributed a few acknowledged pages to the second and third editions of Chamberlain's *Things Japanese* (1891, 1898). No wonder Hearn wrote to Ellwood Hendrick* that "I made one delightful friend here, Professor Chamberlain" (February 1893). Four months later Hearn confided in Hendrick that he and Chamberlain were secretly planning to co-author a book on Japanese folklore, but nothing came of this alleged project.

By November 1890 Hearn felt comfortable enough with Chamberlain to write to him critically about his entry on Japanese music in his *Things Japanese*, for which Chamberlain was preparing the second edition. Notwithstanding Hearn's love of such music, Chamberlain retained Hearn's adverse comments on "the strummings and squealings of Orientals" and how they "exasperate beyond endurance the European breast." Hearn's extensive correspondence with Chamberlain, beginning early in 1890, quickly concerned Japanese words, spellings, and etymologies; religious beliefs, legends, folklore, superstitions, and shrines; travels and landscapes, food, drink, music, dances, and the courtesy of his Japanese associates; and many curious, quirky observations. Chamberlain visited Hearn and his wife, Setsu Koizumi,* at their home in Kumamoto (April 1893). When Chamberlain read Hearn's "Of the Eternal Feminine" (*Atlantic Monthly,* December 1893; *Out of the East*), he praised it as of unique value. In July 1894 Hearn stayed briefly at the Tokyo residence of Chamberlain, who was away on vacation but made him feel welcome, not least by telling him to use his valuable library in any way he wished. On his way home, Hearn met Chamberlain for a stay in a luxurious hotel in Miyannoshita.

Hearn's letters to and discussions with Chamberlain make it obvious that he was assiduously studying Japan, its geography, and its people and, further, that many thoughts expressed in his letters to Chamberlain went directly, sometimes verbatim, into his 1894 *Glimpses of Unfamiliar Japan*. While composing it, he wrote to Chamberlain about problems he was having. When he had read it, Chamberlain praised both its detailed accuracy and its charming style.

When the two began to disagree on politics, Chamberlain being a pro-British imperialist and Hearn the strident reverse, Hearn's letters to Chamberlain began to contain more comments on literature and also more autobiographical data—concerning his background, growing restlessness, and unshakable melancholy. One letter (March 1895) hints at friction between the two men, Hearn's temper having been aroused by Chamberlain's daring to correct Hearn's literary style. In another letter, dated April 1895 and containing well over 2,000 words, Hearn writes extensively about Herbert Spencer, evolution, and heredity in ways that must have tried Chamberlain's patience. Hearn defended Chamberlain when an oblique attack on *Things Japanese* appeared in the *Atlantic Monthly* (June 1895). Although the critic was anonymous, Hearn was convinced that Ernest Francisco Fenollosa,* the learned Japanologist both men knew, was the culprit and therefore blasted him in a letter to Horace Scudder, the *Atlantic* editor. In December 1895 Chamberlain helped get Hearn appointed professor of English language and literature at the Imperial University of Tokyo (1896–1903). Inexplicably, once settled in Tokyo, Hearn broke off his friendship with Chamberlain. They did not correspond again; nor, evidently, did they speak to each other again, although they were both then living in Tokyo and teaching at the same university.

After Hearn's death his wife, Setsu, and Kazuo Koizumi,* their oldest son, visited Chamberlain amiably. Chamberlain wrote a beautiful tribute to Hearn, dated December 1910 and published in a Japanese translation (*Kokoro no hana*, November 1911). Chamberlain left Japan in 1911 and made Geneva, Switzerland, his residence. For his posthumously published sixth edition of *Things Japanese* (1939), Chamberlain ignored his former delight in Hearn's writings about Japan and attempted to discredit him for being a romantic nomad, having imperfect eyesight, romanticizing old Japan, and dreamily preferring it to new Japan. Perhaps Chamberlain was influenced by the conduct of his younger brother, Houston Stewart Chamberlain (1855–1927). Houston Chamberlain preferred Germany to England; wrote and published extensively in German, including a biography of Richard Wagner (1896); in 1907 settled in Bayreuth and for a second wife married Eva Wagner, the only daughter of Richard Wagner. His *Die Grundlagen des neunzehnten Jahrhunderts* (2 vols., 1911; translated as *Foundations of the Nineteenth Century*) advocated pro-Aryan, anti-Semitic racism and influenced German nationalistic thought leading to the Nazi movement. In 1916, during World War I, he became a German citizen and expressed anti-British propaganda. Basil Hall Chamberlain may well have transferred part of his hatred of his brother to Hearn because of Hearn's many anti-British, anti-Christian pronouncements.

Bibliography: Bisland; Richard Bowring, "An Amused Guest in All: Basil Hall Chamberlain (1850–1935)," in *Britain and Japan 1859–1991*, eds. Sir Hugh Cortazzi and Gordon Daniels (London: Routledge, 1991), pp. 128–136; Basil Hall Chamberlain, "Rodriguez' System of Transliteration," *Transactions of the Asiatic Society of Japan* 16 (1889): 10–16, and review of Ernest Satow, *The Jesuit Mission Press in Japan 1591–1610, Transactions of the Asiatic Society of Japan* 17 (1889): 91–100; Cott; Dawson; Hirakawa; *Letters from Basil Hall Chamberlain to Lafcadio Hearn* and *More Letters from Basil Hall Chamberlain to Lafcadio Hearn*, compiled by Kazuo Koizumi (Tokyo: Hokuseido Press, 1936, 1937); Miner; Earl Miner, "Hearn and Japan: An Attempt at Interpretation," in Hirakawa, pp. 58–71; J. F. Moran, "Chamberlain, Rodrigues, and the Morphology of Japanese," *Japan Forum* 7 (Autumn 1995): 317–326; Murray; Paul Murray, "Lafcadio Hearn, 1850–1904," in *Britain & Japan: Biographical Portraits*, vol. 2, ed. Ian Nish (Richmond, Surrey: Japan Library, 1997), pp. 137–150; Yuzo Ota, *Basil Hall Chamberlain: Portrait of a Japanologist* (Richmond, Surrey: Japan Library, 1998); George A. Sioris, "Introduction," *Early Japanology: Aston, Satow, Chamberlain . . .* (Westport, Conn.: Greenwood Press, 1998); Stevenson.

"THE CHARNEL-HOUSE" (1874). Cincinnati news article. The coroner, "with a degree of nonchalance which would put a ghoul to the blush," exhumes a drowned man's corpse at the widow's request and puts his gloved hand past "writhing swarms of white vermin" for an identifying dental examination—then goes home to "a hearty dinner."

"CHEAP FRENCH LITERATURE" (1863). Editorial. We may well judge a society's opinions by the way romance writers present them. British novelists have depicted British aristocrats favorably. Contemporary French authors, however, picture French nobility mostly as "villains or idiots . . . whose least crime is conjugal infidelity." Characters in the works of Alphonse Daudet (1840–1897) and Edmond Goncourt (1822–1896) are exceptions, but those of the French Naturalists are "odious." French readers relish all of this because they hate their own titled folk.

"LES CHIFFONIERS" (1874). Cincinnati news article. Hearn learns about country and city cotton rags, hard wool rags, and soft wool rags and about scrap metal, glass, and bones. He goes to the city dumps, passes several scavengers scurrying "with a noiseless swiftness that seemed goblin-like," and offers to talk to a vulture-like woman who supports two sons. She brushes him off. He interviews a businessman who collects material from 40 or so dump-pickers. He generalizes that most of them are old, crippled, rheumatic, and average 20 to 50 cents a day, and then he offers specific vital statistics on several, including their names, genders, ages, and other details.

Bibliography: Cott.

"CHINESE BELIEF IN GOD" (1884). Editorial. The recent lecture in France by the Marquis d'Hervey-Saint-Denys on Chinese religion dispels the erroneous belief that the Chinese are both superstitious and atheistic. Saint-Denys says that Confucius was a reformer, not the founder of a new religion, and that the Chinese believe in One God, and the immortality of the soul, and not in Buddhistic Nirvana. Hearn quotes extensively from Saint-Denys's translations of the Chinese classics *Chi-King* and *Chou-King*. Marie Jean Léon, Marquis d'Hervey-Saint-Denys (1823–1892), wrote numerous books on China.

CHINESE GHOSTS. *See Some Chinese Ghosts.*

CHITA **(1889).** (Full title: *Chita: A Memory of Last Island.*) Novel, in three parts. "The Legend of L'Île Dernière." The narrator describes a steamboat trip from New Orleans through bayous and lakes, past fishermen's villages into the Gulf of Mexico. As he and his fellow passengers go beyond Grande Isle, with its massive hotel, and other islands, he observes the unending struggle as "the Mississippi strives to build; forever the sea struggles to destroy." They pass Last Island, swept naked by a terrible hurricane in 1856. The narrator hears the tragic story from an old pilot as the two sit on a cypress beached on Grande Isle, while the sea moans as though in a ghostly "rage against the living." A summer day here is matchlessly beautiful, as sky meets sea. But beware of swimming too far out, for fear of the clutch of swirling, nightmarish sea abysmally below. Nature is an "incomprehensible Sphinx." August 1856: Masses of happy hotel guests on Last Island are unaware as a sighing wind raises surges and billows attract breezes. For a week, both winds and waters have been heightening. On the 9th "the sea was one wild agony of foam," and the wind turns weird and pivots, blowing from the south. The steamer *Star*, captained by Abraham Smith, bravely approaches despite the wind's "paroxysmal power." Smith cannot believe his ears when he hears tatters of dance music from the hotel on the evening of the 10th. The nearly four hundred guests seem to hold back half-felt uneasiness by courteous, forced gayety. Handsome, well-schooled young men respond to the witchery of graceful girls. Smith, his several anchors tearing loose, grimly says that the wind is waltzing with the sea. Water suddenly crawls across the dance floor. In a flash, fierce tornado winds and raging waves smash every thing and every body into the sea. Smith ties a rope to himself, saves 40 lives, and is dragged back aboard unconscious. Dawn breaks, "spectral . . . [and] wan." After the "enormous vortex of wreck and vast wan drift of corpses," the dead, washed ashore for a hundred miles, are a feast for vultures. Sicilian, Corsican, Malay, Lascar, and other human vultures forage for toys, clothing, and jewelry from the dead, until the relief boat whistles and steams close.

"Out of the Sea's Strength." Marshy elevations of soil near the Gulf shore resemble little islands. On one are Feliu Viosca and his wife, Carmen. After their daughter, Conchita, died in Barcelona, they left their native Spain. Now a successful fisherman, Feliu founded a little settlement and has luggers and sloops and workers, including Miguel and Mateo. Feliu is enjoying a hard-earned sleep when Carmen awakens him with news of a rising sea on that fatal August 10th. He grumbles; when they sleep some more, she dreams that her image of the Virgin Mary hands her a child. Can it replace Conchita? Next morning, fierce rain and a flooding sea. A dead cow floats by. Mateo lassoes it. Keen-eyed Feliu sees a dead woman floating on a billiard table and clutching a yellow-haired child. He bravely swims out and saves the girl but must let the table and its corpse drift away. Carmen tenderly warms and holds the little girl and revives her. Feliu murmurs, weeps a little. Carmen says the Virgin sent the child, who is now perhaps an orphan. Ten days later the authorities arrive, having buried what they could find and having tried and executed many corpse robbers. Captain Harris, in charge, gets several of his men to try to question the timid, comely little girl. Only Laroussel, who speaks French—and also recently killed someone—can draw from her that she is named Lili, that she is also called by the Creole name Zouzoune, and that her parents are—or were—Julien and Adèle. The child, age 4, sobs when the men leave. Elsewhere other searchers find a drowned woman whose wedding ring has the names Adèle and Julien engraved on it. Returned to New Orleans, she is identified and buried as Adèle La Brierre, the wife of Dr. Julien Raymond La Brierre and the mother of Eulalie, all drowned off "L'Île Dernière, le 10 Août, CCCCLVI." But six months later Julien turns up alive and is aghast to read his family epitaph and—worse—to be ostracized by fellow citizens for returning to life and thus foiling their sorrow. Relatives have even been bickering over his estate. Distraught and thinking of suicide, he "struggles between courage and despair, . . . weakness and force, . . . darkness and light." He reviews his past—home, childhood, university life in Paris, falling in love back home, a duel with a rival named Laroussel who wounded but then spared him, loss of both parents, marriage to that "sweet woman" who gave him Zouzoune. Gradually Julien recovers and regains a sober love of life.

"The Shadow of the Tide." The little girl, now called Conchita Viosca, nicknamed Chita, lives at Viosca Point. Carmen loves her ecstatically and modifies her French prayers with Spanish ones, while Feliu guards, protects, and teaches her to swim. Chita becomes graceful and tall, displaying "hereditary refinement of habit and of mind." One day, against Carmen's orders, she wanders to the weed- and grass-hidden stony tomb of an old Spanish fisherman. Through an aperture she sees his eyeless, grinning skull. Chita rushes home and grows feverish but is comforted when Carmen reassures her that her mother is not like that, is instead now with the "loving God . . . above the clouds." At times, the child seems to see her mother bending over her, smiling, caressing her. Chita gains much by living far from "dusty . . . cities" with their social restrictions and dreary schools. She responds profoundly to "the unveiled magnificence of Nature's moods." Meanwhile, back in New Orleans, it is the summer of 1867. Dr. Julien La Brierre, widowed at age 28 in 1856, now treats malaria cases unselfishly and tirelessly. He served in the Confederate Army for four years in that disastrous war. Laroussel, a cavalryman, by chance met up with him before Chancellorsville, told him of a little Creole girl saved at Last Island, and then was killed in battle. Suddenly, late one August night, Julien is summoned by an Italian boatman named Sparicio, who was paid $100 to fetch the doctor to sail with him to Last Island and treat Julien's grievously sick old friend, Henry

Edwards, who had gone there to rest and was staying with Carmen and Feliu. With great difficulty Julien makes the long sea trip. Gioachino Sparicio and his assistant, Carmelo, pole their vessel, then sail briskly. Sparicio cooks macaroni and fish, he and Carmelo sing beautifully together, and Julien can occasionally relax and rest. But when they get to Feliu's bayou and rush ashore, Julien is told that Edwards's heart gave out and he died. Soon falling ill himself, Julien is cared for expertly by Carmen. Suddenly he sees Chita, with "singularly splendid . . . brown eyes peeping at him from beneath a golden riot of loose hair." They speak briefly. Everything about her reminds him of Adèle—her poise, grace, movement of neck, "bird-tone of her speech." He even notes a tiny birthmark under her right ear. He grows delirious and fatally ill with yellow fever. His mind floods with memories. Carmen recognizes the malady, orders Chita away, and does what she can for Julien; but he dies—before a priest can be summoned. Carmen kneels in prayer.

Hearn developed his interest in Herbert Spencer (1820–1903) and evolutionary thought, much reflected in *Chita*, while talking with his New Orleans physician friend Rudolph Matas* in the late 1870s. Beginning in the early 1880s, Hearn enjoyed vacationing on nearby islands notable for primitive, exotic conditions. At a dinner party in 1883 his host and friend, George Washington Cable,* told about the August 1856 hurricane that ruined Last Island. In June 1888 Hearn wrote his friend George Milbry Gould* a summary of a L'Île Dernière story concerning a little girl rescued after the storm by a fisherman's family, reared by them, but then rescued and returned to New Orleans. Her family sent her to a convent; but, preferring the free and healthy coastal life, she escaped, married a fisherman, and was happy. Timid about undertaking a long piece of fiction, Hearn published two sketches in the New Orleans *Times-Democrat* relating to what became *Chita*. They are "Torn Letters" (September 14, 1884) and "The Post-Office" (October 19, 1884). Details of the destructive storm were available to Hearn in files of several New Orleans newspapers, notably the *Picayune*. He learned, for example, that there was a real *Star* captained by a real Abraham Smith, and that pillagers did rob corpses, and that some were caught, tried, and hanged. Hearn asked Henry Edward Krehbiel,* his musician friend, for information about Creole music; and he asked Matas to help him not only with details about yellow fever but also with Spanish words for use in the dialogue. Interestingly, Hearn argued with Henry Edward Krehbiel and perhaps therefore gave a character in *Chita* the name Henry Edwards and had him killed.

Henry Mills Alden,* Hearn's editor at Harper & Brothers, approved the manuscript of *Chita* in May 1887. It appeared in *Harper's Magazine* (April 1888) and in book form in 1889, considerably revised and dedicated to Matas. Hearn long admired Victor Hugo, uses as epigraph for *Chita* six lines from a Hugo poem, and must have been thrilled when in a Boston *Evening Transcript* review of *Chita* (November 2, 1889) he was compared to Hugo. A closer comparison is to the works of Pierre Loti, whose exotic scenes and lush, sensuous descriptions Hearn longed to replicate in his poetic prose. Clashing with Hearn's romantic, imagistic depiction of tropical sights, sounds, and smells is his esoteric, often scientific, vocabulary, which features such words as "arborescent," "baragouin," "coryopsis," "crepitates," "euphorbias," "flocculant," "morbific," "susurration," "tillandsia," "tumefied," and "tutoiement." *Chita* proved to be popular, was reprinted more than 10 times, and enjoyed a British edition (1890). In citations of *Chita*, "Last Island" in its subtitle is, perhaps understandably, often misnamed "Lost Island."

Bibliography: Murray; Arlin Turner, "Introduction," Lafcadio Hearn, *Chita: A Memory of Last Island* (Chapel Hill: University of North Carolina Press, 1969).

"THE CITY OF DREAMS" (1879). Sketch. Citizens of New Orleans talk to themselves. Is it because they are outraged by stupid laws, high taxes, business losses? Aged people mutter along what policemen call "dead streets." Are they rather streets of the dead? The oldsters mutter about lost fortunes, utter curses, occasionally laugh softly. When summer brings fevers, the voices, between sobs, speak of the dead, sometimes using foreign words. Shadows, thus addressed, may answer.

Bibliography: Cott.

"THE CLAIRVOYANT ABORTIONIST" (1873). Cincinnati news article. When authorities are alerted, "vault-cleaners" on May 22, 1873, drag the privy of Mme. Sidney Augustine, a fortune-telling abortionist. They find an aborted fetus wrapped in the big woman's immense dress. A pregnant colored girl named Mary Williams was recently operated on by the clairvoyant—so says Hattie Sperling, now in the hospital recovering from a long stay with Mme Augustine. "The Clairvoyant Abortionist" is a continuation of "Mme. Sidney Augustine."

"THE COLORED GHOUL" (1874). Cincinnati news article. An African American body-snatcher—called a "resurrectionist"—was arrested for trying to ship a box containing incompletely boiled human skeletons to a local medical college "for articulation." The authorities suspected him of frequently dumping human flesh in a canal near his residence but probably will not arrest him. After all, as he explains, "Doctors must have subjects."

"COLORS AND EMOTIONS" (1887). Editorial. People from the times of Homer, Roman mosaic artists, and Gobelin tapestry weavers to the present have developed a sense, ever more refined, of colors. Gold and sunlight are yellow. Blood red is associated with war, love, hunting, and sacrifice. The whole world is green. Blue is "the color most mysterious and holy." These "primary" colors are too garish and are modified for clothing, uniforms, and decorations. Hearn assigns to red, passion; to yellow, life; to green, labor; to blue, faith and duty. He cites work by his friend George Milbry Gould* on the subject of colors.

"COMPLAINT OF CREOLE BOARDING-HOUSE-KEEPER" (1879). Sketch. A Creole landlady complains about deadbeat tenants. A "capitaine" owed her "seventy dollaire" and left when she removed the furniture in his room. A "coco" Frenchman nailed his valise to the floor to make it seem heavy. When an unmarried couple broke up, the man blamed the Creole. She tells about a sick man whose medicine she bought, a "sage femme," her doctor who was "not so much doctor as my cat," and "tree familee" of thieving squatters. The charm of this piece lies in Hearn's recording of delightful Creole speech. A follow-up sketch is "The Boarder's Reply."

"THE CORPSE-DEMON" (1884). Tale. A Demon tells King Vikramaditya three stories.

1. To the goddess Devi's temple at Dharmpur comes a young pilgrim, with a friend. The youth sees a beautiful damsel. He vows to give his head to Devi if he can marry the girl. Returning home, he grows so lovesick that he asks his friend to determine the girl's identity for him. The friend and the youth's father go to Dharmpur, find the girl's father, get his permission, and bring the youth to Dharmpur, and the two get married. Returning later to Dharmpur for a feast, the joyous youth suddenly remembers his vow, goes to the temple, and beheads himself. His friend finds him, fears he will be accused of murder to gain the damsel, and also beheads himself. The girl finds the dead men, fears she will be accused of wickedness, and would kill herself but Devi restrains her, sprinkles the severed heads with magic nectar, and tells her to reattach them. Because of dizziness, she transposes them. The Demon asks Vikramaditya to tell which man was her husband; if Vikramaditya errs, the Demon will eat him. He says that because the head is the chief of the body, the man with the husband's head is now her husband.

2. In Dharmasthal, a brahman named Kesav, his wife, and their son seek a husband for Madhumalati, Kesav's beautiful daughter. Kesav promises her to a certain Brahman; the mother, to another Brahman; the brother, to a student. The three handsome suitors present themselves at the home of the girl, who is bitten by a snake, dies, and is cremated. One suitor gathers her bones; another, her ashes; Madhusadam, the third, with no relic, becomes a Yogi. Begging at a strange Brahman's home, Madhusadam is aghast upon seeing the Brahman's wife toss their little son in the fire. Though burned to ashes, he is restored when the Brahman reads an incantation from a resurrection book. Stealing the book, Madhusadam returns to the spot where Madhumalati was burned. The two other suitors are there. They pile her bones and ashes together, and Madhusadam reads the incantation and restores her to beautiful life. Asked by the Demon whose wife she should be, Vikramaditya says that one preserved her bones as a son

should his parents'; one reanimated her as a father gives life to a child; the third, memorably keeping her ashes, should be her husband.

3. The wife and daughter of a king slain in battle escape into the forest. The rajah Chandrasen and his son follow their beautiful footsteps. The rajah will marry the larger woman; his son, the smaller. It happens that the rajah weds the big daughter; his son, the small mother. The Demon asks Vikramaditya in what manner the children of the two men are related. King Vikramaditya can't say but is mysteriously "befriended" anyway.

"LES COULISSES: SOUVENIRS OF A STRAKOSCH OPERA NIGHT" (1879). Sketch. Joyously attending "the Creole Opera House," Hearn penetrates the curtain between reality and the "veritable Fair-World" of dancers, actors, actresses, singers, and musicians. They may be "Puppets of mimic passion" creating "mystic anachronism[s]," but for a brief time the show is "visible, tangible, sentient life." Hearn's vocabulary and references are unusually rich here.

"THE CREOLE CHARACTER" (1879). Sketch. Two Irishmen could build a Creole grocery-man's awning in 24 hours. But when he hires four Creole carpenters they take three weeks to make only a good start, because they often interrupt their labor to grin at passing girls, smoke, take off for a few drinks, and sing.

"A CREOLE COURTYARD" (1879). Sketch. The front of an old Creole house is unattractive, but "beyond the gates . . . [is] a little Paradise," with a courtyard, garden, plants and trees, porcelain vases, and a fountain. Outside is "American traffic"; inside, "good old-fashioned people" still reflecting "the epoch of the Spanish Domination."

"A CREOLE JOURNAL" (1879). Sketch. Entries from "Jan. 1" to "December 1" indicate that the diarist borrowed "ten dollaire," promised to repay, was rudely dunned ("I be tramped upon"), will pay "wen sugar come in de market," and finally "not pay ever" the insolent creditor at all.

"A CREOLE MYSTERY" (1880). Sketch. A woman comes from Havana with her servant. The mistress is dark, mirthless, as lithe as a snake. Her servant is a mulatress, tall like a bronze caryatid, mute, as observant as a camera. They begin to live in rented rooms in the French Quarter. When her mistress wants her, the servant simply emerges, like a phantom. Swarthy foreign men visit, pop champagne corks, laugh. One night an argument, in Catalan, is heard. Glasses break. Blows follow, then silence. In the morning a postman tries to deliver a registered letter, but no one is there. Eventually the empty rooms grow musty, with everything covered by dust. Wouldn't you like to read that letter, now in the dead-letter office?

"CREOLE SERVANT GIRLS" (1880). Sketch. "Creole colored girls" are bright, shrewd, and able. They are "consummate actresses," can tell lies prettily, and can make the truth seem false. Once trained, they are "admirable waiting-machines." If paid on time, treated properly, and given the liberty they absolutely require, they will remain permanently with families by whom they are hired. They relay gossip to trusted employers, are polylingual, sing strange songs, and are implacable enemies if riled. Their fascinating type is disappearing.

CREOLE SKETCHES. Part of Volume 1 of *The Writings of Lafcadio Hearn* (16 vols., 1922). Charles Woodward Hutson* selected 31 sketches by Hearn first published in the New Orleans *Item* (1878–1881). *See* Appendix for titles of individual sketches. *Creole Sketches* was reissued, with additional pieces, as a separate volume in 1924.

    Bibliography: Junko Hagiwara, "Lafcadio Hearn and Leona Queyrouze," *Lafcadio Hearn Journal* 1 (Fall 1991): 2–4.

"A CREOLE SONG" (1880). Sketch. Hearn quotes a two-stanza, sixteen-line Creole song, beginning "Moin pas conne' " (I do not know), and then translates. The burden is that pleasant memories trigger present "tormente." Hearn closes by asking readers to send him lyrics of some more such songs.

"A CREOLE TYPE" (1879). Sketch. Hearn begins by contrasting the bustling American element with the quiet French-Quarter Creoles. He illustrates differences between the two groups by describing "a stiff-mannered stranger" when he tries to ask a dark, attractive landlady to rent him some rooms. She has him wait a little, declines to tell him the price when he first asks, but in detail explains her requirements—cash, long-term tenancy, and cleanliness. He is willing to agree. But she gesticulates "gypsy-like," flirts her keys at him, says she will not rent "to the canaille," and finally settles on $25 [a month?]. Mesmerized by her beauty, the "phlegmatic" man faithfully observes her stipulations.

"CREOLE WOMEN IN THE FRENCH WEST INDIES" (1890). Sketch. The well-known seclusion of women in Latin countries is elevated by writers and painters to a romantic realm of happiness. Truly, sunlight in tropical regions is magical, nature there bewitches one in a non-intellectual drowsiness, and social life becomes "indolent and provincial." Time has moved so slowly in the old

French colonies that everything seems like life back in the seventeenth century. If Napoleon's Josephine de la Pagerie could return to her Martinique home in Trois-Islets, she would find almost nothing changed. The birth of a female Creole today is formally announced. She is christened with six names and released to the care of her *da* (black nurse). The *da* teaches her to speak, kiss, and listen to Creole tales told in a "cooing . . . tongue." The child grows, goes to a convent school—then perhaps to France—returns all polished, and is formally presented to Creole society. She then leads a secluded life, like a caged bird, until a gentleman she may have seen only as a solemn visitor asks for her hand. Her marriage is arranged by the two families' heads. Once she has children, she rarely goes out and then usually just to church. In the past, both slavery and wealth created more luxurious lives for these Creole women, especially if they lived near enough to Fort Royal, the capital of Martinique, to visit the governor's court. Within a few generations there, the French colonists were considerably transformed by climate and other tropical influences.

Using complex genealogical data, Hearn details, then counters, the "absurd" legend of a person who allegedly became "the Sultana-Validé of Salim III" from a Martinique village called Robert. Hearn says that the shrunken state of modern Creole life was caused by the "decline of caste dignity and caste prosperity," especially on Martinique.

"CRIMSON MADNESS" (1878). Editorial. Hearn is inspired by an essay on Edgar Allan Poe by Francis Gerry Fairchild ("A Mad Man of Letters," *Scribner's*, October 1875), to support that critic's theory of Poe's progressive insanity by suggesting that Poe's abnormal imagination is demonstrated by his overuse of the word "crimson" in later stories.

LA CUISINE CRÉOLE: A COLLECTION OF CULINARY RECIPES (1885).
Cookbook. Hearn put together a large collection of Creole recipes from leading chefs and several New Orleans housewives, including the charming wife of Rudolph Matas.* The work, first published in New York, was popular; enjoyed a second edition, which was published in New Orleans; and was republished in 1990.

Bibliography: Cott; Alan Rosen, "Hearn and the Gastronomic Grotesque," in Hirakawa, pp. 158–181; Stevenson.

D

"THE DANCE OF DEATH" (1874). Cincinnati news article. When a friend, whom he names Joe Saubohnz, challenged him to visit the dissecting rooms of his medical college, Hearn "jumped at the offer." In the man's "anthropophagical meat-store" he is shown the skeleton of a notorious grave robber, denominated "Cunny the Resurrectionist" and with a pipe stuck "between its grinning jaws." Hearn sees obstetrical illustrations, dried bodies, and skulls and bones. The janitor, a "withered-up gray agony," lets them into a long room with many tables and a swirl of disgusting stenches. After viewing and smelling much putrefaction, Hearn is shown the corpse of a once-beautiful blonde teenager, carelessly chopped and slivered and poked. Hearn sees her torn-out heart, which he is certain must recently have palpitated with rushing passions. He notes her obvious former "slender symmetry" despite her present "hideous semi-denudation." She lacks a head now, a student having taken it home for private study. Thinking she might have been "naughty," Hearn would like to make her faithless lover gaze at this "frightful mass of bleeding flesh and blackened bone." Students assembled alongside a 300-pound black man's corpse resemble "a solemn conclave of vultures about a dead camel." Hearn avoids visiting a bone-boiling room because he still faintly hopes to have a little dinner.

Bibliography: Murray.

"THE DAWN OF THE CARNIVAL" (1880). Sketch. In our prosaic age, the advent of the carnival presents a "kaleidoscopic changing and flashing of colors," often seen by glum spectators.

"DEAD FOR A DUCAT—AND LESS THAN A DUCAT" (1880). After detailing the many modes of executing criminals, Hearn concludes that because we shoot disabled animals we should do the same for especially heinous law-breakers, who, "in this enlightened age," we conclude are "diseased creature[s]." This, not for revenge but to protect society.

"A DEAD LOVE." *See* "L'Amour après la Mort."

"DEATH AND RESURRECTION IN THE SOUDAN" (1884). Editorial. In this editorial published on December 9, 1884, about the siege of Khartoum in the Sudan, Hearn says that no news would be better than the current flood of inaccurate reports. He notes that Arabs and Berbers led by the Mahdi are opposing British and Egyptian troops. He comments sarcastically about inflated casualty figures and false rumors concerning the death of the two opposing leaders—hence his title. In truth, the Mahdi (Muhammad Ahmad, 1848–1885) defeated General Charles Gordon (1833–1885), massacred his garrison, killed him on January 26, 1885, but died in June 1885 of typhus. *See* "The Rise of the Mahdi."

DEDICATIONS BY HEARN. Hearn dedicated most of his books to friends. He dedicated *Stray Leaves from Strange Literature* (1884) to Page M. Baker*; *Some Chinese Ghosts* (1887) to Henry Edward Krehbiel*; *Chita: A Story of Last Island* (1889) to "Dr. Rodolfo Matas" (*see* Matas, Rudolph); *Youma: The Story of a West-Indian Slave* (1890) to Joseph S. Tunison (*see* Tunison, Joseph Salathiel); *Two Years in the French West Indies* (1890) to Léopold Arnoux, a Martinique notary; *Glimpses of Unfamiliar Japan* (1894) to "Paymaster Mitchell McDonald," of the U.S. Navy in Japan, and Basil Hall Chamberlain*; *Out of the East: Reveries and Studies in New Japan* (1895) to Nishida Sentarō, a teacher in Izumo, Japan; *Kokoro: Hints and Echoes of Japanese Inner Life* (1896) to Amenomori Nobushige, Japanese "poet, scholar, and patriot," and Hearn's friend; *Exotics and Retrospectives* (1898) to Dr. C.H.H. Hall, Hearn's friend, formerly stationed with the U.S. Navy at Yokohama; *In Ghostly Japan* (1899) to Mrs. Alice Von Behrens, a friend in Japan; *Shadowings* (1900) to "Paymaster Mitchell McDonald"; *A Japanese Miscellany* (1901) to Mrs. Elizabeth Bisland Wetmore (*see* Bisland, Elizabeth); and *Kottō* (1902) to Sir Edwin Arnold.*

"DESERT OR SEA" (1879). Editorial. Hearn evidently takes seriously the proposal by Ferdinand de Lesseps (1805–1894) "to convert the Sahara into an inland sea." Hearn discusses the effects of the scheme, if brought to fruition, on ocean depths, geography, climates, and even the earth's revolution.

"THE DESTINY OF SOLAR SYSTEMS" (1883). Editorial. Predictions as to when our sun will die, as well as discoveries by astronomers, inspire Hearn to "chat." He posits this progression: A central sun cools, its planets and satellites crumble and scatter, the ashen sun becomes a planet needing warmth from another sun. Because matter and energy are indestructible, new forms and new ruins will continue forever. This intriguing essay is nicely verbalized poppycock less credible than *Eureka: A Prose Poem* (1848) by Edgar Allan Poe (1809–1849), whom Hearn admired. Hearn's essay is also at variance with his pro-Buddhist theorem that matter and energy are illusory.

"THE DEVIL'S CARBUNCLE" (1879). Sketch. On Good Friday, 1547, three sinful Conquistadores in Peru are seeking gold in an Indian cave. They kick a mummy, see a big gem roll out, argue over it, and kill each other. Tradition calls the gem the devil's carbuncle. This piece is a translation by Hearn of "El Carbunclo del Diablo," from a collection by Richard Palma (1833–1919), a *La Raza Latina* correspondent in Lima.

"THE DEVIL'S CATHEDRAL" (1879). Editorial. The Cologne cathedral, "the most magnificent specimen of Gothic architecture in the world," is to be completed soon. Its architect, who began construction in 1247, is unknown although his plans have been exactly followed. Legend has it that his building plans remained hazy in part, until a tall, dark, flashy-eyed stranger visited him, showed him a final plan, and got him to sign a parchment in blood in return for the tempter's plan. The architect repented and was forgiven but was cursed into perpetual anonymity when the defrauded stranger reappeared. Although the construction is virtually complete, many still have their fears that the Devil may revisit them.

"THE DISPUTE OF THE HALACHA" (1884). Legend. To persuade his sage opponents that he is correct in saying the oven is legally clean according to the Halacha, Rabbi Eliezer gets a carob-tree to uproot and replant itself elsewhere, a brook to stop itself, walls to bend, and a heavenly Voice to warn the wranglers. Excommunicated and ill, Eliezer is asked too late by Rabbi Akiva ben Joseph to expound the law. Eliezer rebukes him, predicts a painful death for Akiva, and dies. Later Akiva is tortured to death by Romans for teaching the law in Israel. (Halakah is a legal part of the Talmud.)

"DOLLY" (1876). Cincinnati news article. Dolly is a compactly built, Egyptian-looking girl living in Sausage Row. Her "snakish . . . grace" is accentuated by vivid, home-made dresses. Her hair is so thick and strong that no breeze can move it, especially when it is greased with butter. Dolly rows, shoots, and swims superbly. She seems better than "her sisters of the levee," some of whom think she is stuck up. She loves to see the boats dock, especially when "her man" Aleck, a "good-looking yellow roustabout," puts in his appearance. When he gives her a silver watch, she tries to make it more accurate by removing "a little hair wound round its guts," that is, its mainspring. Aleck gets drunk, is in a wild fight, and is jailed and ordered to pay a $40 fine. Dolly works extra hard, denies herself food and rest, and sells her furniture to scrape together money for his fine. Out comes Aleck, and off he sails. One evening, word circulates that Aleck got married in Maysville. Dolly loses all will to live. The negro preacher is summoned, and musicians strike up "Oh, ain't I mighty glad my Jesus rose / To send me up on high." Tightly gripping her silver watch, Dolly falls into "the Dreamless Sleep."

"LA DOUANE" (1878). Sketch. The gray custom house on Canal Street in New Orleans resembles a musty Egyptian sarcophagus. In its dank marble halls are "hypogea[l]" statues of important "[p]ersonages," which have never been uncrated and set up in place.

"A DREAM OF FUTURITY" (1880). Editorial. It would not benefit society if science produced a human being by artificial means, but what a boon it would be if a lost limb or eye could be replaced. Could science follow by discovering an elixir of perpetual youth? Unless the strong and bright were to hide this potion from the weak and ignorant, overpopulation would follow. The more intelligent the new aristocrats would become, the weaker their reproductive powers would be. Perhaps science would then invent beings uniquely wise and sturdy.

"A DREAM OF KITES" (1880). Sketch. Hearn sees kites caught in telegraph wires; suggests that whereas some boys cry over their lost kites, others laugh, forget, philosophize, and make and lose new ones; and concludes by comparing such kites to adults who fly "toys of love and faith" toward a fickle, ruinous heaven. Hearn's images of dancing, impaled, gibbeted, mummified kites represent his Gothic virtuosity at its best.

"DUG-UP" (1873). Cincinnati news article. A certain doctor asserted that his patient died of spinal meningitis. But the coroner heard that the cause of death was a beating. So, in the presence of six jurors, reporters, onlookers, and the dead man's brother, the body was exhumed and an autopsy performed. It was almost conclusively shown that the cause of death was a blow to the head. After reporting every unpleasant detail of the grisly examination, Hearn concludes that hospital personnel, family members, and detectives will all remain at odds.

E

EDITORIALS. While in New Orleans, Hearn wrote with infinite care a steady stream of editorials, first for the *Item* and then for the *Times-Democrat*. In 1926 his friend Charles Woodward Hutson* edited *Editorials by Lafcadio Hearn*, containing 44 editorials, often short, from the *Item* (1878–1881) and 36, usually longer, from the *Times-Democrat* (1882–1887). In these pieces Hearn combined the style of the journalist and the literary artist, the here-and-now observational power of the newsman, and the vision of the amateur scientist-philosopher. He wrote about architecture, literature, music, and translations; New Orleans city life, civic and political problems, and Creoles; feminism; foreign countries; and scientific topics, including archaeology, astronomy, biology, demographics, eugenics, hygiene, inventions, meteorology, optics, and seismology. *See* individual editorials.

"THE ELECTRIC LIGHT" (1880). Editorial. Writing in the New Orleans *Item*, Hearn expresses surprise that the *Times-Democrat* predicts the lighting of cities by electricity rather than by gas within 10 years. Hearn says it is happening already, because electric lights are cheaper and brighter than gas. He also suggests the Mississippi River as a source of power.

"ELEUSIS" (1880). Sketch. Hearn describes a ballet dancer's boudoir or dressing room in positively diaphanous prose, then realistically details the regimen of her dressing: chemise, tights, drawers, petticoats, corset, bodice, slippers. All is ready. Reader, dream on! Either Eleusis is the dancer's name, or the title refers to an Eleusian mystery dance.

"THE ELIXIR OF LOVE" (1872). Cincinnati news article. Thomas L. Bond tried to kill the Rev. J. L. Thompson with a hatchet and is in jail. The two evidently vied for the affections of Mrs. Shingledecker, now ailing. In remorse, Bond tried to commit suicide by using his pocket knife. He cut his throat but missed the jugular, and he also opened a vein in his arm. He is being watched. Adopting a sardonic tone, Hearn says that Bond "was found guilty of cutting with intent to wound" but adds that the fellow ought to be taken to the hospital, because "our code of justice" should be "tempered with a little more mercy."

"EMBALMING A CORPSE" (1877). Cincinnati news article. Because no Cincinnati undertaker could do a proper job on M. Auguste Labrot, his friends hired two physicians, who saw "the work much in the light of a scientific experiment." Hearn describes in unwelcome detail their handling of various named organs. He comments on Egyptian embalming methods and adds that Labrot now goes on to France in "a double casing of lead."

ENGLISH LITERATURE, HEARN ON. Hearn held the chair of English language and literature at the Imperial University of Tokyo (1896–1902). He lectured without notes, in a slow, deliberate manner, because his more able students took down his words carefully, often verbatim through long passages and even entire lectures. He modestly wrote to Mitchell McDonald (February 1899) that his lectures, adapted to his students' knowledge of English and their thought processes, were basic and not worth publishing even if revised. He suggested in a letter to Ellwood Hendrick* (September 1902) that he taught literature as an expression of emotion and as a representation of life in all its real, romantic, and mystical complexities. After Hearn's death, McDonald obtained at least 400,000 words of Hearn's lectures preserved by his best students; took them to New York; and let John Erskine, literature professor at Columbia University, publish generous samples, minimally edited, in two volumes in 1924. The first volume mainly concerned nineteenth-century British authors; the second, mostly English but some miscellaneous authors. Exigencies of space prohibit any kind of discussion, even summary, of them here.

The lectures reveal Hearn's incredible range of knowledge. The index of the first volume identifies almost 200 writers and just over 100 titles of long or short works; the second-volume index, about 60 authors and almost a hundred titles. The two indexes reveal some overlap. Hearn lectured often on George Gordon, Lord Byron, Samuel Taylor Coleridge, Johann Wolfgang von Goethe, John Keats, Henry Wadsworth Longfellow, Pierre Loti, Guy de Maupassant, Sir Walter Scott, William Shakespeare, Percy Bysshe Shelley, Herbert Spencer, Algernon Charles Swinburne, Alfred, Lord Tennyson, and William Wordsworth. He also at least mentioned such hardly-knowns as Marie Catherine d'Aulnoy, Richard Barnefield, Jacob Boehme, Francis William Bourdillon, Michael Bruce, Henry Thomas Buckle, Charon of Lampsacus, Henry Conscience, Alexander Cruden, Baltasar Gracian, William Habington, William Hamilton of Bangour, Frederick Locker-Lampson, Moschus, Constance Naden, Richard Porson, Frederick York Powell, Emil Rittershaus, Charles G. D. Roberts, Charlotte Perkins Stetson, Gulbrandr Vigfússon, and John Leicester Warren. Hearn left behind his huge personal library when in 1890 he went to Japan, which lacked extensive library facilities devoted to literature in England.

To this day, Hearn's subjective literary criticism is undervalued. Moreover, his position as the professor who first introduced conscientious and devoted students in Japan to great and lesser literary masterpieces in the English language was of absolutely unparalleled value. In 1927 Erskine edited *Life and Literature*, a selection of 23 more essays by Hearn, many on English authors but some on critical theory. *See also* Lafcadio Hearn, *A History of English Literature* (2 vols., Tokyo: Hokuseido Press, 1927; rev. ed., 1 vol., 1930). Lectures by Hearn on English literature and non-American literature, including a few lectures not published before, were also issued in Japan, 1927, 1928, 1929, 1930, and 1932. In these Japanese publications Hearn is identified as Yakumo Koizumi, his Japanese name.

Bibliography: Lafcadio Hearn, *Interpretations of Literature*, ed. John Erskine (2 vols., New York: Dodd, Mead, 1924); *Life and Literature*, ed. Erskine (New York: Dodd, Mead, 1927).

"ENGLISH THE UNIVERSAL TONGUE OF THE FUTURE" (1881). Editorial. Agreeing with the prediction of historian John Fiske (1842–1901) that English will become a worldwide language, Hearn says that American "commercial ascendancy" makes it most likely but that the possible waning of political power would be an impediment.

***ESSAYS ON EUROPEAN AND ORIENTAL LITERATURE* (1923).** Albert Mordell, a distinguished American literary critic and editor, assembled 47 essays by Hearn that first appeared in the New Orleans *Times-Democrat* (1883–1887). Mordell arranged them under the following rubrics: "Essays on Literary Topics," "Essays on French Literature," "Studies in Russian, English, German, and Italian Literature," and "Oriental Literature." Most are of minimal importance, as it may be said that by 1923 earlier posthumous gatherings of material by Hearn had already presented the best. Mordell also deserves praise for publishing *An American Miscellany* (1924) and *Occidental Gleanings* (2 vols., 1925), a book-length collection of 55 minor articles and stories, and 87 minor other pieces, respectively, by Hearn.

"ESTHER'S CHOICE" (1884). Legend. In Sidon, Rabbi Simon ben Yochai, rich and esteemed, is sad that he and his comely wife have no child. A rich merchant, accompanied by his wife, Esther, consults Rabbi Simon and sadly says he has no child and therefore seeks divorce papers. Simon orders the merchant to give a banquet, praise Esther to their guests, and tell her to take away to safety whatever she desires and then return for the divorce papers. Much food and wine are served. When the merchant grows drowsy, Esther has her husband carried to her father's home. The merchant awakens in his wife's loving arms. She says she took away "whatsoever I most desired." Simon appears and blesses their love, which soon proves fruitful. Hearn writes that the guests enjoy so much wine that they hear "a buzzing in their ears as of innumerable bees." Tennyson, anyone? In Alfred, Lord Tennyson's *The Princess, a Medley* (1847, 1853), Hearn surely read about "The moan of doves in immemorial elms, / And murmuring of innumerable bees."

EXOTICS AND RETROSPECTIVES (1898). A collection of six essays called "Exotics" and ten called "Retrospectives." All but one were published in book form for the first time. Hearn dedicated the book to C.H.H. Hall, a retired U.S. Navy doctor whom he knew in Yokohama. Hearn wrote to Ellwood Hendrick* (August 1897) that he thought of dedicating *Exotics and Retrospectives* to Elizabeth Bisland,* their mutual friend, but decided that some of the contents "might be found a little startling."

The first of the "Exotics" is "Fuji-no-Yama": Hearn says the only thing of value he can add to factual data concerning sacred Mount Fuji is a narrative of his climbing in August 1897 via Gotemba, the easiest route. He hires two sturdy guides. They dress him warmly, and at 4:00 A.M., with a "kuruma" (ricksha), three runners, and a horse, they ascend a black, cindery road the first five thousand feet, through woods, past farmhouses, into sudden sunlight bathing a dark slope. The "warm-blue" cone is visible through vapors. Grassy fields have black patches. Fuji shows teeth-like streaks of white snow on nightmarish black. Trudging through black sand, by 6:00 A.M. they reach six thousand feet and the first of ten station houses. They walk zigzag, Hearn, nervously, with a staff, into and beyond a fog. At another station—8:30 A.M., 7,085 feet up—he squats, walks about, and looks down a straight slope. With the guides' help, to 7,937 feet by 10:30 A.M. As the air grows thin and the way more difficult, Hearn suffers and the guides push him along, and when it is 2:07 P.M. they are at 9,317 feet. The land below is dim through ragged clouds. At 10,693 feet it is 4:40 P.M., and Hearn vows to proceed no more. The horizon seems too high, and below is a cottony sea. Inside the eighth station house, the party gets warm and prepares to rest. The guides tell about a meteorologist and his wife who, for scientific purposes, attempted to spend the winter on Fuji's summit and had to be rescued by three daring volunteers. Though told not to, Hearn briefly braves the bitter cold outside at 4:00 A.M. Dawn turns the milky clouds to cotton and then to purple, burning rags. Hearn views the topography beneath. The climbers begin to zigzag through lava blocks at 6:40 A.M., pass the deserted ninth station, and reach the top, upwards of 12,000 feet, at 8:20 A.M. Hearn notes stone huts, a shrine, a tablet, and lava walls, and gazes down "a cavity horrible." Far from resembling the snowy, lotus-like petals viewed from the base, "[n]o spot in this world can be . . . more atrociously dismal than the cindered tip." But the vast, surrounding view! Ah, "immense poetry . . . a thrill . . . no luminous detail can fade" until his eyes turn to dust and join that of millions before him who also gazed "from the summit supreme of Fuji to the Rising of the Sun." This essay has been criticized for combining objective detail and poetic subjectivity in an ersatz manner. But it should be obvious that Hearn took no notes as he climbed and shivered, and was pushed and pulled, until he attained the object of his mission. Relying afterwards on guides, fellow travelers, guidebooks, and his own phenomenal memory, he gives a gripping account, at its best when poetically impressionistic.

"Insect-Musicians": Visitors to Japan should go to a temple festival, with circus-like shows but—better—caged musical insects for sale. These little creatures are distinguished from chattering cicadae, as larks are from sparrows. Hearn summarizes the history of references to musical insects in Japanese fiction and poetry, beginning in the tenth century, then takes up the history of insect hunters (eleventh century or earlier), salesmen (by seventeenth century), and breeders (soon thereafter). Hearn recently acquired a history of the industry, details of which he presents. Chūzō (late eighteenth century) added to his grocery business in Tōkyō when he began to catch, sell, and breed insects. Competitors followed. Chūzō bequeathed his business to a toy-merchant relative (c. 1820). Hearn presents details concerning laws regulating the bug trade, prices charged, and native habitats of various insects, and he describes the 12 most notable varieties—with Japanese names, English translations, line drawings, and write-ups of their songs. For example, *matsumushi*, pine insect, "chin-chironīn, chin-chironīn." Insects are prominent in "countless" melancholy Japanese poems, mainly about love, autumn, separation, and death. Admitting these poems contain "ingenious but untranslatable allusions," he proceeds to offer no fewer than 28 short renderings into English. My favorite: "Parting is sorrowful always—even the parting with autumn! / O plaintive matsumushi, add not thou to my pain!" In a touching runnerup, a wife is frustrated when she mistakes the cricket-like "chirrup" of a *kutsuwamushi* for the jingling of her absent husband's *kutsuwa* (bridle-bit). This essay, loaded with names of Japanese provinces, cities, bugs, bug drummers, and onomatopoetic verbiage, might be read as satirical but for Hearn's conclusion: Westerners, "masters in the mechanical . . . [and] teachers of the artificial in all its varieties of ugliness," will be sorry when their "aggressive industrialism has wasted and sterilized their [Japanese] paradise— substituting everywhere for beauty the utilitarian, the conventional, the vulgar, the utterly hideous."

"A Question in the Zen Texts": A friend shows Hearn a beautiful book with a story studied by Zen scholars. Such stories end with unanswered questions. One concerns a girl named Ts'ing. Her father, Chang-Kien, jokingly promises her to his nephew Wang-Chau, who loves her. When she grows up, Chang offers her to a high-ranking man. Chau angrily prepares to leave. Ts'ing rushes after him; they escape, marry, have two children. Seeking a reconciliation, they return to Chang. Alone, Chau explains events and apologizes to Chang but is told that Ts'ing never left home, fell ill, and became speechless. Chau sees her but then brings in his waiting wife. The two Ts'ings meet and meltingly become one. Hearn's friend poses the question: Given her "separation of . . . spirit," which is the real Ts'ing? If one can decide, he is wise. When Hearn asks whether the two girls' clothes also blended, his friend replies that the doctrinal question concerns Ts'ing personality.

"The Literature of the Dead": Behind Hearn's home is a Buddhist temple made of gnarled wood. Beyond its gate is a cemetery he likes to wander in. Above various graves are planted *sobota* (tall, narrow, unpainted laths) with two-sentence inscriptions. They are about ether, wind, fire, water, and earth, the five elements identical with the five Buddhas, each containing the other four. After providing quotations concerning each element and admitting that explaining all this would require many books, Hearn proceeds to try. Sentences of *sutra* (precepts) are especially attractive on *sobota*, each with the name of the giver and a short prayer. Different sects have different invocations and texts. They may provide praise, address the sect founder, or pray for salvation of the dead in any of several ways. These cheerful, devout, poetic texts proclaim "the eternal and infinite nature of Thought, the unity of all mind, and the certainty of universal salvation." By explication, Hearn demonstrates that seemingly simple texts are really profound, affirming that ultimately everything is unreal but the One Mind, subsuming past-present-future, mind-matter, nonsentient-sentient. Hearn turns to inscriptions on *haka* (tombs). Each may include a floral carving, a mystical sign, the *kaimyō* (posthumous Buddhist name) of the dead and date of death, rank and deeds of the dead, and an invocation. Hearn tediously lists half a hundred *kaimyō*—adult, child, male, female—putting some into Romanji (i.e., converting Japanese words into roman letters) and translating all (by competent Japanese scholars). A single nice example: "Vow-abiding-wondrously-without-fault." Hearn's final remarks are wistful. His "subject [is] wide and deep as the sea." Those who criticize him for beautifying matters are disingenuous. One should be tolerant of "an alien faith." Given the exotica treated, Hearn wisely adds, "Perhaps I have presumed too much upon the patience of my readers."

"Frogs": People often remember sounds associated with travel abroad. In Japan, frogs in flushed rice fields provide a noticeable "exotic accent," which might seem like "the speech of the quickening soil itself." Japanese verse from the eighth century celebrates frog sounds, especially that of *kawazu* (singing frog). One poem praises *kawazu* for resting his hands on the floor and speaking his verse reverently—all this reminds one of "the Far-Eastern etiquette of posture while addressing a superior." Among numerous examples, Hearn quotes and translates what he calls "the first hokku" (haiku). Many frog poems concern love, the watery sounds frogs make, and what they look like; others address the frog directly. Why do no Japanese poems mention how cold and clammy frogs feel? Perhaps because "we Occidentals," unlike the Japanese, "shrink from many purely natural impressions by reason of repulsion developed through a morbid tactual sensibility." Thus once again, Hearn attempts to criticize things non-Oriental.

"Of Moon-Desire": When a little boy asked him to get a bamboo pole and knock down the moon for him, Hearn was inspired to philosophize about the natural desire to have things—whether food, water, or freedom. A higher wisdom makes us want differently. Hearn once wanted to melt into the blue sky, not to have it but to become it. Wishing to have is foolish; wishing to be, wise. Wishing for possessions, for power, is "small and vulgar." Who has not, distinguishing between animate and inanimate, wished to become fire, wild wind, surging waves, even interstellar ether? We should transform "childish . . . personal" senses into an awareness of "Light-as-Unity." Hearn hopes to become "Ether, Wind, Fire, Water, Earth." He read this essay to a friend, who replied that Buddhistic though his "fancies" were, he should realize that "Nirvana is never to be reached by wishing, but by *not* wishing." "Of Moon-Desire" is the last of the six essays in the "Exotics."

"First Impressions" is the first of the "Retrospectives." Hearn begins by saying each face is a composite of innumerable hereditary traits. Every mother sees in her child's face reflections of parent, grandparent, and someone else, as well as expressions unidentifiable. We recognize a familiar face but are often startled by its "fugitive subtleties of expression." These are "ancestral," molded and moved by forebears, by immemorial loves or hates. We respond intuitively to faces before us and call the process having "first impressions." Seeing a face may evoke wordless fear, sympathy, sadness. Our eyes are not any perceiving cause; inherited forces in us are. A dominant personality's aggressiveness has evil, remote, subhuman origins. However, the beauteous dead grant us the power to trust, be inspired, brighten others. It would be revealing if we could take the photograph of a face and "decompose" it into successive traits of the subject's ancestors.

"Beauty Is Memory": When a man sees a certain woman, his heart leaps, his blood tingles. What happens is that the dead in him are remembering having loved many young women like her. Ghosts cause this "witchery" to influence him. He wonders at beauty's "power and mystery." We are born with an ability to see beauty, but what we see is "a composite of numberless race-memories of individual attractions." In truth, beauty itself does not exist. Instead, it is a constant temporary becoming. The dead in "comely bodies" are "easy and happy"; in the ugly, they are "miserable." Thus beauty is the memory of the physical fitness of forebears, a sense of whose joys we inherit.

"Sadness in Beauty": Agreeing with the poet who suggested that "beautiful things bring sadness," Hearn explains that such sadness results from "the sense of beauty . . . of countless anterior lives—and therefore [it] indeed [is] a sadness of reminiscence." Some beautiful things—for example, a tropical, moonlit night—evoke tender, not sad, feelings. Beautiful things that bring sadness do so because they inspire a sense of separation, loss, continued longing. The sudden sight of a beautiful landscape can make former Westerners sad, because their "walled cities" separate them from nature. They miss forests, peaks, plains, mountain springs, and sea breezes. Beautiful scenes do not make us cry; "it is the longing of generations quickening in the hearts of us" that does.

"Parfum de Jeunesse": A friend said that when he was young he could find his girlfriend's coat in the dark because it smelled like "sweet new milk." Hearn ponders the perfume of youth. It can emanate from good health and fine vigor; it can make you think of tropical gums and spices; it may be thin, like a touch of musk. It is natural, vernal, like that of "the wild violet." It may relate, like beauty, to the moral. Just as flower fragrances could lead our ancestors to food, so youth smells may appeal to amorous or parental "tenderness." Odors, like beauty, appeal to what survives in us of "countless memories of countless lives."

"Azure Psychology" (1895): Nature rarely colors birds, flowers, and insects bright blue. It is a color created after "a prodigious period of evolutional specialization." Intense blue is more "pleasurable" than other primary colors. Blue seems transparent, deep. Street vistas in Japan are tastefully colored with blue-grays above and dark blues below, and clothes are usually gray and blue. Fascinating is the "subjective evolutional history" of blue. It generally evokes pleasant thrills. Hearn's first voyage in the Caribbean Gulf Stream was magically splendid. The water seemed a condensation of innumerable summer skies into "flaming azure." The ship's captain said his wife wanted a dress of the same glorious color, and he bought one for her in Canton, China. Blue is the color of the ghost of the earth, the breath of the world's life, "the enormity of day." Blue suggests height, vastness, depth, "Space in Time," distance, vagueness. When mountains and valleys recede, they become blue; approached again, they define themselves out of the blue. So we associate blue with change. Blue, the pantheistic color, belongs to faith's beauty and tenderness. From our forebears we inherit religious feelings, which pulse through us in a blue tide. Peaceful blues make us dream of blissful youthfulness and echo through beautiful prayers.

"A Serenade": Hearn's sleep was made to melt into sudden ecstatic music from outside. The flutes were like doves; the mandolins, like beating hearts. The night was moonlit; the warm air, filled with orange and emerald fireflies. The music caressed him with tenderness and a sense of regret. He was certain, he says, that its "mystery was of other existences than mine." Music evoking a sense of love echoes long-ago pain, delight, conquest, doubt, rivalry, impermanence. The source of this tropical serenade, feminine in tone and forcefully appealing to him, was "the Eternal Feminine." In his past, every man has been many women. Embedded in each sex are remembered feelings of both sexes. Whenever he thinks of that tropical melody, the dead within him shudder softly.

"A Red Sunset": The most spectacular red Hearn ever saw was that of a cloudless tropical sunset, turning from orange to "fervid vermilion" to burned-out crimson. It evoked a nightmarish horror. Why? We associate pink and rose with blossoms, ripe fruit, youthful flesh, fragrant and sweet sensations. Although adults detest "fervid red," children do not, because their instincts and feelings are allied to inborn savage impulses. These are not yet subordinated to "the nobler mental and moral qualities" that develop in disciplined, civilized societies. We inherit all emotions, but "the higher" evolve only with brain development. Children and savages like vivid colors, whereas civilized adults find them jarring, like cheap brasses and drums. Red sunsets induce ancient feelings, including melancholy, sadness, fear, and horror. After sundown come darkness, night enemies, and ghosts. Red reminds the primitive in us of forest fires, volcanoes, lava, pyres, and warmth turning to heat and pain. Gradually, civilized sensibilities condemn literal hellfire, blood sports, and other brutal reds "to the limbo of old barbarities." Will such "evolutional" refinements eventually render the color red useless and hence invisible, and other colors with higher "rate[s] of . . . ether-oscillation" visible? This essay combines Hearn's descriptive talents and his obsession with both psychological evolution and scientific jargon, a harmless example being this: "compensated by superior coincident specializations of retinal sensibility."

"Frisson": A human being can be sympathetic or repulsive and usually independent of the moral nature of aspects of life that impact us. Hearn knew a man who was a fine "poet, soldier, and refugee," and a killer, now long deceased. His handshake used to send a warm, summery, electric glow through Hearn. Having read the Scottish psychologist Alexander Bain (1818–1903) on the tactile sensations, Hearn amplifies. The "pleasurable thrill" (frisson) occasioned by the touch of living skin has to do with its smoothness, warmth, softness, dampness—also, however, with its electricity, its magnetism, as distinct as the uniqueness of every voice. Perhaps subtle "nervous systems" can distinguish "electrical differences of touch." Hearn theorizes that one falls in love at first sight because traits in the object of sudden devotion replicate traits in lovers one had in previous lives. So it is, sometimes, with a touch, which can "sense-echo" a "thrill immeasurable . . . in the fathomless sleep of ancestral memory."

"Vespertina Cognitio": Uniquely terrifying is fear of the supernatural. Children fear it day and night; most adults, mostly when dreaming or ill. Indescribable terror comes not wholly from experience but is "prenatal, ancestral[,] . . . compounded of . . . millions of inherited fears." Such terror, a "projection of a dream-fear into waking consciousness," occasionally occurred to Hearn during siestas in the West Indies, where "merciless sunfire," heat, and silence are stupefying. First would come "a sudden shock of thought," then heat in the lungs and a centipede-like trickle of sweat, and next a voice rebuking him for snoozing instead of enjoying the sunny day and then sneering that many dark days lie ahead. Once, while Hearn was touring "the island" (Martinique?) with Louis, his Creole guide, they stopped overnight at the house of a widow, her two daughters, and their two servants. The two travelers took the upstairs room and locked the door. Bats flapped in and out of the window. Below was a garden of ripe, fragrant fruit. Birds, frogs, and insects made a "night-chorus." Louis was snoring away on a floor mat when Hearn finally fell asleep on his hot bed.

Then: A sudden, pre-nightmare sort of suspicion. Inability to rise. Growing terror. Slow footsteps on the stairs. A tall, feminine "thing robed" opened the locked door, entered, caused the floorboards to creak. Nightmarish moanings emanated from two separate rooms below, then sounds of running and shouts. Louis began to moan, sat up, wondered whether Hearn saw it. Hearn asked him what he was trying to say. "Fenm-là" (that woman), he answered, adding that she was a tall zombie, the locked door was no problem, she was busy touching others downstairs. Seeking a rational explanation, Hearn wonders whether the heat caused the floors to creak, whether Louis's imagination fashioned something out of his "West-Indian superstition[s]," whether Hearn's own comparable vision had been induced by a "horrible Celtic story" improperly told to him when he was an impressionable child. But he has a better explanation. Our human memories are made up in part of "record[s] of extinct forms of pain—pain related to strange powers once exerted by some ghastly vanished life."

"The Eternal Haunter": Of all the recent Tōkyō color prints, the most unusual was the picture of a girl, dainty like "a resting butterfly," with cherry blossoms "falling *through* her form." She is the dream image of the cherry tree's spirit. This drawing of something closer to reality than what is commonplace reminds all honest men of a familiar type of ghost. A guardian angel, perhaps, or a dead sister's soul? Such a "haunter" first appears when boyhood begins to mature. Sadness follows, but "enchantment remains." This sweet, sad thing revisits often. Her like in reality you can never find. Ancient she is, but forever young. All men, though deceived, adore her. You cannot describe her, because "her beauty . . . is a ceaseless becoming." Timeless, when wooed she becomes an echo; when reached for, a shadow. If she smiles, a resulting pain keeps you from smiling in return. She is a phantom, shaped by hearts now crumbled into dust.

In his preface to *Exotics and Retrospectives*, Hearn emphasizes the fact that his thinking is saturated with Buddhist theories and adds, unnecessarily, that hints in his thinking are easier to recognize than they are to define. To most Western readers, his "Retrospectives" are probably more credible than his "Exotics." The book enjoyed a British edition (1908) and several reprintings in England and the United States.

Bibliography: Archie J. Bahm, *Philosophy of the Buddha* (New York: Harper, 1959); Bisland; Kennard; Kunst; Murray; Stevenson.

F

"FAIR WOMEN AND DARK WOMEN" (1878). Editorial. Countering a Spaniard's preference for brunettes as expressed in the New Orleans *Picayune*, Hearn defends "the fair woman" in a bewildering recital—he names 26 females—about Greek goddesses and statues, mythological characters, female Druids and Vikings, and Scandinavian priestesses and sorceresses. Blondes are awesome, queenly, angelic; brunettes invite love and inspire enthusiastic poets. One sees Eve as fair; Lilith, as dark. Solomon's Sulamitess, "black but beautiful," had safe, milk-washed eyes. Hearn elsewhere expressed and lived out his rather steady preference for dark-skinned women.

Bibliography: Cott.

"FANTASTIC POSSIBILITIES OF INVENTION" (1878). Editorial. Hearn follows sensible predictions of electrical weapons and "flying machines" with notions of communications from "astral continents" and chemically crystallized "human flesh and blood."

FANTASTICS AND OTHER FANCIES **(1914).** A collection of 36 sketches from the New Orleans *Item* (1879–1881) and New Orleans *Times-Democrat* (1882–1884). Charles Woodward Hutson* assembled and republished them in 1914. They reappear as part of Volume 2 of *The Writings of Lafcadio Hearn* (1922), with an introduction by Hutson. He indicates which sketches were titled by Hearn, who usually called them "Fantastiques," and which titles Hudson provided. *See* Appendix for individual titles.

Bibliography: Kunst.

"THE FATE OF THE COMET" (1882). Editorial. All comets, like moths around a flame, are probably doomed to fall into the sun. The centrifugal force of planets, vastly heavier than comets, creates steady planetary orbits. The sun, losing fuel, will die, perhaps in 3.2 quadrillion years. By then, our life force may "be reborn under a myriad million forms." Hearn, who was excited by the bright 1882 comet, was no scientist. He pontificates, inaccurately if poetically, that comets, which he says help fuel the sun, travel "through shoals of embryonic nebulae floating in immensity like fish-spawn," that tiny Vulcan may be between Mercury and the sun, that the earth was once a star.

FENOLLOSA, ERNEST FRANCISCO (1853–1908). Orientalist and educator. Fenollosa was born in Salem, Massachusetts; studied art history under the eminent Charles Eliot Norton (1837–1908) and also philosophy at Harvard; was class poet; and graduated at the head of his class (1874). He attended Harvard Divinity School (1874–1877) and took classes at the Boston Museum of Fine Arts (1877). In 1878 Fenollosa married Lizzie Goodhue Millet and accepted a position as professor at Tokyo's Imperial University (1878–1886). Edward Sylvester Morse (1838–1925), his archaeologist friend from Salem, was teaching there and had recommended him. Fenollosa was attracted to Japanese art, helped preserve Japanese temples and shrines, salvaged sculptural pieces from junkyards, and bought paintings carelessly left in furniture stores. He initiated and led a revival in Japanese and Chinese art history studies. He took a Japanese name and became a Buddhist (1885). Critical of Western-style pencils and crayons used in art classes, he helped restore Japanese ink-and-brush techniques (1885). In 1886 he sold his vast collection of Oriental paintings to a wealthy Bostonian on the condition that it go to the Boston Museum of Fine Arts. Also in 1886, accompanied by his wife and their son (who died in 1887) and daughter, he visited the United States and studied art education methods there (and abroad), under orders from the emperor of Japan.

Fenollosa taught aesthetics at the Imperial Museum at Tokyo (1887–1890) and helped form the Tokyo Fine Arts Academy (opened in 1889). Next, he was curator of Japanese art at the Boston Museum of Fine Arts (1890–1896) and curator of the Japanese display at the World's Colombian Exposition (Chicago, 1893). Divorced in 1895, he almost immediately married the twice-widowed Mary McNeil Chester Scott, who was 30 years old and had a child from each earlier marriage. She had lived in Japan in 1890 with her first husband. Returning to Japan with her twice in the 1890s, Fenollosa began to be ill-treated by Japanese authorities, who were turning jingoistic, xenophobic, and militaristic as their culture modernized. Downgraded, he taught English to Tokyo's Imperial Normal School language students (1897–1900). He grew fond of Japanese No plays, translated 50 or so, and helped preserve that art form. In the United States (1900–1908) he lectured from coast to coast; lived in Mobile, Alabama, and New York; and advised Columbia University professors on East Asian studies.

He visited Japan once more, to supervise the publication of *An Outline History of Ukiyoye* (1901), his study of seventeenth-century Japanese wood-block prints. While on a planned European tour to lecture to traveling students visiting art museums, he died of a heart attack in London. Buried there, his ashes were transported by a Japanese warship and reburied at a temple in Kyoto, Japan.

Fenollosa's vast bibliography includes essays, art catalogues, lectures, poetry, and bits of fiction. His *Epochs of Chinese and Japanese Art: An Outline History of East Asiatic Design* is monumental. Left in 1906 incomplete and in rough form, with uncorrected errors, it was scrupulously edited and improved by his widow (by then a novelist publishing as Sidney McCall); she even returned to Japan and enlisted the help of two Japanese art experts. The book, issued in 1912, deals with primitive, Buddhist, idealistic, and modern Chinese art, and with Buddhist, feudal, modern, and plebeian Japanese art. Fenollosa sought to oppose the ramifications of scientific materialism by fusing cultural multiplicity with an ultra-modern aesthetic. His theories influenced many artists, including Max Weber and Georgia O'Keeffe, and many poets, including William Butler Yeats and Ezra Pound (his literary executor). Several American Orientalists and travelers among his personal friends were Henry Adams, William Sturges Bigelow, John LaFarge, and also Percival Lowell,* some of whose work Hearn admired.

Hearn knew of Fenollosa's fame in Japan. The June 1895 *Atlantic Monthly* published an unsigned review of Hearn's *Glimpses of Unfamiliar Japan* that criticized its lack of unity, scientific aim, and philosophical understanding. Hearn was convinced that Fenollosa was the reviewer, who in the same review criticized *Japanese Things* (1890, later *Things Japanese*) by Basil Hall Chamberlain,* Hearn's friend at the time. Hearn grew angry and sent an undated letter to Horace Scudder, editor of the *Atlantic Monthly*, labeling Fenollosa a quack and a fraud. In later letters in 1895 to Scudder, Hearn continued downgrading Fenollosa. In one (July 7), Hearn praised Fenollosa as "an authority on Japanese art" but added that Fenollosa "made a fortune" by collecting it, and Hearn "doubt[ed] his intellectual sincerity, his spirit of fairness, and the sense in him of scruple as to his use of that knowledge [of Japanese art]." Still, the two men made and retained contact. In the spring of 1898 Hearn visited the Fenollosas, both of whom recorded their impressions of him as splendid, delightful, charming. In April 1898 Hearn sent them an inscribed copy of *Gleanings in Buddha-Fields* (1897). When he forwarded to Fenollosa part of his *Exotics and Retrospectives* (1898), Mrs. Fenollosa wrote him to praise it. But Hearn gradually reverted to feeling offended. When on two later occasions the Fenollosas tried to call on Hearn at his home in Tokyo, he was not at home or said as much by a servant, and soon thereafter wrote to Fenollosa that he should give him notice because friends were worse than enemies since they said they admired his work, wanted more of it, but broke into his "habits of industry" somewhat like children hurting butterflies by excessive caresses (December 1898). Hearn did go on to express gratitude for "that wonderful story"—presumably "Mountain of Skulls," a legend Hearn used in *In Ghostly Japan* (1899). Another likely source of discomfiture for Hearn may have been his attempting to discuss the works of Herbert Spencer with Fenollosa, who had founded Harvard's Herbert Spencer Club and may have found Hearn philosophically shallow.

Bibliography: Bisland; Van Wyck Brooks, *Fenollosa and His Circle with Other Essays* (New York: E. P. Dutton, 1962); Lawrence W. Chisolm, *Fenollosa: The Far East and American Culture* (New Haven and London: Yale University Press, 1963); Dawson; Miner; Murray.

"THE FEROCITY OF THE SHOEMAKER" (1881).

Editorial. Ready-made shoes rarely fit, because men have all kinds of differently shaped feet. Custom-made shoes that take corn and bunion positions into account cause new corns and bunions. Stretched shoes shrink. If used shoes sold to another man don't burst quickly, they cause injuries. No wonder customers plan vengeful acts on "diabolical" shoemakers.

"THE FIRST MUSICIAN" (1884).

Rune. Once Wainamoinen has created his three-stringed kantele, old men, young men, and witches are unable to play it. An ancient suggests casting it into water, but it rises all dripping and asks to be given back to Wainamoinen. He sings strong, brave runes, which birds accompany by warbling. The king and queen of the woods, the god of beasts, their followers, more birds, and even the sun, the moon, and fish enjoy the runes. Men and women weep for joy. When Wainamoinen cries responsively, his tears flow through black sands into the sea and become pearls. A seamew gathers the pearls, destined for kings and heroes.

FOLEY, ALETHEA (c. 1846–?).

Hearn's first wife, nicknamed Mattie. She was born a slave near Marysville, Kentucky. Her mother was a slave whom Mattie's white father owned. Mattie became a servant to her Irish father's legitimate, white, married daughter. Freed after the Civil War, Mattie had a son named William by a Scotsman named Anderson. She was a beautiful mulatto cook in a Cincinnati boardinghouse where Hearn lodged in 1873 or so. William, age 4 at the time, was with her. Mattie was illiterate but had a fund of stories to which Hearn listened, often sitting on the kitchen stairs with her. She also kept late meals warm for him and nursed him when he was ill. Soberly recognizing a duty to a lover, but perhaps also thrilled by a dangerous liaison, he proposed marriage. Because of anti-miscegenation laws, it was hard to find a minister; but the two were married in a black woman's home on June 14, 1874, by a black Episcopalian clergyman named John King. Notoriety about the affair cost Hearn his job with the Cincinnati *Enquirer*. He easily found employment with the rival Cincinnati *Commercial*. The couple remained together only until 1875. Meanwhile, she was developing a reputation for violence. She later contended that she deserted him in the fall of 1877 because he was gloomy and also fussy about clothes and food.

After relocating to New Orleans in 1877, Hearn missed Mattie and professed both continued love for her and anguish that he had raised her social status only to allow her to fall beneath her premarital level. Nevertheless he feared that news of his interracial marriage would reach New Orleans and hurt him professionally and socially. In 1880 Mattie married a black man named John Kleintank, although Hearn did not know of this event. In 1906, two years after Hearn's death, Mattie, by then separated from her husband and calling herself a Creole, sought to establish a legal claim on Hearn's estate and published an account of their relationship in the Cincinnati *Enquirer*, but it failed on the grounds that although a wedding ceremony had occurred in 1874, the marriage was illegal. Curiously, both Hearn and his father married attractive women from different cultural backgrounds and considerably less well educated than they; further, both father and son and both of their wives remarried. In "The Pariah People" (1875), Hearn writes about couples in Bucktown (a Cincinnati slum area) "who have lost cast by miscegenation." In "Some Strange Experience" (also 1875), the kitchen worker who tells Hearn about her ghostly visitations, though unnamed, is based on Mattie Foley.

Bibliography: Bisland; Cott; George Hughes, "Lafcadio Hearn and the Fin de Siècle," in Hirakawa, pp. 83–103; Kennard; Murray; Tinker; *Veiled Letters from Lafcadio Hearn*, ed. Kaoru Sekita (Tokyo: Yushudo Press, 1991).

"FOR THE SUM OF $25" (1882). Editorial. A Philadelphia newspaper reported that wretched translations of fine French and German books are prepared in saloons for $25 a volume. It is not surprising that these translations mangle the originals and that no talented linguist will undertake such work. Hearn rhapsodizes on the subtlety of the French language as handled by "the great masters" and discusses the time-consuming difficulty of echoing their "shades of meaning" and their "harmonies of tones." It's no wonder, he says, the French, Italian, and Spanish words for "translator" and "traitor" are virtually synonymous. French Naturalists in particular, hurt by "bogus" translations, deserve better. *See* Translations by Hearn.

Bibliography: Tinker.

"FORGERY IN ART" (1883). Editorial. A recent book by Paul Eudel, published in Paris, warns would-be art buyers to beware of tricks by forgers. After listing upward of two dozen objects often faked—from armor to vellum texts— Hearn describes how forgers can create fake paintings, etchings, and engravings. He commends the French for proposing strict laws against forgers and for organizing detectives knowledgeable in art. Paul Eudel (1837–1911) published *Le Truquage: les contrafaçons dévoilées* (dated 1884).

"THE FOUNTAIN MAIDEN" (1884). Tale. Thieves sing to everything in nature to be quiet, so that the natives of Rarotonga will sleep and thieves can steal bananas, coconuts, plaintains, and taros. One night Chief Aki sees a naked boy and girl emerge from the fountain of Vaipiki. When they sing, everything turns silent and motionless. Aki captures the fountain maiden in a net. The boy escapes. Aki wins her love, but her silvery beauty waxes and wanes with the phases of the moon. Years later, though aging, Aki sires her son, who for 10 years grows tall and handsome. His mother, to avoid death, slips back into the fountain. After a great storm, the lad disappears. Aki lives to be more than a hundred years old. Dying, he is placed on pandanus leaves. A sweet old song is heard. The watchers sleep. A woman whiter than moonbeams glides to Aki and kisses him. Dawn comes. He sleeps forever.

"THE FOUNTAIN OF GOLD." *See* "A Tropical Intermezzo."

"THE FRENCH IN LOUISIANA" (1880). Editorial. Critics of the recent law encouraging the use of the French language in "public affairs and public schools" in New Orleans are prejudiced. The French here display good manners and customs. French businesses are thriving. It would be advantageous if the city became "the central point for America-seeking French emigrants."

"FRENCH JOURNALISM" (1880). Editorial. Boastful though American newsmen are, journalism in Europe is better, especially in France. The French daily is four pages, in clear type, with only one page of advertisements. "[H]asty news" is minimized, thus saving high telegraph costs. Splendid writers are employed as traveling correspondents; their contributions are occasional and are a combination of letters and editorials; they are paid well and have bylines, and if they grow ineffective they are dumped. A given paper usually has a known editorial position. By comparison, American journalists are "unlettered scribblers."

"A FRENCH TRANSLATION OF EDGAR POE" (1879). Essay. Hearn begins by lauding Edgar Allan Poe's "subtleties of language," especially words having to do with colors, and then he praises translations of Poe by Charles Baudelaire (1821–1867). However, no translator can handle Poe's use of certain words, for example, "ghastly" (not quite the French *sinistre, lugubre*), "hideous" (*affreux*), and "duskily" (*confusément*).

"THE FURNACE FIENDS [1]" (1874). Cincinnati news article. This is the fifth of eight articles about the murder of Herman Schilling on Saturday, November 7, 1874, by Andreas Egner, his son Frederick K. Egner, and their friend

George Rufer, in revenge for Schilling's having allegedly seduced Andreas Egner's daughter Julia, about 15 years of age, who later died while pregnant. The other articles, in chronological order, are "Violent Cremation," "Killed and Cremated," "It Is Out!," "The Tannery Horror," "The Furnace Fiends [2]," "The Quarter of Shambles," and "The Furnace Horror." By Thursday, November 12, Hearn has come to tentative conclusions concerning details of the murder, comments on Andreas's viciousness, and sympathizes to a degree with Fred, who is uneducated and was often beaten by his father.

"THE FURNACE FIENDS [2]" (1874). Cincinnati news article. This is the sixth of eight articles about the murder of Herman Schilling on Saturday, November 7, 1874. Friday, November 13: The prisoners are remanded to await grand-jury action. Andreas's weeping wife visits him in jail, only to be snarled at. When Mrs. Egner, somewhat dazed, comes in and shows Egner their baby, he breaks down and cries uncontrollably. Returning home, she attempts a few times to kill her baby but is restrained, held, and declared briefly demented.

"THE FURNACE HORROR" (1874). Cincinnati news article. This is the last of eight articles about the murder of Herman Schilling on Saturday, November 7, 1874. Sunday, November 15: George Rufer tells the sheriff he is Protestant and is prepared for execution. He adds that Andreas Egner pitchforked Schilling through his bowels and also entirely crushed his skull. Hearn concludes his gory reports by saying that Schilling, earlier praised as handsome and hard-working, should have realized he was in danger for having been well known as one of Egner's daughter's disloyal lovers and, instead of waiting for dire trouble, should have left "Cincinnati, at least for a time."

Given today's slow pace of justice, it is remarkable that this hideous murder case was virtually wrapped up—detective work, arrests, inquest, confessions, and cross-examinations—in less than a week. All that remained, evidently, was a speedy jury trial, sentencing, and at least two hangings.

"FURNISHED ROOMS" (1879). Sketch. A male Creole cannot understand why "prizes" for "Room garneesh" are so "elevate." (It must be that the landladies do not want him as a tenant.)

G

"THE GHOSTLY KISS" (1880). Sketch. The narrator describes the theater, with black velvet hangings and filled with a white-clad audience. Palms outside move in the moonlight. No one looks at him. A beautiful woman sits in front of him. His heart beats frantically. He cannot resist kissing her humid, responsive lips. She says that the kiss seals their eternal compact. The seats turn to graves; the dresses, shrouds; the stage, a mausoleum. This is the most hallucinatory of several Hearnean corpse-kissing sketches.

Bibliography: Kunst.

"GIBBETED" (1876). Cincinnati news article. On August 31, 1875, James Murphy, age 19, and some cronies got drunk on beer and whisky and tried to crash a wedding ball in Dayton, Ohio. It was managed by Colonel William Dawson, the employer of the bridegroom. A fracas followed, and Murphy, in a fit of passion, stabbed Dawson to death. Despite his efforts to blame others, Murphy was convicted on April 28, 1876, and was sentenced to be hanged on August 25, 1876. While waiting in jail, he heard his gallows being built. He confessed to his Irish-Catholic priest, made a public confession, and walked to his execution. The authorities used a thin rope, which Murphy's weight caused to break. Stunned and soon hysterical, he groaned, "Why, I ain't dead—I ain't dead!" and then said he could walk up to the platform again. He was hanged once more, with better rope, six and a half minutes later, and was pronounced dead seventeen minutes after that. Hearn was evidently present, may have been "the reporter" who felt Murphy's pulse after the first attempt at his being hanged, and lavishes all kinds of details on Murphy's stated drunken action at the ball, the lad's anguish in jail, relevant official documents and personages, and the final debacle. Touches include a description of Murphy's older brother dancing on the scaffold, Murphy's dreaming of his deceased mother and hearing her "crying weirdly" (other prisoners said they also heard her), and the spiritual comfort the priest provided Murphy. "Gibbeted" has been frequently reprinted.

Bibliography: Cott.

YE GIGLAMPZ. Weekly newspaper. In Cincinnati in 1874, Hearn pooled his savings with those of his friend Henry F. Farny (1847–1916), a cartoonist and artist, to found a weekly newspaper. Hearn did the writing and editing, and Farny furnished the illustrations. They were backed temporarily by the publishers of *Kladderadatsch*, a German-language newspaper. A few other journalists provided slight aid. But Hearn and Farny, chronically arguing, were largely on their own. They produced only nine issues (June 21–August 16). Farny supposedly invented the title of the weekly after noticing the lamp-like reflections of lights off Hearn's owlish spectacles. The two advertised the paper thus: "A Weekly Illustrated Journal Devoted to Art, Literature, and Satire (Published Daily, Except Weekdays)." They poked irreverent fun at physicians, the temperance movement, and the YMCA, and sold ad space to local breweries and saloons. Hearn resigned from the Cincinnati *Enquirer* to try to make a go of *Ye Giglampz*, but when Farny tried to censor his style he quit and returned to the *Enquirer*. A highlight of *Ye Giglampz* was Farny's cartoon of Henry Ward Beecher (1813–1887) on a scaffold and wearing a scarlet letter. (In 1874 Beecher, a prominent Congregational clergyman who had lived earlier in Cincinnati, was charged with adultery. A trial lasting six months the following year resulted in jury disagreement.) Hearn contributed two minor fantasies, a piece on a gynecological butcher, squibs against city officials, and other items. For their eighth issue, Farny furnished drawings of a real-life steamer sinking. This scoop of the bigger daily newspapers could not save *Ye Giglampz*, because the public, already tired of its relentless satirical contents, incorrectly thought the drawings aimed to ridicule suffering. In the final number, Hearn lamented the weekly's death "of inanition and the bad taste of the great American people" and offered "[a] complete file . . . for sale cheap at this office." Anyone now finding such a file could probably sell it for thousands of dollars. The only complete set known to exist is in the Public Library of Cincinnati and Hamilton County, Ohio. Farny later designed a brochure for the Baldwin Piano Company titled *Walks about Cincinnati* (1888).

Bibliography: Jon Christopher Hughes, "Ye Giglampz and the Apprenticeship of Lafcadio Hearn," *American Literary Realism* 15 (Autumn 1982): 182–194; Murray; Stevenson.

"THE GLAMOUR OF NEW ORLEANS" (1878). Sketch. Hearn rhapsodizes on the numberless enchantments of New Orleans that draw visitors from all over the world to its "eternal summer."

"A GLANCE AT GYPSY LITERATURE" (1881). Editorial. A recent book from Seville, by "Demófilo," is a collection of gypsy ballads in the Andalusian dialect. Most are about love, usually unrequited, and are "full of frenzied passion and tortured symbolism"; a few concern revenge. Hearn quotes short passages from two songs in the original and then provides what he calls "line for line" translations of several other wild works. Antonio Machado y Alvarez (1846– 1893; pen name Demófilo) published *Cantes Flamencos* (Madrid, 188?).

GLEANINGS IN BUDDHA-FIELDS: STUDIES OF HAND AND SOUL IN THE FAR EAST **(1897).** Collection of 11 essays, the first five of which were previously published, whereas the sixth is based on an earlier treatment of the same subject. Thus the work may seem to be somewhat padded.

"A Living God" (1896): Shintō temples or shrines, perhaps better called ghost houses, are similar, seem "weird," and, but for dusky symbols, are empty— except for gods within. Hearn feels haunted when he enters one. He imagines himself as a god, impalpable like "ether or . . . magnetism," flitting wherever he will. He would have power, be prayed to for rain or love, enjoy gifts and festivals in his honor, and watch the changing seasons. In olden times Japanese village rules concerning ethics, work, and religion had the force of law. Deadly fights between individual rivals were rare. A girl could be wayward once but, if noticed with a second lover, would be disrobed, humiliated, and banished for five years. In case of fire or sickness, the whole village would turn out to help. Behold Hamaguchi Gohei, and old man a hundred years ago. Wise, rich, char- itable, and revered, one autumn day he felt the "long, slow, spongy motion" of a tiny earthquake. The villagers below felt nothing. Alarmed, Hamaguchi turned and saw the sea creeping back from the land and sensed the coming of a tsunami. Just in time, he set fire to his vast stacks of ripened rice, which were whipped by the sea wind into a gigantic blaze. It warned the entire village of four hundred to rush to Hamaguchi's high land just as the ebbing sea turned and struck five times and destroyed their homes. The grateful villagers converted Hamaguchi, impoverished now as they, into a living god, "for they believed that the ghost within him was divine." The commentary on religion obscures the only abiding value of "A Living God," which is the story about the old man.

"Out of the Street" (1896): Hearn's servant Manyemon, a student of classical Japanese poetry, gives Hearn a roll of songs by ordinary Japanese people. Clas- sical verse is difficult to study because of its subtle "sentiment, allusion, and color." "Vulgar" verse is artlessly simple, direct, and sincere, and it concerns timeless, classless human experiences. Out of Manyemon's 47 poems, Hearn is helped to render "the best" freely (if at times awkwardly). They vary from 17 to 31 syllables, and those syllables are in lines of five or seven syllables each. The poems chosen concern love. Hearn divides his sequence into three groups. The first group, of seven poems, expresses surprise, pain, reproach, weakness, and trust; the second, of eleven, expresses joy and surrender; the third, of six, expresses doubt, pain again, and love's survival to challenge death itself. Hearn offers the Japanese originals of several of the poems, together with touches of explication. For example, he says that in one poem *totaku* (meaning "somehow," "for some reason") adds "a peculiar pathos."

"Notes of a Trip to Kyōto" (1896): In October 1895 Hearn takes a train to see the historical processions celebrating the eleven hundredth anniversary of the founding of Kyōto. Geisha sing delightfully on the way. Kyōto is decorated with lanterns on posts. Hearn visits an exhibition at the imperial summer palace, buys pictures drawn by art students, marvels over the seemingly divinely inspired calligraphy of a six-year-old boy, revels in the palace garden built ten centuries ago, and goes by *jinrikisha* to a third-floor restaurant catering to foreigners—complete with tableware from "a long-defunct English hotel." At a bookstore he finds a copy of an 1860 *Atlantic Monthly* issue, with a commendable essay on Japan. He looks in on some street sideshows until silent darkness descends upon the crowds. He theorizes that the "charm of Japanese amusements" is augmented, as most pleasures are, by its fugitive, evanescent "cheapness." Poor people make beautiful things "out of nothing!" He buys 20 paper dolls made rapidly by a thin girl. Next morning, the procession: vast, friendly, patient crowd; stunningly graceful, dainty women, including one princess; marchers displaying costumes and uniforms from different historical periods. Hearn goes to the government's Shintō temple, has tea, and is given a souvenir cup. He visits the tomb of Yuko Hatakeyama, whose suicide, to repair Japan's honor, tarnished when the Russian czar's son was wounded while on Japanese soil, made her a national hero. (*See* "Yuko: A Reminiscence," in *Out of the East*.) He returns through a city quarter replete with temples. Although the walls are painted mud, the gates are of wood holding up tiles, and the gardens are mere shrubs and rocks and ponds, the harmonious effect is poetic enchantment. In this essay, one of his most charming, Hearn praises the Japanese for making pleasure out of what soon must pass and out of poverty's cheap objects. The essay is a little marred by his gratuitous degrading of most things Occidental: Japanese toys are superior to more expensively, and solidly, built American ones; "the bare walls and foul pavements and smoky skies" found in American cities are there to punish the "unfortunate, or weak, or stupid, or overconfident"; and we "in the West" should "learn our ethics over again from the common people." Hearn's one favorable comparison involving a foreign region occurs when the palace garden "vividly recalls some aspects of tropical nature in the Antilles."

"Dust" (1896): Hearn wandered into a rural area and saw some children "play[ing] at funerals" with wet clay. Japanese and Buddhists are aware of having lived and died a million times and of "the ghostliness of all substance." Hearns feels ghostly and haunted. Only shadow forces are real. Every atom in the universe has felt pleasure and pain. The "Cosmic Apparition" evolves, dissolves, is "metempsychosis" and "palingenesis," and experiences "a resurrection more stupendous than any dreamed of by Western creeds." Each human soul is "quintillions of souls." Nothing is new, only recomposed. Although the present assures us of past and future, we still wonder "Why!" The answer may lie in the Chinese symbol for man—a pair of legs. Its moral value? We live by "getting help and giving help."

"About Faces in Japanese Art" (1896): Edward Fairbrother Strange (1862–1929), a British expert lecturing in London on Japanese art, said that its principles are "the subordination of detail to the expression of a sensation or idea, the subordination of the particular to the general." Despite his noting of the influence of Japanese art on Aubrey Beardsley, James Whistler, and other Westerners, the critic was pooh-poohed, even by the Japanese ambassador, who was too enamored of recent Japanese military successes to be aware that only Japan's excellent "art sense" will enable it to compete commercially. Hearn says it took him two years to appreciate the merit of Japanese depictions of faces. When he saw their "grace and truth," Western pictures of faces seemed "flat, coarse, and clumsy." Greek art has had its fine critics, who have taught us that faces in Greek sculpture "represent . . . impossible perfection, a superhuman evolution." Critics should be telling us that faces in Japanese art, only "seemingly inexpressive," in reality "represent . . . the living, the actual, the everyday." Japanese artists subordinate details to type, to humanity, to feeling. They do so, as well, when depicting insects, flowers, elements of landscapes, and human figures. As for faces, they express boys by smoothness; women by coiffure, dress, and posture; and the elderly by wrinkles expressive of half-hidden "sweetness" or "resignation." Western realistic art fails not by having a multiplicity of details but by lacking significant details. Japanese art scientifically systematizes; Greek art aspires spiritually. Both seek impersonality and agree on the "non-moral significance of individual expression." Occidentals admire artistic depictions of faces showing the reverse of "inward *moral* perfections"—shrewdness, forcefulness, power—and all that not "to create and preserve," but to smash. Hearn concludes thus: Greek art aims to show beauty and wisdom; Japanese, to show joy, nature in flux, and harmony through orderliness. When he showed two Japanese youngsters Western illustrations, they called the people depicted horrible and hellish. Hearn's otherwise helpfully suggestive essay betrays its overall subjective design—to put down the civilization in which he spent a depressing childhood and youth. *The Colour-Prints of Japan: An Appreciation and History* (1904) was Strange's major work on his specialty.

"Ningyō-no-Haka": Manyemon introduces Iné, who tells Hearn her story. Iné, her parents, her paternal grandmother, her brother, and her baby sister lived together. Her father, a paperhanger, and her mother, a hairdresser, died within days of each other. The neighbors told them to build a *ningnō-no-haka* (a third grave) to prevent the often-anticipated third death in a family from occurring. But the brother, a seal-cutter, became feverish and raved that his mother was pulling him toward death. Despite the grandmother's scolding of her meddling daughter-in-law (a humorous touch), the lad also died. Iné says that her sister was nicely adopted, kneels before Hearn to thank him for his sympathy, and will depart once he has struck the warm spot where she knelt to ward off his absorbing of her griefs. But no. Hearn sits there. Manyemon tells the girl that "the master" wants to absorb her grief so as to understand other people's pain.

"In Ōsaka": The seaport city of Ōsaka was founded more than 2,500 years ago. It has not changed essentially since Captain John Saris (?–1646), a British merchant and sea captain, described visiting it almost three centuries ago. Now the empire's financial and commercial center, it is superior to Tōkyō, with factories, shipping companies, and "commercial travelers" unique in appearance and ability. Its citizens are fashion-setters, including geisha in silks of "a burning sky-blue." Because of its narrow streets, canals, and overhanging houses, it has been called "the Venice of Japan." It has numerous bridges and a downtown crowded with tall buildings, theaters, restaurants, hotels, and a foreign corner called "the old Concession." It has a superb newspaper that is managed from quiet, modest offices. Ōsaka is a veritable "commercial school of the empire," in which apprentice-clerks work 15 hours a day, for 12 to 14 years, learning aspects of industrial or trade companies. Predicting that Japan's old ways will continue for another century at least, Hearn visits Tennōji, a sixth-century Buddhist temple. Although saying it "would be hopeless" to try to describe the ancient place, he proceeds to do so: timbers, walls, five-story pagoda, pond, bridge, statues, gates, and spring. Elements of worship there are unusual: bell towers, tapers, incense, and innumerable tablets commemorating deceased children, with a bell rope woven of their bibs. In contrast is a pair of modern temples of pure, dignified Buddhist design. Hearn roughly equates rites therein, with respect to those of old Japan, to Catholicism versus Protestantism. He describes some cemeteries, one with a statue of a famous wrestler and a statue of a wine gourd. On his last day in Ōsaka he shops for toys and silks. While doing so he inquires about the clerks' wages, food, and working conditions. An evening train finally bears him away from "the cheery turmoil" of a city flourishing because of Japanese love, patience, and trust. Hearn is at pains to praise things Japanese at the expense of things non-Japanese. Thus after reporting that Ōsaka is full of little houses, cheaply constructed but beautiful, he adds that American "house-builders have universes of facts to learn . . . from the study of Japanese interiors"; also, foreign travelers who complain about fleas in Japanese inns should instead admire the fresh flowers in them "arranged as no European florist could ever learn."

"Buddhist Allusions in Japanese Folk-Songs": Proofs abound showing how thoroughly Buddhist idealism has "fertilized" the Japanese mind. Toys, industrial products, kitchenware, ceramics, gardens, shop signs, and the like all reveal it. So do literature, drama, narrative poetry, and simple folk songs. Hearn has collected almost 50 typical *dodoitsu*, songs of 26 syllables each, in four lines (7,7,7,5). Many deal with "the ideas of pre-existence and of future rebirths," notably when lovers poetize about post-death reunions. Some poems concern the transmigration of souls, as in the relentless "Wheel of Karma"; others, "the instability of all material things" (including the Ego), the vastness of the universe, and objects inviting witty treatment. Although he annotates and comments well, his translations of many poems presented in Japanese are stodgy.

"Nirvana: A Study in Synthetic Buddhism": Hearn begins this essay by contending that the Western mind has wrongly regarded Nirvana as annihilation, as "soul-death," but is correct in defining part of Buddhist philosophy as espousing "extinction of individual sensation, emotion, thought." One should, however, explain that everything in what we regard as self is temporary, illusory, and hence ultimately false. The "spiritual progress . . . up to Nirvana" evolves through physical necessities into "spheres," where one's self is emptied and proceeds to a state called "infinite bliss." What enters Nirvana, therefore, is one's ultimate karma, absent of self. Nirvana may be reached through what Hearn diagrams as two or three "even" or "uneven" "births," from "man" up to (and sometimes, not always, back down from) "heaven" and finally sidestepping "heaven" and entering Nirvana. In his concluding section, Hearn strains to relate Buddhism to nineteenth-century philosophical and scientific thought, with respect to unstable integrations, heredity, intellectual and moral advances, and— what he is pleased to include—wholesale repudiation of materialism, spiritualism, any divine creator, and personal spiritual immortality. He concludes by inviting us to believe that "One" is the unique reality, that all physical "Substance" is "unreal." Midway through, Hearn hints that acceptance of Buddhism results in "opacities which darkened the reality of Mind within the mirage of mind begin [ning] to [be] illumine [d]."

"The Rebirth of Katsugorō": Hearn presents the translation of a set of official Japanese documents dated from 1823 and concerning the previous life, rebirth, and subsequent life of a boy named Katsugorō. According to seemingly incontrovertible testimony, the boy, son of Genzō and his wife, Sei, in the province of Musashi, and age 9 at the time of the depositions, creditably asserted that in his previous existence he was Tōzō, son of Kyūbei, of a different village but in the same province. He said that as Tōzō he had died of smallpox at age 6 some years earlier. Katsugorō told his sister about all this, in confidence, and expressed surprise that she could not also remember her own previous existence. She revealed the secret to their parents. Katsugorō then sought support by telling his paternal grandmother, Tsuya, and even revealing precise details of his burial and his later being virtually flown into his new mother's womb. Believing him, gentle Tsuya took him to Tōzō's village. Katsugorō immediately ran to his previous home, was recognized and embraced by his previous parents, and pointed out physical changes in their neighborhood, thus convincing various witnesses of the veracity of his account. A translator's note explains that these documents were purchased in 1869 by a collector of unusual stories. Hearn creates both verisimilitude and confusion by flooding his presentation with more than two dozen names of Japanese persons and places.

"Within the Circle": One cannot acceptably describe to anyone else one's pains or pleasures. So, how is it possible to express "the real pain of seeing my former births," asks Hearn, who then tries, with such words as "agony," "anguish, "despaired," "ghastliness," "monstrous," and "shuddered." His past lives provided no pleasures. Then "the voice of the divine one" comforts him by saying that everything seemingly joyful—nature, heroic deeds, fine works, emotions, thoughts—is only sensuous, shadowy, dreamy, phantasmagoric. Everything "in Time must perish." Wake up—to nothing temporal, spatial, or mutable. Without infinite awareness, you cannot learn "the Secret."

Hearn completed *Gleanings in Buddha-Fields* while in Kōbe, but it was published after he began living in Tokyo, a city he hated. By the end of his Kōbe days he was internalizing his experiences to a greater extent. Also, some of the depressing touches in the book may have crept in during revisions accomplished in Tokyo. The book was also published in London and was reissued both there and in the United States.

Bibliography: Edwin Bayrd, *Kyoto* (New York: Newsweek, 1974); Bisland; Dawson; Kennard; Kunst.

GLIMPSES OF UNFAMILIAR JAPAN (1894). Two-volume travel book containing a preface and 27 often disparate essays, six of which had been previously published. Hearn dedicated the book to Mitchell McDonald, a U.S. Navy man and his friend, and Basil Hall Chamberlain,* a Japanologist. In the preface Hearn says that after a residence in Japan of only four years he can offer mere "glimpses." Feeling that Western-style "progress" has been detrimental here, he therefore dislikes agnostic Japanese "intellectuals," Occidentalized Japanese, "modern" developments, and foreign commentators. The cultural implications of Japanese superstitions should be valued. He extols the common Japanese people's charity, courtesy, goodness, happiness, kindness, morality, patience, and simplicity. True, they have their shadowy side, but it is brighter than Western darkness.

In "My First Day in the Orient" (1892) Hearn describes his tour of Yokohama with Cha, a *jinrikisha* runner: narrow streets with small, half-smiling people; colorful ideographs; shops with tempting wares; instinctive touches of art everywhere; and matchless, dreamy Fujiyama. He visits the interiors of two Buddhist temples, where he is offered tea and sugar-cakes. Then he goes on to a shrine, with park, children, and cherry trees. Though neither Christian nor Buddhist, Hearn tells Akira Manabe, an English-speaking attendant, that he admires the beauty of Buddhism and the faith of Buddhists. He sees demonic Ni-Ō statues guarded by a pretty girl. At twilight he heads back to the hotel. Before he sleeps and dreams, he hears a blind woman singing and asking for money to massage one's pains away.

"The Writing of Kobodaishi": Hearn relates how, according to Akira, his friend, Kobodaishi, the most wizard of ancient writers, could write beautifully with five brushes in hands, feet, and mouth, on water and in the sky, and depicting the special "ten" character. When opponents jeered him, they were made to dream of being beaten up.

"Jizō" (1892): Akira takes Hearn to see various Buddha statues. The two read their fortunes by numbered bamboo sticks. At a Buddhist cemetery Hearn sees six Jizō statues. Jizō is a lover and playmate of deceased children. Hearn moves on through the cemetery, seeing statues of Buddha with different symbolic values, figures of animals, a grove of sun-caressed trees, and a sad half-caste child proscribed and hence better off with Jizō. Akira takes Hearn to a village of temples where, beyond several statues, they visit a funereal place. Akira lectures on burial customs. They unroll several paintings—of daylight, ghosts, demons, souls in fire and a lake of blood, and finally a garden of paradise with blue sky above. Akira concludes by reading a child-pitying Jizō hymn from a book two hundred years old.

"A Pilgrimage to Enoshima" (1892): Feeling melancholy under "a speckless azure sky," Hearn joins Akira on a *jinrikisha* trip. They arrive at En-gaku-ji temple, with two-story gate, temples, grove, and a "sacred," thick-lipped bell five feet in diameter, cast 650 years ago. Akira strikes it once, and it "sob[s] and moan[s] for . . . ten minutes." He recounts legends about it. There are hollowed-out chapels in a stony hill, and the Ken-chōji temple, beyond which is a bronze fountain. Another temple houses a thousand Jizō. Akira tells of a woman who made a silk cap for a chilled Jizō; when she died, she was condemned by King Emma, judge of the dead, to a fiery hell for hurting silkworms, but the grateful Jizō rescued her. Next Hearn and Akira visit 700-hundred-year-old Emma's temple; they pass nine statues, after which the surprising tenth is hideous Emma, wrought by a craftsman returned from death. Hearn buys an authenticated picture of Emma. He is impressed when he sees a gigantic statue of Buddha near the big Kwannon temple. Within is a tiny statue of Kwannon, beside which is "the great Kwannon"—seen if one contributes a fee. Her "divine feminity [sic] . . . produces . . . reverence." He goes past dwellings to Enoshima, a sacred island, with a palace for its goddess. Shops are packed. The Benton shrine is hidden by several Shintō temples, but the city has a military museum and a dragon-shaped cavern, which Hearn finds unaccountably charming. At the nearby Kishibojin temple he hears about its female, child-devouring demon. Distressed by "Christian bigotry," Hearn attempts to see only challenging goodness in numberless gods piled into "fathomless" mythologies; he concludes they need "some human love." Surrounded by kind-eyed onlookers, he boards a return train.

"At the Market of the Dead" (1891): Akira invites Hearn to the market where one can buy things needed for the Festival of the Dead (July 13–15). Foodstuffs are offered by torchlight, ever since a Buddhist thus fed his deceased mother, suffering hunger for her sins. Mourners sit before tiny shrines, sip tea, then proceed through streets to obtain real and artificial flowers, votive sticks, dishes, lanterns, bits of decoration, beaded tassels—all taken to a dream-like temple. Gongs clang to command gifts and prayers. Hearn hopes a poor mother will feel her dead daughter's hands. This short essay is unusually unified.

"Bon-Odori" (1892): A four-day journey by *jinrikisha* brings Hearn, with

Akira, past humble Buddhist temples and bigger Shintō symbols toward Ka-miyo. Scenery varies. Temperature grows hot. They stop at a nice little inn. People in Japan's interior are unimaginably courteous. Measured clapping sounds signal "the Bon-Odori, the Dance of the Festival of the Dead." At a Buddhist temple court, it begins. Tall women and girls lead, followed by shorter ones; all resemble birds, "dreams of shapes" seen on Greek or Etruscan vases. Hearn describes the dance motions and gestures, steps, smiles, swayings, cir-clings, bows. The moonlit audience is lulled into silence. Hearn feels bewitched into the past. Crickets are shrill. Two huge males appear, chant, and praise children. At the sound of a temple bell "the witchcraft ends" to the sound of "Sayōnara!" The female necromancers turn into callow lasses who now glance at Hearn's "foreign face." Hearn recalls emotions evoked by European art forms. But this dance was part of something immemorially ancient, vibrating to some-thing universal, akin "to the music of solitudes." This essay first appeared in the New Orleans *Times-Democrat* (March 6, 1892).

"The Chief City of the Province of the Gods" (1891): Hearn describes the first sounds (rice-cleaning pestle, temple bells, street-vendors' cries) and sights ("ghostly love-colors," bridge, junk sail) of a Matsue morning. Residents clap, wash in the river, and offer Shintō sun prayers. People swarm on "twinkling . . . feet" in wooden sandals. Children hurry to school, and lake steamers toot. Rice and beans are offered to propitiate evil gods. An iron-pillared river bridge recently opened to fireworks fanfare. It replaced a centipede-like structure three centuries old, built, washed away, but finally rebuilt after a human sacrifice appeased the flood spirits. Gensuke, the victim, became a legend. A lake islet is sacred to the goddess of eloquence and beauty, but its legend concerns a woman, lovely, pious, and unhappy, who drowned there and was memorialized. Hearn devoutly collects *ofuda* (overdoor papers with "idiographic inscriptions"). Up a narrow street are dwarfish houses made of tinted timbers. Farther along are bamboo poles holding spidery fish nets of black silk. Beyond is the spectral Daisen mountain, called the local Fuji. Hearn continues his rambling itinerary: Jizō temple; other temples with cemeteries, temple courts with wrestling matches, dances, and toy vendors; students studying biology and practicing mil-itary marches; pilgrims with mushroom-shaped straw hats, fed by rice donations from dirt-poor farmers. Hearn adverts to Matsue's layout, its samurai homes and how in feudal times thousands of warriors could muster in a moment by the castle. To sanctify this structure a beautiful maiden was immured alive. Most Matsue temples have their individual traditions. Hearn offers two: A misbehav-ing samurai's child was beheaded; a mother, buried alive and giving birth, died and became a ghost. This disoriented essay concludes with a description of light, dreamy sunsets, a street shop at night, seasonally misty sights, and nocturnal lights and shadows—lamps like fireflies—and sounds—bells and street yells—and finally a dream about children playing with shadows and demons.

"Kitsuki: The Most Ancient Shrine of Japan" (1891): One September morning Hearn and Akira take a tiny lake steamer. Akira answers many questions about

Buddhism but can handle few about Shintō. They pass the temple of a Buddhist treating afflicted eyes. Even though Hearn says he does not care about the god of obstacles, they do discuss the god of poverty. Once on land, they take *jin-rikishas* on a dike-like road past rice fields with bubbly-sounding frogs. There are sparkling lights here in Kitsuki's town. Their hotel landlord points out an avenue with a prayer hall near the temple and tells about the sacred serpent: one being caught each year and brought to the gods' annual assembly to announce the gods' arrival. In the morning the travelers have a smoke and eat breakfast. A Shintō messenger-priest escorts Hearn and Akira past a box for offerings beside the temple. Priests awaiting the visitors remind Hearn of a French print of Assyrian astrologers. A letter of recommendation permits him into the presence, once he kneels in obeisance, of Senke Takanori, the head priest, regarded as of divine ancestry. Young, powerful, bearded, and statuesque, he says Hearn is the first foreigner ever admitted to Kitsuki. He courteously explains that the temple has had to be rebuilt countless times. Hearn asks questions about its present timbers, where the deities assemble, and how many pilgrims come. He gets much information from the head priest, who is also called the Guji, and his assistant, Sasa—about architecture, wrestling, deities' names, relics, furniture, wooden firemaking devices, rice gifts, storms, and musical instruments. He is allowed to observe the graceful walk-dance of a lovely virgin priestess. They visit other edifices and are shown old manuscripts secreted in the Guji's personal residence. As Hearn leaves, his gracious host gives him images of deities and some historical documents. He and Akira are escorted to a beach resort and play host to some local priests. The Guji is venerated more than anyone else except the emperor himself. Hearn learns about some legends of both potent persons. Returning to Matsue, Hearn reviews what he has learned during this dreamlike journey to Kitsuki. Obviously, Shintōism remained a mystery to Hearn, who nonetheless pleasingly and memorably limns his gracious host, Senke Takanori, the mighty Guji.

"In the Cave of the Children's Ghosts": From Matsue by way of rice valleys, Hearn goes to Mitsu-ura, a town near the mountains. Then he goes on by boat to Kaka-ura, with its rough "goblin coast," and to the beautiful sea cave of Kami, with tall, smooth walls. Because Hearn is not evil, no stone from above falls to crush him as they glide in. Light from a side archway provides illumination. Atop another entrance is a Jizō fountain of milk for needy children. Inside, tumultuous waters splash and echo. Hearn decides not to have a swim when the boatwoman screams "Samē" (sharks). She also pounds the bow with a stone to ward off "ma" (goblins). In another grotto is a happy-faced Jizō statue. Hearn learns that the nearby towers of stones and pebbles have been piled up by dead children. Footprints of "infant ghosts" are traced in the sand by drips from the cave roof. Artifacts alongside the statue are both Buddhist and Shintō. When strong waves tumble the towers, they are magically rebuilt the next calm night. Hearn bumps a tower down and is told to rebuild two. Like the murmurs of children are the water's "broken syllables." Then the travelers head back to the drowsy streets of Kaka and to their open, empty hotel. A naiad-like young woman, naked to the waist, runs ahead and admits them, and crowds darken the windows to have a look at the foreigner. The host gently rebukes the "peepers," all "fresh and clean as flower-buds." After dinner Hearn is escorted by a crowd, silent as in a dream, to his boat. He would like somehow to preserve this image of the Kaka natives, silent as in a dream; but, no, "all things pass away."

"At Mionoseki": Residents at Mionoseki tolerate no eggs because the son of the god of Kitsuki was not awakened by his rooster promptly, lost his oars, and had his hands, by which to paddle home from Mionoseki, bitten by "the wicked fishes." Hearn steams into Mionoseki, "the quaintest city of little Japanese cities." The backs of houses face the beach, for ease of mooring. He visits the Miojinja temple. Only its sloping pavement approach is unusual—with lions and lamps of stone, and a gigantic bronze tank. Girls learning needlework offer votive samples to the temple's motherly deity. Hearn admires bargemen plying cross-handled oars and chanting a refrain ending "Ghi!" Nocturnal revelry of "Old Japan" sailors is noisy, with lantern-lighted banquets, dancing and drum-thumping geishas, and saké. In the morning Hearn observes a 500-strong crew of "New Japan" sailors, "manned by brown Latin men" in white uniforms and looking fit and well disciplined aboard an imperial "monster" cruiser with turrets, guns, chains, and the like. Would-be visitors are disappointed when they are told that no more can climb up on deck. As the man-of-war steams out, the little boats all scatter to avoid the wake. Hearn, ever the pacifist, deplores rice-paddy workers' taxes for this "magnificent horror of steam and steel and all the multiple enginery of death." Drowsy little Mionoseki is preferable, especially when that "sinister vision" is again out of sight. This sprightly essay is unified by beginning and ending with local songs. Incidentally, Hearn says here that he has been in Izumo for 14 months.

"Notes on Kitsuki": This essay is a jumble of diary-like entries, some dated in July 1891. Hearn says that although Akira has left he now has other friends and is known and liked. He discusses the Guji again, his swimming regimen, and his people's reverence for him; Miko's face and dance, her residence, and legends about her; strangely rooted trees and horses made of straw; a certain deity's riding through the streets on a bronze horse, which was really a statue; stopping a wooden dragon's movement by cutting its throat; calligraphy and ideographs; sales at temple festivals of toys, including miniature animals, games, and dolls (some lifelike and much revered). Finally, the Hōnen-odori (The Dance of the Fruitful Year) takes place, including supper, crowds in motion, and a sequence of soloists and dancers in two rings; it so captivated Hearn that he thought the seven-hour event lasted only three hours.

"At Hinomisaki": By boat Hearn goes to visit Hinomisaki, a town near Kitsuki, to see its double temples dedicated to the Lady of Light and her divine brother. The water is of variously colored, rock-pierced depths, and the beachless coast is ruggedly fissured. Near the oddly scooped bay are millions of cuttlefish drying on bamboo frames. The two remote temples are so massive that the poor nearby fisherfolk and small numbers of pilgrims cannot support them. Tax money and rich merchants from afar augment the funds needed. The head priest permits Hearn to visit the Sun temple, an example of ancient Shintō architecture "interpenetrated and allied with Buddhism." It is dainty, with carved altar, lacquer work in scarlet and gold, and cloud-and-dragon ceiling—all in "a blended . . . opulent repose." Beyond its gallery is the smaller temple, recently rebuilt in an inadequate manner. At the pontiff's spacious "ancestral residence" in a chamber with a hundred mats Hearn dines on seaweed, wine, and much else. A legend has it that a haughty Izumo ruler, entertained in the seventeenth century in this old Hinomisaki residence, demanded his host's pretty wife for concubinage. Courteously refused, he exiled the host, who died. So the ruler ordered the widow to present herself to him. Instead, her father honorably decapitated her and gave the ruler her head. The humbled ruler's remorse, which included extensive temple building, did not prevent his family's ruin.

"Shinjū": The word means "love-death," the joint suicide of two hopeless lovers. Although Buddhism regards suicide as a terrible sin, it also expresses hope for the transmigration of such souls to bliss. Hearn heard of such a suicide pact. Tashirō-San, a physician's son, fell in love with Kane, a sweet young courtesan who sold herself to support a widowed mother and young sister. When the son was disinherited, the two drank poison and died in one another's arms. Normally such a couple would be buried together, but the physician, more angry than grief-stricken, refused. A newspaper friend of Hearn's prints Kane's touching farewell letter. Visiting the cemetery, Hearn hears a happy laborer singing a birdlike love song.

"Yaegaki-Jinja": Lovers, even those predestined to marry, go to the Yaegaki temple in Sakusa, a village just south of Matsue, where wedlock and love deities are enshrined. The temple name derives from Ya-he-gaki (the Temple of the Eightfold Fence), concerning a maiden-eating, eight-forked serpent made drunk at eight liquor vats and then chopped up. On the way Hearn sees temples, discusses legends about them, and also sees sacred love birds and curious stone paths near little shrines. By the love-temple gate is a monument with "a poem in Hokku [haiku], or verse in seventeen syllables." By the door gratings are wordless paper prayers, also flags signaling amatory victories. To prove he has visited a temple a thousand times, a pilgrim puts a thousand little bamboo sticks in a box by the door. Stepping beyond and back from the gate a thousand times is acceptable. Behind the temple is a holy *tsubaki* tree (Camellia Japonica), with twin trunks entwined "together at the middle," emblemizing "undying wedded love." It is said that this species of tree can walk at night. A nearby shop sells amulets guaranteeing not only love but also happy consequences thereof. A shaded grove is crowded with bamboo, camellias, cedars, pines, and *sakaki* (holy Shintō trees). Big trunks are encased in mats to discourage vandals from cutting off bark for souvenirs. Bamboo surfaces are covered with sweethearts' carved names. The ashes of cremated pond newts are considered aphrodisiacal. However, newts have been known to say that the only love charm is money. Paper boats with sweeties' names are launched on the pond, with varying signs of success or frustration. One lover wrote "I wish You, Haru!" as his plea, on the assumption that Japanese gods know English. "Yaegaki-Jinja" is the liveliest essay in all of Hearn's *Glimpses of Unfamiliar Japan*. He seems to feel that he will be forgiven if, in its pleasant context, he includes more than 125 Japanese words, sometimes without accompanying translations. He did, however, translate the haiku he quoted.

"Kitsune": Hearn visits many temples and shrines dedicated to Inari, an oft-mentioned god. The sites have statues of various sizes of *kitsune* (fox), a sacred animal. Cemeteries are especially full of them. They are graceful, ghostly, "uncouth," moody. Children have broken off the noses of many. When pedestaled, they seem to snicker at the passing centuries. Pilgrims to the shrine at Oba take clay foxes home; if their petitions are favorably answered, they return the statues, with donations if possible. Foxes are elaborately classified by location, good or bad qualities, and shape-shifting ability. Persons possessed by demon foxes can elude one's grasp. Invisible foxes cast shadows on water. If one harbors a fox, he is rightly shunned. Foxes are afraid of wrestlers. Shrewd speculators snap up fox-damaged lands. A man was once pursued by dogs but saved by a fox, which then became a woman and knocked on his door the next evening with gifts. Foxes love tofu. Stories about ghost foxes go back to the eleventh century. Foxes relish making people eat horse manure, thinking it is tasty, and making people jump into cesspools on the assumption they are bathing. Nice foxes can cure people of diseases. Some foxes convert themselves into boys and seek brief companionship with real boys. Nowadays, Hearn says, belief in fox superstitions is crumbling, especially when sick people are treated with physicians speaking German. The writings of evolutionary theorists are potent sources for thoughtful change in Japanese schools. All the same, Hearn concludes, "a superstition outlives a religion." Some readers of this delightful essay, which is essentially a fox anthology, may regard it as too long. "Kitsune" is the last essay in Volume 1 of *Glimpses of Unfamiliar Japan*.

"In a Japanese Garden" (1892) begins volume 2: To escape Matsue's summer heat, Hearn moves to an old samurai house with beautiful gardens. Japanese gardens are usually landscaped—designed for simple charm, not, like American ones, for gaudy show. Some Japanese gardens are immense; others, "microscopic." Naturally shaped stones, some with superstitions, provide a garden its "skeleton." Buddhist monks were Japan's first gardeners. Their gardens expressed the moral values of the owners. Hearn describes his first garden in detail—location, walls, rocks, lamps, stone fish, hills and sanded areas, bees, shrubs, and berry plants. Among trees, cherries are uniquely beautiful when in blossom. Girls are often named for flowers. Hearn discusses superstitions and legends. An Izumo belief is that trees have souls. Goblin trees can walk. Hearn's favorite garden is the second one, which he describes. The third garden is huge and includes a pond, bamboo grove, well, Inari shrine, and chrysanthemums. Topics that follow include frogs, fish, snails, and tortoises. Gardens are training grounds for children of the well-to-do. Without much logic, Hearn then turns to goblin cats, butterflies, noisy cicadae (especially the well-named "minmin-zemi"), dragonflies, and "unbidden" mosquitoes. Legend has it that when an ancient warrior fell in battle into a rice field, he metamorphosed into a rice-eating mosquito that must be burned in effigy to clear the fields of insects. Fever-bearing moths must also be incinerated. After Hearn writes about bugs of other sorts, the reader will likely welcome the next topics: birds (with strange cries), owls, kites, crows by the colony, wild doves (with "plaintive" voice, carefully quoted), and the *uguisu* (delicate songster that in death avoids rigor mortis). Hearn draws to a close. After work at the college, he goes home, dons his Japanese robe, and views his gardens, "within [which] dwell the all-reposing peace of nature and the dreams of the sixteenth century." "In A Japanese Garden" is the first essay in *Glimpses of Unfamiliar Japan* in which Hearn mentions his teaching at Matsue.

"The Household Shrine": Hearn describes objects used and rituals performed in Shintō, and to a lesser degree Buddhist worship in Japanese homes. Ancestors and deified leaders are venerated according to the Shintō religion, which has evolved throughout fifteen centuries. To understand it, one must know history, philology, and anthropology. During the Meiji era of Japan (1868–1912), attempts to cleanse Shintō of every Buddhist "sign or token" were unsuccessful. Hearn praises Shintō virtues, including honor, loyalty, "filial piety," "wish for martyrdom," and especially reverence for the dead. Because conscience is the intuitive Shintō guide, "no decalogue is required." Praising hearth worship, Hearn takes the reader into typical Japanese homes and describes numerous artifacts and devotional practices—shrines with shelves containing items, miniature temples, ropes, paper screens, jars of saké, and lamps (kindled at nightfall by flint and steel). Gods are prayed to in one room; ancestral dead and deceased family members, in another. Hearn distinguishes briefly between Shintō and Buddhist practices, with Shintō believers being in Izumo's majority. Although Buddhism does not countenance suicide, in Japan it is often countenanced, for example, when a servant commits suicide so as to aid a deceased lord or lady in the afterworld. Shintō prayers are silent, whereas Buddhists whisper prayers to those long deceased. Although at the outset Hearn says that "the ethics of Shintō will surely endure," he closes with a poignant word picture of a dying patriarch who "knows happily nothing" about "[s]trange changes . . . coming upon the land" and hence firmly believes that "the children of his children's children" will clap their prayers before his *ihai* (mortuary tablet) with his well-remembered name. Hearn includes a bewildering number of Japanese words, which the index at the end of *Glimpses of Unfamiliar Japan* helps readers to fathom, somewhat.

"Of Women's Hair": The Japanese hairdresser typically shampoos her lady's hair, then combs and shapes it. She shaves off "peachy [facial] floss." Each young girl has a round spot shaved off the top of the head to signify "maidenhood." Diminished until marriage, it then "vanishes." Some coiffeurs, with combs and pins, provide a "nimbus for the features." Hearn gives the Japanese names, with translations, of 14 styles for girls from 7 to 28 years of age. When a girl marries, her hair style changes. A hairdresser named Jin lied about the curiously wrinkled neck of Koto, her professional rival, saying it stretched into the shape of a serpent and scared Koto's first husband into disappearing. More lies jeopardized Koto's second marriage, until the governor published a denunciation of Jin. Some Japanese believe that a jealous woman's hair turns into dangerous snakes and that the hair of a wife and the hair of a concubine, under the same roof, hiss and fight, even wrestle and bite. Widows and corpses of women have hair arranged in certain ways. Japanese ghosts, typically tall, diaphanous, and footless, are seen and depicted as having hair disheveled over "peculiar . . . eyes." Betrayed husbands sometimes resist murdering their wives and cut off their hair instead. Widows demonstrate grief by cutting their hair and burying it with their husbands.

"From the Diary of an English Teacher": Hearn records his experiences, from September 2, 1890, through December 23, 1891, mainly at Matsue's Ordinary Middle School but to a lesser extent at its Normal School. He is aided by Nishida Sentaro, a Japanese teacher of English; meets his superiors, including the big, kind, provincial governor; and delights in the neatness and military-style courtesy of his students, including day boys, boarding boys, and girls. Hearn prefers the middle school, although it is dingy compared to the normal school. On October 15 he witnesses athletic contests involving five thousand students of rival schools and held on the castle grounds. They race, fence, jump, and play tug-of-war. Daily science lessons are taught, mainly in botany and geology. At a certain date, the emperor's message concerning education is read at assembly. Teachers are less like English masters, more like older brothers. Little boys learn to sing and march. Punishment is limited to loss of play time. Students, by refusing to attend class, can cause a poor teacher to be expelled. Each November 3, pupils and teachers assemble to honor the emperor's birthday by singing the national anthem, stepping about and bowing, and hearing the governor extol "His Imperial Majesty." Hearn discusses school finances; the severity of seven years of basic study for students, including lessons in English and fencing; rigorous marching; a beans-and-rice diet; and stiff classroom postures. Explaining that he teaches third, fourth, and fifth graders, he offers samples (often unidiomatic, didactic, and critical of non-Japanese ways) of their English writing and conversation. Students visit him at his home, where they squat and chat with him courteously and show him family possessions, including precious statues and dolls. Exposure to scientific thought makes students skeptical and unsuperstitious but still reverent Buddhistic monists. Hearn describes some of his favorite students: Ishihara, an anti-British superpatriot; Masonobu, a bright scientist; Adzukizawa, "perfect bookworm"; Yokogi, penniless but bright, therefore financed by a rich man, saved a so-so teacher by backing him for trying; and Shida, "whose soul is full of art." September 1891 brings changes. Some familiar students are gone, even dead. The popular governor is transferred. Challenging are the new faces—fresh, frank, childish, neither aggressive nor shy, unlike "the horrible faces" of foreigners, sometimes red-haired at that. A November 1891 entry reports that Shida has died and that Yokogi, dying at age 17 through over-study, is carried to see his school a final time. Hearn describes funeral arrange-ments—body placement, screens, prayers, kimono wrapping, procession, bell ringing, food offering, priests' chant, teacher's eulogy. Hearn's sentimental con-clusion is detailed.

"Two Strange Festivals": During the three-day festival of the New Year, streets are decorated, shops are closed, and straw ropes are hung in front of houses. Lanterns and flags are everywhere. Pines with bamboo cuttings—sym-bols, respectively, of endurance and faith—are erected beside gates and door-ways. Used emblematically also are charcoal and leaves of various kinds. Indoors, temple shelves are decorated. The Japanese celebrate a second vivid festival at the beginning of spring, when they cast out devils by tossing peas in the house, collecting them, and eating them when spring thunder first sounds. Charms placed in doorways keep the devils from returning. As thunder can be dangerous, the thunder animal is caught and caged when possible. Cracked old fire-starting bamboo pipes help in casting out an especially virulent devil called Bimbogami, whose presence is indicated by a certain insect's ticking. Family members rub their bodies with figurines in cutout paper, which are then burned, to ward off a year's worth of misfortune.

"By the Japanese Sea": Hearn begins his essay about a mid-summer vacation at Hōki, a coastal town, by summarizing superstitions about ghost ships, swimmer-eating sea monsters, burying drowned sailors' souvenirs, and good-luck cats aboard ships. These ancient beliefs do not dampen the somber joy of the summer Bon (dance of the dead). Straw models of junks, with lanterns, are launched as "soul-boats" for those lost at sea. Hearn visits a sacred tree, part of a "phallic cult" now officially suppressed. At a hamlet inn he sees a soul boat, interviews a waitress, and learns that her husband and brother drowned in waves "[t]all like hills." She dries her tears and, pressed by Hearn's "attendant," tells about a futon in the village of Tottori. It seems that a futon in one room of an innocent innkeeper's place held the spirits of two dead waifs, who habitually talked in the night to guests sleeping on it. An Izumo legend has it that a peasant drowned six of his children, as soon as they were born, because of poverty. Later well-off, he had another son who at five months of age rebuked his father for throwing him away earlier, then never grew up or spoke again. One evening, Hearn visits the cemetery, admires the well-kept graves, observes a lanquered tray with dainty food, and sees tiny footsteps in the sand nearby. At Hamamura, Hearn dreams of a woman with closed eyes and hair dark, then blue; her chant reminds him of a Celtic lullaby. When he wakes up, the sea speaks of ghosts on a tide. Hearn renders this lengthy essay comic by literally translating much Japanese dialogue, for example, the innkeeper's complaint: "Wherefore that such things be spoken, right-there-is-none!"

"Of a Dancing Girl" (1893): Hearn describes a typical Japanese banquet—

quiet and sedate—then saké, then laughter, and decorous geisha weave in, dance, pour more saké, and gesture enticingly. The typical geisha is bought from an impoverished family and elaborately trained with respect to dress, comportment, and music. She must catch near-fatal colds to render herself hoarse. She pays obeisance to kitten images. By age 18 she is nocturnal, clever with drink and food, often made love to; thereafter, someone may purchase her freedom, or she may die early. Hearn apparently digresses to discuss student artists who wander and sketch. One, lost at night between Kyōto and Yedo, asks for shelter at a cottage. A beautiful woman admits him, gives him food, and persuades him to sleep in her own bed, saying she has work to do that night. He awakens to see her richly clad and dancing as only a *shirabyōshi* can. She explains that she was once an esteemed dancer, was loved by a youth, went into the mountains with him, and mourns his early death by dancing before his *butsudan* (shrine). In the morning the artist leaves. Forty years pass; he is now a master artist. One day an old woman, in tatters, comes to him. At first they do not recognize each other. But then he remembers his dancing hostess. Astonished, she too remembers. She asks him to take her rich dancing raiment and paint her as she was 40 years ago. He does so, wraps his work carefully, and gives it to her. She accepts no money. He has a student follow her; then he does so, only to find her in a riverside hut. He looks in, finds his painting beside her dead lover's shrine, seeks to awaken her, but finds her dead. Memorable is the painter's artistic alchemy: "Under the magic of the Master's brush, the vanished grace returned, the faded beauty bloomed again."

"From Hōki to Oki": Hearn resolves to visit remote Oki, a group of islands a hundred miles north of Matsue, reachable by steamer from Hōki, east of Matsue. Legends tell of seductive women there. While he and a business friend wait in a Hōki hotel, Hearn watches and hears stevedores at work, singing raplike songs to lighten loads. A Nagasaki steamer docks; its sailors eat, drink, and dance on deck. In the morning he boards a "squabby" boat with a stifling gangway, examines his tiny first-class cabin, and threads his way through rolling watermelons and baskets of eels and chickens topside. The powerful engine starts, roaring and spitting like a volcano. His friend says the craft is safe. Hearn digresses to combine a legend, about a nearby god offended and causing storms, with his customary fine geographical description. The peak of Daisen, a mountain, clearly seen, suddenly vaporizes. The "horrid little steamer" races straight across the "lonesome" Sea of Japan. A veritable "ancient mariner" sits on one watermelon and explains why sailors must never sail on the seventh month's sixteenth day. Suddenly before them looms Oki's sacred Takuhizan mountain, where "ghostly fires" appear on certain dates. Fishing boats rush by, with yellow sails like butterflies. The steamer drops mail at a hamlet "in a mountain wrinkle," then passes beautiful islands of a wondrous "irregularity," toward the port of Urago. Meanwhile, Hearn tells about an army captain turned holy monk and living on Takuhizan centuries ago, doing penance for murder. Lusting after a man's decent wife, he persuaded her to let him kill her husband; pretending to agree, she occupied her absent husband's bed, and the sinner sneaked in and beheaded the reclining one.

The first thing Hearn notes at Urago is its cemetery, then the harbor full of naked swimmers. On he goes past Hishi-ura, pretty and prosperous through farming. Finally he reaches Dōgo Oki's main island, and Saigo, its attractive city on both sides of a river, with three main, twisting streets, and a 300-ship harbor. His hotel is excellent, with Occidental food he ignores but with the omnipresent stench of rotting fish entrails used as fertilizer. The local physician invites Hearn, the first foreigner he has ever seen, to dinner and showers him with gifts. A teacher brings him maps. A visitor gives him an elaborate pipe case. The Oki dialect resembles Izumo's, and its people have more "nutritive food" and ply their fishing craft well, but Izumo girls are prettier and Oki live-stock is diminutive. Special in Oki are its dried cuttlefish and *bateiseki* (black stone), carved into costly art objects. A legend about a certain warrior's steed explains *bateiseki*'s horse-hoof shape. Hearn discusses coralline sea-pine and nacre wares. Intrigued by stories, he visits various sights, each of reputed uniqueness: a local god who cures toothaches, noisy tide-rolled boulders, monsters guarding a pool to discourage swimmers, a wide cedar allegedly eight hundred years old, a three-foot temple commemorating an emperor's brief visit. Crime is so rare that in Oki's main islands, with a population upward of 30,000, ten policemen are sufficient. Theft is virtually unknown. Hearn discusses the magic that thieves use in Izumo (an inverted tub will cause residents of a target house to fall asleep) and housewifely countermeasures (put burning weed on an escaping thief's footprints in sand to stop him in his tracks). An Oki superstition has it that intermittent fever is caused by a *gaki* (the soul of one without living relatives) entering one's body, chilling it, absorbing its warmth, leaving, and returning. Hearn discusses connotations of the word *hotoke*, one being that a lover sees his Buddha, not hers, in his beloved's eyes; Hearn relates this to the theory of egotism espoused by Arthur Schopenhauer, one of his favorite authors. Although Oki schoolteachers are pooh-poohing superstitions, many natives firmly believe in fox goblins.

Nearby Hishi-ura is prettier than Saigo. Hearn watches girls weave robes of cotton and silk by hand, and he hears mothers singing lullabies. He sees a child's funeral, the mother perhaps being consoled by her Buddhistic faith; the name of a dead one is called to induce the soul to return. Those who swoon may have near-death experiences. At Amamura, Hearn visits the shabby tomb of an exiled emperor who once commanded the frogs, which were disturbing his sleep, to shut up, which they have done for centuries now. European and American hunters once came here to kill for sport; not now, however, and therefore wild creatures are fearless again. English and Russian naval personnel formerly visited Urago; so when Hearn's being a foreigner became known, he was peeped at by swarms of curiosity seekers. Hearn expounds on the almost total lack of privacy in Japan; ergo, higher morals, no ridicule, no superciliousness. Some descendants of disestablished samurai families are in Oki. Some are humble farmers. Many are in the police force, which Hearn calls "the most perfect . . . in the world." It may be well, he adds, that "Christian bayonets" (albeit "for the holy motive of gain") have occasioned beneficial changes. Suddenly reminded, he describes a reverent ceremony of old, dispossessed, impoverished samurai he witnessed in Izumo. It so tired the old fellows while they were transporting their temple by boat that, some toothless, they could hardly sing the old songs. They carried the temple to the place where their lord once stood. Witnesses thought the oldsters were ghosts. Hearn sadly agrees that "both that which remembers, and that which is remembered," last "only for a day." On the steamer back to Matsue, Hearn, pleased to have briefly escaped "the far-reaching influences of high-pressure civilization," reverently sums up his treasured experiences. What readers of this long essay should delight in most is Hearn's intermittent portrayal of himself as something of an observant clown.

"Of Souls": Hearn queries his gardener, Kinjurō, who says people can have one to nine souls, the number and quality causing individuals' differences. A weak, one-souled person can have a many-souled ancestor. A man whose several souls are separated goes insane. A dead man's soul first ascends to his roof for 49 days. Hearn says he has read that each person has a "rough" soul and a "gentle" soul. Kinjurō never knew this but says the gods can transplant a soul into a priest's heart. When his assistant tortures a pond frog, Kinjurō says the lad is one-souled, hence mean. Hearn includes a long footnote on relevant Chinese astrological data.

"Of Ghosts and Goblins": Kinjurō tells Hearn about a ghostly snow woman in the snow, seen by pilgrims near a winter shrine. At a street festival, Hearn fails to see a woman wearing cold snakes, but he and Kinjurō do note other oddities, including exhibits of life-size people—some artificial but one looking painted until he laughed. In the goblin tent a badger clutches at Hearn, men have misplaced eyes, a nurse is said to eat children, and a footless woman suspended in air flies forward. At another entrance they pay to "go to hell." Inside are a female ghost who takes souls' clothing, the king of hell with decapitated heads, a saw-wielding devil, and the tortured damned. Outside they enjoy a magic-lantern show about a girl saved from a demon by a samurai. Kinjurō tells about a beautiful girl courted by many samurai, all of whom flee after undergoing prescribed secret tests. A final suitor passes her test, which is to accompany her to a cemetery and eat the arm of a dead child. When he professes to relish it, she calls him a man and will marry him. Asked if returning from the dead is ever a good thing, Kinjurō tells of two young lovers. The lad had to fight for his samurai far away but promised to return to his girl in a year. When he did not, she took sick and died. Her parents sold everything and went on a pilgrimage, pausing briefly at Minobu, a village, where they left the girl's *ihai* (mortuary tablet) at a temple. The lad returned late, learned of his girl's death, and visited her grave. She appeared, they were wed, chanced to move to Minobu, opened a shop, and had a child. His wife's parents chanced to return, greeted their son-in-law, saw his child, and wanted to see their daughter. She was gone forever, but near the child sat her *ihai*.

"The Japanese Smile" (1893): It is difficult to generalize in contrasting East and West. The Japanese see anger in non-smiling British faces; Westerners see hypocrisy in Japanese smiles. The Japanese smile, however, is not defiant, insincere, or resigned but happy, heroic, touching. Hearn presents evidence that misunderstanding the Japanese smile can lead to unpleasantness; that to understand the smile one must ignore modern changes in Japan and study its "ancient, natural, and popular life," which stresses love of family and nature, morality rather than artfulness, and politeness. The smile is not a "soul-mask." It "illuminates conversation." In Kyōto one night, Hearn saw a young boy praying before a Jizō statue; their identical smiles made them seem like twins. Hearn's conclusion: "[T]hat which the Buddhist sculptor symbolizes . . . must be the explanation of the smile of the race." The smile connotes self-control and self-suppression, calm, rest. Hearn hopes that Japanese awareness of "Western material superiority" will not result in adoption of Western moral standards; yet his hopes are shadowed by doubts, given current changes in the attitudes of Japan's young people. They should seek to be influenced by the best elements of their "ancient faith."

"Sayōnara!": Wanting a warmer climate (and better pay), Hearn leaves his Matsue teaching post (November 1891) for one at Kumamoto on the island of Kyūshū. Students and faculty send him gifts. There is a farewell banquet and even a Japanese rendition of "Auld Lang Syne." Although an outbreak of cholera in town should have prevented their seeing him off, a crowd materializes at the wharf. He concludes that such courtesy to a foreign teacher—of some five hundred students—would be possible only in Japan. As the steamer moves out, the land, full of magic charms, recedes from view. Spectral Daisen is in the distance. His heart sinks, but he is revived by "happy memories" of the smiles, doves and dogs, gardens, cedar groves, temple bells, lanterns, moonlit dances, and hand-clappings to the rising sun.

Glimpses of Unfamiliar Japan was written mostly in Kumamoto, a place Hearn disliked when compared to lovely Matsue. The book reflects the first phase of his years in Japan, when he was infatuated with impressions of his new country. Perhaps as a result, it has proved to be his most popular set of essays on Japan. It became Volumes 5 and 6 in *The Writings of Lafcadio Hearn* (16 vols., 1922). In it, Hearn links many of the disparate essays by the device of repeated references to such items as *Daisen, guki*, Jizō statues, *jorō* (prostitutes), Caribbean memories, his swimming ability, temples and shrines, and pretty girls. He frequently uses Japanese words, especially names of objects, but sometimes provides translations only in later essays—if at all. This may give the book a local-color flavoring but encourages skip-reading. Hearn refers to the province of Izumo, whereas Matsue was in reality the capital of the Shimane prefecture, which was part of the old province. *Glimpses of Unfamiliar Japan* was reprinted twice in the first year of issue, was published in London (1894), and proved extremely popular.

Bibliography: Bisland; Dawson; Espey; Kunst; Miner; Masaru Toda, "The Western Approach to Shinto: Lafcadio Hearn, Bruno Taut and André Malraux," in Hirakawa, pp. 223–241.

"A GOBLIN TALE" (1875). Cincinnati news article. It is rumored that the Freiberg tannery is haunted by a skeleton that throws its skull at would-be taunters. A bold drover bets he can visit the place after midnight with impunity. Loaded up on beer, he enters. Soon thereafter, his friends call after him. But he is never seen again, nor is his money from a recent cattle sale. The locale is that of the murder of Herman Schilling. *See* "Violent Cremation."

"GOLGOTHA" (1874). Cincinnati news article. Hearn and the coroner, Dr. Maley, visit the sexton at Potter's Field to investigate rumors that Maley permits corpses, left to be buried or already interred, to be stolen and sold to medical colleges. The sexton says that his seven-acre cemetery contains about five thousand graves, many of them empty. His directors have told him not to guard with any unusual care. He calls the ghoulish grave robbers Resurrectionists. One team is composed of two doctors and a black driver with a wagon. Once, when the sexton concealed some "stiffs" in his locked outhouse, the ghouls tore the roof off and got at them that way. When Maley identifies himself, the sexton, although nervous, continues to provide details. He gets $1.25 per grave dug and keeps no receipts. He explains that the Jewish cemetery is never robbed because Jewish families regularly hire watchmen and, moreover, pay the Jewish sexton $3 per burial.

"GOMBO ZHÉBES": A LITTLE DICTIONARY OF CREOLE PROVERBS, SE-LECTED FROM SIX CREOLE DIALECTS (1885). Dictionary. Hearn hastily assembled a dictionary of over 350 Creole proverbs from French Guyana, Haiti, New Orleans, Martinique, Mauritius, and Trinidad dialects. He translated the proverbs into English and provided annotations, an index, and what on the title page he calls "remarks upon the Creole Idioms of Louisiana." The following example shows Creole piquancy: "Derriére chien, c'est chien; devant chien, c'est 'Monsieur Chien.' " The 42-page book had many misprints and sold poorly.

Bibliography: Cott; Murray; Tinker.

GOULD, GEORGE MILBRY (1848–1922). Physician, editor, and author. Gould was born in Auburn, Maine. After his mother's death, he and his father moved in 1855 to Salina, Ohio, where he completed his public school education. During the Civil War he was a drummer boy with Ohio volunteers for 18 months, and then a soldier (1864–1865). He earned degrees at Ohio Wesleyan University and the Harvard Divinity School, and studied in Paris, Leipzig, and Berlin. He was a pastor in Chillicote, Ohio; invested in and worked in a printing shop; ran a book and art store; and married Harriet Fletcher Cartwright in 1876. The couple had no children. Gould successfully studied at Jefferson Medical College (1885–1888) and developed a brilliant medical career as an ophthalmologist in Philadelphia (1888–1908) and as an author of books and articles in his field. His several medical dictionaries sold in excess of 500,000 copies. He also edited medical journals (1891–1906) and wrote biographies, essays, poems, and studies in history, philosophy, and psychology. He practiced medicine in Ithaca, New York (1908–1911) and retired in Atlantic City, New Jersey. He was a member of, and occasionally an officer in, professional establishments. Long widowered, in 1917 he married Laura Stedman, the granddaughter of the versatile man of letters Edmund Clarence Stedman. In 1910 Gould and Miss Stedman had prepared the two-volume *Life and Letters of Edmund Clarence Stedman* for publication. Aggressively conservative and brusquely immodest, Gould antagonized many professional and personal associates.

What proved to be a stormy friendship with Hearn began in 1887 when Gould addressed a letter to him in New Orleans commending *Some Chinese Ghosts*. The two continued to correspond while Hearn was in Martinique. Gould admired Hearn's *Chita* (1888). Becoming frank, Hearn described his partial blindness and much else about himself, thus arming Gould for later attacks. In 1889 Hearn left the West Indies, made his way to the Goulds' home at 119 South Seventeenth Street in Philadelphia in May, and accepted his invitation, offered many times in letters, to stay for five or six months in a spare room and write. Mrs. Gould was less than pleased. Hearn defined Gould as a friend, teacher, brother, even father to him. Recognizing Hearn's artistic brilliance but wayward, ironic personality, Gould let Hearn help with his own early writings, sought to remodel Hearn into something more conservative and hence successful, and studied him as a victim of nothing other than severe myopia. Hearn happily left Gould and his inhospitable wife in October 1889. She was undoubtedly miffed that she was not privy to the lengthy correspondence between the two men. Furthermore, Hearn had been their free roomer and boarder for too long. Leaving for New York, he borrowed $40 from Gould, to whom he soon appealed for $20 more. Once in New York, Hearn joined up with his friend from his former New Orleans days, Elizabeth Bisland,* which made Gould jealous. Gould not only truly asserted that he had partly inspired the moral lesson in Hearn's short story "Karma" (1890) but also falsely asserted that he alone had first encouraged Hearn to visit Japan. In truth, it was Hearn who recommended to Gould *The Soul of the Far East* by the Orientalist Percival Lowell.* Arriving in Japan in 1890, Hearn wrote an angry letter to Henry Mills Alden,* the editor at Harper & Brothers, his publisher. He fancied that Alden owed him money; so, aware that he himself still owed Gould, he urgently asked Alden to send Hearn's books, left with Alden, to Gould as payment. Then Hearn foolishly wrote to Gould, asserting that he owed Gould $500 for unpaid room and board and that his library would be in lieu of payment. Gould accepted, whereupon Hearn accused him of sneaky greed, asked later for some of his books back, was refused, and lost yet another friend. Hearn also contended that he ghost-wrote on three occasions for Gould, who took the credit and pocketed the pay.

Gould got even after Hearn's death in 1904, by unfairly characterizing him briefly in his *Biographic Clinics* (Vol. 4, 1906) and at length in his *Concerning Lafcadio Hearn* (1908). In *Biographic Clinics* he theorized that Hearn was strange because of myopia. Before he wrote *Concerning Lafcadio Hearn*, Gould generously made available to Bisland his letters from Hearn. For her biography, *The Life and Letters of Lafcadio Hearn* (2 vols., 1906), she used the letters in ways of which Gould disapproved, as is manifest in his disparaging *Concerning Lafcadio Hearn*. In it, he defines Hearn as a genius but a peculiarly unpuritanical one because of his myopia. Bisland does not come off well either, though, because she altered some of Hearn's letters to Gould. Gould's treatment of Hearn in his biography, expressing admiration and frustration alike, aroused a whirlwind of critical commentary, some favorable to, others critical of, Hearn. Gould's opening assessment of Hearn hardly did his friend any favor: "He has been spoken of as 'a great man,' which, of course, he was not. . . . Deprived by nature, by the necessities of his life, or by conscious intention, of religion, morality, scholarship, magnanimity, loyalty, character, benevolence, and other constituents of personal greatness, it is more than folly to endeavour to place him thus wrongly before the world." The most valuable elements of *Concerning Lafcadio Hearn* are Gould's extensive use of letters from Hearn to him and, especially, Laura Stedman Gould's painstaking, though badly organized, bibliography of Hearn's writings and also of early books and articles about Hearn and reviews of his works.

Bibliography: Cott; Gould; Murray; Stevenson; Tinker.

"THE GRANDISSIMES" (1880). Review. Hearn calls this 1880 novel by George Washington Cable* "the most remarkable work of fiction ever created in the South." It is half dream, half tale, with unflattering pictures half impressionistic, half real. He praises its evocation of New Orleans, its characters, its "pithily forceable" descriptions, its valuable use of Creole songs. However, he doubts the validity of Honoré Grandissime's ideas concerning society and deplores Cable's dismissal of voodooism as superstition.

GREENSLET, FERRIS (1875–1959). Editor, publisher, and author. Greenslet was born in Glens Falls, New York. He earned a B.A. at Wesleyan University (1897), and at Columbia University an M.A. (1898) and a Ph.D. (1900). After working for a while at the Boston Public Library, he became an associate editor of the *Atlantic Monthly* (1902–1907). Greenslet married Ella B. Hulst in 1905 and with her had two children. From 1907 until his retirement in 1947, Greenslet was associated with Houghton Mifflin, the distinguished Boston publishing firm—first as a literary adviser; then in editorial, executive, and managerial capacities; and next as a vice president. During his long career he was a fine editor and publisher, a scholarly author, and an amateur fisherman. He assisted in securing publication rights to works by Henry Adams, Willa Cather, and many others. Among other subjects, Greenslet wrote books on the Holy Grail, Walter Pater, and Thomas Bailey Aldrich. In his autobiography, *Under the Bridge* (1943), he expresses pride in being acquainted with some 192 authors. His study tracing 11 generations of a New England family, *The Lowells and Their Seven Worlds* (1946), is especially valuable for discussions of James Russell Lowell, the author, educator, and diplomat; Percival Lowell,* the Orientalist turned astronomer; and Amy Lowell, the poet. In Kumamoto, Japan, in 1893 Hearn met Percival Lowell, whose *The Soul of the Far East* (1888) he had already read. Soon after Hearn's death, when Houghton Mifflin began issuing selections of his works, Greenslet provided introductions. The first were *The Romance of the Milky Way and Other Studies and Stories* (1905) and *Leaves from the Diary of an Impressionist* (1911). Later, the decision was made to publish a multi-volume edition of Hearn's work. It became *The Writings of Lafcadio Hearn* (16 vols., 1922), with Greenslet its scholar-editor and author of the general introduction to the first volume. In it, he outlines Hearn's life, discusses phases of his literary production, praises *Chita* and *Two Years in the French West Indies* highly, and suggests the importance of Lowell's book on East Asia to Hearn. Greenslet objects to labeling Hearn "decadent." In truth, Greenslet avows, Hearn was a humanist, loved words for their own sake, was never robust, was occasionally morbid and "ghostly," and because of severe eye trouble observed minutiae. He says that Hearn's early death cut short his much-evidenced literary development. Greenslet compares Hearn to Sir Thomas Browne, Thomas De Quincey, and Pater. Hearn, he concludes, "portray[s] the human spirit caught in a magic web of necessity."

Bibliography: Cott; Murray.

"THE GYPSY'S STORY" (1881). Sketch. As they languidly sail one summer eve through warm seas, wafted by lemony southern breezes, an Andalusian gypsy plays his guitar, improvises a song, and tells the narrator his story. Orphaned when tiny, he often dreamed sadly of his dark-eyed mother now gone, thought of oceans and winds strangely fragrant and often cold, hated noisy cities, and liked reading about mysterious skies and seas. He felt his blood to be strange, unlike that of his father, who blanched when the boy asked, once only, about his mother. The lad ran away from home; one night a tall, swarthy girl came to him in shadowy woods, spoke to him in a strange dream language he understood, and said his mother was a member of her wandering race. He would be forever with the people of this girl, who promised to be his sister. This sketch has autobiographical overtones, as Hearn hated his selfish father, remembered his dark mother when he was tiny, and fancied that he and she shared the blood of gypsies.

H

"HACELDAMA" (1875). Cincinnati news article. *Haceldama*, a word found in the New Testament, means "field of blood" (from Aramaic *hagel dema* and Greek *Ákeldamá*). People like to watch slaughters; further, "the higher the organization of the victim," the more intense the pleasure. Ancient Romans enjoyed seeing the death, in descending order of delight, of elephants, hippopotamuses, bulls, boars, ostriches, and chickens. Best was a human being. By analogy, "we" would rather see a bullock slaughtered than a hog. Describing his visit to foul, reeking, gory slaughterhouses, Hearn provides enough details of the suffering of the kicking, bellowing, grunting victims to turn most stomachs. He half-humanizes a pair of cows; one watches her "sister" die and then is noosed and follows. Some workers, wading barefoot in blood, entrails, and offal, are described as deliberately clumsy sadists. By contrast, Hearn's visit to a neat, spacious, well-ventilated Jewish slaughterhouse is "a pleasant relief." He details the training, skill, and implements of the Shochet (a rabbinically licensed slaughterer). Whereas nine blows are sometimes needed to fell a vicious butcher's quarry, the Shochet is as swift as lightning and humane in dispatching sheep and bullocks with special knives. His stamp of "cosseher" (Kosher) signifies meat sought by the smartest shoppers. The blood of his animals is ruddy, whereas the gutters of filthy slaughterhouses are toxic. A Jewish slaughterhouse proprietor tells Hearn that sick people regain their health by drinking blood fresh from his slaughtered bullocks. Hearn tries some, as an experiment and to complete this report to the public. He observes "the clear, ruddy life stream," drains a brimming glass, and describes it as "the richest cream, warm, with a tart sweetness." Ordinary human blood should be avoided, he says, as it would be ruinously tainted with cheap liquor and tobacco. *See* "A Slaughter-House Story." In a few reprints of this essay, "haceldama" is misspelled "hacledama."

Bibliography: Cott.

"THE HAUNTED AND THE HAUNTERS" (1874). Cincinnati news article. Rumor having it that the city stables are haunted, "an *ENQUIRER* reporter" (Hearn) proceeds through darkness, rain, and dangerous streets to the scene, hoping to "interview . . . a ghost." At the stable he thinks he sees a face and a yellow light. He raps at the office door, arouses some dogs, and identifies himself as a reporter seeking news of the night sounds. The cheery private watchman admits him, persuades his dogs to be friendly, and admits that he has heard sounds resembling "the ghost of a nigger minstrel . . . running all round . . . rattling the bones." His friend the saddler heard the sounds and started the rumor about ghosts. When asked about his own "theory," the watchman says the rattles are caused by defective gas pipes. Leaving sadly, the reporter vows not to return unless the watchman first sends him a photograph of the ghost.

"THE HEALING OF WAINAMOINEN" (1884). Rune. Hiisi the Evil causes Wainamoinen to gash his knee with his steel axe. He cannot pronounce the healing "Words of Blood." He drives his steed-drawn sledge to the sorcerers' land for help. A child fails to aid. A three-toothed hag fails to aid. An old man says that "the Three [Original] Words of the Creator" will stop the blood flow. Only then does Wainamoinen recall and recite the origin of iron and the birth of steel: Ilmarinnen the smith used fire to smelt iron. Iron promised to cut trees and stones but never people. Ilmarinnen felt that water would not harden iron into steel, so he asked Hiisi's supposedly friendly bird Herlihainen, to bring honey and flower pistils for the purpose. Instead, it brought worm and toad poisons. When Ilmarinnen used them, Iron quivered, forgot its oath, and turned into murderous Steel. This recitation jogs the memory of the old man, who recites the Original Words, curses Iron, stanches Wainamoinen's wound, and reknits his veins, muscles, flesh, and bones. Hearn introduces distracting commentary about the milk of virgins having something to do with the birth of flexible iron, fragile iron, and steel.

HEARN, CHARLES BUSH (1818–1866). Lafcadio Hearn's father. His father and grandfather were officers in the British Army. Hearn, an Anglican, graduated with a B.A. from Trinity College in Dublin, Ireland, in 1839 and with a medical degree from the Royal College of Surgeons, Dublin, in 1842. A handsome swordsman, tenor, and guitar player, Hearn was appointed assistant surgeon with the 45th Regiment of Foot, in the British Army, April 15, 1842. Between 1846 and 1850 he was assigned to various islands in Greece, which were under British control until 1864. He was stationed on Zante, Ithaca, Corfu, and, beginning in April 1848, at a Venetian castle on the island of Cerigo, near the town of the same name. In his free time he began to notice Rosa Antonia Cassimati in town, followed her, was encouraged, and quickly became intimate with her. When she got pregnant, her respectable and close-knit family disapproved. According to a family story, her brother followed Hearn, stabbed him repeatedly, and left him for dead in an alley. Rosa rescued him, nursed him back to health, and in July 1849 bore him a son, George Robert Hearn,* at Charles's new post at Fort Santa Maura on the island of Leucadia, to which they had traveled when he was assigned there in June. On November 16 Hearn was promoted to staff surgeon, second class. On November 25 he married Rosa (*see* Hearn, Rosa Antonia Cassimati) in a quiet Greek Orthodox ceremony on Leucadia. On February 27, 1850, he was transferred via England to Dominica and Grenada, British West Indies, with the First (Royal) Regiment of Foot. In June, Rosa gave birth to Lafcadio Hearn.

During these years Charles Hearn kept knowledge of his marriage secret from the British War Office, for two reasons. He feared that the marriage might impede his military advancement; and his mother, Elizabeth Holmes Hearn,* found details of the marriage so distasteful that she was reluctant to make her son an heir to part of her substantial estate in Dublin. But on July 30, 1852, Hearn by letter to the War Office in London reported his marriage and children. Hearn's younger brother, Richard Holmes Hearn,* then living in Paris, probably made transportation arrangements for Rosa and Lafcadio Hearn to migrate from Greece to Dublin. They may have proceeded via Malta, where Robert Hearn, another brother of Charles, was stationed. Arriving on August 1, mother and child were cared for at first by Elizabeth Hearn, who was living with her daughter, Jane Hearn Stephens, and Jane's solicitor husband, Henry Cloclough Stevens. This curious ménage was always unstable. Charles contracted yellow fever in Grenada, was sent home to Dublin on sick leave in October 1853, was soon healthy again, and obtained housing for himself, Rosa, and Lafcadio near his barracks at Portobello, a Dublin suburb. By this time Charles was vacillatingly indifferent to Rosa, who had grown unattractive to him. Leaving Rosa pregnant, he was happy to be sent to the Crimea in March 1854. At this time Sarah Holmes Brenane,* Elizabeth Hearn's younger, widowed sister and a Roman Catholic convert, welcomed Lafcadio into her home. He soon called her "Auntie."

Leaving Lafcadio Hearn in Dublin, Rosa returned in the summer of 1854 to Greece, where she gave birth later that year to James Daniel Hearn.* Charles Hearn returned to Dublin in July 1856 and terminated his marriage by annulment on the spurious grounds that Rosa had not signed the original wedding document. She never could have signed it, as she was illiterate. At some time in 1856 also, Rosa married Giovanni Cavallini in Greece. Because Cavallini adamantly demanded that she disavow her sons Lafcadio and James, she sent James to his relatives in Dublin.

Early in the 1840s Charles Hearn had wanted to marry a Dublin sweetheart named Alicia Goslin. Because of her petite beauty, she was called "The Pocket Venus." Lacking funds at that time, Charles went with the army to Greece and was saddened to learn that she had married a judge named George John Crawford and migrated with him to Australia. In 1853, back from the West Indies, Charles despite being married to Rosa renewed his friendship with Alicia, by then widowed with two young daughters and living in Dublin again. One day he boldly took little Lafcadio to meet sweet Alicia. Years later Lafcadio could still recall her bright hair, angelic beauty, nice kiss, and gifts to him of a pretty book and a toy gun. He also remembered, however, that when he returned to Mrs. Brenane, she took his presents away from him and pronounced his father and his girlfriend wicked.

On July 18, 1857, Charles and Alicia Crawford, age 33, were married in Dublin. He was assigned to the First Infantry Regiment, Secunderabad, India, and on August 4 left Ireland and took his new wife and her daughters with him. The couple had three daughters before Alicia, shortly after delivering a stillborn child, died in India in the autumn of 1861. In 1865 Mrs. Brenane started legal proceedings to force Charles to repay loans she had advanced to him over the years. But he died of malaria, financially ruined, in the Gulf of Suez on November 21, 1866. His daughters were Elizabeth Sarah Maude Hearn (1858–?), born in Secunderabad; Minnie Charlotte Hearn Atkinson* (1859–?), also born in Secunderabad; and Posey Gertrude ("Lillah") Hearn (1860–?), born in Trimulgberry, India. Years later the three wrote to Lafcadio Hearn, their half-brother, but he evidently replied only to Minnie Atkinson. Lillah visited the United States and made contact with James Daniel Hearn,* another half-brother.

In later years Lafcadio Hearn permanently blamed Charles and Alicia Hearn for abandoning Rosa; he also downplayed the Anglo-Irish blood in his heritage and preferred to regard himself as gypsy-like, even believing there was something of a dark and wandering element in his unloved father's family. In his short story "Karma," it is possible that the unnamed heroine, who forgives the mother of her would-be lover's dark-eyed boy, is Hearn's slightly recognizable depiction of Alicia.

Bibliography: Cott; Murray; Stevenson.

HEARN, DANIEL (1693–1766). (Full title: The Venerable Daniel Hearn.) Lafcadio Hearn's great-great-grandfather. He studied for four years at Trinity College, Dublin, and graduated in 1713. His brother-in-law was a lieutenant colonel in the British Army in Ireland. Daniel Hearn was archdeacon of Cashel, in Munster (1728–1766), but probably lived instead in Dublin, where he was also rector of the fashionable St. Anne's. He had seven children by a second marriage. His oldest son, Robert Hearn, had thirteen children with two wives; his oldest son was Daniel James Hearn.* Many Hearns served in Anglican churches and British military units. Also, many Hearns, both before and after Daniel Hearn, held to the story that they had gypsy blood. *See* "Among the Spirits."

Bibliography: Murray; Stevenson.

HEARN, DANIEL JAMES (1768–1837). Hearn's grandfather. The son of Daniel Hearn,* he graduated from Trinity College, Dublin, in 1789, and qualified as barrister three years later, but he joined the British Army instead. He rose in the ranks through combat, and as a lieutenant colonel he commanded the 43rd Regiment of Light Infantry at Victoria in Spain (1813), under Wellington, during the Peninsular War against Napoleon. Retiring in 1815, Daniel James Hearn married Elizabeth Holmes (*see* Hearn, Elizabeth Holmes). He was appointed sheriff of County Westmeath in 1828. He and his wife had seven children, including Lafcadio Hearn's father, Charles Bush Hearn,* and Lafcadio's uncle, Richard Holmes Hearn.*

Bibliography: Murray; Sean G. Ronan and Toki Koizumi, *Lafcadio Hearn (Koizumi Yakumo): His Life, Work and Irish Background* (Dublin: Ireland Japan Association, 1991); Stevenson.

HEARN, ELIZABETH HOLMES (c. 1790–?).

Lafcadio Hearn's grandmother. She was the daughter of Richard Holmes, a well-to-do landowner in Streamstown, County Westmeath, Ireland. She was a great-niece of Dr. John Arbuthnot (1667–1735), M.D., of St. Andrews, Queen Anne's physician, and the recipient of "An Epistle to Dr. Arbuthnot" (1735) by Alexander Pope. Elizabeth Holmes married Daniel James Hearn* in 1815. Sarah Holmes Brenane,* Mrs. Daniel Hearn's younger sister, deserted the Anglican faith of her family by marrying a Catholic. She converted to Catholicism and was a widow for many years. Her seven children, in addition to Hearn's father, Charles Bush Hearn,* included one of Lafcadio Hearn's uncles, the painter Richard Holmes Hearn,* and two of his aunts, Catherine Frances Hearn (Mrs. Thomas Elwood) and Jane Hearn (Mrs. Henry Stephens). From the start, Elizabeth Hearn opposed her son Charles's marriage to Rosa Antonia Cassimati Hearn* but tried to make a home for Rosa and Lafcadio in Dublin when they arrived there in August 1852. At that time Elizabeth Hearn was living with her daughter Jane and Jane's husband, Henry Cloclough Stephens, a successful solicitor. When that arrangement proved impossible, the pair moved in with Mrs. Brenane, who was more receptive.

Bibliography: Cott; Murray; Stevenson.

HEARN, GEORGE ROBERT (July 24, 1849–August 17, 1850).

Lafcadio Hearn's older brother, born on the Greek island of Leucadia to Rosa Antonia Cassimati Hearn* and Charles Bush Hearn.* Many of the islanders suffered from malaria. The sickly infant George died on Leucadia when Lafcadio was only two months old.

Bibliography: Cott; Stevenson.

HEARN, JAMES DANIEL (1854–1935).

(His name is sometimes given as Daniel James Hearn.) Lafcadio Hearn's younger brother. James Hearn was the son of Charles Bush Hearn* and Rosa Antonia Cassimati Hearn,* and was born in Greece, probably on the island of Cephalonia, after Rosa returned from Dublin home in 1854. Rosa never saw Charles or Lafcadio again. When she married Giovanni Cavallini in Greece in 1856, Cavallini demanded that she relinquish all rights and responsibilities to both Lafcadio (then in Dublin) and James, so she immediately sent James to her Hearn in-laws in Dublin. Charles took Lafcadio and James to a military barracks in Cavin, near Dublin. Lafcadio recalls beating up little James during an argument over possession of some toy soldiers. Soon thereafter, and later, he did not know of James's whereabouts. When Charles was assigned to India in 1857, James was sent to a boarding school run by a Dr. Stewart in Alton, Hampshire, England. In 1871 he migrated to the United States; lost part of his luggage in the Great Fire of Chicago that year while on his way to visit Henry and Tom Turvil, friends in Wisconsin, where he worked in market gardening; and returned to England in 1875. Dr. Stewart had a son who was a civil engineer for a tea company, for which James was to work. To this end he was to travel to India but first to return to the United States to study tobacco growing at Poquonock, Connecticut. He worked in Connecticut for several years; but when the younger Stewart died, James settled in Gibsonburg, Ohio. In about 1879 he bought into a mill there, quit for health reasons, and turned unsuccessfully to farming. At this time he got married.

During this time James also wrote for a Cincinnati newspaper. After Lafcadio Hearn returned from the French West Indies in 1889, James saw his brother's name in a Cleveland newspaper, wrote to him from Bradner, Ohio, and started a correspondence. James said Lafcadio promised to visit him in Ohio but never did. Their correspondence ended in 1892, by which time Lafcadio was in Japan. Lafcadio was critical because in his view James had never had the curiosity to try to learn about their mother. The two brothers never met in adulthood. In a letter (probably 1890), Lafcadio informs James that their great-aunt, Sarah Holmes Brenane,* was victimized financially by Henry Hearn Molyneux, whom he called "a Jesuitical adventurer." In another letter, Lafcadio expresses a vain hope that he might see Gracie, James's daughter.

At one point James Hearn, while living and farming in Bethany, Michigan, welcomed to his home Posey Gertrude Hearn, who was one of their deceased father's three daughters by his second marriage. The other half-sisters were Minnie Charlotte Hearn Atkinson* and Elizabeth Sarah Maude Hearn. In 1998 Margery Bebow of Michigan posted a note on the Internet reporting that she was James Daniel Hearn's granddaughter.

Bibliography: Cott; Henry Trace Kneeland, "Lafcadio Hearn's Brother," *Atlantic Monthly* 131 (January 1923): 20–27; R. M. Lawless, "A Note on Lafcadio Hearn's Brother: With Text of Letter from Japan," *American Literature* 10 (March 1938): 80–83; Murray; Stevenson; Tinker.

HEARN, RICHARD HOLMES (?–1890). The brother of Charles Bush Hearn,* Lafcadio's father, and hence Lafcadio's uncle. He lived with his mother, Elizabeth Holmes Hearn,* and his aunt, Sarah Holmes Brenane,* in Dublin, at least until 1849. He became a painter, studied in the Thomas Couture teaching studio in Paris, was a member of the Barbizon school, and knew Jean François Millet and also some American art students there. When Rosa Antonia Cassimati Hearn,* Lafcadio's mother, took Lafcadio from Greece to Dublin in 1852, Richard may have arranged transportation and accompanied them, perhaps only from Paris, to Dublin. In 1891 Richard Hearn published an essay on Jean-Paul Laurens (1838–1921), a French painter, illustrator, and teacher, in *Toilers in Art*, edited by Henry C. Ewart. Laurens had a special interest in gruesome subjects and distasteful aspects of church history—as did Lafcadio. When Lafcadio wrote to his brother James Daniel Hearn,* he referred to "Uncle Dick," by then long out of touch with both nephews. He was a professor at the École des Beaux-Arts in Paris (from 1886). In 1904, the year of Hearn's death in Japan, artists from Japan were studying in Paris under Laurens, the subject of Hearn's uncle's essay.

Bibliography: Kennard; Murray; Stevenson.

HEARN, ROBERT (1734–1792). Lafcadio Hearn's great-grandfather.

HEARN, ROSA ANTONIA CASSIMATI (1823–December 12, 1882).
Lafcadio Hearn's mother. She was born on Cerigo (known to the Greeks as Cythera), the most southern Ionian island of Greece. Her father, Anthony Cassimati, was of noble Cerigote lineage. Never formally educated and illiterate, Rosa grew up speaking Romaic, Italian, and Greek. She was a devout member of the Greek Orthodox Church and always retained a childlike, semi-superstitious faith. In 1848 she met Charles Bush Hearn* when he was stationed with the British Army on various Ionian islands under British control. She responded naively to his advances and soon became pregnant. Her father noticed, whereupon, according to an unsubstantiated family story, his son Demetrius, bent on vengeance, followed the culprit while he was doing his medical rounds, stabbed him several times, and left him for dead. Rosa found Charles, however, helped him recover, and accompanied him in June 1849 to Fort Santa Maura, on the island of Leucadia, where she gave birth to George Robert Hearn* (July 24, 1849). Charles decided to formalize his relationship with Rosa, so they were married in a private Greek Orthodox ceremony on Leucadia (November 25, 1849). Concealing his marriage from British authorities, he was transferred via England (February 1850) to Dominica and Grenada, British West Indies, leaving Rosa pregnant again. She gave birth to the son she christened as Patricio (Patrick) Lafcadio Tessima Carlos Hearn (June 27, 1850). She cut each of his calves three times, as a prayer, in accordance with her beliefs. She was crushed when her older little boy, George, died (August 17, 1850), and she only partially

recovered her mental equilibrium by lavishing a sad young mother's love on little Lafcadio.

On August 1, 1852, Rosa and Lafcadio Hearn arrived in Dublin, Ireland, to make their home with Charles Hearn's family. His mother, Elizabeth Holmes Hearn,* was unable to provide a warm welcome to the pair, who spoke no English, rattled away in Greek, Italian, and Romaic instead, and had other foreign ways as well. Rosa was soon befriended by Elizabeth's younger sister, Sarah Holmes Brenane,* a Catholic convert who was widowed and wealthy. Not until October 1853 did Rosa see her husband again, when he was sent to Dublin on sick leave. By this time she had grown plump, was mentally unstable, and shortly before Charles's return had attempted to jump out of a window to kill herself. He moved his wife and their child into a house near the Portobello Barracks where he was stationed outside Dublin. He evinced little affection, and Rosa threw tantrums and grew manic. In March 1854 he was transferred to the Crimea; Rosa, pregnant yet again, left Lafcadio with Mrs. Brenane and that summer returned to Cerigo. Mrs. Brenane paid for the voyage and also that of a colored woman accompanying Rosa as both midwife and wet nurse. Before reaching Cerigo, Rosa gave birth to James Daniel Hearn* in 1854, probably on the nearby island of Cephalonia. In 1856 Rosa, at home on Cerigo, learned that Charles had obtained an annulment of their marriage. She quickly married Giovanni Cavallini, an Italian-Greek who was later appointed by the British to be governor of the nearby island of Cerigotto. Cavallini ordered Rosa to give up custody of both Lafcadio, then in Dublin, and James, who was dispatched with the wet nurse back to Ireland and to his father, Charles. Rosa secretly visited Ireland a final time, hoped to see Lafcadio and James again, but was denied access to them. She returned to the Ionian islands, had two sons (Angelo and George) and two daughters (Ziza and Catherine) with Cavallini, and grew more unstable mentally. In 1872 she suffered from severe religious dementia and was institutionalized by Cavallini in the National Mental Asylum of Corfu. She died there on December 12, 1882.

Lafcadio Hearn had only the vaguest memories of his mother. He had self-induced visions of her beautiful face and dark eyes. He wrote once that in response to her leaning over him he unaccountably slapped her and was probably disciplined for doing so. He wrote to his brother James that he would rather have a picture of her than a fortune. Hearn occasionally enjoyed pointing to what resembled a thumbprint-like mark on his hand, which he said was proof that he had gypsy blood from her.

Bibliography: Nicholas Andromedas, "Ancestry of Lafcadio Hearn's Mother," *Athene* II (August 1950): 28–29, 62; Cott; Murray; Stevenson.

HENDRICK, ELLWOOD (1861–1930).

Chemist, businessman, and author. Hendrick was born in Albany, New York; studied chemistry at the University of Zurich (1878–1881); managed an Albany chemical works (1881–1884); and became a successful insurance agent. In 1897 Hendrick married Josephine Pomeroy, and they subsequently had two children. He worked with his two brothers-in-law as a broker (1900–1915) with access through them to the New York Stock Exchange, of which they were members. Hendrick worked with a consulting firm based in Cambridge, Massachusetts (1917–1922). He was a consulting editor of a chemical and metallurgical journal (1918–1923), a lecturer in chemistry at Columbia University, and the curator of its chemical museum (1924–1930). He wrote successful books on chemistry and published a book of essays, a biography of the inventor-philanthropist Lewis Miller (1829–1899), and several short biographical essays.

Hendrick was huge, attractive, genial, and generous, and he had a legion of loyal friends, one being Hearn. The two met in 1889 at a dinner party given in New York by Alice Wellington Rollins,* a well-to-do writer who rented apartment space to Hendrick. Mrs. Rollins was a friend of Elizabeth Bisland,*who was Hearn's friend from his New Orleans days and whom Hendrick considered the most beautiful woman he had ever seen. Hendrick rescued Hearn, who was somewhat disheveled, from embarrassment at the party. The two went to a beer garden and until 2:00 A.M. had a fine conversation, which they resumed at Hearn's hotel later the same morning. Hendrick was fascinated by Hearn's conversational brilliance. The two remained close, loyal, and contrastingly balanced friends. Hearn spent part of his last day in New York with Hendrick before departing for Japan in 1890. Once there, he wrote informative letters to Hendrick about his marriage, his growing Japanese family and friends, his finances and writings, his travels, his observations, his religious and ethical opinions, his health, their mutual friends, and his becoming a Japanese citizen. After Hearn's death, Hendrick served him in two ways. He defended Hearn against criticism by George Milbry Gould*; and at the request of Hearn's widow, Setsu Koizumi,* he, as well as Bisland, handled business matters with Ferris Greenslet,* Hearn's editor at the publishing firm Houghton Mifflin.

Bibliography: Cott; Ellwood Hendrick, *Percolator Papers* (New York and London: Harper & Brothers, 1919), and "Lafcadio Hearn," *The Nation* 116 (April 11, 1923): 432–433; Murray; Stevenson; Tinker.

"HEREDITARY MEMORIES" (1880). Sketch. The Doctor says we inherit memories. A stranger responds by saying that although he is well traveled he has a recurrent dream of a place he never saw in reality, of strange tongues spoken, and of a foreign port with a domed edifice. In response to the Doctor's queries, the stranger says his father was born in India, which he has never visited. The Doctor regards all this as proof of his theory.

"HIOUEN-THSANG" (1882). Sketch. In seventh-century China, after his mother receives favorable signs, Hiouen-thsang is born. He studies with Buddhists until he is uniquely learned. When times turn troublesome, he wants to find more profound wisdom in India, "the land of the Savior of Man," but the emperor of China denies him permission to leave. He goes anyway, past frontier guards, into the desert and to the land of the Oigour Tartars. The Khan welcomes him and guides him toward the Himalayas. He proceeds to Benares, exempt through holiness from all dangers, to the dragon cave of Purashapura. He weeps and thrice prays there. Though long in Nirvana, Buddha appears—radiant, smiling, but silent. After 16 years of study, copying law books and collecting many volumes, Hiouen-thsang, a gray-haired old man, returns to China and the emperor's welcome. After translating hundreds of books, he dies and is mourned by millions. He dutifully devoted his life to the pursuit of truth, and his writings exerted a widespread influence. We are wrong to think that Christians have a monopoly on goodness.

" 'HIS HEART IS OLD' " (1882). Sketch. The perusal of a quaint old archaeological volume evokes in Hearn's troubled nineteenth-century persona phantoms of joyful, beautiful classical creatures. In response, a phantom whispers of him that "His heart is old!" He quotes but then rejects the dour counsels of "Ecclesiastes." Another phantom whispers that their world was gloriously lovely but that his wisdom has produced sorrow. When he cannot weep, the final whisper is that his heart is that of Medusa. Hearn's high-density, verbose prose here is lightened by an occasional fine rhythm, as in this galloping 14-syllable line: "the noiseless flow of marble waves from urns that gurgle not."

HISTORICAL SKETCH BOOK AND GUIDE TO NEW ORLEANS AND ENVIRONS, WITH MAP... (1885). Guidebook. Hearn was one of the editors of this work, which was advertised as containing accounts of traditions, legends, and localities of "the Creole City."

"HOME" (1881). Sketch. Hearn dilates on the difficulty a bachelor, if not rich, has in trying to make a home for himself. In truth, "A woman is the soul of home." This short piece has obvious autobiographical overtones of a sad strain.

"A HORROR FROM SHAKER LIFE" (1877). Cincinnati news article. On April 24, 1877, Sallie Dill, 36, and her daughter Ida May, 16, checked into a hotel, went out and returned a couple of times, and left word to be awakened at 11 o'clock the next morning. When they could not be aroused then, authorities entered their room and found Ida dead and Sallie dying, both of morphine overdoses. Letters and cards found on them, along with investigative work, revealed that Sallie Dill, an unwed mother, with her child Ida May, one or two years old, had joined a nearby Shaker community. Fourteen years passed, and Ida innocently sought young men's companionship; she was gossiped about and forced to leave. Sallie accompanied her. They got to Cincinnati about three weeks before, were hired by a woman as housekeeper and nurse, respectively, but found the chores too difficult. Sallie wrote a friend explaining that they would meet in heaven; Ida May added a few words of farewell. Hearn blames the Shakers for turning an unskilled, defenseless girl "into a strange world, . . . where her . . . sensitive nature might be blasted by the first frost of unkindness."

"HOT BATHS IN THE MIDDLE AGES" (1884). Editorial. Albert Lecoy de la Marche (1839–1897), a French journalist-historian, having studied archival material, is publishing articles that present a "scintillant picture of the gorgeous toilets of the [European] aristocracy." He shows that, contrary to comments by the liberal historian Jules Michelet (1798–1874), not only the elite but also members of the middle class and travelers had access to warm baths in the thirteenth century.

"HUMBLE FARE AND HIGH LIVING IN ANCIENT ROME" (1880). Editorial. Hearn cites *Business Life in Ancient Rome* by Charles G. Hebermann. It was already known that "social conditions" in ancient Rome resembled ours more than they did those of medieval times. Now Hebermann shows that the wealthy Romans were extravagant, the needs of their poor were simple and cheaply accommodated, and the "free working classes" did "pretty well," in part by forming guilds. Food for the middle classes was inadequate by modern standards, while slaves survived on corn, oil, and wine. The luxuriously rich, however, could spend the equivalent of $400,000 for one banquet. Hearn's account includes other adjusted figures in dollars and cents. Information on Hebermann is scarce to the point of being unknown.

HUTSON, CHARLES WOODWARD (1840–1936). Educator and artist. He was born in McPhearsonville, South Carolina; received an A.B. from South Carolina College (1860); studied law briefly; and joined the Confederate Army, was wounded, was captured, grew ill, and was exchanged. Hutson tried to practice law but soon became a teacher in Georgia and then Louisiana. From 1873 to 1908 he taught classical and modern languages and did administrative work in various institutions of higher learning—in Louisiana, Alabama, North Carolina, South Carolina, Kentucky, Mississippi, and Texas. Thereafter he made his home in New Orleans and turned to producing prize-winning art work in oils, water colors, and pastels. Hutson also wrote several books dealing with history, French literature, and languages, and published short pieces in periodicals. In 1871 he married Mary Janes Lockett, with whom he had eight children.

Hutson, who evidently never met Hearn, assembled and published three collections of his miscellaneous newspaper pieces. They are *Fantastics and Other Fancies* (1914), *Creole Sketches* (1924), and *Editorials: New Orleans Journal-*

istic Writings (1926). In his introduction to the "Creole Sketches" section of Volume 1 of *The Writings of Lafcadio Hearn* (16 vols., 1922), Hutson mentions Hearn's connection with the *Item* and the *Times-Democrat* in New Orleans; discusses Hearn's friendship there with persons both notable and ordinary, all of whom made allowances for his eccentricities and found him lovable; shows that Hearn wrote about Creole life in ways that approximate literature rather than journalism; and praises a few tangential sketches. In his introduction to the "Fantastics and Other Fancies" section of Volume 2 of *The Writings of Lafcadio Hearn*, Hutson discusses the rationale behind his selections of *Item* and *Times-Democrat* sketches and comments in some detail about their literary merit.

"THE HYPOCRISY OF THE FACE" (1884). Editorial. P. Mantegazza of Florence, Italy, writes that efforts to hide our true feelings—because of bitterness, bravery, fear, humiliation, or pride—through employing exaggerated gestures or dissimulation, can often be detected. Our eyes may give us away. If we control our eyes, we sometimes cannot control "vasomotor nerves" causing pallor or blushing. If we avoid turning pale or red, we may twitch revealingly. Finally, Mantegazza says that one who completely controls body language still runs the risk of suddenly talking foolishly. Paolo Mantegazza (1831–1910), a prolific author, published studies of the physiognomy of love, marriage, sex, genius, and so on and was once well known for his *La physiognomie et l'expressione des sentiments* (1885).

"IDOLATRY" (1906). Autobiographical essay. As a child, Hearn disliked the Catholic Church and his overly zealous Cousin Jane (*see* "My Guardian Angel"). So, when he was taught that the early Church accepted heathen gods as demons, he happily prayed to them. He relished looking at pictures of Greek mythological creatures in "our library." He concluded that because they were beautiful, they were hated and demonized. By comparison, he regarded pictures of saints, prophets, and patriarchs as squalid. The sight of something beautiful began to evoke a "dim deep memory" of something generations back—"the phantom of rapture forgotten." He was anguished when the illustrated mythology books disappeared and then reappeared with the breasts of lovely "dryads, naiads, graces, muses" having been removed by a penknife, and with underwear having been drawn on gods and Cupids, by his "early tutors." Modern nude paintings and statues are imperfect when compared to the idealized representations by Greek artists. Hearn has gradually shed most of his old terrors despite lingering sadness and pain, and he has learned to thrill in the presence of human and natural beauty.

"THE IDYL OF A FRENCH SNUFF-BOX" (1881). Sketch. An old Creole man accidentally leaves his snuffbox in the narrator's home. Its lid is an ivory carving of a nude, sleeping dryad approached by an amorous faun who while lifting her robe is kept back by a topaz-eyed snake wound around the dryad's smooth thigh. The narrator so delights in the scene that he dreams of its continuation. The faun is excited. A dove coos. The snake follows the dove, a creature sacred to Aphrodite. The dryad awakens, stretches, embraces and kisses the faun, and— suddenly the Creole knocks on the door and asks for his tabatière. The narrator's dream remains incomplete. This delightful item rings changes on the legend surrounding Samuel Taylor Coleridge's unfinished "Kubla Khan: Or, a Vision in a Dream. A Fragment" (1798).

Bibliography: Kunst.

IN GHOSTLY JAPAN **(1899).** A collection of 14 essays, none previously published, and dedicated to "Mrs. Alice Von Behrens," a woman whom Hearn and his friend Mitchell McDonald knew in Japan. The book was republished as part of Volume 9, after *Exotics and Retrospectives*, in *The Writings of Lafcadio Hearn* (16 vols., 1922).

"Fragment": At sunset a young pilgrim, who has asked to climb to "the place of the Vision," trudges with his guide, a Bodhisattva (i.e., a religious leader not yet of Buddhahood status), up a lifeless mountainside. It is cold and stony. The frightened pilgrim is reassured that there is no danger. Finally he sees that the mountain is composed entirely of skulls. His guide says they are the youth's skulls, remnants of "the billions of his former lives." Hearn originally called this sketch "Mountain of Skulls," the title of a legend told to him by Ernest Francisco Fenollosa.*

"Furisodé": Hearn sees a long-sleeved robe (*furisodé*) hanging in a shop. It is purple and is decorated with five crests. The robe reminds him of a legend. Some 250 years ago O-Samé, a rich wine merchant's singularly beautiful daughter, saw a handsome, gorgeously garbed samurai. She had a robe made like his, to attract his attention; but she could never find him again. She fell ill and died. Her family gave their priest the robe, which he sold. The girl who bought it died at once. Sold again twice, it caused two more girls to die. So the priest burned the robe. Its dazzling flames set fire to the temple, then other buildings, and finally most of Tōkyō. The catastrophe occurred in the year 1655.

"Incense": Incense odors make Hearn see a lotus in a vase and also remember his first day in Japan. The perfumes of incense permeate homes, temples, and wayside places. Incense varies greatly in price. The history of Japanese incense would make an enormous volume. It would cover the sixth-century introduction of incense from Korea, tenth-century incense classifications, awareness of thirteenth-century Chinese incense lore, preservation of ancient forms of incense, sources of imported incense, and names of 130 varieties, recipes, and similes in romantic literature in which incense figures. Hearn describes "the religious, the luxurious, and the ghostly uses of incense." It aids pilgrims, priests, and those praying for divine help. It is central in *kō-kwai* (incense parties), in which hosts and guests try to name various incenses by their subtly differing fragrances. Hearn tabulates efforts by seven *kō-kwai* contestants sniffing four different incense odors: A fellow named Young Pine, batting .800, won, partly because he liked inhaling Wakakusa (Young Grass). To resharpen their olfactory edge, contestants used vinegar mouthwash during intermission. Hearn offers recipes for two types of incense; one has ten ingredients, two of which he names while confessing he does not know what they are. The cost of envelopes of party incense varies from $2 to $30, and accoutrements—desks, boxes, stands, pincers, censer—can total "thousands of dollars." Mourners burn incense beside corpses to ward off demons and goblins and to summon beneficent spirits, seen and unseen, of the adored deceased.

"A Story of Divination": Hearn knew a fortune-teller who believed in his ability. His four predictions for Hearn were frighteningly accurate. Although people pooh-pooh fortune-tellers, "something of inherited superstitious tendency" makes many believe in them. The fortune-teller told Hearn about Shōko Setsu, a phenomenal Chinese fortune-teller. One day Shōko threw a tile at a rat, and in a tile fracture it was written that he would break the tile by throwing it at a rat, and the correct date had been added. He consulted the tile maker, was told the address of the fortune-teller who had written on the tile, went there, and found that man's students. They told him that their master was dead, had predicted Shōko's visit, and willed him his fortune-telling manual. It told Shōko where to find a fortune, which he happily did—in the form of a jar of gold. When Hearn's friend the fortune-teller died unexpectedly in a snowstorm, Hearn recalled the Japanese saying that a fortune-teller does not know his own fate.

"Silkworms": The phrase "silkworm-mother eyebrow" puzzles Hearn, who therefore goes to his friend Niimi, a silkworm keeper, for help. Niimi shows him a sleepy silkworm-moth, which has antennae arched over its eyes like pretty eyebrows. Niimi and his family raise silkworms, feed them mulberry leaves, put fat ones in boxes when they are ready to spin, and let them "swathe themselves . . . in white floss." They have been cared for so long that they would be helpless if left alone. While Niimi lectures, Hearn muses thus: Western faiths contend that our earthly lives are larva-like in "greedy helplessness," that death "is a pupa-sleep," and that we will emerge with wings and soar to "perfect bliss." Hearn contends that such "celestial domestication" would resemble a silkworm existence of total comfort and no struggle. If the gods accorded us this kind of life, we would degenerate into "amorphous sacs, mere blind stomachs." Only pain enables us to know pleasure, to evolve. When Hearn tells Niimi about his reverie, Niimi replies with the story of Nanda, a disciple of the wise Buddha Shaka. Nanda was smitten by his girlfriend's beauty, so Shaka showed him a bunch of female apes. When asked, Nanda said he much preferred his girlfriend. Shaka took him to a heavenly sphere of desire and showed him some incomparably beautiful dancing women. Oh, yes, Nanda would prefer any of them to his girlfriend. Shaka transported him to hell, where a devil was waiting to boil his next victim alive. Nanda wondered who it would be. "Nanda, one of Shaka's disciples," was the devil's answer. The devil explains that Nanda's good actions merited his rebirth into paradise but that when there he indulged himself and must now be reborn in hell.

"A Passional Karma": Hearn attended a Tōkyō performance of *Peony-Lantern*, a play based on a novel by Enchō. Hearn and a Japanese friend translate part of the novel dealing with ghosts. In the eighteenth century O-Tsuyu, the beautiful teenage daughter of Iijima Heizayémon, and handsome young Hagiwara Shinzaburō meet through his physician friend Yamamoto Shijō. They immediately fall in love. Her maid is O-Yoné. Fearing Iijima, Shijō keeps the lovers apart, and O-Tsuyu dies of grief; O-Yoné also dies. When Shinzaburō learns this, he grieves and offers prayers for O-Tsuyu. One evening two women, carrying a lantern decorated with silk peonies, approach Shinzaburō's veranda. They are O-Tsuyu and O-Yoné, both, they say, now living in a tiny dwelling in Shitaya. Shijō tells O-Yoné that Shinzaburō is dead. He says Shijō told him they were. They conclude that Iijima's second wife, O-Kuni, told Shijō to lie. The women remain with Shinzaburō, who embraces O-Tsuyu. Shinzaburō's servant, Tomozō, spies on the couple and sees Shinzaburō hug a skeleton whose lower form is a shadow. Tomozō discusses this with Hakūdō Yusai, a scholarly fortune-teller, who visits Shinzaburō to save him from a ghost's deadly kiss. Shinzaburō goes to Shitaya, cannot find evidence of O-Tsuyu's living there, but finds the tombs of O-Tsuyu and O-Yoné, decorated with a peony lantern. Yusai sends Shinzaburō, now terrified, to Ryōseki, a holy priest, for advice. Ryōseki explains that O-Tsuyu loved Shinzaburō in previous lives, means him no harm, but is dangerous. He gives Shinzaburō several charms, to block O-Tsuyu from re-entering his house, and an amulet. She and O-Yoné promise Tomozō some gold if he will remove a charm from a window. When he does so, shadows of the two women enter, and in the morning Tomozō finds Shinzaburō in the agony of a horrible death and two female skeletons beside him. Tomozō tells Yusai, who consults Ryōseki, who, being prescient, already knows; and Ryōseki tells Yusai not to worry, because Shinzaburō was foredoomed. However, Yusai should make sure that the two lovers are buried side by side, because Shinzaburō's karma for the girl was strong. Here the story ends. Hearn and his Japanese friend agree, although for different reasons, that Shinzaburō was contemptible. The two visit the couple's cemetery. It is desolate, with potato patches and frog ponds. When asked, a woman points out the Peony-Lantern tombs. But they are of an innkeeper and a Buddhist nun. Hearn's friend says Hearn surely never supposed this ghost story was true. "A Passional Karma" is Hearn's most complex story within a story and is bulwarked with 17 learned footnotes. It is one of his best ghost stories, enlivened by a rare touch of humor at the end. (Information about Enchō seems to be unavailable.)

"Footprints of the Buddha": The feet of Buddha figures in Japan are often represented in monuments, paintings, and carvings of footprints. The first such footprint in Japan was a copy of a Chinese copy of an Indian original. It is said that looking at the Buddha's footprint purifies one and delivers one from evils caused by bad behavior. Hearn includes drawings of Buddha footprints. Typically they are decorated with swastikas and pictures of fish, maces, seashells, flower vases, wheels, and crowns. Each design has symbolic value. Twenty-four centuries ago an Indian pilgrim meditated and expressed the highest truths— concerning unity, illusions, and universal cycles. People worship his very footprints because his philosophy has survived the waxing and waning of many empires.

"Ululation": Hearn's "white bitch" is a gentle guard dog, fed and protected by everyone nearby. Her only fault is her nocturnal howl. In succession it is moan, wail, chuckle, "wild" wail, "atrocious laugh," and childish sob. It combines "piteous agony" and "goblin mockery" in a way that symbolizes her split personality. If Hearn died, she would mourn and then eat him up, bones and all. Other dogs, understanding her "extraordinary vowelings," answer from the hills. We cannot translate, but we may imagine that dog cries arise from fears. Perhaps the smell of a "ghostly terror" evokes them. Maybe this white bitch "*mentally* sees . . . the ghoulish law of life." To her, "Nature" is not loving or merciful. All living things live "by eating each other." From this concept, Hearn makes a curious leap: All matter is "self-devouring." So are planetary systems, and the cosmos itself. But this is all illusory. If Hearn's bitch could speak, the existence-tormented thing would discuss little but smells, smell-based judgments, the joy of eating, and the fear of being eaten. Her "notion of apparent realities must be worse than sepulchral"; so let her howl. In some ways she is more virtuous than we are and deserves a better condition when reborn.

"Bits of Poetry": Hearn calls this item "gossip on poetry." Japanese poetry is heard and seen everywhere. People sing and chant verses at play and work, and they print them on countless objects. Hearn offers samples of tiny poems from a manuscript collection. They are responses to all sorts of trouble, and he says that they are both pleasingly artistic and dutifully moral. Evocative, revivifying, suggestive, they "stir imagination without satisfying it." He quotes and praises a haiku by "the famous poetess Chiyo" (Chiyo-Ni Fukuda, 1703–1775). While complaining that all translations are disappointing, Hearn presents more than a score of poems in Japanese and then in English. Hearn is quite correct: The originals relate to Japanese feelings and experiences in ways Westerners have almost no way of sharing. How can, for example, "Mi ni shiniru" or "Sakura chiru" resonate aesthetically and didactically in Occidental ears? Moreover, Hearn is offputting when in the first paragraph he contends that lower classes in Japan are in every way superior to "our own lower classes" because they are surrounded by poetry.

"Japanese Buddhist Proverbs": Proverbs reflect the "moral experience" of people and are little altered by social changes. Philosophers find them of "special psychological interest." Japanese sayings that by derivation or allusion concern Buddhism seem especially noteworthy. Hearn presents 100 such proverbs, in Japanese and English (courtesy of a Japanese friend), and annotates 77 of them. They mostly concern living with care, restraint, and stoic awareness of this life's difficulties and their evanescent if usually dangerous ingredients. Sufficiently illustrative are the following examples, with words within brackets reflecting Hearn's explications. "Life is a lamp-flame before a wind [Buddhist wind of death]," "Never let go the reins of the wild colt of the heart," "This world is only a resting-place [or travelers' inn]," "The mouth [uttering unguarded speech] is the front-gate of all misfortune," "The blind man [one ignorant or vicious] does not fear the snake," "The devil [any wicked man] takes a goblin [wicked woman] to wife," "The fallen blossom never returns to the branch," "To become an abbot one must begin as a novice," and (perhaps Hearn's favorite) "Only by reason of having died does one enter into life." Peculiarly, Hearn alphabetizes his hundred selections by the first Japanese word of each, "to facilitate reference," he avers.

"Suggestion": A learned man visiting Tōkyō on his way to India theorizes that because "man desires woman, and woman man" more than anything else except life itself, it follows that when reborn a man ought to become a woman, and vice versa. When Hearn wonders what sort of person who through knowledge and behavior would become "superior to all weaknesses of sex," the answer is that such a person would be reborn in a higher form of humanity than we now know. The traveler gives Hearn permission to publish his ideas, and here they are.

"Ingwa-Banashi": In 1829 the wife of a feudal baron lies dying. She asks her husband to bring Yukiko, his teenage concubine, to her. She tells Yukiko that she wants the embarrassed girl to become her husband's new wife, because he will love and promote her. The wife fervently begs Yukiko to carry her on her shoulders to the garden so she can see its double-blossoming cherry tree before she dies. The husband nods his approval. But when the wife mounts Yukiko's back, she reaches over her shoulders and firmly grasps her breasts, cries out, "I have my wish for the cherry-bloom," and dies. Her hands cannot be removed from their clutch. A skillful physician is summoned and amputates the hands at the wrist; but, withered and black though they are, they remain squeezing Yukiko for the next 17 years, despite the fact that she becomes an itinerant nun and prays for the repose of the wife's spirit. Yukiko is last heard of in 1846. *Ingwa* means the evil results of sins committed in a former life. Does the first wife combine jealousy and destructive lesbian tendencies?

"Story of a Tengu": One summer day a priest living near Kyōto bribes some naughty boys with a fan to stop beating a bird, which he then lets fly away. On his way home he sees a monk, who thanks him for saving his life. The monk explains that he was the rescued bird, has supernatural powers, and will grant the priest any favor. When the priest says he would like to see the assembly in India at which the Buddha appeared, the monk is agreeable. But he warns that when the priest sees the Buddha, he must say nothing. Agreeing, the priest opens his eyes to a vision of the Vulture Peak, a holy Indian mountain. When the Buddha appears amid glorious lights, the priest forgets his promise and says, "O thou Blessed One!" Darkness instantly falls, and the priest finds himself back on his way home. The "goblin-monk" reappears, upbraids him, and laments that in punishment for deceiving the priest, he has a broken wing preventing any more flights. A *tengu* is a beak-nosed, winged man, or a bird of prey.

"At Yaidzu": Yaidzu, a coastal town, has a rough surf worked through by 50-man, flatbottomed boats, uniquely designed for fishermen to catch bonito and supply the entire empire. Remarkable too are their enormous bamboo bait baskets, metal-shod anchors, and other implements. The people are frank, honest, innocent, kind, and loyal to ancient traditions. Hearn visits Yaidzu during the three-day festival of the dead. Late during the third night he swims alongside a fleet of miniature boats, each with a lighted candle and painted paper sides, launched to commemorate the dead. We too are launched on a "blind current . . . bearing . . . [us] into the outer blackness," Hearn says. Ashore again, he is warned by his landlord and landlady of the dangers of swimming too far. His landlady tells him the story of a bold Yaidzu lover-swimmer whose fate reminds him of that of Leander in the Greek legend of Hero and Leander. The next morning, Hearn watches the "formidable" waves crashing into the sea wall and concludes, once again, that the sea is "a conscious and a hostile power." Swim underwater at night, and you will feel "enveloped by . . . an infinite soft cold Ghost," he cautions. That night Hearn hears the surf roar and also a "further surf," like that of the massing of cavalry and artillery. His being terrified by "the voice of the sea" when he was a child and again during his adult visits to sea coasts prompts him to conclude that such emotions are "the inherited sum of numberless terrors ancestral." Sea sounds include battle noises, bestial roars, fire cracklings, earthquake rumbles, and screams of the drowning. Sea depths call to our own depths and make us serious. But superb music, a veritable "psychical storm," moves us still more by appealing to "billions of prenatal memories" of every "ancient pleasure and pain." They ultimately rise in "perfect harmony" as "the music of the Gods." Because we combine the varied feelings "of dead generations," we too "are as Gods" and will furnish music to "other hearts" after our departure. This essay is one of Hearn's most representative concerning psychic evolution.

The persistent Buddhist strain running throughout the 14 sketches comprising *In Ghostly Japan* provides a degree of unity and made some contemporaries assert that Hearn had converted to Buddhism, which was not true and which he denied. In December 1898 Hearn wrote to McDonald that contrary to his advice, he had just packed up his unique copy of the manuscript of *In Ghostly Japan*, labeled it, addressed it in various languages, and shipped it—"doubly-registered"—to his publishers (Little, Brown and Company in Boston), whom, he added, he "told . . . just to do whatever they pleased about terms." He was evidently sick and tired of worrying his manuscript into the better shape McDonald had persistently suggested. The book was issued in England (1899, 1905) and enjoyed numerous reprintings there and in the United States.

Bibliography: Bisland; Michiko Iwasaka and Barre Toelken, *Ghosts and the Japanese Cultural Experience in Japanese Death Legends* (Logan: Utah State University Press, 1994); Kennard; Kunst; Murray.

"INSECT POLITICS" (1878). Editorial. A New York newspaper editorial titled "Communism among Ants" triggers Hearn's comment on ant "civilization"— its architecture, warfare, and use of aphids as slaves. Recently, socialistically inclined ants have been observed attacking rich ants that have selfishly hoarded "honey, or other wealth."

"IS THE SEA SERPENT AN EEL?" (1878). Editorial. Notwithstanding earlier hoaxes, the existence of sea monsters is being more widely believed. Hearn discounts sightings of big serpents and counters with the theory that they are actually enormous eels, which are ferocious and have been seen 50 feet long in French rivers.

"IT IS OUT!" (1874). Cincinnati news article. This is the third of eight articles about the murder of Herman Schilling on Saturday, November 7, 1874, by Andreas Egner, his son Frederick K. Egner, and their friend George Rufer, in revenge for Schilling's having allegedly seduced Andreas Egner's daughter Julia, age about 15, who died while pregnant. The other articles, in chronological order, are "Violent Cremation," "Killed and Cremated," "The Tannery Horror," "The Furnace Fiends [1]," "The Furnace Fiends[2]," "The Quarter of Shambles," and "The Furnace Horror." Fred Egner has confessed to helping his father, Andreas, and their friend Rufer kill Schilling. Tuesday, November 10:Rufer's story that his wife Frederika, who lies ineffectively for him, scratched him is disproved by the testimony of others. Andreas maintains a sphinx-like silence. Fred and others testify that Schilling slept with Fred's sister Julia and that her father abused her afterward and sent her to a hospital, where she died. Rufer maintains a glittery-eyed silence at first. Fred amplifies his testimony to a full, dictated, and signed confession: Rufer clubbed Schilling; Andreas thrust a pitchfork through him several times; and Fred tried to shove Schilling's probably dead body into the tannery furnace, but only Rufer succeeded in doing so. When Fred's confession is read to Rufer and Andreas, Rufer says that Andreas and Fred feared he would blame only them, and Andreas says that Fred is crazy. Curiously, it is asserted that Julia's death from cancer of the vulva was caused by her father's kicks.

J

JAPAN: AN ATTEMPT AT INTERPRETATION (1904). A collection of lectures on Japan. In 1901 Elizabeth Bisland* interested J. G. Schurman, president of Cornell University, in having Hearn lecture there on Japan. On December 24, 1902, Schurman sent Hearn an invitation to deliver 20 lectures and gave him freedom to lecture elsewhere in the United States on the same subject. Hearn was delighted. But on March 9, 1903, Schurman sent a letter of cancellation, saying that typhoid had hit the campus and that the university lacked funds to pay Hearn the $1,000 promised. Hearn continued working on and revising his lectures, prepared them for publication in book form, and added a first chapter and a last chapter. In a 1903 letter to Bisland, he explained that he wanted this book to be "a serious work upon Japan, entirely unlike anything yet written. The substantial idea [he continued] . . . is that Japanese society represents the condition of ancient Greek society a thousand years before Christ. I am treating of religious Japan—not of artistic or economical Japan, except by way of illustration." The book, in 22 titled but unnumbered chapters, was published in September, the month of Hearn's death. *Japan: An Attempt at Interpretation* is Volume 12 of *The Writings of Lafcadio Hearn* (16 vols., 1922).

"Difficulties": There is no balanced study of Japanese religion, which is necessary for an complete understanding of Japanese art and literature.

"Strangeness and Charm": Foreigners observe that Japan's outward strangeness (architecture, dress, habits) is beautiful; its inner strangeness (speech patterns, courtesy, manifestations of joy), charming. Religion is joyful. Old ways, resembling the aesthetic and moral culture of ancient Greece, are disappearing as Japan enters "the world's competitive struggle."

"The Ancient Cult": Japan's "real religion," Shintō, is based on worship of family, tribal, and imperial ancestors. Elements of its evolutionary development (ghosts, power of the dead, sacrifice) resemble those of Indo-European religions.

"The Religion of the Home": Propitiating deceased family members came first, followed by sacrifice to clan leaders and, finally, by worshipping national rulers. The three forms exist together. Hearn discusses details of funerals, mourning, sacrifice, and reverential service (filial piety, patriotism).

"The Japanese Family": A family's welfare depends on that of dead ancestors. Family bonding is more religious than affectionate. Family structure is patriarchal: Fathers and brothers outrank mothers and daughters; Wives obey husbands; children obey parents and grandparents; younger brothers obey older ones; younger sisters obey older ones. Family chiefs resemble rulers and priests. A person marrying into a family is "adopted," subject to dismissal. Getting married proves filial piety. Monogamy strengthens families, but concubines are tolerated—and then some. Following divorces, children remain with the patriarchal family. Patriarchal power has diminished. Modern thinkers regard Japanese women, always "under tutelage," as oppressed. Servants, slavelike in former times, are "inferiors" but also "trusted familiars," with loyalty demanded. Old-time families were happier than this discussion suggests.

"The Communal Cult": Just as religion controls family, so religion mandates conduct toward the outside world by village and district families, through belief in the power of the Ujigami (clan deities), to whom worship is due. Most villages have individual Ujigami, with appropriate temples, customs, and laws. Each young man is subservient to the community, even in the choice of spouse. When he becomes a household head he defers to communal judgment, as does even the commune's "headman." A man's time, money, and effort are for the village and are not exclusively his. Violations of rules, including infractions of work habits, are severely punished by flogging or, worse, banishment. In exercising his authority the Shintō priest represents "communal sentiment" and is deferred to in many ways, for example, by shrine-bearers and festive dancers. Hearn cites John Henry Wigmore (1863–1943), a prodigious American legal scholar, as one of his sources here (and later in this book).

"Developments of Shintō": Worship of a supreme deity (or group of deities) evolved from ancestral-spirit reverence, first in family, then clan, groups. The supreme-ruler cult gave rise to the earliest Shintō histories, largely mythological and starting in the eighth century. Primitive accounts combine "pathos with nightmare-terror." In explicating Shintō evolution in Japan, Hearn relies heavily on the works of the anti-Buddhist Hirata Atsutane (1776–1843). Imperial-ancestor worship is significant but less so than worship of the Sun-Goddess and of her brother's offspring, "first ruler of the Province of the Gods." Old Japan's God of the Living was the Mikado ("deity incarnate"). When Hearn turns to worship of gods of "crafts and callings," he confesses a lack of information but mentions temples throughout Japan devoted to agricultural deities (e.g., the silk-worm goddess). He discusses household gods and mentions the fact that slowly evolved animism in Shintō was influenced by Chinese practitioners.

"Worship and Purification": Given the pervasive influence of the dead, which haunted and made holy everything everywhere, the individual in Old Japan faced awesome difficulties identifying and praying to multitudinous deities, attending public rites, participating in festivals, and attending public Shintō-cult rites. Demanded were cleanliness, *o-harai* (ceremonial purification), communal lustration by burning *kitogata* (papers cut into human forms), and various ascetic practices (cold-water baths; use of a civil representative to atone vicariously), and appointment of diviners. Hearn personalizes part of this chapter by reporting that he witnessed certain ceremonies in Izumo.

"The Rule of the Dead": These beliefs led to and influenced ceremonies, social relations, and family behavior. Obedience was pious; disobedience, impious. Results of such discipline, at which foreign sociologists may smile, admirably combine affection, cleanliness, diligence, kindness, respect, reverence, tenderness, and thrift. At first coerced, all became habitual. Law prescribed details at every level of existence: house size and interior features; wedding protocol, including gifts; clothing and hairdressing; modes of speech, smiles, bows, and breathing; and funeral, burial, and veneration rites. The consequence became self-imposed moral rigidity. Hearn reveals two personal proclivities here. After reporting that the shogun Tokugawa Iyéyasu (Ieyasu, 1542–1616) authorized samurai to execute any artisan, farmer, or merchant deemed to have violated "prescribed etiquette," he first says that Old Japanese punishments were "almost as savage, as those established during our own [Christian] mediaeval period" and, second, relishes quoting the description by Captain John Saris (?–1846) of a horrendous punishment in 1613 of quarreling adulterers.

"The Introduction of Buddhism": Shintō was established before any Chinese or Korean influences. Buddhism entered Japan after difficulties, including bloodshed, from Korea (A.D. 552) and spread by the ninth century, after Confucianism, promoting the love of learning, had reorganized Japanese administrative procedures. After overlying Shintō for nearly a millennium, Buddhism, which almost absorbed Shintō, was disestablished (1871) and Shintō "resumed its archaic simplicity." But meanwhile, Buddhists promulgated belief in metempsychosis; demystified the birth-life-death cycle; urged belief in the present consequences of good-bad actions in one's previous existence; and preached about Heaven and Abuda (eight hells) rather than Nirvana, wisdom in everyone (usually dormant), the duty for kindness and pity, and the value of education. Shintō priests were not teachers. Buddhist priests introduced Chinese art, calligraphy, literature, and more.

"The Higher Buddhism": Many Westerners wrongly believe that Japanese intellectuals are atheistic and that ordinary Japanese define Nirvana as extinction. One can study Buddhism by reading "the more important sutras" in European-language translations. The Chinese Buddhist canon is a formidable seven thousand volumes. Hearn calls *Buddhism in Translations* (1896) by Henry Clarke Warren (1854–1899) the best resource in English. Some Buddhist concepts are analogous to Western thought (including Monism). Buddhism is most notable for teaching that there is one reality, that consciousness is not the essential self, that acts and thoughts create phenomena that create matter, and that Karma makes all existence (with past creating present, and both determining future conditions). Hearn relates these doctrines to "modern thought," relying on publications by Herbert Spencer (1820–1903). The implication at the most personal, individual level is that "the human consciousness is but a temporary aggregate—not an eternal entity." There is, Hearn continues, no permanent self; there is but one eternal principle in all life—the supreme Buddha. Modern Japanese call this Absolute the "Essence of Mind."

"The Social Organization": Patriarchal families, ancient Japan's original social units, were divided into greater and lesser clans, each with its own territory, leaders, dependents, serfs, slaves, and freedmen. Clans claimed descent from deities or were "plebs." Clans combined for protection. Strict hierarchies evolved over centuries, with samurai and soldier-farmers. Iyéyasu reorganized and subdivided the samurai. The nobility and the military ruled the nation severely. Commoners, in descending order, were farmers, artisans, and merchants. Beneath all were the *chōri* (pariahs, "things"); they dug wells and graves, slaughtered and cured hides, made sandals, and so on and were ghettoed. At the bottom were *hinin* (non-persons), including beggars, entertainers, prostitutes, and those outlawed; the *hinin* were organized, had chiefs, and were left alone by the government. Anyone killing *hinin* was merely fined. Such a society is distinct from anything in the Occident. It exemplifies "religious communism doubled with a military despotism of the most terrible kind." Hearn closes by correcting modern commentators who regard Japanese organizational ability and democratic enthusiasm as proof of "fitness for representative government in the Western sense." Fundamentally different are compulsory cooperation and voluntary cooperation, despotism and individually exercised rights. It might be thought that constant moral and physical coercion would create "a dismal uniformity" throughout Japan, which, however, has never turned "homogeneous." The result is that the social customs and work habits of each despotic region have evolved uniquely. Travelers in Japan find everywhere "the novel, the unexpected, the unimagined." In this essay, Hearn makes use of the expertise of Japanologist and translator Karl Adolf Florenz (1865–1939).

"The Rise of Military Power": Japanese history from the reign of Jimmu Tennō (660?–585? B.C.) until the reign of the Empress Suikō (A.D. 593–628) is "little better than fairy-tales." Despots followed, and with them luxury, corruption, and militarists. Authorities inheriting their power delegated the conducting of wars to rival clans, notably the Minamoto and the Taira. The worst war in Japanese history ended in 1185 with Taira extermination. Hearn summarizes centuries of shōgun, regent, and militant Buddhist history—with many names and dates. Enter Tokugawa Iyéyasu, "the most remarkable man that Japan ever produced"—aristocrat, diplomat, scholar, soldier, statesman. Victorious at Sekigahara (1600), he consolidated his power, distributed fiefs, and balanced would-be rivals into impotence; the Tokugawa shogunate, totaling 15 military sovereigns, gave Japan peace and prosperity and lasted until 1867. Japan's history proves Herbert Spencer's assertion that conservative, cohesive religious dynasties resist change and survive, whereas military dynasties depend on individuals and disintegrate.

"The Religion of Loyalty": In Japan, filial piety "widens in range" to "political obedience" within communities, and then to "military obedience" to war lords. Ultimately the individual submits not through "the sense of obligation, but the sentiment of duty." This feeling, initially religious, evolved into affectionate self-sacrifice. Retainers owed their all to "divinely descended lord[s]." When a *daimyō* (feudal lord) died, a score of his retainers often practiced *junshi* (mass suicide). Although Iyéyasu ordered the custom stopped, it persisted. In 1664 a vassal disemboweled himself, whereupon the government seized his lands, executed two of his sons, and banished the remnants of his household. Hearn discusses military suicides, suicides of condemned officials' wives, samurai harakiri, dependents' killing their children to save their *daimyō*'s children, killing killers of one's parents or *daimyō* (a requirement according to Confucian ethics), and theatrical tragedies adumbrating these activities. The Chinese vengeance code gained acceptance in Japan, there called *kataki-uchi*. Iyéyasu decreed that written notice of vendetta plans be filed beforehand in court. Striking a parent or a teacher ("the father of the mind") was a capital offense. When Japan began to "face . . . the unexpected peril of Western aggression," diffuse social units were fused into one national mass, with obedience solely directed to "the Heavenly Sovereign." Here and elsewhere Hearn makes use of *Tales of Old Japan* (1871) and other works by Algernon Bertram Freeman-Mitford (1837–1916).

"The Jesuit Peril": Landing at Kagoshima, Japan (1549), Jesuits built more than two hundred churches (by 1581). Politician-soldier Nobunaga (1534–1582) tolerated Christianity in order to oppose Buddhism, which he hated. Hidéyoshi (1536–1598) succeeded him, regarded foreign priests as dangerous, but remained busy centralizing his power. When Jesuit forces killed Buddhist priests and destroyed their temples and art works, Hidéyoshi struck back, destroying mission churches (1587) and ordering the Jesuits to leave. They merely scattered. Spanish Franciscans arrived from the Philippines (1591) and broke their promise not to preach, so Hidéyoshi crucified several priests and followers (Nagasaki, 1597). Iyéyasu succeeded Hidéyoshi, tolerated the Jesuits until he had consolidated his power (by 1606), prohibited further missionary work, was disobeyed, and encouraged "pitiless" persecution (beginning in 1614) eliminating "every outward trace of Christianity." Hearn presents anti-Jesuit evidence: plots to control the Japanese central government; intolerance of both Shintō and Buddhism; fears that Will Adams (1564–1620), an English pilot of a Dutch ship landing in Japan (1600), would tell Iyéyasu about Spanish Catholic conquests in America and the West Indies. Iyéyasu questioned him, trusted him, made him a samurai, but never let him return home. Iyéyasu finally defined Roman Catholicism as "a 'false and corrupt religion.' " When Hidéyoshi's son, Hidéyori, favored the Jesuits, Iyéyasu stormed his fortress and Hidéyori committed suicide (1615). When Iyéyasu's son, Hidétada, became ruler, he ordered the execution of every Catholic priest and friar found in Japan (1617). Sizable numbers of Christians remained, eventually organized defensively at Shimabara, but were massacred (1638), thus ending "the real history of the Portuguese and Spanish missions." Hearn laments the hideous fate of Japanese converts to Christianity (he reports that two Jesuit priests were tortured into denying their faith and marrying Japanese women) but insists that Catholicism—"this black creed," "this pitiless faith"—"brought to Japan nothing but evil." Hearn grimly imagines what the Pacific rim would have been like had Catholicism spread from a Japanese foothold. He is glad that Japan was spared, to preserve "its traditions, beliefs, and customs," all of which Catholicism would have extirpated, he opines. Western industrialism, he adds, is wrecking Japan's wonderful "art-world"; still, "industrial influence, though pitiless, is not fanatic." The adventures of William Adams inspired *Shogun: A Novel of Japan* (1975), the bestselling novel by James Clavell (1925–1994).

"Feudal Integration": Iyéyasu's "Legacy" (legal code) established laws weighing more heavily on the upper classes and less and less so "as the social scale descended." It protected peasants and the poor from cruelty above. Insubordination was never tolerated. Ancestor worship was required; marriage, virtually so. The Tokugawa rule, lasting two and a half centuries and ending when the Meiji period began (1868), "compelled peace and encouraged industry." Individual ambition was restrained. Accomplishments, pleasures, and etiquette formerly reserved for the upper classes became more common elsewhere. Art products were marvelous. But best was the completion and perfection of womankind, evolved thus by nature, tradition, and artifice. Japanese women are childish, courageous, dutiful, forceful, gentle, moral, tender—and angelic.

"The Shintō Revival": Shintō Satsuma and Chōshū clans, being conservative, chafed for two centuries under Tokugawa regimes. Three eminent Shintō scholars—Mabuchi (1697–1769), Motowori (1730–1801), and Hirata (1776–1843)—helped disestablish Buddhism and thus led to the Shintō revival (1871). It was possible only during times of peace. The three were sponsored by naive patrons. Tokugawa officials feared that admitting to the Imperial Court their inability to face down Western aggression would result in their personal ruin. Tokugawa shōgunate enemies persuaded the Court to evict foreigners; a prince fired on naval vessels, commanders of which took successful action against Shimonoséki and demanded a heavy indemnity; the Court abolished the shōgunate. Total military and civil power returned to the Mikado (i.e., the emperor) (1867), Shintōism became the national religion, and Buddhism was abolished. The successful clansmen advocated meeting Western challenges by studying Western science and Europeanizing Japanese society. Changes led to the first Japanese Parliament (1891). Shintō "save[d] the country from foreign domination." Hearn's ominous close: Shintō's appeal to duty, loyalty, and national patriotism "will not be vain . . . in another hour of national peril."

"Survivals": With the advent of the Meiji period, feudalism was abolished and the military class was suppressed. But remnants of Old Japan remain. Family, communal, and tribal clan laws abide. The average man is still coerced socially by his superiors, his equals, and his inferiors and thus is "confronted by the despotism of collective opinion."

"Modern Restraints": Coercion restrains "individual energy and capacity." But those in authority have to guard against applying excessive pressure, which might trigger peasant revolts. Similarly, every household head must limit the imposition of his will on family members and servants. Also, too much pressure from community leaders is "likely to prove mischievous" because it suppresses necessary competition. The government remains strong because it conserves "ancient methods," modified though they must be. Meanwhile, the people are brave, patient, and uncomplaining. This is good, because "Japan is in danger, between the terrible friendship of England and the terrible enmity of Russia."

"Official Education": The government has organized national education on a European curriculum (absent Greek and Latin), with Chinese study still required. Despite these changes, Japanese schools—revering Occidental procedures—treat small children tenderly but older ones severely. Little children never become bullies. In middle schools, students grow serious, coalesce, and pressure teachers. In schools for older students (mostly preparing for universities and then governmental work), class discipline is strict and teachers are generally promotion-minded "officials"; throughout, a "sinister silence" prevails. For the finest students, who leave home forever, the gates of the university open and life within is deadly serious. Failures used to be called criminals. Students study hard, are gawkily courteous to faculty, mostly graduate to merit governmental employment, and metamorphose into "dignified, impassive, easy-mannered official[s]." The system works. The government rarely fails to appoint skillfully. A well-minted official, seemingly "amiable," in reality turns "secretive and inscrutable," alert, quick at decision making, ever cautious. All his learning is "oil to make easy the working of certain official machinery." Totally lacking moral freedom, he is the system's slave. Success causes career advancements; failure, once followed by *hara-kiri*, now results in absolute ostracism. Teachers, traditionally underpaid, or not paid and instead self-sacrificial, deserve praise. Recent scandals and alleged shortcomings are caused by political interference with innovations or attempts to mimic foreign methods alien to Japanese "moral experience." Lamentable has been the fate of exceptionally brilliant Japanese students sent abroad. Armed with prodigious memories, they study literature, philology, modern philosophy, and psychology, but they return to Japan not to use what they have learned but to advance in government. Upon coming home again, they should have tried to "reconstruct . . . their patriarchal society to meet the sudden peril [of Western encroachment]."

"Industrial Danger": After comparing and contrasting stages of Japanese social evolution to revolutionary phases in Greek, Roman, and European civilizations, Hearn suggests that Japan would be in trouble if it had followed those sociological models. Instead, in 30 years it legally dissolved its patriarchal system and shaped an industrial system in its place. But the dangers of anarchy are near, and many in Japan's expanding population are already suffering misery caused by industrial conditions. In subsidizing national industries, the government has let wither family-production methods, with their beautiful and famous artistic and industrial items. Capitalism has reinstated cruel servitude. Humane reforms, when called for, are opposed by industrialists claiming reforms would hurt competition with foreign companies. Japan's loyal soldiers and sailors cannot save the country, which will lose the fight against free and intelligent workers abroad. Japan's "ancient social experience" is now an incubus. It would help if officials could order its obedient citizens to adopt useful Western traits while retaining their own kindest ones. Hearn fears the consequences to Japan of combinations of aggressive greed entering from beyond its shores.

"Reflections": Hearn has sought to explain Japan's social history. He has contemplated the country with pleasure. Its old civilization is unspeakably charming. Much is attractively illusory but may foretell a better future. Old Japan was near the pinnacle of morality. To survive, the Japanese must become less amiable. Writing while the "terrible" Russo-Japanese war was raging, Hearn praises Japanese courage but warns Japan, if victorious (which it was a year later), not to assume any victory over an invasion of foreign money. The New Japan has strengths and weaknesses. Ancient morality will probably "loosen"; however, despite outward danger signs, it remains true that "a religion [fortunately] decays slowly." Requisite new individualism in Japan surely should not rest on Christian foundations. Would-be Occidental missionaries should be warned that Japan still practices ancestor worship, will repel Christianity, and will see it as a cover for foreign "industrial . . . aggrandizement." Turning away from Japan, Hearn writes prophetically: "With the return of all Europe to militant conditions, there has set in a vast ecclesiastical revival of which the menace to human liberty is unmistakable; the spirit of the Middle Ages threatens to prevail again; and anti-semitism has actually become a factor in the politics of three Continental powers." Those intolerant at home should not preach tolerance abroad. Only compromise with East Asia can prevent evil.

In an appendix added to the fourth printing (also 1904), Hearn reprints a letter from Spencer to a Japanese statesman named Baron Kanéko Kentarō. It is dated August 26, 1892, and urges Japan to avoid Americans and Europeans as much as possible.

Japan: An Attempt at Interpretation was often reprinted and was issued in England (1904). Modern scholarly pronouncements on *Japan: An Attempt at Interpretation* vary from calling it weary and cynical to regarding it as Hearn's finest study of his adopted land.

Bibliography: Dawson; Espey; Dennis Fox, "Requiem for a Recluse," *Lafcadio Hearn Journal* 3 (Spring 1993): 3–6; Kunst; Earl Miner, "Hearn and Japan: An Attempt at Interpretation," in Hirakawa, pp. 58–71; Murray; Masaru Toda, "The Western Approach to Shinto: Hearn, Bruno Taut and André Malraux," in Hirakawa, pp. 223–241.

"JAPANESE FAIRY TALE SERIES." Hearn translated four Japanese fairy tales for inclusion in this popular series, published by Takejirō Hasegawa in Tōkyō.

Individual little numbers were published in multiple editions with colored illustrations, some from woodblocks. Some editions after being bound were tied with blue silk threads; some were printed on paper that was then crêped. Hearn's contributions, each a separately published number, are "The Boy Who Drew Cats" (1898), "The Goblin Spider" (1899), "The Old Woman Who Lost Her Dumpling" (1902), and "Chin Chin Kobakama" (1903). Each was frequently republished in Japan, and each was issued in England (1902; 1925; and 1903? and 1925, respectively). Hearn's translation of "Window of the Temple," in the first edition of "The Goblin Spider," was omitted from later editions. In addition, Hearn's translation of "The Fountain of Youth," another Japanese fairy tale, was scheduled for publication as part of the series, was mislaid, and was separately issued (in 14 pages) in 1922. Because the stock was destroyed in the 1923 earthquake and subsequent fire, remnants of the original printing of two hundred copies have become collectors' items.

***JAPANESE LYRICS* (1915).** Collection of lyrics translated by Hearn and divided into "Insect Poems," "Lullabies and Children's Verse," "Love Songs and Lyrics," "Goblin Poetry," and "The River of Heaven," with notes. Posthumously published in Boston and New York, the small book was reissued in England (1915).

***A JAPANESE MISCELLANY* (1901).** A collection of 15 stories and other prose pieces under three headings: "Strange Stories," "Folk-Lore Gleanings," and "Studies Here and There." The book was dedicated to "Mrs. Elizabeth Bisland Wetmore," Hearn's old friend Elizabeth Bisland.* *Shadowings* and *A Japanese Miscellany* comprise Volume 10 of *The Writings of Lafcadio Hearn* (16 vols., 1922).

"Strange Stories" has six tales. "Of a Promise Kept" begins when Akana Soyëmon plans to visit his birthplace in faraway Izumo and promises his brother Hasébé Samon to return home on the ninth month's ninth day. But on that day, although Hasébé plans a celebratory feast, Soyëmon does not appear. Hasébé waits until after the moon sets. Suddenly a tall man enters "lightly and quickly." It is Soyëmon, who, however, refuses food and wine. He begins to explain. A usurper named Tsunéhisa took command of a certain castle in Izumo and ordered Soyëmon's cousin Akana Tanji to keep Soyëmon, because he had been loyal to Tsunéhisa's rival. Soyëmon says he retained his sword, pauses, and disappears. Deducing that Soyëmon killed himself and traveled back home in spirit, Hasébé rushes to Izumo, learns the truth about his brother's *hara-kiri*, kills the treacherous Tanji, and is forgiven by Tsunéhisa, who, though cruel, respects Hasébé's filial courage. In a footnote, Hearn cites *Ugétsu Monogatari* (Tales of Moonlight and Rain, 1858) by Ueda Akinari (1734–1809) as the source of this gripping story, which in the original concerns the devoted love of homosexuals, not brothers. *See* "The Story of Kōgi the Priest" later in this entry.

"Of a Promise Broken": A sweet, childless wife lies dying, and fears her samurai husband will remarry, but when he solemnly vows he will not, she asks to be buried in their garden with a Buddhist bell in her coffin. She would otherwise have wished to be interred elsewhere, so as not to be near a second wife. All is done as promised. But within a year the widower is persuaded by relatives to remarry and have children. Seven days after the wedding, he is ordered to the castle on duty. That night his wife is disturbed by the ringing of a bell. Dogs howl, and an eyeless, shrouded corpse glides in, announces that she is mistress of the house and the interloper must go, telling no one, or be torn to pieces. This warning is repeated the next night. When the husband returns, his wife says she must leave. He demands an honorable explanation, so she tells what has happened and also expresses her fear of imminent death. Because he has to report to the castle again that night, he posts two stalwart bodyguards. While they sit and play *go* (checkers), the wife sleeps well—until early morning, when a bell sound approaches her. She shrieks but cannot awaken her guards, who sit frozen and staring. When the husband returns he finds his wife's corpse, with its head torn off and held dripping outside in the garden in the claw-like hand of "a nightmare-thing that chippered like a bat." With one sword blow, a guard reduces "the long-buried woman" to rags, bones, and hair. Hearn complains to a friend that vengeance should have been directed against the man but is told that Japanese women do not feel that way. Hearn manages point-of-view shifts excellently in the last part of this gruesome tale.

"Before the Supreme Court," an eighth-century tale, begins with the observation that prayers to "unjust gods" oftentimes bring misfortune. In a district called Yamadagori, a girl named Kinumé gets sick. Her parents pray to the Pest-God for her recovery. The girl has an elaborate dream: To help, the Pest-God must kill some other girl also named Kinumé; a girl named Kinumé in the district of Utarigori is suggested; going there, the god plunges a knife in that girl's forehead. The Yamadagori girl wakes up after three days, tells her parents that they are not hers and their home is not her home, and rushes out. Meanwhile, the Utarigori girl dies, her body is cremated, and her spirit visits the Judge of Souls. He orders her to be returned to the world. But she explains that she has been cremated. The Judge says not to worry, that he will put her spirit into the Yamadagori girl's body. It is at the moment of that transformation that the Yamadagori girl tells her parents that theirs is not her home. She escapes to the house of the Utarigori girl's parents, calls them her parents, and while not recognized is humored as a lunatic. She explains what the Judge of Souls did for her. When the other parents, having followed her, arrive, all four parents quiz the girl and believe her. The Yamadagori girl's mother explains to the other mother and her husband that this girl's spirit is their child's spirit, whereas her body is the other parents' daughter's body. The four adults accept the girl as the daughter of all four. Later, she even inherits from both sets of parents. For some inexplicable reason, Hearn adds that the author of this story says it can be found on the left side of sheet 12, Volume 1, of a book he names.

"The Story of Kwashin Koji": In the sixteenth century Kwashin Koji, an old man in Kyōto, preaches Buddhist doctrine and exhibits a scary painting by Oguri So-tan, a famous fifteenth-century artist. It depicts torments of the damned in various hells. Oda Nobunaga, Kyōto's ruler, sees the picture, covets it, but refuses to pay Kwashin Koji the hundred pieces of gold that are demanded. Arakawa, one of the ruler's retainers, follows old Koji, kills him, and grabs the carefully wrapped picture. But when he unrolls it before Nobunaga, it is blank. Arakawa, after a prison term, hears that Koji is exhibiting his painting again, pursues him to a tavern, lets him drink 12 bowls of wine, and then takes him to the ruler's palace. To an officer there, Koji says that he is guiltless and that Arakawa stole the picture, showed the ruler a blank, and has the real one, whereas what Koji has recently shown is only a copy. The officer tortures Arakawa to get at the truth, but the man becomes unconscious. Saying he will reveal all, Koji explains that any really superb picture has a soul and won't tolerate being separated from its creator or even from a rightful owner. It vanished when displayed before the ruler but probably will reappear if he pays the requested gold. He shells out the hundred, and behold! the painting is there again, although with slightly faded colors. Koji explains that because its value exceeds a mere hundred pieces of gold, it now seems less lustrous. Arakawa is freed; but his brother, Buichi, determines to kill Koji for revenge. He finds the artist in a tavern, beheads him, wraps up both head and coins, and takes them to Arakawa. Unwrapped, his bundle is nothing but a wine gourd and "a lump of filth." Found drunk later, Koji is jailed and sleeps for 10 days and nights. The ruler is killed by a treacherous captain, who, when he hears about Koji, summons him and offers him all the wine he can drink. After 10 huge cups, Koji in gratitude displays a picture of his that depicts the lake of Ōmi. While everyone looks on in astonishment, Koji beckons to a boat and boatman in the pictured lake. They come closer; waters flood the captain's dining room, and Koji climbs into the vessel. As the waters recede from the room, he is rowed out of sight and is never seen again. This nicely unified story is one of Hearn's best creative redactions from Japanese sources.

"The Story of Umétsu Chūbei": A young samurai in Dewa province has considerable strength and courage. He is on guard duty at the castle of his lord during a pre-dawn watch when he sees a strange woman on the road. She approaches with a baby in her arms, and he fears she may be a goblin. But when she sweetly asks him to hold the infant while she goes away briefly, he agrees. The child begins to grow heavier, until it weighs fully six hundred pounds. Holding it with great difficulty, he repeats "Namu Amida Butsu," a holy invocation, three times. Not only does the weight decrease, but the child disappears. The woman returns, saying she is the parish divinity and was assisting at a difficult birth. Only when he spoke the invocation was the child born. As a reward, the samurai will have children of inordinate strength. And thus it happens, down to his descendants now residing in Dewa.

"The Story of Kōgi the Priest": Almost a millennium ago, Kōgi, a priest, lived in Ōmo. This is his story. Though painting everything well, he is best at depicting fish. Fishermen catch fish in a lake for him; he paints pictures of them, feeds them, and returns them to safety. One day, after dreaming he was playing underwater with some fish, he paints "Dream-Carp" from memory. He sells his pictures of birds, flowers, and landscapes, but never fish pictures, because all would-be buyers are fish-eaters. He falls ill and seems dead, but at his funeral service his disciples find his body to be warm. After three days he revives and tells an acolyte to request that guests of Taira no Suké leave their feast and come over to hear a wonderful story. They arrive. When Kōgi asks Suké if Bunshi the fisherman sold him a big fish this day, the answer is yes. Kōgi explains that he was never dead and that after his funeral he seemed to get up and go to the lake for a swim. When he expressed the wish that he could swim like a fish, a big fish popped up, told him to wait, and returned with a man ceremonially robed and riding on the fish. The man said that the Dragon-King, out of gratitude for Kōgi's kindness to fish, was going to change him into a Golden Carp so he could swim like the fish he loves. But he must not eat fish or get caught by fishermen. For three days he enjoyed swimming away, seeing sunlight on water, an island's coast, and the depths in bad weather. After three days he got so hungry that he ignored his promise and bit some fish bait off Bunshi's hook. He was hauled in despite verbose protests, which Bunshi seemed not to hear. Taken to Suké's house screaming, he was carved up—and awakened and was at his temple. Suké sends orders for the remains of the fish to be thrown into the lake. Kōgi lives for years and paints more fish. When some of his fish paintings fall into the lake, the fish detach themselves and swim away. In a footnote, Hearn identifies *Ugétsu Monogatori* (Tales of Moonlight and Rain, 1858) by Ueda Akinari (1734–1809) as the source of this story. *See* "Of a Promise Kept" earlier in this entry.

"Folk-Lore Gleanings" has three pieces. In "Dragon-Flies," Hearn is concerned with the poetry and folklore of the Japanese dragonfly. He expresses delight "[i]n the dazzling rapidity of its flight—invisible but as a needle-gleam of darting color." Such motion may symbolize the Japanese notion of life's "impermanency." Japan, once called the Island of the Dragon-Fly because of the shape of the island of Yamato, has more kinds of dragonflies than any other country. With loving care Hearn describes the color, wings, body, head, thorax, eyes, and legs of an exquisitely beautiful dragonfly he once briefly captured. Gleaning material from old books and drawings, he names and discusses 32 species; one example is "Yanagi-joro (the lady of the weeping-willow)." Ancient authorities divided dragonflies into four classes: black, green, red, or yellow. Most poems about dragonflies are *hokku* (17-syllable haiku). Rarely are they in *tanka* (31 syllables), and few are in *dodoitsu* (26), the latter form being largely reserved for love verse. Typically a dragonfly *hokku* is a picture intended to revive a sight or a feeling. Modern is the appeal of this one: "Only ten dragon-flies—all clinging to the same withered spray!" Menacing is this: "O the expression of that cock's eyes in the sunset-light—trying to catch a dragon-fly!"

Hearn finds modern dragonfly *hokku* less appealing than naively picturesque old ones, which reflect their writers' "patience and . . . freshness of curiosity [,] impossible to this busier generation." To suggest the range of these poets, Hearn presents more than 60 poems, mostly *hokku*, under the following rubrics: picturesque, sunshine, flight, love, strangeness and beauty, lightness, stupidity, spiders, and indifference to flowers. As for stupidity: "Ah! the poor dragon-fly, sporting beside the spider's web!" Admitting that Western poets outdo the Japanese in describing nature, Hearn nevertheless lauds Japanese writers of dragonfly *hokku* because "they could feel the beauty of the world without its sorrow, and rejoice in that beauty, much after the manner of inquisitive and happy children." He reports that during the Festival of the Bon (a kind of All Souls' Day) children are forbidden to molest dragonflies, but at other times they catch them, often ingeniously. One device is a bolo made of pebble-weighted hair, tossed as a lure. Although Hearn does not hint at *hokku* he preferred, it seems likely that this one must have had particular appeal: "Happy dragon-fly!—never self-consumed by longing—never even uttering a cry."

"Buddhist Names of Plants and Animals": Hearn wanted to prepare a glossary of Buddhist names given to animals and plants in Japan. But the task proved impossible, partly because different provincial folk speech appeared in such names. Still, he hopes his efforts here will help "future explorers in this unfamiliar region of Far-Eastern folk-lore." He shows how the name "Buddha" and names of Buddhist gods appear in the names of animals, birds, fish, insects, plants, and trees. For an example of arid prose in this essay: "There is a bird . . . called 'buppōsō,' because its cry resembles the sound of the word 'buppōsō.' This word is a Japanese equivalent for the Sanskrit term 'triratna' or 'ratnatraya' (three jewels);—the syllable 'bu' standing for Butsu (the Buddha); 'po,' for hō (the Law); and 'sō' for the priesthood. The bird is also called sambōchō (the sambō bird);—the word 'sambō' being a literal translation of triratna."

In "Songs of Japanese Children," the longest essay in the group titled "Folk-Lore Gleanings," Hearn laments the fact that because in Japanese public schools little children are taught new songs, the traditional songs their grandmothers used to teach them "will cease to be sung" soon. Folklorists are working hard, however, to preserve this wonderful oral literature. Out of generous selections copied and translated for him, Hearn presents examples of six types: weather and sky songs, songs about animals, play-songs, narratives, songs about battledore and ball games, and lullabies. He admits that the translations resemble dried flowers pressed in books compared to the originals, which are "living blossoms"—fresh, naive, queerly rhythmic, rhymeless. Nursery rhymes the world over are similar in subject matter; still, the unique aspects of Japan's "child-literature" are interesting. A hundred or so selections follow, in Japanese verse, with English translations and explanatory notes. One example from each category should suffice to indicate range and quality: "Snow is fluttering—chira-chira! / The clouds are full of ashes." "Hare, hare! what do you see that makes you jump?" "Clink! clink!—the child of the blacksmith." "From the swamp . . .

rose up a serpent, in the likeness of the . . . daughter of . . . Hachiman." "Hi ya!
/ Fu ya!" (strike one, strike two). And "Sleep, my child!—My love of this child
is incalculable as the number of the trees in the mountain-forest." Hearn says
that if you should stroll through a Japanese street, your impressions would be
vague and later you would remember little and understand less. Similarly, after
reading these poems you will be vaguely "surprised and pleased . . . without
knowing why." To you, the Japanese "race-soul [will remain] strangely alluring,
yet forever alien to your own."

"Studies Here and There" has six sketches. "On a Bridge": His Kumamoto
rickshaw man, Heishichi, takes Hearn to a bridge. The sunshine beautifies the
river and its surroundings. Heishichi reminisces. Twenty-three years ago he was
on the bridge during a civil war and watched Kumamoto burn. Three enemy
samurai, disguised as peasants, were there too and ordered him not to move.
Separately, three cavalry officers from Kumamoto galloped up, and the samurai
beheaded them. When Hearn asks whether Heishichi ever reported the incident,
he is rebuked by being told that doing so "would have been ungrateful."

"The Case of O-Dai": For their transmuting, transubstantiating potency, O-
Dai reverences the *ihai* (mortuary tablets) of two of her grandparents, both
parents, and a little brother. That is, until two missionary women bribe her by
money, room, and board to become a Christian. They persuade her to throw the
ihai into the river. Her friends, tolerant at first of her foolishness in seeking a
foreign religion, ostracize her after her sacrilegious act. The missionaries soon
abandon her and leave town. Even local pimps ignore her as tainted. She sells
herself into prostitution in faraway Ōsaka. Into this anti-Christian tale Hearn
inserts an explanation of the thinking of O-Dai's inimical neighbors, whose
religion is substantially based on reverence of the dead and respect for *ihai*. One
wonders whether remnants of Christianity in Hearn should not have caused him
to be critical of Japanese pimps and more sympathetic with O-Dai, of whom,
to be sure, he does admit that "an amiable weakness and a childish trustfulness
were the worst of her faults."

"Beside the Sea": Hearn attends a July service for drowned Yaidzu fishermen.
Beside a mortuary tablet at the shore are placed food, candles, incense, and
much else. Bamboo posts have banners naming guardian divinities. Under awn-
ings Hearn squats on matting and makes a sketch. Priests and acolytes come.
Accompanied by tolling bells, a sonorous hymn is chanted to help the spirits of
the "long dead" to achieve Buddhahood. Rites follow, involving sprinklings,
food offerings, recitations, invocations, and finally finger-snappings to disperse
ghosts. During the ceremony the tide turns and the sea surges and hisses toward
the worshippers. Hearn muses on the "dim relation of the dead and the sea."
Reluctantly, he believes that "the grosser substance of vanished being" is "scattered . . . flickering in the light of waters," perhaps to be "tossed on some desolate coast." After the ceremony, fishermen shower the crowd with rice cakes,
and all trappings are removed. Hearn, again alone on the shore, fears that the
temporarily comforted souls of the drowned are in pain again.

"Drifting": While sitting on a sea wall looking at the scary surf, Hearn hears the story of his friend Amano Jinsuké. When he was 19 years old in 1860, he was part of an eight-man crew sailing from Yaidzu for Sanuki. During a typhoon the ship sank and all but Jinsuké were drowned. He heard the doomed men shout "Kocchi é koi!" (Come this way!), to lure him to death too. He floated until dawn on a plank, grew hungry, and was disoriented. Night fell, and it rained. Again he heard "Kocchi é koi!" and saw four of his fellow sailors standing beside him. One upbraided him for sleeping on duty, but another unrolled a religious scroll and persuaded him to pray. He was bitten by a jellyfish, and the intense pain revived him. Daylight was clear, and he saw a mountain and paddled toward it, encouraged by seabirds thumping on his head. Toward sunset he spotted a passing junk, swam toward it, and was hauled on deck. He slept, was fed some boiled rice, and was told by his rescuers, who salvaged his plank, that he had drifted 60-odd miles in two days and nights. Generously tended, he was put ashore at Kuki and was taken home aboard a Yaidzu vessel. Alone among the crew saved, he goes annually to a Sanuki temple and more often to another in Yaidzu, to which he has gratefully offered his plank. Hearn opens this tale with a description of angry waters in a dozen lines of uncanny energy.

"Otokichi's Daruma": Hearn delights in the "grotesqueries" that snow creates when it decorates pine needles, evergreens, bamboos, and garden verdure in the lovely Japanese wintertime. Children make a *yuki-daruma*, a snowman with a big bottom sphere, a smaller upper sphere, and charcoal facial features. The name "Daruma" in Snow-Daruma comes from Bodai-Daruma, the Japanese rendering of the Sanskrit Bodhidharma, a Buddhist patriarch. He went to China in A.D. 520 as a Buddhist missionary and founded the Zen sect. Daruma meditated for nine years, and his legs fell off; hence, there are a number of legless pictures, toys, and snowmen of him. Hearn recalls Darumas he has seen. While Hearn was summering in a fishing village some years ago, his landlord, a man named Otokichi, showed him a one-eyed Daruma in his fish shop. It is said that Darumas do wonderful things to gain eyes. People who worship such gods are laudable because such simplicity is close to "pure goodness." At breakfast on his final morning at Otokichi's place, Hearn notices that the Daruma has two eyes. Hearn, blind in one eye, stoically avoids mention of his own affliction in this essay.

"In a Japanese Hospital": A boy with a broken arm is fibbed to, is told he is going to the theater, but winds up in a hospital. Scared and angry, he fights to avoid lying down, but he is subdued, and when anesthetized he becomes calm and even smiles. The fracture is expertly set. Hearn philosophizes. A fatal blow on the head can also render one silent and smiling. The "eternal consequences" of a passionate act can be a "sudden passionless beauty of the stricken." Ether has "the very touch of death," and the medicated body becomes a smiling "doll of plastic flesh," like a little stone Buddha. To "a God," this event—child crying, personality disappearing, utter calm—is like the sequence of a person's life. Gnats measure time in seconds; we, in years; but "the God of a system" might see with relative speed a boy's smile devolve into his skull's laugh. Still, that God could not understand that over the eons human sentience has emerged from "primordial slime" and will dissolve timelessly into the infinite One.

In *A Japanese Miscellany* Hearn continues his effort, manifest in its immediate predecessor, *Shadowings*, to explain Japan's distinct culture to Western readers. Best in doing so, perhaps, are his "Dragon-Flies," "Songs of Japanese Children," and "Of a Promise Broken." Notable are the implicit autobiographical revelations in some pieces. *A Japanese Miscellany* was reprinted several times and was issued in England (1901, 1905).

Bibliography: Hirakawa; Kunst; Murray; Edward Putzar, *Japanese Literature* (Tucson: University of Arizona Press, 1973).

"A JOURNALISTIC OUTLOOK" (1881). Editorial. A recent development in American newspapers is the humorous sketch. It is "sharp, strong, vivid, . . . satanic." Without realizing it, young journalists improved on reports of minor events with humorous touches, thus creating something unique. Their doing so may help create a taste in the reading public for better literature in our dailies.

K

"KARMA" (1890). Short story. The narrator proposes marriage to a lovely, cool girl. She tells him first to write down everything she would not like to know about him. Thoughts of his task veer from rationalizing to confidence to fear to gratitude to bewilderment. Her order implies acceptance of his imperfections. Remembrance proves difficult. He writes a draft he quickly realizes he cannot show her. He tries another, with "stony hardness," lies down, but cannot sleep. If he can forgive past deeds, should she not? Suddenly he remembers one "unmistakable wickedness" long blotted from memory. Telling it would mean losing the girl. However, could she not complement his darkness, fire, and weakness with her light, snow, and strength? Surely that "black falsehood in his life" would doom him. Should he write it, and die? Or write nothing, and leave her? She suddenly appears "like luminous ivory," dressing to marry him. Others are around her. He confesses every blemish in his past. She listens, smiles, looks angelic. The audience commends him. When he reveals his "last avowal," all turns dark and empty, and his dream ends. For days and nights he writes honestly, fears she may have given up on him, mails the manuscript to her, then wishes he had not. Two days later she writes him one word: "Come." He arrives, is asked if he wants her to burn his letter, says "Yes." Upon doing so, she asks if the woman has died. Yes, five years ago. And the child? Alive. And the friend he wronged? Alive and in the same place. She withers him with scorn. He feels incomparable shame. She tells him he has committed "transcendent sin," not to be called "a painful error." No pardon is possible, only atonement and God's demand for expiation. Losing her is only partial punishment. She orders him to go to the friend he betrayed, confess all, and care for the child regardless of cost. Better if the friend kills him than for her to know he was a coward as well as a criminal. He blanches, recovers, promises. A year passes. He assumes care of his son, lives far away, returns to his angelic beloved's region, writes to her requesting to show her his son. She permits it, kisses the lad, murmurs to the spirit of his mother to rest in peace knowing that only excess of love caused her to sin, and tells her would-be lover to be strong and enlightened through suffering. She will shield him and love his child. They kiss for the first time. She becomes his dream angel again.

This story has autobiographical implications. The "shy dark orbs" of the boy nominate as his mother Rosa Antonia Cassimati Hearn,* Hearn's mother. The sympathetically portrayed, if goofy, narrator of "Karma," however, can hardly be taken for Hearn's philandering father, Charles Bush Hearn.* Or did Hearn fantasize a reunion among himself, his father, and that man's second wife, Alicia Goslin Hearn? Anyway, why does the "angel" figure forgive the wayward mother so sweetly after having put the anguished narrator through such torture? Alicia never tortured Charles; she only went after him. When Hearn submitted "Karma" to his editor friend Elizabeth Bisland,* she was critical of it. George Milbry Gould,* Hearn's physician friend, contended that he gave Hearn the encouragement necessary for him to write "Karma."

Bibliography: Bisland; Cott; Gould; Kunst; Lafcadio Hearn, *Karma*, ed. Albert Mordell (New York: Boni and Liveright, 1918); Murray; Tinker.

"A KENTUCKY COLONEL RENTING ROOMS" (1879). Sketch. Lacking "fait' in peoples military," the Creole landlady demands rent in advance on learning that "monsieur" is a colonel.

"KILLED AND CREMATED" (1874). Cincinnati news article. This is the second of eight articles about the murder of Herman Schilling on Saturday, November 7, 1874, by Andreas Egner, his son Frederick K. Egner, and their friend George Rufer, in revenge for Schilling's having allegedly seduced Andreas Egner's daughter Julia, age about 15, who died while pregnant. The other articles, in chronological order, are "Violent Cremation," "It Is Out!," "The Tannery Horror," "The Furnace Fiends [1]," "The Furnace Fiends [2]," "The Quarter Shambles," and "The Furnace Horror." Monday, November 9: While jailed as suspects, Andreas is excited, Fred cries, and Rufer is nonchalant. When a gory broom is mentioned, however, Rufer gets scared and, interviewed by Hearn, says Andreas and Fred are trying to cast suspicion solely on him. At the coroner's inquest, Freiberg, Rufer's employer, praises Schilling, says Schilling was afraid of Rufer and also Andreas (whom he calls Andrew), admits he slept with Julia but says other men did also, and persuaded Freiberg to discharge Rufer. A neighbor named Hollenbach testifies about hearing the fight, seeking assistance vainly, being afraid, and examining the tannery the next morning with others. Testimony is taken about fresh scratches on Rufer's face. Suddenly Fred confesses he killed Schilling.

"THE KING'S JUSTICE" (1884). Short story. A Persian king orders the execution of a prisoner of war. Sad to be losing life and its joys, he curses the king

in a foreign tongue. The king has his first vizier translate. He lies that the man quoted the Holy Book about pardoning injury. So the king pardons the prisoner, whereupon an ambitious vizier translates accurately. The king, comforted by the first message although it was dishonest, lets the pardon stand and banishes the truthful but malevolent second vizier.

"A KISS FANTASTICAL" (1881). Sketch. "[L]iving apparitions" of lovely women entice men to wish to touch, kiss, even bite them. To an assembly of men, a traveler mentions such a vision in a bath house in Yokohama, Japan. In response to a Spanish guitarist's dance melody, a lovely female vision glides in, accompanied by an ugly Mexican hag with a passionate mouth, white teeth, and a neat foot and ankle. She dances like a hummingbird. At farewell time, she kisses the traveler. What a kiss!—warm as lava, biting, sucking, then cool and supple, creating volcanic fire in its recipient. Six months later the traveler returns from a trip to Honduras, queries his host, and is told that the unforgettable woman married the guitar player and is gone. The reference to Japan is an early one, almost a decade before Hearn's departure for that country.

KOIZUMI, IWAO (1896–?). Hearn's second child and second son, born in Tokyo. Always favoring Kazuo Koizumi,* his oldest son, Hearn paid less attention to Iwao's upbringing, as well as that of his third son, Kiyoshi Koizumi.* When Nina H. Kennard, accompanied by Hearn's half-sister, Minnie Charlotte Hearn Atkinson,* visited the family of Hearn, then deceased, in Japan in 1909, she said "Iwayo," whom she incorrectly called Hearn's third son, was visiting ships in the harbor. As Iwao Inagaki, he edited Lafcadio Hearn, *Lectures on Shakespeare* (Tokyo: Hokuseido Press, 1928); these lectures Hearn had delivered at the Imperial University in Tokyo in 1899.

Bibliography: Cott; Kennard.

KOIZUMI, KAZUO (1893–?). (Full name: Leopold Kazuo ["The First of the Excellent"] Koizumi.) Hearn's oldest child and oldest son, born in Kumamoto, Japan. As a foreigner, Hearn faced difficulties in registering Kazuo as a Japanese citizen. He solved the problem by becoming a Japanese citizen himself, thereby also protecting his Japanese family's right to inherit his property. He taught Kazuo, always his favorite child, the English alphabet, grammar, and conversation, and also arithmetic, geography, gymnastics, and swimming. He took Kazuo, and later his other children as well, on summer vacations to Yaizu on Suruga Bay by rail from Tokyo. Hearn died when Kazuo was not quite 11 years old. So Kazuo's memories of his father were not those of an adult. Nevertheless he wrote *Father and I*, a charming book of recollections about Hearn. In the introduction, Kazuo apologizes for his own limited writing skills; praises his father for loving Japan and its varied literature; and says that Hearn avoided discussing bad personal memories, believed in severe punishment for wrong-doing, loved small things in nature, praised moral samurai over Lord Horatio Nelson, admired the courage of decent widows, detested hypocrisy and wick-edness and cowardice, maintained a demeanor of outward serenity, valued ed-ucation more than money, and deplored interracial marriages despite that of his parents and his own. The book that follows is a five-chapter reminiscence. In 1909 Nina H. Kennard went with Hearn's half-sister, Minnie Charlotte Hearn Atkinson,* to Japan to meet Kazuo in the unavailing hope to implement Hearn's wish to have him educated abroad and enter a profession as an Occidental. When both Hearn and his friend Basil Hall Chamberlain* were dead, Kazuo Koizumi edited Chamberlain's letters to Hearn. Notes posted on the Internet (October 19, 1997; April 3, 1999) report that the home and gardens designed and built by Kazuo Koizumi in Tokyo in 1955 were to be destroyed and the leveled land converted into a car lot; then that they had been demolished.

Bibliography: Cott; Kennard; Kazuo Koizumi, *Father and I: Memories of Lafcadio Hearn* (Boston and New York: Houghton Mifflin, 1935); Koizumi, ed., *Letters from Basil Hall Chamberlain to Lafcadio Hearn* (Tokyo: Hokuseido Press, 1936) and *More Letters from Basil Hall Chamberlain to Lafcadio Hearn* (Tokyo: Hokuseido Press, 1937); Murray.

KOIZUMI, KIYOSHI (1899–). Hearn's third son, born in Tokyo. Hearn pinned his hopes on Kazuo Koizumi,* his oldest son, and seems to have ne-glected not only Kiyoshi but also his second son, Iwao Koizumi.* When Nina H. Kennard, with Minnie Charlotte Hearn Atkinson,* Hearn's half-sister, visited Japan in 1909, they saw Kiyoshi, whom Kennard called "Idaho" and who she incorrectly said was Hearn's second son.

Bibliography: Kennard; Stevenson.

KOIZUMI, SETSU (1869–?). Hearn's Japanese wife. "Setsu" means "The True." She was the granddaughter of a retainer-class samurai, whose principles and manners survived the 1867 social revolution ushering in the Meiji era, but whose more tangible fortunes, and those of Setsu's father as well, did not. Nishida Sentarō, a teacher at the secondary school in Matsu where Hearn taught, thought that Hearn, his admired colleague, was lonely and susceptible to illness. Deciding that a wife would be the solution, Nishida approached Setsu's father, who was accommodating and whose daughter had been trained to be agreeably obedient; accordingly, Hearn met Setsu. In a matter of weeks, perhaps days, the two were married, probably in January 1891. Details of place and date are uncertain. Setsu brought order and comfort to the Spartan regimen that had marked Hearn's first nine or so months in Japan. She combined decency, com-mon sense, delicacy, refinement, and—when needed—firmness of will. She worried about his health, was perplexed by his eccentricities, and took over the management of his initially chaotic handling of his—their—limited income. He knew very little Japanese and taught her a little English. They developed a secret lingo all their own. She called him "Papa-san"; he addressed her as "Mam(m)a-sama." She regaled him with Japanese folktales and ghost stories. They had four children—Kazuo Koizumi,* Iwao Koizumi,* Kiyoshi Koizumi,* and Suzuko Koizumi*—so they loved each other tenderly but more important for Hearn, they became devoted, caring friends as well. Hearn wrote to his friend Ellwood Hendrick* (November 17, 1892) suggesting that his marriage was "a haven," in which he was protected from the dangerous "sea currents" of his old "hunger for the eternal feminine." He accepted the legal requirement that he be responsible for Setsu's immediate family members. In 1896 he became a Japanese citizen and assumed the Japanese name Yakumo Koizumi, partly to ensure that Setsu and their children would inherit his worldly goods and royalties. But now and then he chafed and sought opportunities to get away, far away, to the United States for a time. In 1918 Setsu published her reminiscences of life with Hearn. Nina H. Kennard, who met Setsu in 1909, described her as restrained, with a sad face, and generally having an English housekeeper's mien. Yone Noguchi, however, called her beautiful and sweet of heart; Basil Hall Chamberlain* said she was both noble and remarkable.

Bibliography: Dawson; Yoji Hasegawa, *Lafcadio Hearn's Japanese Wife: Her Memoirs and Her Early Life* (Tokyo: Microprinting, 1988); Kennard; Setsu Koizumi, trans. Paul Kiyoshi Hisada and Frederick Johnson, *Reminiscences of Lafcadio Hearn* (Boston and New York: Houghton Mifflin, 1918); Murray; Yone Noguchi, *Lafcadio Hearn in Japan* (London: Kelly and Walsh, 1910); Stevenson.

KOIZUMI, SUZUKO (1903–?). Hearn's youngest child and only daughter, born in Tokyo. He loved her dearly, worried about her future because of his precarious health, and died when she was only a year old. When Nina H. Kennard and Hearn's half-sister, Minnie Charlotte Hearn Atkinson,* visited Hearn's family in Tokyo in 1909, they saw Suzuko, whom Kennard calls "Setsu-ko."

Bibliography: Kennard; Stevenson.

KOKORO: HINTS AND ECHOES OF JAPANESE INNER LIFE (1896). Collection of 15 essays, four of which had been previously published. Hearn dedicated *Kokoro* to his friend Amenomori Nobushige, whom he calls a "poet, scholar, and patriot." He and Hearn corresponded voluminously, mostly about Buddhism. Hearn explains that *kokoro* means "heart," a word signifying mind but also connoting spirit, affection, and even inner meaning, as in the phrase "the heart of things."

"At a Railway Station": Nomura Teïchi robs a house in Kumamoto, is arrested by a policeman, but kills him and escapes. When discovered under a false name in a Fukuoka prison four years later, he is returned to Kumamoto. At the railway station he is forced to look at the tiny son of the policeman he murdered. The boy stares at him and weeps. The killer falls to his knees and asks for forgiveness. The crowd at the station also weeps. Hearn opines that the killer was moved to remorse by the typically Japanese love of children.

"The Genius of Japanese Civilization" (1895): Japan, recently extending its military and political influence in the East, is trying to remain unchanged emotionally. Compared to things Western, things Japanese are small, dainty, delicate: Gothic cathedrals, Wagnerean opera, epic poetry in the West; in Japan, temples, geisha dances, short poems. Japan lacks outward signs of change; cities remain frail and quiet. Western cities have huge buildings, high-rent apartments, elevators, and mazes of electric wires. We build for "endurance"; the Japanese, for "impermanency." A Japanese house, built of bamboo, mud, wattle, plaster, and mats, rises in five days. Some Japanese temples and fortresses are exceptions to the Japanese ideal of change. Earthquakes make the land, rivers, and even mountains shift into "new forms." The gods remain, and only family shrines and burial places are "permanent." Although Buddhist temples give evidence of "material stability," Buddhism teaches "the doctrine of impermanency"—all is an illusory, fluid, fleeting, "despicable" dream proceeding toward "the eternal Vanishing." Western civilization's vibrations are the result of artificially applied forces; Japanese tremblings, by small and natural forces. We think of ourselves as great travelers; but the simple Japanese inexpensively clothes, feeds, and readies himself for vast travel by foot. Western shoes, which cramp both foot and mind, are abominable compared to healthy Japanese throw-away straw sandals. Clean, sweet-smelling itinerant Japanese are not to be compared to our beggars and tramps. Japanese productions, notably rice, tea, porcelain, and silk, are simply managed but immense and profitable. Huge amounts of "industrial capital," unlike in the West, are not needed in Japan. Its national simplicity is also evidenced in its governmental institutions. Politicians, civil servants, military leaders, and educators, loyal only to the emperor, are relocated in nothing less than a "whirl." Stability in such a system is explained by the fact that Shintō demands faithful unselfishness, and Buddhism teaches that all loved things vanish. Hearn concludes ominously: New Japan is selfishly hardening and may be cursed by "officialism" and "aggressive egotism." Still, he regards as safest not only "the old Japanese" preference for "moral beauty" over "intellectual beauty," but also their trust in education toward an unselfish absence of individualism.

"A Street Singer": An ugly woman comes to Hearn's house, tunes her instrument, and sings a ballad having incredible emotional appeal. Blind from disfiguring smallpox, she supports a paralyzed husband and their child. The singing brings tears to the eyes of neighbors, who have come to listen. Reading the words of the commonplace ballad, which is about the suicide of unhappy teenage lovers, Hearn concludes that the singer's "primitive natural utterance of feeling" appeals "to something wide as human life, and ancient as the knowledge of good and evil." He recalls the simple "Good-night" he overheard a girl utter in London decades ago. Her voice, full of "incomprehensible . . . pleasure and pain," has appealed not only to him personally but also to his inherited racial memories. This is one of Hearn's most poignant short pieces.

"From a Travelling Diary" (1895): Hearn records diverse observations from April 15 to 23, 1895. Seeing Japanese women shield their faces when napping on the Ōsaka–Kyōto train reminds him that he saw his habitually smiling servant looking pained and angry when supposedly alone. Shadows in his Kyōto hotel room make him theorize that all art is inspired by studies of shadow forms. Approaches to "high places of worship or of rest" are uniquely beautiful. One such approach led him to a Buddhist cemetery. Ah, what message? A national exhibition at Kyōto features Japan's new industrial products, with attractive artistic enhancements. A London correspondent remarks that Japan, with its low-paid employees, will destroy competition. The quality of art exhibits, inferior to those of the 1890 Tōkyō Exhibition, suggests the turn to industry in the Japanese economy. A friend expresses fear that the Chinese, if they adopt Japanese methods, will undercut them; Hearn's rebuttal is that quality items, such as those that the French sell, are more in demand than cheap items are. He inveighs against Japanese oil paintings, especially one of a female nude. The human figure is not attractive until idealized, in the mode of ancient Greek sculptors. Two new religious buildings in Kyōto strike his attention. The government gave the people the Dai-Kioku-Dan, a Shintō temple modeled on a palace and commemorating the revered city founder. Finer is the Hogashi Hongwanji, an enormous building financed by the people, costing $8 million and taking 17 years to build. For its inauguration 100,000 peasants sat in the sun, with nurses and physicians standing by to minister to those falling ill. At a lavish garden, aquarium, and zoo a lad asks his father if the place is the world's most beautiful. Hearn silently replies: The paradise-like Garden of Amida is better yet, but something still higher—eternal peace—is best of all.

"The Nun of the Temple of Amida": O-Toyo, married and with a small son, is sad when her husband is ordered to go to the capital. Living with her parents, she prepares tiny trays of food for her absent husband, joyfully teaches her son to pray, tells him tender stories, and takes him on a pilgrimage to a mountain peak, where there is a shrine to a princess whose lover's death caused her to die also. Suddenly, within three days, her husband and her son die. Mourning dreadfully, O-Toyo arranges for a priest to call her son's spirit back briefly. The son tells her that they died of a disease meant for her and that he must return to the underworld at once. Her parents try to advise her, but O-Toyo, reverting to childishness, begins to long for tiny objects. She happily agrees to become a nun and live in a little temple with miniature furnishings. When her parents die, people call her the nun of the temple of Amida and children play courteously with her. She lives long enough to play with the great-grandchildren of her first friends. When she dies, the narrator helps finance a tiny *haka* (tombstone) for her, and children say they will continue to play in her temple court, where she will hear their voices.

"After the War" (1895): In Hyōgo, in May 1895, Hearn sees innumerable paper fish on bamboo poles, normally signifying a son's birth in the home beneath but now celebrating Japan's victory in the Sino-Japanese War (1894–1895). The moment war was declared, toy-makers created objects of a bellicose nature, historians wrote, plays were staged, songs were composed, and artifacts and clothes were produced—all to encourage patriotic and militaristic emotions. When Russia, France, and Germany tried to bully Japan, it "played jiujutsu, and foiled expectations by unlooked-for yielding." Although it had a weak navy, Japan felt strong, with its thousands of schools doubling as army "drilling-machine[s]." Russia was "checked" by a pro-Japanese British pronouncement. The Japanese government restrained the people's desire to battle Russia, France, and Germany anyway, proceeded with "faultless wisdom"—by giving China some peninsular land and more indemnities—and thus secured peace. But the Japanese people continue to hate Russia. The 4,000-ton ironclad *Matsushima Kan*, back from China and in the Hyōgo harbor, is swarmed over by visitors. With special permission, Hearn goes aboard and enjoys a graphic guided tour. In Kobé in June, he sees victorious regiments returning but remembers fresh young soldiers marching off the previous year in their white summer uniforms, recalls the "plaintive" bugle calls, and feels again the fear he had then for casualties yet to come. The town now fêtes the returning veterans, no longer young and fresh in appearance, but instead tough, in frayed winter garb, un-smiling. Their "quick-searching eyes . . . had seen . . . the things which make men serious." When Hearn laments the dead, a friend replies that they are present with the crowd and will hear bugles summoning more Japanese soldiers in the coming war with Russia.

"Haru": Raised mostly at home, Haru becomes simple at heart, naturally graceful, obedient, and dutiful and thus an ideal of Old Japan, not the new. At the mercy of her husband—often a good situation in Japan, under the right circumstances—she is better than her husband, who really never understands her. This "beautiful silver moth" ministers to his every need, at home and outside. As he prospers in business he loves her less, though not because they are childless. Suddenly, after five years, he turns cold, but not brutal in act or word, merely neglectful and indifferent. A geisha has snared him in a sensual web. He habitually stays out late, finally overnight. Haru, gossiped to by their servants and now feverish and ill with jealousy, must speak. When her husband returns, she says "Anata?" (Thou?) to him and falls, smiling in death. Military physicians query him sharply and explain the cause of death. He now sits among his shipments, perhaps visited by her "slender shadow" and hearing her last word.

"A Glimpse of Tendencies": Japan gave concessions to rude foreign merchants, whose ugly factories sprang up like mushrooms. Then foreign companies, lodged in Japan, began competing against each other. Learning their aggressive methods, the Japanese soon began to take over foreign shops and firms. Foreign-born employees had to rely on Japanese workers, butchers, cooks, photographers, tobacconists, vintners, and doctors. Foreign-owned businesses will soon disappear. "[M]utual dislike," expressed in newspapers, grew. Japa-

nese politicians gained support from an "anti-foreign league." Foreign-run papers dangerously supported China in the Sino-Japanese War. Racial animosities,
with some amiable exceptions, remained insurmountable. Foreign customers
were overcharged or ignored. Even as the Japanese grew more and more ex-
asperated that foreign agents, financed by foreign investors, controlled import-
export trade, native merchants, engineers, lawyers, and the like were learning
European and American methods and strengthened home-grown businesses.
Boycotts ensured foreign compliance. This "evolution in Japan" is socially and
commercially significant, and more foreign settlers may be expected. But, just
as foreign objects in living bodies must be "eliminated naturally or removed
artificially," so must these intruding foreigners. Although it is hard to do so,
Hearn ventures some predictions: Japan will soon grow "superior" because of
military and gymnastic training, more meat-rich diets, and delays in marriage
and therefore healthier children. Brutal crimes will increase in number; and
moral standards will fall, including those relating to sexual activities—though
more for men than for women. Education will improve, even as science and
mathematics in the West will remain pre-eminent. It is foolish for Japanese
academic authorities to impose difficult requirements, especially with respect to
an almost universal study of English. Even so, although English has actually
harmed Japanese morality, it has enriched the Japanese language through considerable assimilation. Japan volunteered decades ago to learn from the Chinese
and was therefore grateful to China. Not so with Western "wisdom" thrust upon
it. Christian missionaries have given Japan nothing of beauty. Once again, Hearn
reveals in "A Glimpse of Tendencies" his pro-Japanese and anti-American and
anti-European biases.

"By Force of Karma": Buddhism says that at times we may "recollect our
former lives." Modern science, though denying this, does suggest that when a
tumescent young man happens to see a girl, he is certainly aroused because of
traits inherited from the dead and perhaps aroused because the girl has subsumed
"the multitudinous charm of all the women" his ancestors vainly loved. Today's
desires echo those of past centuries. A Buddhist priest whose temple was near
Ōsaka was so handsome that girls were drawn to him, worshipped him, and
begged to be loved. He resisted properly, but then came a letter from a lowly
girl expressing her hopeless love for him and asking for pity. The priest wrote
to his superior, went to the railroad station, knelt in the tracks, and was killed
by the Kōbé express. When appealed to, a Buddhist scholar tells Hearn that
suicide to escape sin is unacceptable. He offers a story. A woman asked a priest
to let her become a nun. He refused, saying that she was too beautiful to resist
life's temptations. So she burned her face with red-hot tongs. She was accepted
into the order because disfiguring oneself, though sinful, was nothing like suicide. Queried further, Hearn's holy friend says that if the priest killed himself
only to avoid sin, he would have to face identical temptations in his next life.
Pondering all this, Hearn wonders whether a death caused by love may be a
punishment for forgotten sins.

"A Conservative": A samurai's unnamed son is reared severely despite the samurai culture being outmoded. He is taken to public executions and is taught archery, fencing, wrestling, swimming, rowing, and riding. Lightly dressed, he studies Chinese classics in a cold, unheated room. The young samurai grows up pure, simple, dutiful, and fearless. American ships come, so threatening to Old Japan that he and others vainly pray for "Kami-kazé—the Wind of the Gods" to destroy the intruders. The Western invasion begins, with factories and even compulsory English Occidental-science courses. Most Japanese people are dismayed, and elderly samurai are furious. Westerners strike the natives as bright and fearful but also grotesque, animal-like, and with the "moral ideas . . . of goblins." A British teacher is hired by the young samurai's prince. The unattractive fellow's pupils behave courteously, scrutinize him with "superstitious fear," and criticize him in their own language. The samurai accepts social and political changes without foolish regret, cuts his hair, puts his sword away, works in Yokohama with rude English-speaking merchants, and observes their few good and and many bad features. In a friendly old missionary's library he reads the New Testament and sees resemblances between Christ's and Confucius's teachings. The civilization of the so-called Christian races seems overwhelming. Does their material and military success signify divine approval? Despite opposition, the samurai resolves to become a Christian; however, his Buddhist "religious emotions" can never be converted. After years of study the samurai, wiser than his Christian mentors, renounces their creed. Still, seeing the value of comparing religions, he begins to wander, at last stoically spending years in Europe and America, inevitably with incomplete comprehension. Great cities seem grimly mountainous. In Paris, art, especially nude paintings, surprises but does not charm him, and French writers seem worthless. Pleasure places strike him as foolish and effeminate. The abyss between rich and poor makes a mockery of Christianity. In England, ports display goods plundered from abroad, church leaders are blind and ignorant, and poverty, crime, and harlotry abound. To be sure, the British are courteous and friendly. America, though racially more diverse, is otherwise hardly different from Europe—mechanical, greedy, cruel, hypocritical, immoral, degraded, "all one great wolfish struggle." Old Japan was better in every regard. "Western science" is going to inundate the world in pain. Japan must adapt or perish. One cloudless April dawn, the sumarai, sailing home again, sees Mount Fuji "pinkening like a wondrous phantom lotus-bud." The captain tells puzzled foreign passengers that to see Fuji, its base mist-shrouded, they must look "higher up—much higher!" Yes. The returning native sees not Fuji now, but Old Japan and everything he thought he had abandoned. "A Conservative" contains Hearn's most vicious denunciation of virtually all things Western, including much he once professed to love.

"In the Twilight of the Gods" (1895): A cocky curio dealer invites Hearn to visit his warehouse of old statues, Buddhist and otherwise, and Chinese, Indian, and Korean as well as Japanese in origin. Some are of gods, humans, and animals; others are symbolic. The dealer says the collection cost him $50,000.

Hearn reckons the cost in terms of pilgrimages, prayers, and other acts of devotion—all spoiled by this mercenary dealer. He points out a particular statue, that of a figure seated on a golden lotus, identified (by Hearn) as a Kwannon, specifically of "Emmei-Jizō, . . . the giver of long life," and says with a chuckle that it cost him an unusual sum and its original owner a prison term for illegally selling it. The dealer plans to put on "a show of josses" in England of a sort well advertised by churches there. You know, "Heathen idols from Japan!" He will then sell everything to the British Museum. The two men discuss lively wooden statuettes, infant Buddhas, huge Devas, and the like, and the value of the bronze, gold, and silver in some. While the dealer thinks of his sale, Hearn wonders what will happen to the pieces. Will they be "immured" in foggy London with "forgotten divinities of Egypt or Babylon"? Will they inspire painters, illustrators, poets? Perhaps, but also "[t]he soft serenity, the passionless tenderness, of these Buddha faces might yet give peace of soul to a West weary of creeds transformed into conventions, eager for the coming of another teacher to proclaim" measureless, universal sympathy. The irony, though heavy here, is effective when Hearn, the Westerner, can identify various art objects by their Japanese names and can also describe their significance in Eastern culture, whereas the Japanese dealer is concerned only with their marketability.

"The Idea of Preëxistence": The "fundamental idea" of preëxistence, differentiating Oriental and Occidental thought, permeates all aspects of East Asian actions, emotions, language, and thought. Long-time foreign residents are influenced by it. Herbert Spencer (1820–1903), "the greatest of all [psychological] explorers," helps us understand that our so-called instincts, intuitions, first impressions, and quick passions are all "super-individual" and result from millions of years of "psychological inheritance." "[T]he idea of Soul as an infinite multiple" is contrary to the Christian notion of individual souls. But acceptance of the theory of evolution has caused changes in theology and harmonizes with ancient Eastern beliefs. Fear not. Religious feelings are deeper than dogmas. Meanwhile, increasing familiarity with "Sanscrit, Chinese, and Pali scholarship" will make Western thinkers modify their intellectual positions. The selfish fiction of the Ego will yield to an acknowledgment of "the composite nature of Self." Hearn concludes with a lengthy footnote not only on denotations and connotation of the words "ego," "heredity," "self," "soul," and "transmigration" but also on Nirvana, sensations, the mind as substance, and phenomena emerging from "immaterial Unity." Once again, Hearn displays here his preference for Buddhistic thought, his veneration of Spencer, and his contempt for Christianity.

"In Cholera-Time": After the Sino-Japanese War, cholera followed the victorious veterans home to Japan. Some 30,000 have died and are being cremated. Hearn writes about the costs of "burning" an adult and a child. Mentioning the death of a lad, he digresses about the mystery of stones, some of which the boy played with. Now he is playing with dry, shadowless stones in the River of Souls. A pipemender comes by, carrying his little boy with the shadow of his dead mother's *ihai* (mortuary tablet) falling on him, in accordance with her dying request. The pipemender says the boy is healthy because his dead mother's milk still nourishes him. Hearn offers a startling metaphor to suggest the "warm, sympathetic" wrinkles around the pipemender's mouth. They are "dry beds of old smiles."

"Some Thoughts about Ancestor-Worship": Critics too hastily condemn the Japanese for worshipping their ancestors, because some civilized Europeans do the same. Shintō doctrines are in some ways more reconcilable with modern scientific discoveries than are orthodox Christian doctrines, especially those regarding heredity and justice. According to Kami, the human spirit is empowered by death, becomes "above," "upper," akin to Western notions of ghosts although less democratic. Shintōists believe that the dead, although distinguished from highly creative "primal deities," live here, rule, and influence nature, humans, and their fortunes. Related to much of this are tenets of modern psychological evolution. Thus, figuratively, "every mind is a world of ghosts," influenced by devils and angels. Shintō respects both good and evil Kami, the latter naturally requiring propitiation. In the East the past is gratefully loved, the dead revered, and cruel people sacrificed for because of their ancestors. We Westerners would be improved if we similarly exalted our dead. We are born into an enigmatic world, must use "bequeathed knowledge" to get along, should preserve antique elements of society, should foster a "cosmic emotion of humanity," and should recognize our "duty to the past." A man is attracted to a woman not because of herself but because she has inherited feelings and intuitions from "millions of buried hearts." Further, the maternal instinct, far from being personal in each new mother, comes to her from "myriads of millions of dead mothers." True, too, is the fact that jails are filled with persons who have "inherited evil." The dead live on inside us all. Yet we began not with them nor in the sun, but somewhere more remote still; "we are one with that unknown Ultimate."

"Kimiko": On a street of geisha houses is Kimika's establishment. She trained two geishas and named both Kimiko. When a geisha is celebrated, her successor may be given the same name. If you have reason to enter her house, Kimika will regale you with many stories. One such is about two Kimikos. The first Kimiko is exceptionally beautiful and also clever, accomplished, creative, genteel. Her debut startles "the fast world of Kyōto." She is so well trained that she is dangerous, though never malicious. She rebuffs swooning men sweetly, is briefly generous enough to one man to gain freedom for herself and wealth for Kimika, but continues as a geisha. Making no permanent contracts, she is naughtily gracious with many, receives lavish gifts, and gains money for Kimika's firm by letting her photograph be used on product labels. Then, one day, Kimiko leaves Kimika for love of a loving fool. The second Kimiko, originally called Ai, is nicely educated in a samurai family until social changes reduce it to poverty. Ai goes to Kimika and becomes a geisha on the condition that Kimika will support her widowed mother and tiny sister. Ai, now called Kimiko, does well, gains "wicked knowledge of men," and hence is able to marry her sister off, happily, to a good, plain merchant. Wealthy parents indulge their love-touched son, who wants to marry Kimiko. She lives in the family's gardened palace for four months, is prepared for marriage, but suddenly tells her lover that she has lived in hell, been scorched by its fires, is unworthy to be his wife, and will merely comfort him for a time—until a wife, suitable to bear his son, is found. Two months later she vanishes. Diligent searches fail to find her. Years pass. Her former lover marries well and has a son. One day a mendicant nun stops at their palace and asks for alms, and a servant allows the little boy to give her some rice. The nun asks him to tell his father that the heart of one whom he will never see again in this world has been gladdened by seeing his son. When given the message, the father secretly "knew who had been at the gate" and is aware that she will move through death's darkness to the light-surrounded Teacher, who commends her for accepting "the highest truth" and who welcomes her.

Kokoro, Hearn's third Japanese book, was written in Kobe. In a letter to his close friend Nishida Sentarō (January 1895), he called *Kokoro* "a terribly 'radical' book—at variance with all English conventions and beliefs." In a letter to Page M. Baker* (January 1896) he called it "rather a crazy book." By 1902 he wrote to other friends that Japan was changing so fast that parts of *Kokoro* were already out of date. The work, however, has been received as containing in-depth treatments of the customs and folklore of ordinary natives, too often formerly rendered prosaically rather than poetically. "The Genius of Japanese Civilization" is the most significant essay in the book. Hearn's devotion to Spencer led him astray and into wrongly predicting that the Japanese mind could not quickly match the accomplishments of the West in science. The book was issued in London (1896) and enjoyed later editions.

Bibliography: Bisland; Kennard; Kunst; Murray.

KOTTŌ: BEING JAPANESE CURIOS, WITH SUNDRY COBWEBS (1902).
A collection of 20 essays, the first nine of which are under the rubric "Old Stories." Hearn dedicated *Kottō* to Sir Edwin Arnold.* *Kottō* means curio. *Kottō* was reprinted as part of Volume 11 of *The Writings of Lafcadio Hearn* (16 vols., 1922).

"The Legend of Yurei-Daki" is the first of the "Old Stories." In it, five young women are working in a hemp factory in Kurosaka. When four express fear of the nearby waterfall, called Yurei-Daki (The Cascade of Ghosts), the fifth, who has a baby in wrappings on her back, accepts the challenge of visiting the waterfall that night, for a bribe. She goes there, is warned by a voice to stay away, but takes the money box at the nearby Shintō shrine as proof she has been there. She hurries back and is welcomed by the other four women. But when they unwrap her backpack, they find a little corpse all bloody and headless. The source of this story was Setsu Koizumi,* Hearn's wife, whose telling and retelling of the plot caused him to turn pale and practically hypnotized him.

"In a Cup of Tea": We often walk up stairways or onto a cliff, only to find—

nothing. Here is a similar story. In Yedo 220 years ago Sekinai, a samurai's guard, sees the reflection of a living face on the surface of his cup of tea. He throws the tea away, but the face is there for a second cup, and a third, which he drinks. Has he swallowed a ghost? That night Shikibu Heinai, the owner of the face, appears, says he was insulted, and when Sekinai tries to stab him vanishes through the wall. The next night Sekinai is visited by three retainers of Shikibu Heinai, who, they say, will return 16 days hence to exact revenge. Here the story ends. Hearn says he can think of no ending that would "satisfy an Occidental imagination."

"Common Sense": A priest near Kyōto prays fervently at his mountain temple. One day he tells a hunter, who helps provide him with food, that each night he sees Fugen Bosatsu, a Buddhist divinity, approach his temple riding a white elephant. The hunter stays, to see the elephant also. That night a starlike light appears from the east, comes closer, and takes the shape of a divine being riding a six-tusked, white elephant. While the priest and his acolyte prostrate themselves, the hunter shoots an arrow at the Buddha's breast. All becomes dark. In the morning the hunter escorts the priest along a trail of blood to a big, dead badger, felled by the hunter's arrow. The narrator concludes that the priest was deceived by a mere badger, whereas the hunter, armed with common sense, "destroy[ed] a dangerous illusion."

"Ikiryō": In Yedo, Kihei runs a successful porcelain shop. For 40 years Rokubei has been his faithful assistant. Business expands, and with Kihei's permission Rokubei hires his nephew as a clerk. The fellow is capable and loyal, but after seven months he grows mysteriously ill. Rokubei asks him if he is lovesick. The clerk denies this but says that he is being tormented by a Shadow, namely, that of Kihei's wife. Because the wife is alive, the shadow is an *ikiryō* (the spirit of someone living and visible only to that person's target). Kihei, when informed, learns from her that she fears that Kihei's business, which should go to their "simple-hearted" son, could be jeopardized by Rokubei's nephew, whom she wishes she could kill. Saying such a deed would be sinful, Kihei transfers uncle and nephew to a branch office, and all is well.

"Shiryō": Nomoto Yajiyémon, a governor in Echizen, has died. To discredit him, his clerks falsify his papers and send them to the Saishō, a high official, who orders Nomoto's widow and children to prepare for banishment as family punishment. But her maid immediately goes into convulsions, grows calm, and tells the Saishō's agents and his crooked clerks that she has become Nomoto. His voice upbraids the clerks and demands an auditing of his accounts. It is ordered. "She" corrects all false entries in "his" very handwriting. She falls asleep for two days, awakens, regains her girlish voice and mien, and remembers nothing. Hearing of this extraordinary event, the Saishō punishes the guilty and rewards the house of Nomoto, which prospers.

"The Story of O-Kamé": In Tosa, sweet O-Kamé dearly loves her young husband, Hachiyémon, but grows mortally ill and reluctantly asks him not to remarry after her death. He solemnly promises, and she dies happy. But then he gets sick. To his despairing mother he confesses that O-Kamé returns nightly to him and will find no rest until he too dies. However, he says he owes devotion to his parents now. His mother consults a priest, who orders O-Kamé's corpse to be secretly exhumed. The corpse smiles and is found to be warm. The priest takes O-Kamé to a mortuary chapel, writes some holy words on her brow and elsewhere, and has her reburied. All is well again. Whether Hachiyémon remarried is not recorded.

"The Story of a Fly": The scene is Kyōto two hundred years ago. Kazariya Kyūbei, a merchant, and his wife have a dutiful maidservant named Tama, who dresses carelessly. After five years, Kyūbei asks why. Tama says she has been saving money for a mortuary tablet honoring her deceased parents. Tama finally erects the tablet, gives Kyūbei's wife some leftover savings to keep for her, and then dies. A large fly soon buzzes around Kyūbei, who catches it, marks it, and takes it far away. When the same fly persists in returning, his wife thinks it is Tama and says she will take the girl's savings and have a Buddhist service said. The fly falls dead. A priest reverently recites prayers over its boxed body and buries it in the temple grounds.

"Story of a Pheasant": A farmer and his wife live in the province of Bishū. One night her deceased father-in-law comes to her in a dream and asks her to save him from danger tomorrow. In the morning, she tells her husband. While he is in the field and she is weaving, a pheasant enters. Thinking it is her father-in-law, she hides it from the district governor's hunters. When her husband returns, he agrees that the calm pheasant, blind in its right eye, must be his father, also thus blinded. With an evil grin, he kills the pheasant for food. The wife, aghast, runs to the governor and tells all. He banishes the farmer, rewards the wife, and later gets her a better husband.

"The Story of Chūgorō": Young Chūgorō is a retainer of Suzuki, the shogun's vassal in Yedo. When it is seen that Chūgorō sneaks out nightly and returns looking "unwell," an old friend asks for an explanation. Last spring, Chūgorō reveals, he was returning from visiting his parents when a beautiful woman appeared by the river, proposed marriage, and lured him into the water. He was suddenly in a palace, wined and dined lavishly, and persuaded to pledge marriage to her through seven lives. In the morning she explains that this arrangement will continue nightly but must remain secret or else misfortune will befall them. The old friend accepts the explanation even while suspecting a wicked illusion. Chūgorō tries but fails to meet the woman again, fears her disappearance was caused by his revealing their secret, returns to his friend, and lies down all in a chilly tremble. A Chinese physician, unable to prevent Chūgorō's death, certifies that his veins are full of water and that his blood has been sucked out by "a great and ugly Frog" long haunting the river.

"A Woman's Diary" and the following 10 pieces are separately listed and are not part of "Old Stories." "A Woman's Diary" is the diary of an ordinary woman in Tōkyō. Hearn tells us that she was plain in appearance, was well educated, was married to a night doorman, and made cigarettes for a tobacconist. Her 17-

sheet manuscript was loaned by a friend. The translation, with commentaries, follows. In 1895 the diarist, age 29, writes that Okada-Shi, a matchmaker, gets her to agree to marry Namiki-Shi, age 38 and widowered for almost a year. Two days later, accompanied by her mother, she meets him for the first time through Okada. Two days after that, she and Namiki marry. His previous father-in-law warns the diarist that Namiki is strict and that she must not "cross his will." A week later the two call on her parents. A pleasant life begins. The couple attend the theater for the first time, pray at their temple, and dine out. In a poem the diarist compares herself and her husband to enviable love birds and says they both pray for continued "concord." They visit her parents' house at the time of a festival. She records joyful poems she and her husband have written, and also some by her sister, O-Kō, and that woman's husband, Goto. In August 1897 the diarist gives birth to a baby boy. He dies the next day. In January 1898 she falls ill for some time. In August she has a baby daughter, born with a double thumb, which surgery repairs. The child grows ill in April 1899. They have trouble finding a doctor. In May the baby dies of incurable nephritis. The wife feels that something might have been wrong in their previous lives. In September O-Kō dies "of consumption"; a week later Goto marries the diarist's sister, Toshi. Late in September Okada dies. Funeral expenses cause Namiki financial embarrassment. In February 1900 the diarist has another baby boy. Eight days later he falls ill and dies before a doctor, though summoned, has time to get there. The diarist fears her husband will reject her because of some failing in her former life. However, he accepts "the decrees of Heaven." The diarist records her own illness and only apparent recovery, and then the record breaks off. She died late in March 1900. Hearn summarizes her sad life; calls it not exceptional but typical of that of many a heroic Japanese woman; and lauds her bravery, docility, loyalty, gratitude, piety, "capacity of unselfish attachment," poems she wrote "when her heart was breaking," and "Buddhist interpretation of suffering as the penalty for some fault committed in a previous life."

"Heiké-Gani": An environment different from that of the West produces flora, fauna, and people different from those in the West. Two varieties of *gani* (crabs) in Japan are the Heiké-gani and the Genji-gani. The Heiké clan killed their rivals, the Genji clan, in a naval battle seven centuries ago near the coast of Shimonoseki. Heiké-gani crabs living there have grim faces on their backs resembling the faces of slaughtered Heiké warriors. A Japanese friend draws Hearn pictures of two such crabs, but Hearn cannot see the resemblance. *See* "Fireflies" next in this entry and "The Story of Mimi-Nashi-Hōïchi" under the entry "Kwaidan."

"Fireflies": For the beginning of this essay, Hearn relies on the scientific lectures on fireflies by Shozaburo Watasé, a graduate of Johns Hopkins University and professor at the Imperial University of Tōkyō. Watasé knows about firefly morphology, physiology, photometry, chemistry, and spectroscopy. The bitter taste of fireflies makes them unpalatable to birds but not to frogs, who gulp them down until their bellies positively glow. Hearn discusses the etymology of the Japanese word *hotaru* (firefly); says that the two main types of Japanese fireflies are Genji-hotaru and Heiké-hotaru; says they are reputedly the ghosts of rival Genji and Heiké warriors who battled in the twelfth century; and reports that on April 20 rival fireflies replicate that battle on the Uji River. Genji fireflies are larger; Heiké's range farther north and emit feebler light; both species radiate tea-colored (yellow-green) light. Swarms of fireflies in a valley near Ishiyama used to be dazzling from 1688 until 1703. Now the best swarmings are outside Uji, in Yamashiro, and attract trainloads of spectators. Many people make money in the summer by catching and selling fireflies. They stir them out of trees with bamboo poles and net them when they fall to the ground. Experienced hunters put the temporarily helpless insects in their mouths, bag them by mouthfuls, and corral three thousand per night. Fireflies are graded by luminosity, are sold accordingly in plain or fancy cages, and are often supplied to the well-to-do for garden parties and to restaurateurs for display purposes—often in carefully netted gardens. Dead fireflies are converted into poultices, pills, "grease" to harden bent bamboo, and talismans to ward off robbers, poisons, "devils," and enemy soldiers' weapons. Children sing charming songs while they hunt fireflies. Fireflies frequent clean water, favor weeping willows, and avoid pine trees and rose bushes. Hearn says that in Izumo he heard about a young man who saw a firefly, struck at it, and later was told by his betrothed that she dreamed she was flying at him when he suddenly approached and tried to hit her. Hearn summarizes an episode in *Genji-Monogari* (*Genji monogatori*, The Tale of Genji, by Murasaki Shikibu, [978–c. 1016]), in which a lover is able to find his lady in the dark by catching and releasing fireflies. Hearn includes a virtual anthology of 40 or so poems, usually *hokku*, about fireflies—catching them, their light, love songs, miscellaneous pieces, and the "Song of the Firefly-Seller." Hearn theorizes that "the particular miracle of the machinery" that produces light in insects does so because "Matter, in some blind infallible way, *remembers*; and that in every unit of living substance there slumber infinite potentialities . . . because to every . . . atom belongs the . . . indestructible experience of billions . . . of vanished universes." In saying so, Hearn mentions Herbert Spencer (1820–1903), his favorite philosopher. Hearn also cites "Folk of the Air" (the title is "The Host of the Air," 1893) by William Butler Yeats (1865–1939), which contains a line similar to one in a Japanese firefly poem Hearn quotes. Hearn, who here calls Yeats's poem "that most remarkable of modern fairy-ballads," wrote to Yeats (September 24, 1901) to voice his dislike of the 1899 revision of the poem and to urge him to return to the original. *See* "Heiké-Gani" earlier in this entry.

"A Drop of Dew": A drop of dew, with inverted images in prismatic colors, reminds Hearn that "Buddhism finds in such . . . the symbol of that other microcosm which has been called the Soul." Each one of us is "just such a temporary orbing of viewless ultimates . . . [that] combine again with countless kindred atoms for the making of other drops[,] . . . of blood and sweat and tears."

One's "personality signifies" no more than "the shivering of any single drop." Hence "the idea of death as loss" is a delusion; whatever was, now is, and soon will become; personality and individuality are "ghosts of a dream in a dream"; all things are come-and-go shadows of infinite life.

"Gaki": Near the beach on the Suruga coast, Hearn feels at one with everything and thinks that "the Soul of me must have quickened" with all past forms of life and will do so in future lives. What we now do will determine "the future state of our sentiency." By force of thought and action we shape our "future bliss or pain." We may "reënter existence" in lower forms, perhaps as insects or as *gaki* (goblins). The two forms are related in Buddhism. Insects, some horrible, others beautiful, are akin to spirits. Hearn catalogues Buddhist *gaki*, which are one degree up from hell. In Japanese Buddhism are 36 *gaki* classes, one division seen by humans, the one other, not. All suffer one or more of three degrees of hunger and thirst. One *gaki* group eats impurities. Buddhists used to think *gaki* caused different human diseases. Most *gaki* are linked to disease, putrescence, and death; others are linked to specific insects, whose activities relate to superstitions concerning spirits. Spirits specialize in eating blood, corpses, fire, flesh, poison, smells, and wind; some spirits are even—as Hearn modestly puts it—"Jiki-da-gaki, or . . . [*sic*]-eaters" or "Jiki-fun-gaki, or . . . [*sic*]-eaters." He identifies more *gaki* as eaters of garbage, wigs, and funeral and grave leavings. Hearn tells of a man who boldly cut down a goblin tree, only to have its branches avenge the onslaught by strangling him and rendering his widow insane. *Gaki* can assume lewd human shapes. Not all insects are *gaki*, but most *gaki* can assume insect shape. Old myths conflate insect history, dreams, and dead vegetation. Insects are miraculously structured, with X ray-like eyes, ears oddly located, and spectrally potent brains—seeing magnetic waves, smelling light, tasting noises. Beyond the power of our unaided imagination, insects' organs—hand-like lips, drill-like tongues, scissor mouths, and the like—become the stuff of horror and ecstasy. Yes, "there is something spectral, something alarming, in the very beauty of insects." Do our actions and thoughts requicken our dead dust into insect life? Hearn reckons that his "stupidities in this existence" may foredoom him to be an insect in his next life. This would be fine if he could be "an independent, highly organized, respectable insect"—say, an ephemera "dancing in golden air" or a skater able "to slide upon water." It is no "inestimable privilege to be reborn a human being." He would prefer to "clash my tiny cymbals in the sun" as a dew-sipping cicada or haunt "some holy silence of lotus-pools" as a compound-eyed dragonfly. Earlier in the essay Hearn mentions "The White Moth" by Arthur Quiller-Couch (1863–1944). It concerns a soul becoming an insect, which Japanese readers would find appealing. "Gaki" combines Hearn's love of Japanese nomenclature, scientific mumbo-jumbo, obsession with filth, and poetic prose.

"A Matter of Custom": A Zen priest tells Hearn that he does not believe in ghost stories but does have one to tell. While on a pilgrimage he stopped at a village temple, where he was allowed by a nun to stay overnight even though the priest was away at a funeral. During the utterly dark night the Zen priest heard someone chanting. In the morning the nun said the voice was that of the man whose funeral the priest was attending.

"Revery": It is comforting to believe that when we die we will be embraced by a god that is maternal. Still, the earth eventually will crumble; so will the other planets; then the sun will vaporize. But we should not worry, because "nothing essential can be lost." All energy, including ours, inherited from innumerable, long-gone worlds, will go into "the making of the future cosmos." Love that survives former pains and deaths "shall rise again," nourished by the ever-smiling mother. Thus Hearn dismisses, yet again, the patriarchal Western god of his miserable upbringing.

"Pathological": The "soft trilling coo" emitted by Tama (translation; Jewel), Hearn's tricolored cat, inspired this essay. Tama nursed and trained her first kittens well and brought them mice, other creatures, and once a muddy sandal, for toys. When pregnant again she was hit by someone, and her litter was stillborn. Feline instinct—to care for kittens, to hunt, to fight—is planted in a cat's "organic memory . . . accumulated through countless billions of lives." Tama, still missing her dead kittens, "plays with them in dreams, and coos to them."

"In the Dead of the Night": In the black night, the clock strikes three. Ah, Hearn will see the sun again. But not forever. You can doubt much, but not the inevitability of death. If Hearn believes he exists, he must believe he will die. But must he believe he exists? Suddenly "Darkness" walls him in and says that shadowy darkness will be followed by "Reality," containing nothing, certainly not hope. For others, "above," there will be light, warmth, joy for eons. Hearn counters that, awake now, he can think again and concludes that death is the absence of sensation. Darkness replies that when he is dust, burned-out passions may still cling to his atoms. Hearn shouts that he is awake, remembers, and is timeless. Dawn breaks. A bird twitters. The sun rises, "symbol sublime of that infinite Life whose forces are also mine!"

"Kusa-Hibari": In a tiny cage only two inches tall is a *kusa-hibari* (grass lark) the size of a mosquito. Hearn bought the creature for 12 cents. Why keep him, feeding him eggplant and cucumbers? Well, because from sunset to dawn he sings a delicate song—ghostly, silvery, rippling, sweet, elfishly resonant. Although hatched in an insect-merchant's jar, he sings out of his "organic memory" of loves long before even his ancestors personally experienced love. Hearn knew that if he bought him a mate and the two made love, he would soon die. The merchant laughed and said he would soon die anyway. And he did, when Hana, Hearn's housemaid, neglected to find him food. Hearn's responses are complex. He felt a kinship with his grass lark. He is sorry he scolded Hana. When he notes that the hunger of his insect, which sang to the moment of death, caused him to eat his own legs, Hearn concludes with an unusually personal and poignant touch: "There are human crickets who must eat their own hearts in order to sing." Hearn here may be inviting his wide audience of Western readers to see him as a little songster imprisoned in the cage of his Japanese expatriation.

"The Eater of Dreams": The Baku, a composite of different animal parts, guards dreamers by eating their evil dreams. One hot night Hearn dreamed he saw his own corpse. The atmosphere grew heavy. Female watchers silently departed in fear. Hearn saw his body elongate and its eyes open and stare at him. Seizing a handy axe, he reduced it to "a shapeless, hideous, reeking mass." He asked the Baku to eat the dream. But the Baku says that Hearn used "the Axe of the Excellent Law" to destroy "the monster of Self" in what was therefore a splendid dream. Then the Baku flew away over the houses of the city.

Kottō is composed of odds and ends, concentrates on insects and horrific plots, and reveals much about Hearn's late-life personality. It was reprinted and also issued in England (1901).

Bibliography: Bisland; Cott; Dawson; George Hughes, "W. B. Yeats and Lafcadio Hearn: Negotiating with Ghosts," in Hirakawa, pp. 114–129; John Kelly and Ronald Schuchard, eds., *The Collected Letters of W. B. Yeats, Volume Three, 1901–1904* (Oxford: Clarendon Press, 1994); Kunst; Murray; Stevenson.

KREHBIEL, HENRY EDWARD (1854–1923). Music critic and historian. Krehbiel was born in Ann Arbor, Michigan. He was the son of an itinerant German Methodist minister. Henry Krehbiel attended public schools in Michigan and, after 1864, in Cincinnati. He studied violin and harmony there, and he also conducted the choir in his father's church. He was a reporter for the Cincinnati *Gazette*, covering sports and crime stories. He was its music editor (1874–1880), moved to New York in 1880, wrote for the *New York Tribune*, and was its long-serving music critic (1884–1923). Self-educated in music aesthetics and history, Krehbiel competed successfully with numerous formally trained music critics not only in New York but also in Boston and elsewhere. He wrote reviews and essays for the *Tribune*, more than 20 books in his field, and programs for New York's Philharmonic Society; prepared opera libretti; was an adviser for the Grove *Dictionary of Music and Musicians* (2nd ed., 5 vols., 1904–1910); and lectured. Internationally known, he was awarded the French Legion of Honor (1901). Krehbiel set high standards but over the years grew conservative in his taste. Notable, however, were his laudatory analyses of Chinese musical theory (1891) and African American spirituals (1914). Krehbiel married Helen Osborne, an organist and writer, in 1880. They had one child. After Helen Krehbiel's death, Krehbiel married Marie Van, a soprano from Cincinnati (1896).

Hearn met Krehbiel in Cincinnati in the early 1870s. The two were members of a group of lively journalists, including Joseph Salathiel Tunison.* Hearn especially respected Krehbiel for his scholarly achievements. When Krehbiel organized a musical concert played by Chinese laundrymen in the city, Hearn happily attended. Hearn wrote about the event in "A Romantic Episode at the

Music Club" (*Cincinnati Commercial*, October 1, 1877), mentions it and praises Krehbiel in an 1878 editorial titled "Romanticism in Music" (*Cincinnati Item*, July 20, 1878), and dedicated *Some Chinese Ghosts* (1887) to Krehbiel. When he moved to New Orleans in 1877, Hearn wrote to Krehbiel a revealing sequence of modest letters in which he described and praised life there, offered information about Creole musicians and their songs, and adversely criticized the phonetic transcription of Creole verse by Hearn's friend Adrien Emmanuel Rouquette.* When Krehbiel sought to rebuke Hearn for growing lazy in the Deep South and challenged him to write more substantial work than local-color stuff on New Orleans, Hearn defended his enjoyable new way of life, called his epistolary adversary a "son of Odin," and said he was likely to continue producing trivia. In 1887, while in New York on his way to Martinique, Hearn stayed with Krehbiel and his wife, Helen, and evidently wore out his welcome. His hosts turned cool toward him. (It may not be too much to suggest that when Hearn wanted to name an old man in *Chita* (1889) who goes to Last Island and promptly dies, he called him Henry Edwards, in a kind of vindictive move.) In 1890, back in New York, Henry Edward Krehbiel and Hearn, who was about to voyage to Japan, had a ruinous quarrel. Hearn had left a pair of shoes with Krehbiel, went to his apartment to retrieve them, and was denied entrance by a maid who may have regarded the shabby caller as a banshee. When Hearn wrote to demand an explanation, Krehbiel replied that Hearn could "go to Japan or go to HELL." This terminated what might have been a permanently rewarding friendship with the often irascible Hearn. In *Afro-American Folksongs: A Study in Racial and National Music* (1914), Krehbiel quotes Hearn, calls him "musically illiterate," but manages to praise him for being keenly observant and penetratingly intuitive about matters musical.

Bibliography: Edward Downes, "The Taste-Makers: Critics and Criticism," in *One Hundred Years of Music in America*, ed. Paul Henry Lang (New York: Grosset & Dunlap, 1961); [Henry Edward Krehbiel], "Letters of a Poet to a Musician: Lafcadio Hearn to Henry E. Krehbiel," *Critic* 48 (April 1906): 309–318; and Joseph A. Musselman, *Music in the Cultured Generation: A Social History of Music in America, 1870–1900* (Evanston, Ill.: Northwestern University Press, 1971); Stevenson; Tinker.

***KWAIDAN: STORIES AND STUDIES OF STRANGE THINGS* (1904).** A collection of 17 items under the rubric "Kwaidan" (Strange Tales), followed by three essays under "Insect-Studies." Two of the "Kwaidan" pieces were previously published. In a preface, Hearn says that most of his *Kwaidan* tales are from Japanese books, some perhaps being Chinese originally; that "Yuki-Onna" was a village legend told to him by a farmer in Musashi province; and that "Riki-Baka" is a retelling of a personal experience. *Kwaidan* was reprinted as part of Volume 11 of *The Writings of Lafcadio Hearn* (16 vols., 1922).

"The Story of Mimi-Nashi-Hōïchi" (1903) is the first "Kwaidan" piece. The Genji clan slaughtered the Heiké clan at the Straits of Shimonoséki seven hundred years ago. Sea and shore have been haunted. Fires hover, and battle sounds are still heard. A temple, built to appease vengeful Heiké ghosts, helps but little. A few centuries ago a blind lute player named Hōïchi lived in the temple. One hot summer night, while the priest is away, Hōïchi is practicing on his lute when a samurai guides him to a palace, where he is ordered to play and sing of the Heiké defeat. He performs so movingly that he hears loud lamentation all about. The lord, impressed, orders Hōïchi to be escorted home, return, and perform for the next six nights—and tell no one. Back at the temple, the priest grows worried and has some servants follow Hōïchi. They find him chanting in a cemetery lighted by fires for the dead Heiké there. They drag Hōïchi back to the temple. The priest wrings a reluctant explanation from him and concludes that the concert was not in the nearby lord's palace but at the Heiké cemetery. Warning him of grave danger, the priest and his acolyte paint holy sutra texts all over Hōïchi. Ordered to sit motionless on the veranda, Hōïchi does so, and when the samurai comes he sees only the lute and Hōïchi's ears, which the acolyte neglected to paint. The samurai tears off the ears for his lord. Hōïchi recovers, becomes a tourist-attracting performer, and is known thereafter as Mimi-Nashi-Hōïchi (Hōïchi-the-Earless). Hearn demonstrates consummate narrative skill in expertly handling the point of view of the blind Hōïchi. *See* "Heiké-Gani" under the entry "Kottō."

"Oshidori": A Mutso hunter named Sonjō sees a loving pair of *oshidori* (mandarin ducks) at Akanuma and shoots, cooks, and eats the male. That night in "a dreary dream" a beautiful woman appears to him and asks why he killed her guiltless husband. Sobbing a lament about loneliness at Akanuma, she predicts her own death. Out of curiosity, Sonjō next morning goes to Akanuma and sees a female *oshidori*, which swims toward him and commits suicide by tearing herself with her beak. Sonjō subsequently becomes a priest.

"The Story of O-Tei": In Echizen province a medical student named Nagao Chōsei, age 19, is betrothed to O-Tei, who at age 15 is dying of consumption. She tells him she will be reborn as a girl, will grow to adulthood 16 years hence, and will reappear to him for marriage. She cannot tell by what sign he will know her. Nagao agrees to wait. O-Tei dies. He places a written promise at her tomb. But his family persuades him to remarry. Years pass. His parents, his wife, and their child all die. When he goes to a spa at Ikao, a young girl approaches who looks just like O-Tei. Queried, she says she is O-Tei, he is her betrothed Nagao, she died 17 years ago, and he placed a promise of marriage at her shrine. She faints, recovers, remembers nothing of her speech, and they happily wed. Rare for Hearn, this tale comes to a joyful climax.

"Ubazacura": It is three hundred years ago in a village in Iyō province. When the rich Tokubei and his wife pray for a first child, a daughter is born. They name her Tsuyu. Her wet nurse, O-Sudé, is devoted to her. At age 15 the girl, now called O-Tsuyu, falls ill. O-Sudé prays hard. O-Tsuyu recovers. But O-Sudé gets sick, reveals she prayed in the Saihōji temple to die in place of the girl, asks that a cherry tree be planted in her honor there, and expires. The parents plant a beautiful tree. For 254 years it blossoms on the anniversary of O-Tsuyu's death. Its petals resemble milk-bedewed nipples. The tree is called Ubazakura (milk-nurse's cherry tree).

"Diplomacy": A samurai is about to behead a criminal, who protests that his bad action was merely the result of his Karma causing him to be born stupid. He should be forgiven; if not, he will get revenge. The samurai, heard by his retainers, challenges the man to offer proof of resentment by biting a stone down where his severed head will roll. He agrees and is executed, and his head does indeed bite the stone briefly. When the retainers express fear of sounds amid the bamboos and shadows in the garden, the samurai explains that he diverted the condemned man's attention to biting the stone and nothing else. True, he then forgot to try for revenge.

"Of a Mirror and a Bell": It is eight centuries ago, in the village of Mugen-yama in Tōtōmi province. The priests persuade women to donate bronze mirrors for a big bell. A farmer's wife gives her great-grandmother's mirror but soon so regrets doing so that when the heap of mirrors go to the foundry hers will not melt. Gossipers recognize her mirror by its markings and make her feel so ashamed that she drowns herself. Her suicide note says that her mirror will now melt but that her ghost will give much wealth to whoever breaks the finished bell by ringing it. Taking this promise seriously, multitudes ring away at the bell. The din annoys the priests, and they roll the bell into a deep swamp. Remembering the suicide promise, a woman named Umégaë takes a bronze wash basin, pretends hard that it is the big bell, and beats it to pieces while asking for money. An innkeeper wonders what caused the racket, and when told he gives her three hundred gold pieces. A farmer hears of this miracle and fashions a bell out of clay, and when he smashes it a beautiful woman appears and hands him a covered jar. The farmer rushes home and shows his wife. They open the jar. Hearn says he cannot reveal its contents. Hearn makes this tale somewhat inartistic by digressing at midpoint to discuss the Japanese verb *na-zoraëru*, having to do with imagining one object for another—in this case, a basin for a bell.

"Jikininki": In Mino, a Zen priest named Musō Kokushi is lost in the mountains, encounters a solitary old priest in his *anjitsu* (hermitage), is refused shelter, but is directed to a nearby valley. He is welcomed at the headman's house. That night he hears weeping. The headman's son tells him that his father just died and everyone must go elsewhere to pray for him. His corpse must remain in the house. Despite warnings, Musō says he fears no evil and will stay. That night he prays before the corpse, then meditates. Suddenly "a Shape" enters; devours the corpse, its shroud, and all offerings; and departs. Everyone returns in the morning; when told of events, all knowingly agree that both corpse and offerings disappeared according to custom. When Musō asks why the priest in the *anjitsu* does not handle funeral matters better, he is told that there has never been such a priest or any *anjitsu*. Musō politely leaves, finds the old hermit, and receives his apology. The hermit identifies himself as a *jikininki* (man-eating goblin). He was formerly a priest but thought materialistically about bodies and offerings while performing funeral rights, and therefore when he died he was reborn as a *jikininki*, doomed to eat corpses. He asks for Musō's efficacious prayers, disappears, and leaves Musō kneeling at what seems to be a mossy tomb.

"Mujina": On a certain road in Tōkyō there is a place called the Slope of the Province of Kii. On one side is a moat; on the other, palace walls. It is considered dangerous to walk on that road at night, on account of the Mujina (a badger, with supernatural shape-shifting talents) walking there. Here is the story of the last man who walked there, 30 years ago. One night while walking there he saw a graceful young woman, crying and perhaps about to drown herself in the moat. Courteously offering to help, he saw her turn toward him and stroke her face. She had no eyes, nose, or mouth. The man ran away, headed for the light of a buckwheat seller, cried out, and told the fellow he had seen a woman with . . . When he paused, the fellow asked whether what was seen was . . . And he stroked his own face, which turned as smooth as an egg. Then the light went out.

"Rokuro-Kubi": It is five hundred years ago. Isogai Héïdazaëmon Takétsura, a samurai in Kyūshū, serves his lord until his master's fortunes fail, becomes a Buddhist priest, calls himself Kwairyō, and travels to preach in dangerous regions. One night, while sleeping in a forest in Kai province, he is disturbed by a woodcutter who expresses wonder that Kwairyō is unafraid of Hairy Things. Kwairyō cheerfully accepts the woodcutter's invitation to sleep in his hut. Inside, four people greet him so eloquently that he asks his host whether he once belonged in higher society. Yes, he once served a fine lord but through dissipation caused death to visit his employer's house. He would like to repent. Everyone retires except Kwairyō, who prays for his host. But when he goes for a drink outside, he walks past five headless bodies, including that of his host. He recalls reading that a *rokuro-kubi* (headless goblin body), if moved, will never recover its head. He puts the host's body outside, hears voices in the grove beyond, goes to it, and hears five talking heads. His host says they will gobble up their priestly visitor once he quits praying. Another head flies to the house to check and reports the priest missing. For revenge, they all fly at Kwairyō, who, however, grabs a tree, beats off four, but cannot dislodge his host's head from his sleeve. In the house he finds the four bruised heads reattached to their unmoved bodies. When they see him, they flee. In the morning he walks to the village of Suwa, is charged with having a murder victim's head on his sleeve, but laughingly narrates his adventure. Nevertheless the magistrates order his execution. When an old man examines the head, he identifies marks on it proving it is a Rokuro-Kubi's and guesses that brave Kwairyō was once a soldier. He identifies himself as Isogai of Kyūshū and is complimented and welcomed. A couple of days later Kwairyō, still a happy priest with the head dangling as a souvenir from his sleeve, is accosted by a robber who demands to buy both head and robe. Kwairyō warns him but accepts. The robber learns the truth about the head when he passes through Suwa, goes back to the goblin hut, and buries the head for safety. To this day it is still there, under the tombstone of the *rikuro-kubi*.

"A Dead Secret": A rich merchant's bright, beautiful daughter, O-Sono, is sent from their rural region to Kyō to be nicely educated. Her father then marries her to his merchant friend, Nagaraya. They have a son, but O-Sono dies after having been married for only four years. After her funeral, the little boy sees her standing in front of her *tansu* (chest of drawers). Although her family removes her clothes from the *tansu* and donates them to their temple, O-Sono revisits the *tansu*. They consult a priest, who stands one night in her room, sees her staring at the *tansu*, and finds a letter under its lining paper. When he promises to read and then burn it, O-Sono smiles and vanishes. He keeps his word, revealing to no one that the letter was a love note from a student during the girl's student days in Kyōto.

"Yuki-Onna": Old Mosaku and his apprentice, Minokichi, age 18, are woodcutters. One night beside a river near their forest, they are caught by a snowstorm and huddle in the absent ferryman's hut. While Mosaku sleeps soundly, Minokichi is aroused by snow in his face and the vision of a woman in white. She blows her breath on Mosaku, turns to Minokichi, decides not to frost him, but orders him to say nothing of this experience or she will kill him. Next morning the ferryman returns, finds Mosaku dead, but revives the senseless Minokichi. He continues cutting wood, which his mother sells with him. Next winter in the forest he encounters a gorgeous, tall young woman. She is O-Yuki, an orphan on her way to Yedo. He persuades her to visit his mother, who likes her immediately. Minokichi and O-Yuki marry. Five years later the mother dies, praising her daughter-in-law. The couple have 10 children, and O-Yuki retains her youthful looks wonderfully. One night Minokichi tells her that she reminds him of someone as beautiful and white as she. When O-Yuki, sewing carefully, asks for details, he foolishly tells her about "the White Woman," whereupon O-Yuki says she is that woman, he broke his promise of silence, and she would kill him but for the children. Her voice trails away, and she turns into "a bright white mist" and vanishes through the overhead smoke hole.

"The Story of Aoyagi": Tomotada, a handsome, personable samurai, serves the fifteenth-century Lord of Noto. When he is about 20 years old he goes on a mission to Hosokawa, a feudal lord of Kyōto and the Lord of Noto's kinsman. Permitted to visit his widowed mother in their native Echizen, he is delayed en route by a snowstorm. He accepts shelter at the willow-bordered hut of humble peasants, whose daughter, Aoyagi (Green Willow), attracts his attention. She is beautiful, graceful, and modest. By an exchange of recited poems, they pledge themselves to one another. The aged parents are honored by their samurai visitor's promise to cherish them, courteously decline his offer of gold, cheerfully say they will soon die, and watch the happy couple leave. Hearn says that his original text breaks off here with nothing but a "startling end." It seems that Tomotada could not marry without his Lord's consent; so the pair live together secretly. One of Hosokawa's retainers sees the gorgeous Aoyagi and reports her association with Tomotada, and he is summoned to Hosokawa. Although Tomotado fears death as punishment for his disobedience, Hosokawa blesses him, and he and Aoyagi are married. One day, after five happy years, Aoyagi, suddenly stricken with a sharp pain, tells her husband that a previous Karma relation brought them together and a future one will reunite them. She confesses that she is not human, is a willow tree, and is even now being cut down. She falls and vanishes, leaving only her robe and hair ornaments. Tomotado becomes an itinerant Buddhist priest, visits Aoyagi's home, and finds three willow stumps—two old, one young. He then prepares a tomb with sacred texts.

"Jiu-Roku-Zakura": In Iyo province, there is a cherry tree called Jiu-roku-zakura (Cherry Tree of the Sixteenth Day) because it uniquely blooms every year on the sixteenth of the first month (by the old lunar calendar). This is because a man's ghost is in it. It grew in a samurai's garden. He loved it, grew old, and so lamented its death that he committed *hara-kiri* before it, to let his soul go into it. Thus it occurred, on that sixteenth day of the first month. It blooms on that day every year, in the snow.

"The Dream of Akinosuké": Miyata Akinosuké, a *gōshi* (soldier-farmer), lives in Yamato province. While drinking with two friends in his garden under a cedar, he falls asleep and has an elaborate dream. In it, a feudal lord's procession is marching toward his house. A rope-drawn carriage approaches. He is asked to get in and is taken to the palace of the Kokuō of Tokoyo (the King of Fairyland), who orders him to wed his daughter on this day. Appropriately robed, Akinosuké is taken to a gigantic room, shown his bride, and married before an assembly of guests. A few days later the King names him governor of Raishū, an island in Tokoyo. The couple go there; and Akinosuké, ordered to rule benevolently and improve social conditions, finds his duties pleasant for the next 23 years. He sires seven children, but then his wife suddenly dies. They place a Buddhist monument at her grave. The King sends condolences but then gently orders Akinosuké to go back alone to Yamato. He sails away from Raishū, which he sees turn gray and vanish. He wakes up in his garden and tells his friends about his dream. They say he was asleep for only a few minutes, during which they saw a butterfly flutter over him, be dragged by an ant into its hole, but then fly up again near his mouth. Digging out of curiosity under Akinosuké's cedar, the three find an elaborate ant colony. In it are miniature towns, a huge ant resembling the King of Tokoyo, and a dead little female ant, her grave marked by a water-worn pebble shaped like a Buddhist monument. *See* "Ants" later in this entry.

"Riki-Baka": Riki (meaning strength) is called Riki-Baka (Riki the Fool) because he was "born into perpetual childhood." He plays harmlessly, in part by riding a broomstick like a hobbyhorse, until he is 16 years old. By then too noisy, he is a sent away and later dies. His mother writes "Riki-Baka" on the palm of her left hand and prays for a better later life for him. When a baby is born in a region nearby, with Riki-Baka plainly legible on his left-hand palm, his mother learns about the deceased Riki-Baka and sends for clay from his grave. It is explained that "characters [letters] that come in that way" on a baby can be removed only by rubbing its skin with clay from the former person's grave.

"Hi-Mawari": The narrator, age 7, and Robert, age 8, seek "fairy-rings" one sweet August day. The narrator mentions the tale of a Welshman who slept inside a fairy-ring for seven years. Robert sees a harper approach. Though dark and ugly, the fellow sings a song beginning "Believe me, if all those endearing young charms" so captivatingly that the narrator, at first annoyed because he remembers an especially dear one who sings it, surrenders to its charm. When the harper leaves, Robert says he was a gypsy and gypsies steal children. Forty years pass. The narrator, now in Japan, sees a *hi-mawari* (sunflower) and re-members that the gypsy's song continued about a sunflower. He thinks of Robert again. This sketch ends with the narrator quoting the old comment that no greater love does anyone have for another than to die for him. Hearn begins "Hi-Mawari" in the present tense but shifts to the past when the scene shifts to Japan. By using this device Hearn suggests that the past is more present to him than the present is. The beginning scene is in Ireland. The character Robert is based on Hearn's cousin Robert Elwood, who joined the navy and drowned off the coast of China while trying to save a comrade who had fallen overboard. The dear one who sang "Believe me . . . ," the lovely melody of Thomas Moore (1779–1852), was Hearn's well-remembered aunt, Mrs. Thomas Elwood, Rob-ert's mother and the daughter of Elizabeth Holmes Hearn,* Hearn's maternal grandmother. The coarse harper is based on Dan Fitzpatrick of Congo, County Mayo.

"Hōrai": A certain Japanese painting is of "sky and sea—one azure enor-mity"—and in the center are "the glimmering portals of Hōrai the blest." Now, Hōrai is a "not believable" place of utter bliss, with magic viands and water conferring eternal youth, no suffering, no crime or sin. Its atmosphere is com-posed "of quintillions of generations of souls blended into one immense trans-lucency"; they never, ever thought the way Westerners do. Once inhale that atmosphere, and you alter your "notions of Space and Time." It induces the sort of hope that finds "fulfillment . . . in the sweetness of Woman." Hearn sours this saccharine piece by concluding thus: "Evil winds from the West are blowing over Hōrai," the intangible vision of which is fading and soon will be available only in paintings, poetry, and dreams.

The first of the three "Insect-Studies" is "Butterflies." A certain Chinese scholar was told butterfly stories by "spirit-maidens." But Hearn knows they won't favor him because he is too skeptical. Many Japanese butterfly stories originated in China. Some suggest that living humans' souls fly in butterfly forms. Some people believe a butterfly is a dead person's soul. Paper butterflies at a wedding "express the joy of loving union." Hearn presents 22 *hokku* (each of 17 syllables) about butterflies. They comprise epigrammatic pictures, fancies, and suggestions. Three seem especially vivid: While sleeping, a butterfly quiv-ers, perhaps dreaming of flight; what seems like a petal returning to its stem is really a butterfly alighting; all butterflies seem 17 years old (graceful as nubile girls). Hearn offers a didactic, allegorical piece to the effect that the butterfly, beautiful and sought after, should never forget it was born a grubby, wormy creature gnawing farmers' crops. Here is a Japanese story, with no Chinese source: Takahama, an old bachelor, lies dying. His widowed sister-in-law and her son help him. A butterfly lights on the old man's pillow. The nephew drives it away with a fan. It flies to a tomb. Its nearby monument bears the name Akiko. The nephew returns, finds Takahama, and tells about the butterfly. The sister-in-law says the butterfly is the soul of Akiko, whom Takahama would have married 50 years ago but for her untimely death. The Japanese have dancers costumed as butterflies and performing in the Imperial Palace. This late essay suffers from being unusually choppy.

"Mosquitoes": Hearn is plagued by a certain type of "diurnal" mosquito with "wailing" hum and "needly" bite. He cites the advice of the entomologist Leland Ossian Howard (1857–1950), which is to kill mosquitoes by pouring kerosene into their breeding pools. But Hearn sadly notes that his neighborhood cemetery has tens of thousands of *mizutamé* (water tanks) and watered flower vessels, for the refreshment of the deceased. There "mine enemies are born . . . by millions." Tōkyō officials would find it impossible to order such expensive use of kerosene, to say nothing of the proscribed killing of life—even when "invisible." Besides, Hearn whimsically adds, he wants to be buried in the Buddhist cemetery behind his garden, with all its old-fashioned accoutrements, including a bell he hopes to hear, stagnant votive water, and "the chance of being reborn" as a mosquito to bite some of his enemies. (Despite not being a Buddhist, Hearn had his wish, partly; he was buried in accordance with Buddhist rites.)

"Ants": During a storm that wrecked trees, houses, and roads, the ants were able to block entrances to "their subterranean town" and thus survive. This inspires Hearn to write an essay on ants. As a preface, he offers this Chinese story. A man so worshipped a goddess that she anointed his ears so he could understand ant talk. An ant tells him where a treasure is buried. He digs and finds gold coins. Experts, including the well-traveled entomologist David Sharp (1840–1922; his many works include *The Staphylinidae of Japan*, 1874) and the philosopher Herbert Spencer (1820–1903), conclude that the civilization of ants is economically and ethically superior to ours. Ants sacrifice themselves for the good of the community. Ants are fine horticulturalists, agriculturalists, engineers, and meteorologists. Ants in well-evolved societies have practical minds, meet challenges cleverly, and are unselfish and incapable of sinning. Imagine this human society: mostly women; building, planting and harvesting, eating, manufacturing, storing, caring for the young; and staying neat and tidying themselves, their homes, their young. Women who are to be mothers—few in number, royally treated, maternal—must consort momentarily with men, who are otherwise useless. Some women have evolved into gigantic defensive warriors. Men do their function and die off. The sex urge is limited to renewing the race, by suppressing it in most of the young. Religions teach that no civilization is possible unless people are persuaded to hope for rewards and fear punishments; "irreligious Nature," however, teaches otherwise. Ants are naturally beneficent, instinctively moral, unselfish, and "energetically good." So we too may evolve beyond any need for "moral idealism." Spencer hopes that we may become like such social insects as ants and bees. He says that population explosions will cause dreadful human suffering, that intelligence will grow and fertility decline, but that "social equilibrium" will not be achieved unless humankind solves its economic problems by suppressing sex, just as social insects have done. Voluntarily practicing celibacy would help and could also increase people's longevity. Higher evolution seems possible only if humankind stops being cruel, lustful, and egoistic. Forces shaping "all forms of being" are "more exacting than gods." In "Ants," Hearn calls Spencer "the greatest philosopher that has yet appeared in this world." *See* "The Dream of Akinosuké" earlier in this entry.

Kwaidan was immensely popular, especially with Japanese readers, was often reissued, and enjoyed English editions (1904, 1927).

Bibliography: Bisland; Hirakawa; Kennard; Kunst; Yoko Makino, "Hearn's 'Yuki-Onna' and Baudelaire's 'Les Bienfaits de la Lune," in Hirakawa, pp. 199–209; Murray; Yone Noguchi, "Lafcadio Hearn's 'Kwaidan,' " *Bookman* 20 (October 1904): 159–160; Alan Rosen, "Hearn and the Gastronomic Grotesque," in Hirakawa, pp. 158–181; Leonard Wolf, *Horror, a Connoisseur's Guide to Literature and Film* (New York and Oxford: Facts on File, 1989).

L

"LAST OF THE HORSE" (1872). Cincinnati news article. Hearns visits "the horse-frying works at Delhi," just outside Cincinnati, to observe how horse carcasses are hauled in, flayed and dissected, boiled, and turned into various products, including soap, candles, Prussian blue, fertilizer, and even scrap metal (removed from their hooves). Surprisingly, the employees, far from being society's misfits, are "good-looking young men" of "elegant bearing." Most of this article is stomach-wrenching in its gory grisliness.

"LATIN AND ANGLO-SAXON" (1880). Sketch. Hearn gives reasons why he believes that the French Canadians will resist better than Creoles the fate of being absorbed by Anglo-Saxons. Anglo-Saxons are not stronger or more intelligent than those with Latin blood, but they are more prolific. This sketch seems wrong-headed today.

LAVEAU, MARIE (1794?–1881). Voodoo queen. She was born in New Orleans, the natural daughter of Charles Laveau, a Creole planter, and Marguerite Carcantel, one of his mulatto slaves. Marie turned out to be part black, part white, and partly American Indian. She was a Roman Catholic, a free "fille de couleur," and possessed statuesque beauty, refined features, and curly hair. She married Jacques Paris, a free quadroon carpenter from Haiti, but he soon disappeared and was regarded as deceased. Marie Laveau became a hairdresser for well-to-do New Orleans women. From 1824 or so until his death in 1855, Christophe Duminy de Glapion, another Haitian quadroon, was her live-in companion; they had 15 children. By 1830 Laveau was a respected, and feared, voodoo queen. Her ceremonies combined elements of African and Caribbean voodoo and Catholic prayers, music, statuary, incense, and holy water. She hired female voodoo assistants, terrorized the opposition, bribed the authorities to ignore her felonious conduct, and reaped great financial rewards by inviting rich whites to participate in orgies, both lakeside and elsewhere. She obtained revealing gossip from informants and used it to pretend she was a mind-reading fortune-teller. She dazzled a judge to acquit a generous man's son of rape and blackmailed a New Orleans attorney to obtain advice and secrets from him. Her Maison Blanche was half-brothel and half–voodoo shrine. She offered a measure of comfort to parish prison inmates. In 1875 she retired and, according to one legend among many, never emerged. At this time a new Marie, called Marie II and most likely her daughter by Glapion, became the new voodoo queen. The New Orleans *Picayune* published old Marie's obituary (June 17, 1881) a day after her death.

Although legends contend that Marie Laveau never died but instead survived as a crow, dog, snake, or old street hag, it is assuredly true that she did know both Hearn and his friend George Washington Cable.* Hearn never attended her wild annual voodoo celebration, held on St. John's Eve, June 23, where Bayou St. John flows into Lake Pontchartrain. But he did interview her and Marie II, was impressed by the old woman's seemingly inexhaustible energy, received information also from the daughter, and provided details about Laveau in "New Orleans Superstitions" (*Harper's Weekly*, December 25, 1886). Adrien Emmanuel Rouquette,* a New Orleans priest who disliked Cable for his treatment of Creoles in his 1880 novel *The Grandissimes*, included the following Creole ditty in his *A Critical Dialogue between Aboo and Caboo on a New Book; or, A Grandissime Ascension* (1880): "Savan Missie' Kabri/ . . . Li té dansé Kongo / Avec Mari Lovo" (Wise Mr. Goat [the bearded Cable] . . . he danced the Congo with Marie Laveau). Hearn also knew Jean Montanet,* who was known as the King of Voudoo and was Laveau's occasional rival.

Bibliography: Cott; Raymond J. Martinez, *Mysterious Marie Laveau, Voodoo Queen and Folk Tales along the Mississippi* (New Orleans: Hope Publications, 1956); Robert Tallant, *Voodoo in New Orleans* (New York: Collier Books, 1962); Tinker; Edward Larocque Tinker, *Creole City: Its Past and Its People* (New York: Longmans, Green, 1953).

LEAVES FROM THE DIARY OF AN IMPRESSIONIST (1911). A posthumous collection of essays by Hearn, edited by Ferris Greenslet.* Eight were reprinted as part of Volume 1 of *The Writings of Lafcadio Hearn* (1922), under the rubrics "Floridian Reveries," "Creole Papers," and "Arabesques." A limited edition was issued in 1911. *See* Appendix for titles of individual entries.

Bibliography: Kunst.

"A LEGEND" (1881). Sketch. A plague spares females but kills all males except for one handsome man, who is as strong as an elephant. Untemptable women philosophers surround and protect him. Not allowed to exercise his mind, he looks only at beautiful things, hears only nice music, and is approached only by super-lovely females. He enjoys "a life . . . the angels might envy" for 50 years, then dies leaving 15,273 children and 91,638 grandchildren. The third generation has two million males but few females, "so great was the universal desire for males." By the tenth generation, males equal females in number. This "legend" is weakened by Hearn's anti-female crack that his nonpareil male is left alone 65 days a year so he would not be "talked to death." Moreover, is Hearn hinting that selective abortion was used to reduce his fictive female population? (Note: The elephant-man scored an impressive 1.02 conceptions per working day [or night].)

"A LEGEND OF LOVE" (1884). Tale. In a beautiful Moslem city are many Christians. May their bones be ground up and their names forgotten—with one exception. Her name is known only to "Him who never forgets." This well-born Christian maiden loved an impoverished Musselman. They could converse only through her lattices. Frustrated, both fell ill. He went temporarily insane and moved to Damascus to recover. She sent him money. They corresponded. He returned home, got sicker, asked to become a Christian, but died too soon and was buried among Moslems. His friend told the girl, who renounced Christianity, embraced Islam, and, dying, asked to be buried with her feet toward his, to rise facing him on Judgment Day. Hearn creates considerable irony by having the narrator be a loyal Moslem.

"A LEGEND OF RABBA" (1884). Legend. Rabbi Rabba and Rabbi Zira ask Bar-Hedia to interpret their identical dreams. Because Zira pays Bar-Hedia well, his dream is said to portend joy. Because Rabba pays nothing, his dream is said to portend misery, as is a second one, portending Rabba's wife's death. Things happen thus. When Rabba pays well for the interpretation of a third dream, Bar-Hedia explains it nicely. Later, Rabba finds Bar-Hedia's magic book, which says that all dreams are fulfilled according to the interpreter's interpretation. He curses Bar-Hedia, who runs off to Rome. Bar-Hedia plies his evil trade there and interprets the king's stingy treasurer's dream disastrously for the king, who orders Bar-Hedia to be torn into halves. Rabba's malediction worked. Hearn weakens the unity of this piece by adding an introductory paragraph explaining that Rabba created a speechless man out of dust.

"THE LEGEND OF SKOBELEFF" (1884). Editorial. The reminiscences of Skobeleff (Mikhail Dmitrievich Skobelev, 1843–1882), a Russian general, adds to his heroic stature. Did his speeches contribute to his puzzling death? A reporter with him during the Russo-Turkish War (1877–1878) wrote about him glowingly. Skobelev was a pro-peasant Slavophile opposed to imperialistic Russian aggrandizement. He sought to conquer Constantinople in the name of Christianity and wept when the armistice was declared. Worse was news that Austria was to control Bosnia and Herzegovina for German rule and that Turkey was to get control of Macedonia. In effect, these political reverses killed Skobelev. It is ironic that in 1884 Hearn was writing about religious and nationalistic tangles that are deeply troubling the world more than a century later. An early translation of Skobelev's 1881–1882 autobiography is *Die memoiren des Generals Skobelew . . .* (1883).

"THE LEGEND OF TCHI-NIU" (1887). Ghost story. To pay for his father's proper funeral, Tong-yong becomes a rich farmer's slave. He works hard for three years, gets sick, but is restored to health when touched by a plainly dressed, beautiful woman named Tchi, who gently orders him to wed her and pray with her. He works well. She stays at home weaving gloriously illustrated silks with nimble fingers for much silver. She buys Tong's freedom. They have a house, land, and happy servants. Tchi bears a son and devotes herself solely to him. He becomes precocious. Tong is joyous. One autumn night Tchi tells him that she is a goddess sent from heaven to aid him because of his filial devotion, then departs forever. The sleeping child remains. Golden dawn comes. Hearn cites his modified source: a tale in *Kan-ying-p'ien* (Book of Rewards and Punishments), attributed to the Chinese philosopher Lao-tseu.

Bibliography: Murray.

"THE LEGEND OF THE MONSTER MISFORTUNE" (1884). Tale. It is ages ago, when everything was better and gems and gold were plentiful. Ah, how musically the Yellow River flows. The king calls ministers and mandarins, tells them he read that Misfortune once stalked the land, and orders them to buy Misfortune. A god hears of this, walks like a man, and has a sow labeled Misfortune with him. A minister buys her for a million gold pieces and must feed her a bushel of needles daily. Then the supply of needles for the sow's food diminishes; unemployment, famine, and rebellion follow. Misfortune must be killed. With their axes and arrows failing, the people try to burn it up; but it waxes white hot, runs everywhere, and burns up everything, including the king. Hearn cites his source: an 1860 translation by Stanislas Julien (1797–1873) from a Chinese encyclopedia, the sources of which are Sanscrit texts.

"THE LION" (1884). Tale. Of four affectionate, Brahman-caste brothers, three study science deeply, whereas the fourth is idly intelligent. When they come upon the bleached bones of a lion, the three, despite warnings from the fourth, bring the lion to life again. The fourth intelligently climbs a tree and safely watches the lion devour his wise brothers.

"THE LITTLE RED KITTEN" (1879). Sketch. A red kitten, made tough by a varied diet, protects a little tawny kitten until it is killed by the movement of a rocking chair and tossed out. The red one seeks her sister but is killed by a fire engine.

"THE LOTUS OF FAITH; OR, THE FURNACE OF FIRE" (1884). Tale. The Bodhisattva, the Buddha-elect, is educated in the city of Benares. He sees a holy Buddha who has just perfected himself and to whom he offers a dish of rice. But flames open the ground, darkness comes, and the Bodhisattva and the Buddha stand on each side of a fiery abyss. To defeat the powers of evil, the Bodhisattva dutifully walks into the fire. The Buddha smiles; a lotus flower rises from the flames; and the Bodhisattva crosses safely and gives nourishment to the Buddha, who rises into the rosy air.

"LOUISIANA PEOPLE NOT GAY" (1879). Sketch. A Parisian says that Parisians are merry but that Louisianians are sad and cynical, despite their nice climate. An Englishman agrees, adding that mountain people, nearer the stars, are also happier.

LOWELL, PERCIVAL (1855–1916). Writer and astronomer. Lowell, a member of the distinguished New England Lowell family, was born in Boston, graduated from Harvard with a specialty in mathematics (1876), traveled in Europe and the Middle East, and returned to be an accountant in his grandfather's cotton mill and then in another mill. Having invested shrewdly, Lowell visited East Asia many times, and in the 1880s and 1890s he wrote several books about Korea and Japan. By 1894 Lowell was more interested in astronomy, especially in an ambition to prove the existence of canals on the planet Mars; to that end, he founded an observatory in Flagstaff, in the Arizona Territory. His theories regarding the evolution of intelligent life on Mars were presented in articles, in lectures, and in two books, *Mars* (1895) and *Mars as the Abode of Life* (1908), which were popular but were almost immediately discredited. In 1908 Lowell married Constance Savage Keith; the couple had no children. After Lowell's death at Flagstaff, his widow went to court to void his gift of $1 million to his observatory. By an odd coincidence, Ferris Greenslet,* who was an executive at Houghton Mifflin, the firm that published *The Writings of Lafcadio Hearn* (16 vols., 1922), and who wrote the general introduction to its first volume, also wrote *The Lowells and Their Seven Worlds* (1946), which includes an excellent biographical sketch of Percival Lowell.

Hearn read Lowell's masterpiece, *The Soul of the Far East* (1888), with intense pleasure. It probably helped him decide to go to Japan in 1890. In 1893 Hearn met Lowell in Kumamoto. He half-envied Lowell for the wealth that enabled him to travel six months a year in the Orient. In "The Japanese Smile"

(1893), an essay reappearing in *Glimpses of Unfamiliar Japan* (1894), Hearn calls *The Soul of the Far East* a work demonstrating "consummate genius." But Hearn waxed critical about Lowell's *Occult Japan; or, The Way of the Gods: An Esoteric Study of Japanese Personality and Possession* (1894), which Hearn judged to be an unworthy attempt to amuse American readers by ridiculing Japan's popular beliefs. In " 'Ultimate Questions,' " Hearn says that Lowell's *Mars* makes one wonder about interplanetary communication. Modern scholars praise Lowell for coming to clear conclusions about Japanese culture and religion even though such conclusions are based on limited observation, whereas the scholars more highly esteem Hearn for seeking to feel his way into Japanese experiences so as to be able to express the results for the elucidation of Western readers. Lowell, however, had one enormous advantage over Hearn: His knowledge of the Japanese language was phenomenal, whereas Hearn called the language "unspeakably difficult to learn" (letter to Bisland, 1890).

Bibliography: Cott; Dawson; Ferris Greenslet, *The Lowells and Their Seven Worlds* (Boston: Houghton Mifflin, 1946); Murray.

M

"A MAD ROMANTIC" (1884). Editorial. The subject is the French symbolist poet Gérard de Nerval (1808–1855; real name: Gérard Labrunie). Théophile Gautier wrote about Nerval's youth, whose works bear comparison to those of Edgar Allan Poe. Nerval called his women "filles du feu." He translated Johann von Wolfgang Goethe's *Faust* brilliantly. His insanity, of which he was aware, made his world seem dreamy. Hearn delights in summarizing some of Nerval's most bizarre plots: A wine bottle breaks and becomes a nude woman in a pool of blood; a felon's severed hand runs through the streets and up walls; and more. Tolerated in the Middle East as deranged, Nerval traveled, observed, and wrote much there; he also bought and married an Abyssinian slave (who beat him and left him). Home again, he sold more articles, grew worse, and borrowed from friends "who loved him for the ruined beauty of his mind and the exceeding goodness of his heart." After living in the Orient, he gradually found life in Paris to be impossible, and he hanged himself. Hearn was unhealthily attracted to Nerval.

"THE MAGICAL WORDS" (1884). Rune. Wainamoinen, an old magician, wants to woo the virgin daughter of Louhi the witch. To do so he builds a warship, but to make its prow he needs three magic words. An old shepherd tells him to find them in birds. He slaughters not only birds but animals too; finding no words in them, however, he proceeds to Tuonela, where the daughters of the queen of death refuse to help any living man. He lies that weapons, fire, water have killed him. No use. When he explains his need of words to complete his prow, they sail him over their river, give him nourishment the dead take, and let him sleep. Children of death make a net to catch him, but his unsleeping magic garments turn him into a rolling stone, then an iron viper that severs the net. Outside again and alive, Wainamoinen goes to his brother, the smithy Ilmarinnen, for iron shoes with which to walk safely over otherwise deadly needles, swords, and axes to the earth-giant, Kalewa, for help with the magic words. Wainamoinen finds only the giant's grave. He tears out whole trees growing from the corpse and thrusts a mighty steel and iron staff into its mouth. After Kalewa fails to bite the staff, Wainamoinen enters the giant's stomach, builds a big fire there, ignores the giant's curses, and says he will not leave until Kalewa sings the three magic words. Kalewa sings unceasingly for days and nights, then finally emits the three magic words. Satisfied, Wainamoinen departs. Kalewa dies again into the loving earth's embrace. And the forests reweave knotted nets over the grave.

"THE MAKING OF TILOTTAMA" (1884). Tale. Sounda and Oupasounda, evil twin brothers, resolve to dominate the three worlds. To gain ability, they practice austerity for some years and then ask Brahma for the arts of magic and war, for beauty and strength, and for immortality. Brahma gives them all but immortality and warns them that only they can harm each other. They go and sin excessively, and conquer both sea and earth. The holy ones of the air appeal to Brahma for succor. He summons Viswakarman to create a uniquely wondrous woman. He makes Tilottama out of vapors, sunbeams, and a million priceless things. Brahma orders her to visit Sounda and Oupasounda. She distracts them from wicked females, whereupon they fight over her and kill each other. In gratitude, Brahma grants Tilottama's request to live among the splendors of the blessed. Hearn weakens this legend in two ways. He bewilders the reader by an infusion of almost countless Indian names from the *Mahabharata*. And he has Tilottama pause in her mission to pass by "the seven orders of the rishis" and by mirror-like magic make them see her, despite their averted gaze, and thus turn into four-faced gods with a thousand eyes each.

"MANUFACTURING INTERESTS AND ROWDYISM" (1880). Editorial. In an *Item* column, Hearn agrees with a *Times-Democrat* article saying that an increase in manufacturing in New Orleans would help eliminate idleness and crime there. However, he doubts that the city's bullies, bums, rowdies, and "aristocratic rascals" would accept any honorable employment or, if they did, be able to learn a job and be productive. Still, if the city were a manufacturing center, businessmen would become influential enough to force civic leaders and the police to guarantee public safety.

"MARTINIQUE SKETCHES ." *See Two Years in the French West Indies.*

MATAS, RUDOLPH (1860–1957). Physician. He was born on a plantation near Bonnet Carré, Louisiana. His father, a Creole, was a pharmacist and a physician who lived with his wife and children in France, Texas, Mexico, Spain, and finally New Orleans, Louisiana. Matas grew up speaking English, Spanish, and French. He graduated from St. John's Collegiate Institute in Matamoros, Mexico (1877), and studied medicine at the University of Louisiana (now Tulane University) until 1880. In 1879 he clerked and translated in Cuba for the Yellow Fever Commission. While there, he associated with Dr. Carlos M. Sternberg, who in 1881 theorized that the *Aedes aegyptii* mosquito transmitted yellow fever. Dr. Matas published his translation of Sternberg's study in the *New Orleans Medical and Surgical Journal* (1882), long before the American medical team in Cuba validated his discovery. Matas's professional career was astounding. He was a journal editor, physician, surgeon, anatomist, and professor at the Tulane Medical School, and he became a pioneer in various kinds of anesthesia and surgical procedures, notably vascular operations to repair aneurysms (beginning in 1888). During World War I, Matas served as a major specializing in treating fractures and wounds. He was a member, often as an officer, of many professional associations. Matas's wife was Adrienne Goslee, a widowed mother of two; Matas had no children with her.

Matas, who read voraciously, admired Hearn's columns in the New Orleans *Times-Democrat*; so he arranged through Charles Whitney, a reporter for that newspaper, to meet Hearn. Matas provided Hearn with aspects of Arabian medical practice, called him "Leocadio," and was addressed in turn as "El Beithar ben Matas" and "Rudolpho." During strolls through the Spanish Quarter of New Orleans and at fine restaurants there, Hearn poured out uniquely frank reminiscences to Matas, whom he called an ideal brother, who was intrigued by the almost incredible contradictions in Hearn's personality and who defined him as literary genius, unconventional hater, victim of imagined persecutions, and tender-hearted sensualist. The physician diagnosed his eccentric patient as morbid and abnormal. Mrs. Matas shared Creole recipes and herbal nostrums with Hearn. When Hearn left in 1887 for Martinique, he stored his books with Matas and ignored Matas's persistent warnings about the consequences of contracting syphilis in Martinique. When Hearn was writing *Chita*, Matas helped him with some of the colloquial dialogue and was the model for Chita's beautifully limned father. Hearn dedicated *Chita* to "Dr. Rodolfo Matas." Matas later dedicated a room to the memory of Hearn in the medical school of Tulane University. Matas's collection also became the foundation of the Lafcadio Hearn Room and Hearn Collection in Tulane's Howard-Tilton Memorial Library.

Bibliography: Isadore Cohn and Hermann B. Deutsch, *Rudolph Matas: A Biography of One of the Great Pioneers in Surgery* (Garden City, N.Y.: Doubleday, 1960); Cott; Dawson; Albert Mordell, "Lafcadio Hearn and Dr. Rudolph Matas," *Today's Japan* 6 (March 1961): 61–68; Stevenson; Tinker.

"MDCCCLIII" (1882). Sketch. The dead heat is oppressive. A funeral bell sounds, indicating hundreds of deaths. The narrator finds himself in a place of death. A black-robed Sister approaches. With sweet voice and cool hand she leads him past tomb-like beds through darkness to light. Asked if he is afraid, he is told he cannot reclaim "her," as he would like, but should leave her to God. Outside again, he is aware of faith, rekindled but briefly. When death approaches and memories fade, she—that Sister of Charity, now deceased herself—will take his hand and ask again if he is afraid.

Bibliography: Kunst.

"A MEMORY OF TWO FANNIES" (1884). Editorial. Fanny Ellsler was a dancer whose beauty and grace seemed almost immortal. "The frosts of age never touched her looks." She was adored from a distance by an Italian army captain named Cerrito. His only desire was that he and his wife would have a daughter who might learn to dance as well as Fanny Ellsler. They did. Named after Fanny Ellsler, Fanny Cerrito became a brilliant dancer who was celebrated throughout Europe. At age 30, however, she had an accident, not fatal, hardly minor even; but it ended her career. Surely Hearn might have chosen a better title for this piece. Fanny Ellsler (1810–1884) was a celebrated Austrian ballerina who toured in the United States triumphantly (1840–1842) and retired in 1851; Théophile Gautier called her "the Spaniard from the North."

"METEMPSYCHOSIS" (1880). Sketch. A stranger in a Creole house in New Orleans describes the cosmos of atoms living and reliving events in an endless cycle. A doctor and one other character mainly listen.

"MEXICAN COINS" (1879). Sketch. A stranger returns from backward Mexico with many coins. He shows a listener one with an eagle strangling a serpent. He opines that lawless Mexico is serpent-like. He turns to show a unique "Thing" from Mexico, but the listener has departed.

"A MEXICAN'S GRATITUDE" (1880). Sketch. A Mexican crew leaves a fever-stricken sailor ashore at Algiers, a New Orleans suburb. A girl and her mother nurse the fellow back to health, and he thanks them by means of gestures and then departs. Years later he sees the girl, married and vacationing in Montezuma, Mexico, and gives her flowers and fruits that are perfumed as passionately as his unspoken gratitude.

"MIGRATIONS OF THE HUMAN RACE" (1878). Editorial. Indubitably, "a mighty gulf stream in the sea of human life" has propelled people ever westward. Indians have gone into Egypt. African evidence permeates Pacific Ocean islands. But westward migrations recoil eastward again, and the East gets weaker while the West remains stronger. Eventually, "American Aryans" may go west right around the earth.

"MME. SIDNEY AUGUSTINE" (1873). Cincinnati news article. On May 21, 1873, Madame Sidney Augustine, a fortune-telling abortionist, is jailed. Hattie Sperling, recovering in the hospital after undergoing Mme. Augustine's handiwork, had to toil 10 weeks for her to earn the $25 fee. She will testify against the evil creature, about whose house and activities therein is much gossip from neighbors. "The Clairvoyant Abortionist" continues Mme. Augustine's story.

"THE MOCKERS" (1884). Legend. Rabbi Simon ben Yochai has been condemned to die because he has been critical of the Romans. So he and his son hide out in a cave for 12 years. Elijah tells the two that the Roman emperor has died and they are safe. Emerging, they mock the materialism of people outside. So the Holy One sentences them back to the cave for another year. Rabbi Simon emerges, treats his ulcers with water from the land of Tiberias, and announces that he will purify Tiberias in gratitude. Mockers deride him. Simon scatters chopped-up lupines on the land of Tiberias, and up come corpses for proper burial. A doubting Samaritan buries a dirty body where Simon had already been, scoffs at Simon for not causing it to rise, but receives Simon's fatal rejoinder. Another mocker jeers from a tower. Simon replies, and man and tower crumble into smoke.

"THE MONDAY NIGHT MURDER" (1874). Cincinnati news article. Hearn follows up his "Assassination" news article by reporting that a mulatto named Joe Brooks was arrested on suspicion of murdering Mary Lee. Evidence against him included his boot tracks, blood on a sleeve of his coat, and a bloody razor he was said to have borrowed. In addition, he recently had a racially motivated argument with Mary Lee's fiancé. In this hasty article, Hearn spells three names given in "Assassination" differently.

MONTANET, JEAN (c. 1787–1885). Voodoo king, a.k.a. Doctor Jean, Jean Bayou, Jean Grisgris, Hoodoo John, Jean Macaque, Jean La Ficelle, Jean Latanié, Jean Racine, and Voudoo John. He was born in Senegal, Africa, and said his father was a Bambara prince. While very young, Montanet was kidnapped by Spanish slave traders, shipped to Cuba, taught the art of excellent cooking, and freed by his owner. After sailing extensively as a cook on a Spanish ship, he settled in New Orleans, where he handled cotton bales, began to exert occult powers over other black workers, gained renown as a fortune-teller, and amassed enough money to buy property on Bayou Road and build a house on it. Here he expanded his lucrative practice to include Creole medicine. Whites and blacks, and men and women all flocked to him, and they paid $10 to $20 for herbal cures and poultices, hair-growing ointments, and advice concerning family squabbles, gambling, love affairs, and how to work revenge on enemies. The stage effects in Montanet's office included bones, candles, cards, shells, string, the tusk of an elephant, and a picture of the Virgin Mary. His nonprofessional accoutrements included a saddle horse, a Mexican saddle, a carriage and pair, expensive claret, and 15 wives—legitimate, he averred, according to African rituals. He even had one white wife. He sired countless children. He was charitable to the poor and sick. He was a partner in several ventures and was frequently cheated. He lost even more money by playing the lottery. Although worth $50,000 at one time, he was impoverished at last and died destitute in the home of the daughter he had by his white wife. He was always held in reverence by black people when they saw Hoodoo John come by with his "elephant's toof [sic]." At one time Montanet was considered a potent rival of Marie Laveau,* the reigning voodoo queen of New Orleans. Hearn met both Montanet and Laveau. When Montanet died in New Orleans, Hearn wrote an extended obituary and biographical tribute titled "The Last of the Voudoos" (*Harper's Weekly*, November 7, 1885).

Bibliography: Cott; Robert Tallant, *Voodoo in New Orleans* (New York: Collier Books, 1962).

"A MORNING IN THE POLICE COURT" (1877).

Cincinnati news article. Hearn describes the police court, with judge, prosecutor, clerk, deputies, court officers, attorneys, reporters, and spectators. At 8:30 A.M. "an odorous, tattered, ill-favored, unhappy throng" of prisoners is marched in and seated on a bench. This morning, the accused are two teen-aged prostitutes, two drunks, a woman who threw a brick at someone, a slanderer, and a vagrant. Justice in this crowded court depends on the experience and wisdom of the judge, who gives each case about 10 minutes. Hearn quotes the muddled testimony of two people and concludes that it would have been better if these unfortunates, displaying ignorance, sin, shame, vice, evil, deceit, and treachery, were born as monkeys and put in a zoo, fed on peanuts and crackers, and made to hop about for the amusement of spectators. Does God indeed love us all?

"A MOTHERLY MURDER" (1874).

Cincinnati news article. Hearn calls this "the saddest" and "most piteous" story he has covered in his "somewhat extended reportorial experience." In their rented house, Julia A. Snell Perkins, age 28 and married for five years, quarreled beginning Tuesday night, September 29, 1874, with her husband, Charles L. Perkins, a prosperous saddlery-firm businessman. Joseph Claire, a visiting saddle-tree manufacturer, was involved. Although Julia had tried to kill Clara, the Perkinses' baby, age 2, with a razor in the night, she promised not to do so and agreed to go visit friends the next day; so the men left for a while. Julia locked the house, drank paregoric, turned on the gas, and fatally gashed Clara's throat with broken glass. Charles returned home, found the house locked, and summoned his landlord, who forced an entrance. Julia had cut her own throat but was alive. Admitting all to the coroner and his empaneled jury, she said she wanted to die and had not wished to leave the child behind. Although no one provided details, Joseph Claire was evidently involved. Julia was charged with murder and sent, temporarily, to a hospital under a suicide watch. "A Motherly Murder" is the first of a series of four articles dealing with the Perkinses, dated October 1–6, 1874. The others are "The Perkins Tragedy," "Wife and Mistress," and "The Perkins Horror."

"MR. CABLE'S *DR. SEVIER*" (1884). Review. Hearn lauds his friend George Washington Cable,* author of *Dr. Sevier* (1884), for combining in his novel fine word pictures of Louisiana, specifically New Orleans scenery, with suggestions as to how one can make a success of oneself. He quotes passages of special beauty, says that the novel is more effective than *The Grandissimes* (1880), also by Cable, but adds that both works have weaknesses—specifically in handling dialect. Still, Hearn concludes that *Dr. Sevier* is "one of the most remarkable of recent American literary productions."

"MY GUARDIAN ANGEL" (1906). Autobiographical essay. Hearn says he was adopted by a Roman Catholic woman (*see* Brenane, Sarah Holmes) who taught him some prayers, gave him a painting of Virgin and Child (who he thought were his mother, "almost completely forgotten," and himself), and made him speak of Father, Son, and Holy Ghost. Someone's explanation of "ghost" scared him. Cousin Jane, who used to visit the family in the winter, seemed to Hearn to represent Sorrow. One morning she told him to behave and please God. When he wondered who God was, she terrified him by telling him that God made everyone, everything, Heaven and Hell, and could send him to burn in Hell forever. Believing this, he hated her for making him irreparably unhappy. When she left, he hoped she would die. The next summer Hearn, then age 5, went to the third floor, perhaps for a toy, and saw Cousin Jane robed in black. Although he called her name, she walked past him into a bedroom. She wheeled, had no face, and vanished. The next winter Jane returned, caressed the timid, silent Hearn, took him for a walk, smiled, and bought him toys. They went home at twilight, her smiles ceased, and he felt a chill. The next morning she did not leave her bed; indeed, she had contracted consumption and soon died. Hearn wondered if she knew he hated her and wanted her dead. She had told him there were no such things as ghosts and goblins. A lie! Would she now, like other dead people, be transformed by death and seek revenge? Even though she bequeathed him her well-stocked library, he could never reproach himself for despising her. Her terrible words years ago destroyed the beautiful world for him. Many of the personal events recalled in this essay found their way into several of Hearn's later, more imaginative pieces. It is likely that Hearn's title was inspired by *The Guardian Angel* (1867) by Oliver Wendell Holmes (1809–1894). Holmes's novel, though happier, theorizes that one body can house multiple personalities; Hearn would probably agree.

Bibliography: Bisland.

N

"A NAME IN THE PLAZA" (1885). Revery. Fancying ineffable connections with his more primitive life forms, Hearn writes on June 3, 18—, of wandering on his last day in Florida and coming upon a monument to "Our Dead" in the Saint Augustine Plaza. One alien name stands out. "[M]nemonic necromancy" fails to identify its owner. That night he dreams of a tree bending leafy stems away from the sun toward him. Did it grow from another's flesh, another's blood? He associates it with the "blond name," and "the story of the dead" is clarified.

"THE NAME ON THE STONE" (1880). Sketch. She whispers to the narrator that he will return to her because of unforgettable love. After years, he does so one windy, cloudy night. She leads him to a cemetery and tells him not to read the name on a certain gravestone. But he does, and shrieks. Her phantom kisses him and tells him that love is stronger than death.

NAMES, NICKNAMES, AND PEN NAMES, HEARN'S. At St. Cuthbert's College, Hearn was called "Paddy" and "Jack," and he signed himself "P. L. Hearn." He signed letters to his Cincinnati friend Henry Watkin* "The Raven," because of his love of the works of Edgar Allan Poe. He signed himself "Hearny" in some personal letters. For some Cincinnati *Commercial* pieces he called himself "Ozias Midwinter." New Orleans typesetters called him "Old Semi-Colon" because of his almost obsessive use of semicolons, as well as other punctuation marks. Minor pieces, perhaps by Hearn, were signed "Fiat Lux." He was introduced to Japanese students as "Herun-san." Other Japanese called him "Sensei" (Master). His legally adopted Japanese name was Yakumo ("The Place of the Issuing of Clouds") Koizumi.

"NATALIKA" (1884). Tale. Amid ruins, a temple inscription says that only one's virtue accompanies one beyond the grave. After a thousand years, a traveler there sees a black-granite statue of Natalika, a beautiful princess. Here is her story. Khalif Oualed's Arab horsemen defeat Dir-Rajah of Sindh, kill his soldiers, kill him, and capture his daughter, Natalika. Kassim, the Khalif's lieutenant, grabs her for Oualed. Seeing her, Oualed proposes to make her his favorite wife, but she only weeps and tells him that Kassim did her "grievous wrong." Oualed sends orders for Kassim to proceed to Bassora, where he is strangled and his head is carried to Oualed. When he shows it to Natalika, she laughs, says that Kassim was innocent but she wanted him dead as vengeance against his successful war against her people, and stabs herself to death. Her betrothed, Udayah-Rajah, lays waste to Oualed's lands; but, missing her dreadfully, he becomes a mendicant, orders her statue to be made, dies, and is buried beneath it. Out of nearby roses of stone comes perfume after a thousand years.

"A NEW POMPEII" (1885). Editorial. Hearn is delighted that the predictions by the linguist François Lenormant (1837–1883) have proved accurate. Excavations in Taranto, Italy, are revealing ancient Tarentum to be "a Roman city seated upon the corpse of a Greek city"—and with glorious artifacts and art objects.

NEWS ARTICLES. While in Cincinnati, Ohio, Hearn wrote many newspaper articles for the Cincinnati *Enquirer* (1872–1875) and the Cincinnati *Commercial* (1875–1878). They cover a variety of subjects, from grossly unpleasant to nauseatingly horrifying. Hearn resolutely visited, closely observed, and graphically described activities in slaughter houses, hospitals, police courts, houses of prostitution and drug dens, murder and execution scenes, and dreary slums. He alludes to himself in several pieces as "an ENQUIRER reporter" and thereafter "the reporter." Some 51 of these gruesome news articles may be found, briefly considered, under their individual titles in this volume. They occasionally reveal hasty composition and an ingrained bitter irony, sometimes lack an aesthetically pleasing structure, but are unforgettably gripping with touches of poetic phrasing and an undercurrent of numbing sorrow. All are uncompromisingly honest. Many of Hearn's other news articles have been collected. Some of the best, and many others, may be found in Edward Larocque Tinker, *Lafcadio Hearn's American Days* (New York: Dodd, Mead, 1924); Lafcadio Hearn, *An American Miscellany*, ed. Albert Mordell (New York: Dodd, Mead, 1924); and Lafcadio Hearn, *Occidental Gleanings*, ed. Albert Mordell (New York: Dodd, Mead, 1925). Exigencies of space prevent consideration of many of these pieces in detail. *See* "Newspaper publications."

Bibliography: Cott; Murray; *Period of the Gruesome: Selected Cincinnati Journalism of Lafcadio Hearn*, ed. Jo Christopher Hughes (Lanham, Md.: University Press of America, 1990); Stevenson; Tinker.

NEWSPAPER PUBLICATIONS. From 1872 to 1894 Hearn published a staggering number of items of various sorts in several newspapers. Most, however, have never been collected and reprinted. Totals, perhaps not quite complete, are nevertheless almost unbelievable. While he was in Cincinnati, Hearn wrote at least 135 pieces for the Cincinnati *Enquirer* (1872–1875) and then 200 for the Cincinnati *Commercial* (1875–1878). Moving to New Orleans, he wrote for two newspapers—31 pieces for the New Orleans *Democrat* (1878–1881) and 333 for the New Orleans *Item* (1878–1881). For some of his *Item* pieces, Hearn drew his own cartoons. After the New Orleans *Times* merged in 1882 with the *Democrat* to become the New Orleans *Times-Democrat*, Hearn wrote 336 for it (1882–1894). One item ("The Creole Doctor") found a place in the *New York Tribune* (1886). Once in Japan, Hearn had occasion to publish five newspaper pieces in the *Japan Mail* (Yokohama, 1891–1894) and 48 in the *Kobe Chronicle* (1894). A small percentage of this total, over 1,089 contributions, was reissued as parts of books both before and after his death. Most, however, have never been collected and reprinted—nor are they likely ever to be. One must respect Hearn, who, often while impoverished and as often busy writing less ephemeral items, averaged almost a journalistic piece a week for almost a quarter of a century. *See* "News Articles."

   Bibliography: Tinker.

NICKNAMES. *See* Names, Nicknames, and Pen Names, Hearn's.

"THE NIGHT OF ALL SAINTS" (1879). Sketch. One moonlit night the West Wind stifles the cemetery flowers' perfume, but the Wind of the South revives it. The perfume of dead flowers resembles the immortal good deeds of the dead.

"NORODOM THE LAST" (1885). Editorial. Hearn is critical of France for recently deposing King Norodom of Cambodia, to increase its power in Indo-China. He goes on to praise Cambodia's illustrious long history and its jungle-hidden archaeological splendors, especially "Ongkor-Wat." Norodom (1834–1904) was king from 1854 until his death but placed his country under French control in 1863.

"A NOVEL LITERARY ENTERPRISE" (1881). Editorial. Hearn highly praises the forthcoming *Histoire Universelle* being edited by Marius Fontaine in sixteen 500-page volumes. It is to be "ethnological, climatological, and geological," will reflect the philosophy of Hippolyte Taine, will be both compact and thoroughly informative, and will show how science can be applied to history. The first volume, *L'Inde Vedic*, now available, is admirably thorough. Hearn naively implies that these works will never need to be supplanted.

NOVELS BASED ON HEARN'S LIFE. Roger Pulvers, *The Dream of Lafcadio Hearn* (n.p.; translated into Japanese, 2000); Dennis Rose, *Lafcadio Hearn: His Sun Was Dark* (Lewes, Sussex: Book Guild, 1987); Harry E. Wedeck, *Mortal Hunger: A Novel Based on the Life of Lafcadio Hearn* (New York: Sheridan, 1947).

O

"OLD-FASHIONED HOUSES" (1881). Sketch. Most old New Orleans residences are now unaffordably palatial unless converted into boardinghouses. New houses built like big old ones—for example, double cottages—are unlivable because they lack privacy.

"THE ONE PILL-BOX" (1881). Sketch. The yellow plague burns and silences the land. Even the stubborn English mill-master succumbs, lies ill with fever, and sees his past in shadowy images. He imagines difficult problems with lumber and is troubled by dancing numbers and then a tiny pillbox on the nearby table. It becomes three, multiplies, doubles to 162. He seems to be in a sun-baked cemetery, with dark wall space reserved for him. Such fatigue. Can he take a gimlet to bore a hole for sunlight, for outside voices? Now there are 366 pillboxes. Because it is leap year? He breathes commercial thoughts into the boxes, and up they float. The sick room door opens and closes. The boxes disappear. Night comes. He cannot speak. The lamp shines on a solitary pillbox.

"THE ONEIDA COMMUNITY'S ANNOUNCEMENT" (1879). Editorial. Leaders of the Oneida social experiment have abandoned "the practice of complex marriages and 'stirpiculture' " (specialty breeding and rearing). It is rare for a religious sect to quit its practices voluntarily. The Oneida people were in no real danger. Some preachers and journalists have inveighed against them, but others predicted the movement's demise with its founder's. Perhaps adverse public sentiment is causing its collapse. Next, property will be divided, the communist members will educate their children, and the farming combine will break up into small properties. Hearn hopes that the Oneida experiment will inspire eugenists to take steps to eliminate "physically diseased or morally deformed" children.

"OPIUM AND MORPHIA" (1875). Cincinnati news article. Last spring Jewish women marched and prayed to end alcohol consumption. They should work to stop the opium trade. Everywhere you can recognize "opium-slaves" by their faded skin and glittering eyes. They suffer depression, feel the "incubus," rarely recover, and are usually buried without an inquest. Hearn provides details as to drug sources (China, India, Smyrna), stockpiles (7,500 pounds in New York City), overbooked legal morphia merchants (in Philadelphia), price (opium at $775 per pound), favorite method of use (needle injection), and legal dispensers (physicians and druggists). Last week "a reporter" interviewed 13 wholesale druggists in Cincinnati and learned that they dispense 4,310 pounds of opium and 11,250 ounces of morphia annually, sell both drugs at cost to retailers, and would support a law against the drugs' nonmedicinal uses. Calling such addiction a disease, Hearn identifies types of addicts, ranging from high-society ladies and clergymen to "demi-mondes" and sorrowful men seeking temporary bliss by means of monumental overdoses. He compares drug addicts and "slaves to rum," and he finds the former to be in a tighter grip but less prone to violence.

"THE OPIUM HABIT" (1876). Cincinnati news article. Interviewing physicians, druggists, patrolmen, and addicts, Hearn learned the following: Opium is used mostly by Chinese immigrants, whereas morphine is "eaten" by more varied types. Some doctors encourage their patients to dose themselves with morphine as a painkiller, and they become addicts. Prostitutes use morphine, and many women take drugs, including arsenic and belladonna, to enhance their beauty. Addicts need ever-bigger doses. Drug dealers make fluctuating profits. Hearn presents anecdotal evidence of advanced addiction, quantities and prices, preference by Chinese for damp opium, moderate popularity of hasheesh, effects of arsenic, extensive use by women of all classes, and reticence of Chinese consumers. Non-addicted Chinese are ashamed of Chinese addicts, who hide their "opium dens" behind respectable businesses, such as laundries and grocery and tea stores. Hearn describes the typical den: addicts lying on bare floors with heads on bundles, lamps, weird shadows, infernal smoke, foreign odors. He gives names and addresses of dens and tells how he visited them with two friendly policemen, inspected opium pipes, and watched as Sam Wah obligingly demonstrated by lying down on a laundry table, expertly preparing his accoutrements, lighting up, and inhaling and exhaling thrice. To his "Ah!—smokee!—nicee!," one policeman smilingly replied, "Makee sickee."

OUT OF THE EAST: REVERIES AND STUDIES IN NEW JAPAN (1895). Collection of 11 essays, five of which had been previously published. Hearn dedicated the book to Nishida Sentarō, his friend and companion in Izumo. Hearn wrote to Basil Hall Chamberlain* (March 1895) that the title, *Out of the East*, was suggested from "Ex Oriente lux," the Oriental Society's motto;

he rejected these possible titles: "The Far East," "Most Eastern East," and "Out of the Uttermost East."

"The Dream of a Summer Day" (1894): Hearn leaves a hotel called the House of Urashima and is taken by *jinrikisha* along the coast partway to a new residence. While riding through nice scenery, he muses on the story of a fisher-boy named Urishama, living fourteen hundred years ago. Urishama caught and released a sacred tortoise and for reward was allowed to marry the Sea God's beautiful daughter. He returned home only to find his family graves, including his own, all filled in some four hundred years ago. Violating a promise to his wife, he undid the strings of a box she gave him that would have safely guided him back to her, and fell dead. Hearn also recalls the story of a couple finding the fountain of youth. Although the husband drank only enough to get peppy, his wife drank excessively and turned into a baby, which the husband took home, thinking "melancholy thoughts." Along the way Hearn sees telegraph wires, evidence of unattractive modernism. In real life, part of Hearn's journey was from Nagasaki to Kumamoto in 1891. "The Dream of a Summer Day" was one of five essays Hearn published in the *Japan Daily Mail* (July 28, 1894).

"With Kyūshū Students": Hearn finds Kumamoto students to be older, and more plain and direct, than his Izumo students were. The town of Kumamoto is "vast, straggling, dull, unsightly," with no distracting sights. Students have an indefinable "Kyūshū 'tone.' " Call them hard, rugged, outwardly impassive. Their "inner . . . individuality," however, comes out in written compositions, which evince an "absence of . . . false shyness." Examples: When asked about what one remembers longest, two students wrote about the death of parents. When asked about their first day at school, two wrote of loneliness, another of being challenged to become scholarly. Older students, suffering under harsher regulations, wrote about strict masters; others wrote of homesickness, fears, naughtiness, joys. For a test in summer 1893, Hearn asked what is everlasting in literature. Answers concerned truth, patriotism, filial devotion, goodness over evil, reason, noble action, and great teachings. Hearn evoked good oral discussions by recounting Greek myths, "Rappaccini's Daughter" by Nathaniel Hawthorne, and Edgar Allan Poe's "Silence." The students dismissed Mary Shelley's "Frankenstein" as mere Western horror. Plots involving Admeteus, Alcestis, Hercules, and characters in Sir Thomas Malory's "Morte d'Arthur" provoked anti-Christian and anti-Western responses. At recess, one student requested a difficult subject and then proceeded to wonder why "men" have to be born, eat, drink, work and rest, are happy and unhappy, have families, grow old, die, and leave nothing but bones. One mentions the high, wide sky. They talk about dragonflies. Hearn ends this essay by describing an old professor of Chinese in the school. He was a samurai, was jailed when the feudal system ended, but is now revered for teaching the "wisdom of the Chinese sages" about loyalty, honor, and manliness. He visits Hearn, brings gifts, and comports himself with genuine humility. (In "Jiujutsu," the old professor is called Akizuki of Aidzu.)

"At Hakata" (1894): One autumn day Hearn travels to Hakata by *jinrikisha* past boring scenery. Vital greenery appears. Its meaning has "evolved by pain." The desire to know, however, may have created the power to do so. In Hakata is a huge seated Buddha, being built all of mirrors. Ghostly values are ascribed to mirrors. Can one catch a glimpse of the past in a mirror? This reminds Hearn of the story of a man in Matsuyama who gave his wife a mirror. Never having seen one before, she asks him whose smiling face is in it. He laughs, tells her it is hers, and makes her feel ashamed. Dying, she gives the mirror to their daughter and tells the child she will see her mother in it. When asked, the child tells her father the image is her mother. He scorns her. Hearn feels that the child's "innocence . . . was nearer to the eternal truth than the feeling of the father," that "[o]ne are we all—and yet many, because each is a world of ghosts," that "[e]ach of us is truly a mirror, imaging something of the universe— reflecting also the reflection of ourselves," and, finally, that death will melt us all into Eastern rest. In "At Hakata," Hearn's vacillation between one thought and its opposite is perhaps revealed by no fewer than 21 appearances of the words "but" and "yet."

"Of the Eternal Feminine" (1893): Foreign observers, wrongly judging the Japanese as childish or materialistic, are unaware that their nature is rooted in "ancestral habits" and that their conservative minds are rarely influenced by Western ways. Their love of parents, who arrange their children's marriages, makes it impossible for them to understand, for example, British novels featuring love and marriage, actions involving which, if ignoring filial piety, they would regard as indecent. Japanese males, who dominate society, know about passionate love but habitually reserve it for dancing girls. Japanese men are dutiful, first to emperor and then to parents. They rarely speak to an outsider about their wives and children, and even more rarely do they show them. If invited to dinner, the outsider will be served by the host's wife and should treat her with quiet respect. Daughters may entertain the guest with music. Any gallantry by the guest would be regarded as grossly rude. Japanese etiquette is puzzling: Talk about family is "barbarous"; husband and wife do not walk side by side; words of endearment, embraces, and kisses are absent in Japanese daily life and therefore in Japanese literature. Understanding Japan results in re-seeing Occidental culture, especially its veneration of woman as unattainable, incomprehensible, divine. Japanese nouns have no gender, cannot be personified, are rarely used in metaphors. Hearn had trouble explicating to his students the process of calling a day beautiful, feminizing it as a girl, and calling her beautiful. Critics are wrong to contend that Shintō and Buddhism oppose women's rights. Those religions, as evidenced by shrines, esteem "the memory of woman as wife and mother." The ancient Hebrew faith and "monkish Christianity" have treated women worse. True, Buddhism and early Christianity warn of the tempting loveliness of females, and Paul accords "social and spiritual supremacy to the man." But Western culture, a complex mix, esteems human beauty, includes worship of the Virgin Mary, exalts chivalry, idealizes sensuousness, and anthropomorphizes nature into something maternal and aesthetically proportioned—all in ways alien to Eastern culture. Westerners masculinize only the grim, forceful aspects of nature, contrasting them with the overwhelming, more acceptable "witchcraft" of "a feminine pantheism." Hearn asks whether Japanese art may not contain elements unregistered in Occidental forms. Its nature is neuter and is reality- and not fantasy-based. Japanese drawings of insects and fish show their shapes and motions exquisitely. Simply stroked Japanese drawings of flowers are superior to laborious English and German efforts, as French artists and critics, alone among Westerners, have begun to sense. The Japanese reveal their aesthetic tendencies in the way they position and plant trees, place art objects and arrange flowers in family alcoves, obtain uniquely irregular stones and place them in gardens, and design and place *fusuma* (sliding screens of opaque paper) in homes. Hearn views patterned regularities in Western homes as a mechanical, ugly, "horrible vulgarism." Buddhism teaches that one is wise to recognize that "nothingness is law."

Hearn's friend Basil Hall Chamberlain* held Hearn's "Of the Eternal Feminine" in very high regard. In it, Hearn reveals many of his prejudices—against Christianity, Occidental mechanization and standardization, and conservative Euro-American art. He also over-stresses his only semi-rational acceptance of most things Japanese and, incidentally, would have his readers forget his former gross sensuality, as evidenced in his behavior in Cincinnati, New Orleans, Martinique, and elsewhere. Hearn would likely disapprove of the current habit of politically correct meteorologists who assign a female name to every other hurricane sweeping westward from his beloved French West Indies.

"Bits of Life and Death": This piece is in diary form, with dates from July 25 to December 29. In one week Hearn's well is cleaned and blessed, firemen hose down his roof to prevent fire, and children ask for money for their Jizō festival. Next Hearn visits his neighbor, a dyer of silk and cotton fabrics. The man's garden and Buddhist chapel are delightful. He tells about robbers who believed an absent dyer's truth-telling Buddhist wife and stole only what she said her husband owned, not his customers' kimonos; then they slugged a servant who lied that some employees were in the establishment. It is thought that a throat bone left after cremation foretells the dead person's future life. O-Masu, the daughter of Hearn's deceased Matsue pipestem maker, kept herself from testifying against her father, accused of minor theft, by biting off her tongue. A merchant admired the act, married her, and supported her father. At precisely 2 years of age, a child will utter one word about its previous life; if enigmatic, the word can be explained by an expert. An angry act by A against B results in B's smile, followed in due time, first, by revenge managed against A by B, and second, by B's suicide. In a story, part play dialogue with stage directions and part prose narrative, Hearn tells of Ichirō, a Japanese husband threatened by Kasaku, the ex-convict uncle of O-Noto, Ichirō's wife; the couple hack the uncle to death and then execute a suicide pact. Hearn explains that the typical Japanese woman is gentle, submissive, and sweet; but "let one particular nervestring be touched, and fire shall forgive sooner than she." Next door to Hearn are some poor houses. In one, a man lies dying. Moved by the "ghastly timbre" of his groans, Hearn sends over some money for a funeral when the man dies. He learns that the fellow made a suicide pact with his girlfriend when she refused a rich merchant's offer to her parents for her hand. The fellow killed her but survived his own throat-cutting effort. Cancer developed in the wound, but his loving family sacrificed everything to keep him alive for seven years and wept at his passing. Hearn moralizes that perhaps "we . . . love most that which causes us most pain."

"The Stone Buddha": Between classes at Kumamoto, Hearn visits a nearby cemetery, which has a smiling stone Buddha. With the sun at Hearn's back, the scene resembles a Japanese picture, with spectral mountain peaks and banded colors and the shadowless Plain of Higo. Occidental aesthetic innovations have caused Japanese artists to introduce black shadows in their paintings, to their detriment. Western-style telegraph poles, chimneys, factories, and machinery have cast shadows even into people's hearts. When Hearn sees a farm couple toiling with their ox—a scene repeated over the centuries—it prompts a lament that we are evolving social perfection only to die. Is life only a "phantom-flash between darknesses"? The West proclaims the post-mortem advent of "another universal life," to which Buddhists instead "write . . . something of . . . innumerable births, . . . and of the unity of life." When the West urges belief that pain produces thought and that sorrow teaches duty, the East answers that "Science" only confirms what that peasant already believes. Abruptly suspending this confused see-sawing, Hearn turns to an anecdote. Its moral is that we suffer from thoughts out of a previous existence and that our present-day errors will hurt our future lives. The house in which Hearn now lives is supposedly haunted by an *iki-ryō* (ghost of a living person). This person, a woman, was hired by the former owner of the house to produce his heir, did so, and was abruptly sent away. Her anger, secretly indulged in, produced a ghost that visited the father of their child and caused his death. Hearn asks that we interpret the *iki-ryō* only "as a strong form of conscience." Simply not resenting a wrong does not nullify the strong evil force generated by the wrongdoer. Hearn and the stone Buddha, looking together at the college, are equally sad, because its faculty is concerned only with the scientific "systemization of human experience." Denying Christianity, Hearn prefers to believe that "the Unknowable . . . is inaccessible to prayer" and that he must instead, following Buddha's revelation, be his own lamp and use it to find the truth. Perhaps his—our—task is only beginning.

"Jiujutsu": A one-story building on the college grounds in Kumamoto has a huge room devoted to the slow and careful instruction of *jiujutsu* (jujitsu), the art of using an opponent's strength to defeat him. This system of defense is more than scientific. It is philosophical, economic, ethical, and moral; indeed, "it is, above all, the expression of a racial genius as yet but faintly perceived by those Powers who dream of further aggrandizement of the East." Japan has used the strength in American, English, French, and German procedures to improve its own commercial, communication, educational, financial, legal, lighthouse, military, mining, and police activities—all for "intellectual self-defense"; hence Japan's strategy is "a marvelous national jiujutsu." Photographs of some samurai and barons who adopted "nondescript" foreign haberdashery look foolish alongside the picture of a warrior in feudal costume, a veritable "War beetle, all horns and mandibles and menace despite its dazzlings of jewel-color!" The "mania" for foreign clothes is only partial and, moreover, is waning. Japanese soldiers hate leather shoes and prefer sandals. Adopting Western ways would require ruinous changes in home furnishings. Japanese architecture has resisted foreign influence, except for the use of fireproof materials in municipal structures. Port buildings, far from changing, are ultra-conservative and even adapt strong Japanese features. Hearn criticizes Christianity and the failed efforts of missionaries to convert the Japanese. He commends Buddhists, once they arrived in Japan, for absorbing aspects of Shintō already there, instead of employing Christian "power and menace" techniques. No new religion should expect to alter the social and ethical practices of a target nation. Hearn quotes "the world's greatest philosopher," Herbert Spencer (1820–1903), to support his belief that Japan would never open its interior to foreign capitalistic takeovers. Such influence, augmented by aggression and the impact of alien ideas, would dissolve the national fabric; political reaction therefore stopped it. Americans and Australians fear the superior Oriental way of life, as evidenced by their anti-immigration laws. The constant economic pressure applied by Western nations against Japan was recently countered by a treaty denying the British permanent commercial footholds in Japan. Hearn does wonder whether Japan "will ultimately win all her ends by Jiujutsu" alone. He praises the Japanese military buildup at home and its inroads in foreign markets. Helpful to its national purpose is the Japanese notion of duty, which is so ingrained as to make the word "patriotism" insufficient. Hearn reports a conversation he had with a university student. The student was pleased when Hearn told him he admires ancient Japanese manners; but the lad expressed fear that having to compete with the West will degrade Japanese morals and that members of its new generation must abandon their past, enact laws requiring moral behavior, and "learn to be moral by reason" rather than by emotion. In an update written after Japan's victory in the Sino-Japanese War (1894–1895), Hearn praises Japan; endorses predictions that "the future belongs to the Orient"; says that "we" may be superior but that not necessarily the fittest will survive; and that whereas some races have overlived feebler ones, "we" may be eliminated by people "capable of *underliving* us," adapting "the best" in us, and never missing us in the process. Hearn's pro-Japanese, anti-Christian, anti-Western proclivities climb to their zenith in this propagandistic essay.

"The Red Bridal" (1894): A Western couple's suicide for love is generally frenzied; a Japanese *jōshi*, on the other hand, "involves a marriage of which the certificate is death." The two pledge sacredly before the gods, write goodbye letters, and die. If the man should survive somehow, he must die soon or be regarded as a disgraceful perjurer, killer, and coward. In a village by a river,

Tarō, a dyer's son, is born on an unlucky day. At age 6 he goes to school, where he is frightened, is laughed at, and cries at recess until O-Yoshi, a nice little girl, comforts him, goes home with him, and shares his cake. O-Yoshi lives with her father, a shopkeeper named Miyahara, who when his samurai wife died married O-Tama, an illiterate but controlling and cunning peasant. Tarō and O-Yoshi remain at school together until she turns 11 and begins to work at her family's shop. At age 14 Tarō leaves to work for his father, whose wife bears another son and dies. Now 17, Tarō visits O-Yoshi, and the two are smitten and pledge their love. But a matchmaker is arranging for O-Yoshi to wed Okazaki, an old, wealthy, dishonest rice speculator. O-Tama persuades Miyahara that it is all in the interests of his daughter and demands much money from Okazaki. O-Tama even encourages Tarō and his father to visit, to make Okazaki worried and offer more. The young lovers occasionally meet and fret over memories of their previous lives together. When O-Tama tells O-Yoshi she must wed the old man, O-Yoshi surprisingly surrenders with a bow. The girl, of samurai blood, is shocked at first but instantly makes courageous plans. She meets Tarō, and the two, having left letters to their families, go to the nearby railroad tracks, run toward the approaching train, lie down in an embrace, pledge their future union, and are sheared in two by the screeching wheels. Mourners decorate their single grave, while lovers, gently defying Buddhistic condemnation of *jōshi*, pray to them in devout memory of their suffering. This long, poignant story is well modulated and contains many local-color touches.

"A Wish Fulfilled" (1895): The emperor declares war against China. Troops head north, through Kumamoto. Buddhist and Shintō ceremonies are held. Prayers are offered to the memory of Kato Kiyomasa (1562–1611), who conquered Korea and was the Jesuits' enemy. Kiyomasa's weaponry had disappeared from his old monastery, perhaps gone ahead to help him lead new armies. Citizens' patriotism is quietly evident. Kosuga Asakichi, a former student at Izumo and now a 19-year-old army sergeant, calls courteously on Hearn. They discuss views of death and of the soul. Asakichi, eager to die in combat, explains that Japanese families both worship the dead at home and believe the souls of the dead are everywhere, like wind, electricity, light. Further, the living must love the dead and offer their souls food and drink for precisely one hundred years. Hearn is reminded of ancient Greek and Roman beliefs. Asakichi explains that soldiers killed in battle are cremated, their ashes sent home, and their spirits regarded as *kami* (gods) and prayed to in times of national danger. He says he prays and weeps at old shrines. At twilight, the two hear 10,000 soldiers chanting the "Kumamato Rōjō" (The Song of the Siege). Leaving his photograph and saluting, Asakichi departs. Later, in Hearn's guest room are the photograph and a shrine, with a little food, for his dead student-soldier. Hearn's words of prayer remain a secret.

"In Yokohama": Hearn and a young student seek the Jizō-Dō (a certain temple), make their way past the usual Buddhist trappings and some Western gimcracks, and confer with Mu-myo, an old priest who is writing volumes on Japanese religious history, with stories of miracles and fairies. In a deep voice, with "bronze tones in it," he tells Hearn that we are reborn improved if our former good deeds outweigh our former evil ones. He denies Hearn's fear that spiritual progress is impeded by love of "things of the senses." While Mu-myo attends to other visitors, Hearn ponders the swarm of lives becoming thoughts unendingly. He tells the returning priest about the gap in the West between rich and poor, and he says that Western thinkers wonder about the whence, whither, and why of their lives and are restless until science answers these unanswerables. Mu-myo replies that out of the universal mind come our minds, which create phenomena we call substances, but that mind and substance are "only two phases of one infinite Entity." He discusses the universal mind's unique reality, illusions as misdirected ideas, pre-beginnings, the universe's cyclical nature, and Nehan (Nirvana) as total self-sufficiency and not "infinite stillness." When Hearn wonders about "sexual love," Mu-myo replies that marriage may help or hinder progress toward spiritual betterment, depending on one's handling of sexual dangers, which celibates also confront. He says that attaining the ability to see the future requires much knowledge. Hearn and the student, who is slightly contemptuous, depart. Hearn wants to see Mu-myo again but never does. Five years pass. In Yokohama again, he is entranced by "the divine spectre of Fuji." As a ghostly sweetness wafts away, he thinks of Mu-myo, goes to his temple, but learns of his death. The new priest leaves Hearn before Mu-myo's *ihai* (mortuary tablet), where he prays silently, although not "for the return of lost illusions." Hearn's writing here combines the style of the inquisitive reporter and that of the conscientious researcher.

"Yuko: A Reminiscence": It seems that while visiting in Otsu, Japan, a son of the Russian czar was wounded. This caused the emperor of Japan to announce that he "augustly sorrows." Some samurai send a keen sword to the official in charge of guarding the prince with the suggestion that *hara-kiri* is in order. Meanwhile, in faraway Kanagawa, a beautiful young orphan girl named Yuko, a servant although of samurai extraction, to alleviate her emperor's sorrow puts her life in order, has her small razor sharpened, writes a letter to her brother and a petition to an official, dresses appropriately, kneels before dawn at the gate of a government building, slits her throat, and dies. Hearing of her sacrifice, the emperor "augustly ceases to mourn."

Hearn wrote to Nishida Sentarō (January 1895), shortly before becoming a naturalized Japanese citizen, that *Out of the East* was quickly proving to be more impressive in England than *Glimpses of Unfamiliar Japan* had been. *Out of the East* was published in England (1895, 1902) and in Germany (1910). However, *Glimpses of Unfamiliar Japan* was steadily more popular in the United States and abroad. *Out of the East* was included as part of Volume 7 in *The Writings of Lafcadio Hearn* (16 vols., 1922).

Bibliography: Bisland; Dawson; Espey; Kennard; Kunst; Murray.

"OVER-EDUCATION IN GERMANY" (1886). Editorial. The critic Ernst Eckstein (1845–1900) theorizes well that preference among Germans for French

literature over their own has resulted in poor German writing. But he is incorrect when he says that the French like only their own literature. In truth, they "devour" American, English, Russian, and other foreign books, and also translate many of them well. German authors are not paid sufficiently, and the result is mediocrity. In addition, Germans are so over-educated that even though they excel in the sciences and in "dead" and Oriental languages, they lack a corresponding emotional development, which is more necessary in an author than being learned.

P

"A PARABLE BUDDHISTIC" (1884). Parable. A Brahman is surprised to observe that when a hooded serpent bites a man, his father, mother, sister, wife, and slave are all reconciled to his death. They explain that they cannot alter destiny and continue with their lives.

"PARIAH PEOPLE" (1875). Cincinnati news article. Bucktown, an unsavory district, used to be worse than it is now. Today, policemen can freely enter, search, and make arrests. But even now, "[t]he harlot's bully, the pimp, the prostitute, the thief, the procuress, the highway robber—white, tawny, brown and black—constitute the mass of the population." In addition, some white women live with black husbands or lovers there, as do black levee hands with their girls. For the most part, only the old, worn-out, and crippled inhabitants are ugly. Many nonwhite females are remarkably beautiful, graceful, and strong. Ever eager to observe, Hearn accompanied two policemen in search of a female thief. They rapped at doors, were courteously admitted, looked around by candlelight through ground-level and underground "dens," and sought information by asking short and simple questions. Hearn took careful note of various hovels, streets, wells, sewers, and people—especially women with nice hair, delicate profiles, and lithe limbs. He indicates his thoroughness by recording at least 30 names of Bucktown residents. Notable are Chestine, Detroit Dolly West, Hunnykut, Crooked-back Jack, Limber Jim, Long Nell, Fatty Maria, Mrs. Ham, and Pocahontas. Hearn begins this graphic article by commenting that authorities in Paris "some years since" walled up subterranean dens of its hopeless poor, partly to prevent the birth of "deformed . . . monsters." He thinks that in 10 years Bucktown will cease to exist. When Dolly died, a dance was held, with music provided by banjos and bass viols and women chanting "Oh, ain't I mighty glad my Jesus arose / To send me up on high." Limber Jim was featured in a profane song, a mild part of which goes thus: "Limber Jim, / Shiloh!/ . . . You turtle-dove, / Shiloh!" Hearn was also escorted through this district by Denny Cor-coran, the 300-pound nephew of Mrs. Margaret Courtney, who was of Irish descent and whose popular boardinghouse Hearn regularly frequented, as did many young medical students. Hearn liked Mrs. Courtney and her cooking so much that he moved a couple of times to lodgings nearer to her boardinghouse.

Bibliography: Cott; Stevenson; Tinker.

"PARTHENIA SULLIVAN" (1874). Cincinnati news article. Parthenia Sulli-van, the owner of a boardinghouse, performed an abortion on Carrie Davis, who then died. During the inquest a physician innocently boarding with Mrs. Sullivan said that a man visited Carrie frequently but after her death said he was her lover, not her husband, and never returned. Another witness also boarding with Mrs. Sullivan was a single woman. She gave birth to her baby instead of having an abortion, saw Carrie after what must have been her abortion, and was slapped by Mrs. Sullivan and warned to say nothing. This witness added that she was sure Mrs. Sullivan concealed five women at one time in her house, "for the worst of purposes." Hearn says that he is "suppressing some passages too filthy and disgusting for publication."

PEN NAMES. *See* Names, Nicknames, and Pen Names, Hearn's.

"PENITENTIARIES AND PUNISHMENTS" (1880). Editorial. Even when the general public is made aware of "cruelty in houses of correction," it is unable to improve conditions. This is because when a different political party takes over control of the state government, its leaders appoint new but not more enlightened penitentiary managers. People of intelligence know that prisoners should not be mistreated; prisons "serve no correctional purposes"; criminals incline toward illegal, immoral acts because they have "inherited mental dis-ease"; and recidivist statistics support these conclusions. Keeping criminals in-carcerated is expensive, but the evil that ex-convicts inflict on society is more costly still. Moreover, criminals on the loose "too often" bequeath evil tenden-cies to their children. When a person first breaks "any important ethical law," swift, painless execution should follow to protect society.

PERIODICAL PUBLICATIONS. Beginning in 1882, Hearn augmented his mea-ger income by placing work in periodicals. The first such items—a translation from Théophile Gautier (1811–1872) and another from Alphonse Daudet (1840–1897)—were published in the San Francisco *Argonaut*. In the 1880s Hearn published at least two dozen other pieces in periodicals—one in the *Century Magazine*, one in the *Southern Bivouac*, and the rest in three magazines issued by the Harper Brothers (*Bazar, Magazine,* and *Weekly*) under the editorship of Henry Mills Alden.* In the 1890s Hearn cracked *Lippincott's Magazine* (once), the *Cosmopolitan* (twice), and continued with *Harper's Monthly* (twice). Once in Japan, he placed an item in the San Francisco *Chrysanthemum* and began to treat *Atlantic Monthly* readers to what eventually totaled 30 works, counting posthumous ones. In addition, he placed a piece on Japanese ballads in *Transactions of the Asiatic Society of Japan* (Yokohama, 1894). Two of his papers appeared in *Transactions of the Japan Society* (London, 1904, 1905). Most of these periodical publications reappeared in Hearn's various books. For example, much of *Two Years in the French West Indies* and all of *Youma* first appeared in *Harper's Monthly,* and many of his essays on Japan that first saw light in the *Atlantic Monthly* were reissued in successive books. Correspondents jumped on the bandwagon created by Hearn's popularity in succeeding decades to publish letters of his in various periodicals; and editors and others gathered some of his minor items and a couple of short translations, previously unwanted, for issuance.

"THE PERKINS HORROR" (1874). Cincinnati news article. This is the fourth of four articles dealing with the Perkinses, dated October 1–6,1874. The others are "A Motherly Murder," "The Perkins Tragedy, and "Wife and Mistress." On Wednesday, September 30, 1874, Julia A. Snell Perkins murdered her 2-year-old daughter, Clara, and tried unsuccessfully to kill herself. Facts have gradually emerged: Julia's husband, Charles L. Perkins, had a mistress, Pauline "Susie" Payne; and Julia had a lover named Joseph Claire. Julia knew for a long time about Susie; but when Perkins ambushed Julia and Claire, he demanded a separation. On Monday, October 5, Hearn learned through a woman who knew both Perkinses and Pauline Payne that Pauline was no Creole at all but instead was a stupid, conniving woman. For three years she wanted to split up the Perkinses. She tried, without success, to lure Julia to a house of ill repute and have witnesses there to discredit her. Hearn quotes, in full, a mealy-mouthed letter sent by Perkins to his editor, undoubtedly written on October 5. In it, he admits his marital infidelities but blames Claire for being Julia's shameless lover and says that he caught the two, they admitted everything, and he left them together at 6:00 A.M., on September 30, before the murder of his child, on the understanding that Claire would put Julia on a train to go to her father.

"THE PERKINS TRAGEDY" (1874). Cincinnati news article. This is the second of four articles dealing with the Perkinses, dated October 1–4, 1874. The others are "A Motherly Murder," "Wife and Mistress," and "The Perkins Horror." On Wednesday, September 30, 1874, Julia A. Snell Perkins killed her 2-year-old daughter, Clara, and then tried but failed to kill herself. New facts have come to light. For two years Julia's husband, Charles L. Perkins, had a mistress in Covington, Ohio. His wife knew about it and felt humiliated. When Julia and her husband moved to Cincinnati, the "courtesan" followed, occasionally even rang their door bell, and asked for "Charley." On the night before the child's murder, Joseph Claire, a friend of both Perkinses, tried to quell their argument, which, however, concerned Julia's brief flirtation with a man during her vacation the previous summer. Julia, cared for by one of the Sisters of the Poor, has expressed a desire to die and a hope for God's forgiveness. Hearn's description of little Clara, "the little flaxen-haired beauty" in whose home "the sweet child's voice" rang "with laughter and music," is worthy of the most sentimental Victorian novel, of the sort Hearn habitually deplored.

"POMPEII" (1878). Editorial. The announcement that the destruction of Pompeii and three other cities eighteen hundred years ago will be "celebrated" next year ought to have read "commemorated." But Vesuvius should be thanked for thus preserving art works and evidences of ancient domestic life. Specialists have learned much from items found in the ruins. Specialists will gather next year, and valuable publications will follow.

"POOR MUMMIES!" (1878). Editorial. "Frankish speculators" (i.e., Germans) propose to pay the Egyptian Khedive substantial sums to remove thousands of tons of mummy wrappings and use them to manufacture paper. But no one should disturb the thirty-century rest of "kind-hearted old Egyptians," many of whom, it has been discovered, were buried with childish toys to please them in their next world.

"THE POST-OFFICE" (1884). Sketch. Hearn takes a trip by mail-packet from New Orleans through a waterway to a summer resort on a little island. The passengers go ashore and are welcomed by friendly "brown island people" and a thunderous sea surge not far away. Hearn describes buildings, accommodations, vegetation, water creatures, birds, and pure bright air. Evidence of vitality is everywhere. "But the mighty blind sea" is ominous. A Spanish-speaking black points out the location of the post office—"a dark red stain against the green distance." Hearn walks over and talks to a 12-year-old girl caring for two babies (Valentine and Léonie) and chanting a Creole song to them—with its "tiquiti . . . tocoto . . . tacata" refrain. With touching courtesy, the child sells him stamped envelopes but is deeply troubled when she lacks the proper change. Hearn fears that this girl, this "dainty sea-land flower," will drift to the city, work, worry about money, but still—perhaps with a pale child in her arms— think at sundown not of mists, clouds, and noisy street vehicles but of seas, her island, and the mule going "tocoto, tocoto, tocoto." Contrasting effectively with the primitiveness of life once the city-dwellers land on the island is Hearn's deliberate overuse in his opening paragraph of such scientific words as "anchylosed," "frondescense," "geniculated," and "macurating." Hearn's handling of his visit to Grand Isle prefigures much subject matter used later in *Chita* (1889). "Torn Letters" was another sketch, part of which made its way into *Chita*.

"PRESENT STATUS OF THE GERM THEORY" (1882). Editorial. Hearn agrees with the statement of Louis Pasteur (1822–1895) that germs are not created by "spontaneous generation." Hearn cites the popularizing physicist John Tyndall (1822–1893) in support, and he discounts the opposition mounted by "Dr. Bastian" (the English bacteriologist Henry Charlton Bastion, 1837–1915). Hearn summarizes the convincing experiments proving Pasteur's germ theory. Although the controversy continued into the 1870s, Hearn, even while describing splenic fever and other germs in sickening detail, seems to be beating a dead horse: Pasteur's theory had been officially accepted in 1864 by a commission of an academy of sciences, and Tyndall's experiments were found to be convincing five years later.

"PREVENTION OF CRUELTY TO WOMEN" (1880). Editorial. Recent laws in Kentucky against seduction, although probably inefficacious, renew concern about wife-beating. We are more eager to prevent cruelty to animals. Women, delicate and sensitive, have only their "beauty, affection, and gentleness" as defenses. Let us make it a crime to strike or ill-treat a woman. Although no law will prevent women from being seduced, a law may help. Otherwise, a girl who is a mistress of a man typically gets abandoned, and she lives with another man and then another, until she falls into "degradation." If a man has lived with a woman for a certain period of time, make him legally "*ipso facto . . .* the husband."

"PROLIFIC CRIME" (1880). Editorial. We are too squeamish to execute persons "with strong criminal tendencies" or even to castrate criminals. In olden times, weak children were slain. Why should we build asylums for lunatics and prisons for murderers? It is more cruel to give them life sentences. In France recently, a whole family was condemned for committing unspeakable crimes. The chief culprit had 47 children—"strong and healthy but morally diseased." This nest of vipers should never have been allowed to develop. The Chinese condemn the entire family of a person "wholly barbarous and brutal." *See* "Penitentiaries and Punishments."

"PUNDARI" (1884). Tale. A beauteous city has lacy palaces, the breath of flowers, and dancing ladies. One girl, named Pundari, grows tired and escapes to seek a reclusive life with Buddha. But she sees her lovely form in a mountain spring and decides to return. Buddha presents himself as an even more gorgeous female to Pundari, whose kiss and adoring gaze, however, transform the vision into a revolting hag. Buddha persuades Pundari to extinguish all desires so as to attain happiness. Hearn's prose is poetic here, as in this line: "Fierce was the heat of the sun, and rough the dizzy paths."

"THE PUNISHMENT OF SILENCE" (1884). Editorial. The French criminal justice system has three types of punishment: execution, hard labor for life, and solitary confinement. Measures are afoot to abolish the last, which in many ways is the worst, because persons so condemned are forbidden to speak or to see daylight. Women so condemned sometimes became insane. Hearn notes that *La Fille Elisa* (1878) by the naturalist novelist Edmond de Goncourt (1822–1896) has helped provoke abolition of this cruel punishment.

Q

"QUAINT NEW ORLEANS AND ITS INHABITANTS" (1884). Sketch. Old New Orleans, called French-Town by steamboatmen and Le Carré by its inhabitants, was once a fortress but is now mostly lined by bird-filled trees. Hearn describes half-ruined old mansions and buildings, the products of French and Spanish settlers, like their descendants, who are called Creoles. Their skin is surprisingly cool, like tropical fruit, even in burning sunlight. Hearn details racial differences in Creoles, those mislabeled "colored Creoles," " 'American' colored folk," and those of Latin blood. The New Orleans climate has given its Creoles supple limbs, deep-set eyes, and lustrous hair. They have nervous temperaments, seeming listlessness, and considerable linguistic ability. But American commercial energy is changing the old city.

"THE QUARTER OF SHAMBLES" (1874). Cincinnati news article. This is the seventh of eight articles about the murder of Herman Schilling on Saturday, November 7, 1874, by Andreas Egner, his son Frederick K. Egner, and their friend George Rufer, in revenge for Schilling's having allegedly seduced Andreas Egner's daughter Julia, age about 15, who died while pregnant. The other articles, in chronological order, are "Violent Cremation," "Killed and Cremated," "It Is Out!," "The Tannery Horror," "The Furnace Fiends [1]," "The Furnace Fiends [2]," and "The Furnace Horror." On Sunday, November 15, Hearn published a description of the tannery where the murder was committed, as well as its environs. The murder scene, a shambles, is surrounded by slaughterhouses, rendering factories, soap and candle factories, hog pens, and other tanneries. Foreign workers labor in the midst of blood, entrails, offal, and dung. Schilling's brother takes charge of his estate and begins suit against the Egners and also Rufer, who is tardily identified as a murderer who escaped from jail in Germany. It has been suggested that when Hearn describes the slaughterhouse as a "labrynthine perplexity" he may well be thinking of himself, trapped in Cincinnati, in 1874—in fact, from 1872 until 1877.

Bibliography: Stevenson.

"THE QUESTION IN GERMANY" (1878). Editorial. Germany has devoted such national energy to producing a mighty army that its farms are barren, its factories idle. Reduction of arms would tempt the French to seek revenge. Socialism is only an indirect threat. But soldiers, if disbanded, would find such difficulty seeking employment that they might join communist clubs. The solution: a weapon of mass destruction, handled by only a very few soldiers, "an electric battery" able to "pulverize a city . . . with a random flash."

R

"RABBI YOCHANAN BEN ZACHAI" (1884). Legend. Wise Hillel, who taught Jesus, gathers disciples. Though considered "least" of a "middling" group, Rabbi Yochanan ben Zachai is holy, humble, and learned. For 40 years he earned money; for the next 40, he studied; during the last 40, he has been teaching. Rabbi Yochanan explains to a cocky disciple that Isaiah said he would place huge gems and pearls at Jerusalem's gates. The disciple laughs at Yochanan, sails away, but sees angels quarrying monstrous gems and pearls under water, and returns to tell Yochanan. The rabbi, however, rebukes him for his earlier wicked mockery of sages, and with a flaming glance he reduces the disciple to ashes. Yochanan then continues to teach.

"RABYAH'S LAST RIDE: A TRADITION OF PRE-ISLAMIC ARABIA" (1887). Arabesque. Brave Rabyah is escorting a caravan of women, including his bride, Raytah, and his mother, Oumm Saiyar, through the desert to their country when they are attacked. Rabyah points the women toward a safe pass and kills many enemies with arrows, spear, and sword; but he is mortally wounded by Nubaishah. Rabyah remains mounted on his mare and when dead still stands guard. The women ride on and alert their tribesmen, who counterattack. Rabyah's fame spread in a poem by Hafs called "Kamil." Hearn cites as his source *Translations of Ancient Arabian Poetry* (1885) by the distinguished linguist Sir Charles James Lyall (1845–1920). An English teacher named C. H. Hinton in Yokohama, Japan, offered Hearn hospitality there in 1890 because he had read and admired "Rabyah's Last Ride"; Charles Howard Hinton (1853–1907) was a writer-scholar of science fiction. Why did Hearn describe the enemies of Rabyah abusing his corpse by spearing it in one eye? Perhaps while writing thus Hearn was thinking of his own blinded eye. In 1887 Hearn corresponded with his friend Henry Edward Krehbiel,* a music critic, and discussed the possibility of studying Arabian chronicles dealing with Rabyan's courtship and marriage, with a view toward helping someone make an opera on the subject. Nothing came of the idea.

Bibliography: Murray.

"RAINBOW BIRDS" (1881). Editorial. A recent essay on hummingbirds explains their origin in the Andes, says they may be the oldest of all bird species, describes their beautiful colors, explains the functional evolution of their several sorts of beaks, and asserts that although tiny they fight fearlessly. Hearn details their colors lovingly and laments the fact that they are killed to provide gaudy feathers for thoughtless women.

"RAT ROW RANCHES" (1874). Cincinnati news article. Rat Row is an area of dilapidated riverfront properties, many allegedly owned by H. Thane Miller, whom Hearn designates "our great Y.M.C.A. Boanerges." Miller is said to be renting some "tumble-down premises" to a man named Pickett, who has converted one unit into a saloon and two other units into nefarious "sleeping apartments." Investigating, Hearn learns that Miller is indeed a big Rat Row owner. So, one evening he gets himself escorted to Miller's saloon by a levee worker. Miller is evasive when questioned and soon orders Hearn to get out, which he does "with an unwonted celerity of peripatetic motion." Pickett was a colorful, illiterate former slave and an associate of criminals. When times on the levee were flush, he made money; when the river froze and people were unemployed and starving, he freely dispensed food and drink, and he housed the unfortunates for free.

Bibliography: Stevenson.

"RECENT AMERICAN NOVELS" (1881). Editorial. Few are the "novels illustrating American life proper." Publishers have tried to be encouraging, but "fulfillment has been . . . difficult." Most such efforts imitate English and French fiction, and most results emanate from Boston and are "pedantic." Suggestions: Present life on farms, in shops and factories, in mining and frontier regions, and in quaint old towns; dramatize the personalities of the uncultured rich and the cultured poor; give us "beautiful and . . . picturesque" aspects of both "upper" and "lower strata of society." Hearn praises the work of Bret Harte, Oliver Wendell Holmes, Washington Irving, and Elizabeth Stuart Phelps.

"THE RESTLESS BOARDER" (1879). Sketch. A male boarder gets the narrator, his Creole landlady, to switch rooms for him, back and forth, because of "noise abominable at make dose infants." He rents elsewhere but comes back. The other landlord returns his "one mont advance."

"THE RETURN OF YEN-TCHIN-KING" (1887). Ghost story. When evil Li-hi-lié begins to revolt, the emperor commands the wise and brave Yen-Tchin-King to intervene. Tchin-King rides north, finds Hi-lié, reads aloud an imperial order for him to submit, but is executed and buried. His spirit goes south and manifests itself simultaneously to both the emperor and Tchin-King's gray-haired servant. Allies aid the imperial armies. Tchin-King's body is found, uncorrupted by worms, and is borne in triumph to a mausoleum in his homeland. Hearn says he may have anachronistically treated *Kan-ying-p'ien* (Book of Rewards and Punishments), his source.

"THE RISE OF THE MAHDI" (1885). Editorial. Despite recent news about the "Arab revolt in the Soudan," little is known concerning the Mahdi, its leader. In this March 29, 1885, editorial, Hearn identifies him as the Mahdi, Mohammed Ahmed; says he was born in 1843 in Dongala (Dunqulah, a Turko-Egyptian city in the Sudan), with birthmarks on each cheek predicting greatness; and knew the Koran by heart at age 12. His brothers sent him to study at a Moslem seminary. After 25 years there, he devoted himself to prayer and meditation on a White Nile island. Venerated as a prophet by Moslem tribes, he began in 1881 to assemble numerous sheiks and their cohorts in an effort to overthrow Turkish domination. When two hundred Turkish soldiers attacked him on his island, his dervishes slaughtered them all. Hearn summarizes the Mahdi's successes thereafter, including his killing of Charles Gordon (1833–1885), whom the Mahdi called "Antichrist." Warning of the fanatical heroism of "the children of Mahomet," Hearn says that to date the British fleet bars the Mahdi's essential visit to Mecca. In truth, Muhammad Ahmad (1848–1885) died of typhus in June 1885. *See* "Death and Resurrection in the Soudan."

"A RIVER REVERIE" (1882). Sketch. A Walt Whitmanesque catalogue of sights, sounds, and changing colors at and beyond the port of New Orleans is followed by mention of the rheumatic, retired "Captain ———." He used to sit near a steamboat agency and watch. Is he still there? The river evokes varied memories. Also reminding Hearn of previous thoughts was the recent visit of a former river pilot, who is now a famous author. He still has the cheerful ways and keen-eyed glance of a pilot. Is he prompted by old feelings to go sit at the wharf, like Captain ———, and watch and dream? The distinguished visitor was Mark Twain, who in 1882 visited George Washington Cable,* the popular New Orleans author whose 1880 novel *The Grandissimes* Hearn had reviewed favorably.

"THE ROAR OF A GREAT CITY" (1884). Editorial. Artists have depicted cities of the past as noisy. They are worse now, what with steamboat and locomotive whistles, engines, machines, and the New York Elevated railway system. The wind at night creates "a buzzing metallic sound" as it passes around telephone, telegraph, and electric power lines. These wails and shrieks of today will only get worse in the future.

ROLLINS, ALICE WELLINGTON (1847–1897). Author and hostess. Mrs. Daniel M. Rollins (nee Alice Marland Wellington) was the author of books of aphorisms, travel books, books for children, and poetry. Two of her most popular titles are *The Story of a Ranch* (1885) and *Uncle Tom's Tenement: A Novel* (1888). She was a popular hostess at her suite in the Cordova and Navarro Apartments, West Fifty-Eighth Street, on Central Park South, in New York City. Other residents included the author-editor Mary Mapes Dodge (1831–1905), the influential editor Richard Watson Gilder (1844–1909) and his wife, and the versatile man-of-letters Edmund Clarence Stedman (1833–1908). When Mrs. Rollins was planning a dinner party in the fall of 1889, one of the several persons she had invited, Elizabeth Bisland,* persuaded her to invite Hearn, whom Bisland had known in New Orleans. Another guest was to be Ellwood Hendrick,* a successful New York businessman. On his way to the party Hearn got lost, arrived looking seedy, was directed by the snooty doorman to the service elevator, and entered the dining room via the kitchen. He looked so out of place that Hendrick in due time rescued him by whisking him away to a tavern. The two became permanent friends. Mrs. Rollins invited Hearn to stay with her and her family. Hearn accepted but soon departed when he saw that remaining there would displace her son from his room. Shortly before Hearn departed for Japan in 1890, Mrs. Rollins gave him a delightful farewell party. Hearn regarded the Navarro Apartments as gigantic, overly elegant, and costly, at $5,000 per annum for a lofty suite. When in 1891 Mrs. Rollins was in Yokohama, Japan, he ungraciously declined her invitation to proceed from his residence in Matsue and see her.

Bibliography: Cott; Stevenson; Tinker.

THE ROMANCE OF THE MILKY WAY AND OTHER STUDIES AND STORIES (1905). A posthumous collection of seven essays, five of which had been previously published. When this work was reprinted as Volume 8 in *The Writings of Lafcadio Hearn* (16 vols., 1922), an eighth item, "Three Popular Ballads," an 1891 lecture also previously published, was added.

"The Romance of the Milky Way" (1905): A delightful festival in Old Japan was Tanabata-Sama (the Weaving-Lady of the Milky Way). It took place on the seventh day of the seventh month. Tanabata, the daughter of the god of the firmament, was a weaver; Hikoboshi, her husband, was a herdsman. Their excessive devotion to one another so displeased her father that he placed them on opposite sides of the Celestial River and let them get together only one night a year, and then only if her magpies and his crows formed a bridge over the river for them, and—to make matters more frustrating—only when it was not raining. Their love obviously required patience, but fortunately it was also always young. The first poem celebrating the eager weaver, awaiting her lord's coming, is dated A.D. 723. The first recorded observation of the Tanabata festival is dated A.D. 755 and was held by imperial order. The oldest collection of Japanese poetry, dated A.D. 760, names the loving pair. There is also a Chinese version. When the lovers meet in the skies above, keen-eyed observers on earth can see their stars sparkling in five colors. Such happy reunions signify good luck to farmers. The festival evolved into a national holiday in Japan; and when it was held in the emperor's court it included offerings to the star deities (food, wine, incense, flowers, music), five-eyed needles for Tanabata, poems written in dew-ink for the occasion, and much else. Hearn indicates that ceremonial customs differ according to region. He regarded the Izumo festival as especially interesting, and that of Yédo (now Tōkyō) as the most picturesque. He presents many selections of ancient Japanese Tanabata poems. They are from an anthology of more than four thousand compiled in the eighth and ninth centuries by imperial order. Although some are long narratives, most are *tanka* (31-syllable compositions). Hearn compares a *tanka* by "Yamagami no Okura" (Yamano[u]e Okura [660–c.733]) to an even earlier epigram by "Deodorus Zonas of Sardis," from the Greek Anthology; discusses the remarkable stability of the Japanese language over a thousand years; and presents "forty-odd tanka," often with careful footnotes. He contends that his choices are of interest for revealing "the human nature of their authors," for showing Tanabata as "the Japanese wife worshipfully loving," and for providing proof that the Japanese adore the beauties of nature and its seasonal changes. One might add that the poems also regularly express the controlled impatience of long-separated lovers. Hearn rarely lets the erotic creep into his writing, but he must have regarded this expression of Tanabata's eagerness as a permissible exception: "The moment of loosening my girdle is nigh!" Hearn might have felt that this long essay would not greatly appeal to Western readers: He introduces the selections by saying that "my readers ought to be interested" but at its close admits that probably "the legend of Tanabata . . . can make but a faint appeal to Western minds."

"Goblin Poetry": Hearn says he recently puchased a three-volume collection of so-called goblin poetry, that is, *kyōka* (crazy verses). Although they are all in *tanka* form (31 syllables, with lines patterned 5,7,5,7,7), they are anti-classical in content. Many are worthless in Western eyes, but some cleverly mix grim, playful, and terrifying elements. Some are "too gruesome for Western nerves." Hearn presents samples under 14 rubrics: will-o'-the-wisps, ghost-sicknesses, toads, mirages, necks that twist or detach, the Snow Woman, ship ghosts, spirits turned into crabs, Yanari (the sound a house makes when an earthquake shakes it), unluckily reversed house posts, Baké-Jizō (children's shape-shifting divine patron), Umi-Bōzu (a cuttlefish that looks like a priest), home-protecting text-charms, and Tsubaki (unlucky goblin trees). Hearn provides a running commentary on the implications of the various categories, including summaries of other poems. He also annotates the selections, often with solemn modesty but now and then hinting at his knowledge of the Japanese language. For example, "the puns are too much for me" and "Zotto [thrilling] is a difficult word to render literally." But later he glosses "Nam'mai da?" as "How many sheets are there?" and suggests that the question may be a contraction for "Nam[u] A[m]ida," meaning "Hail, O Amitâbha," a Shin-sect invocation. All this implies considerable linguistic expertise. Not surprisingly, he likes poems about goblins and flowers best; he summarizes a narrative poem in which a scholar so loved peonies that he was visited by a gorgeous girl who, when he fell in love with her, turned into a colored shadow and explained she was "only the Soul of a Peony."

" 'Ultimate Questions' " (1905): This is Hearn's premier essay on his intellectual debt to Herbert Spencer (1820–1903), the English philosopher whom he calls here "the world's greatest thinker," "this mightiest of thinkers," and "[t]he greatest mind that this world has yet produced." Hearn says that 20 years earlier he read Spencer's *First Principles* (1862) and subsequently read publications that became Spencer's *System of Synthetic Philosophy* (1862–1893). Hearn was especially inspired by "Ultimate Questions," an essay in the final volume of *System*. In this essay, Spencer reveals that toward the end of his life he became profoundly concerned with death. Although, as Hearn phrases the matter, "there exists no rational evidence for any belief in the continuance of conscious personality after death," he finds a bit of optimism in Spencer's statement that "we seem obliged to relinquish the thought that consciousness [then] continues." Hearn wonders if humankind may later develop "knowledge [that] might help us to a less forlorn prospect." If all suns and planets perish, "[w]e have at least the certainty that the energies of life cannot be destroyed." Further, "the ultimate nature of consciousness remains inscrutable." It must be "a manifestation of the Infinite Energy" and "will return to the timeless and measureless Source of Life." Spencer hypothesizes that "consciousness may belong to the cosmic ether" and hence in some simple form be *"omnipresent"*; it is probable, therefore, that individual consciousness is part of "the infinite Energy," is dissolved by death, and returns to the Source. Meanwhile let's surrender to "the eternal law," give up superstitious beliefs, and yet find comfort that "the Unknown Power" although merciless is not vengeful. Awful thoughts about infinity and timelessness may be mitigated by the awareness of being touched by "the Nameless" and also by the hope that when the human mind is ethically evolved sufficiently for it, superior intelligence from outer space, perhaps by "some method of ether-telegraphy," may provide us with "higher knowledge" that is currently too "dangerous" for us to handle. Hearn found encouragement for this final hope in *Mars* (1895) by Percival Lowell*; this book is now discredited.

"The Mirror Maiden": A Shintō priest named Matsumura Hyōgo wants to rebuild his shrine, seeks help from the Kyōtō shōgun, is told to wait a while, and does so with his family in an "unlucky house" he rents. When he finds a corpse in the well, he investigates and sees in the water the reflection of a beautiful young woman. With difficulty he resists being drawn to her and drowning. A week later, during a storm, the young woman comes to his door, identifies herself as Yayoi, and reveals that she has been lured into the well for centuries by a dragon requiring her to get people to fall in so he can drink their blood. Because the Heavenly Ruler has just ordered the dragon to go jump in another lake, she can be saved if Matsumura will retrieve her body from the well. At dawn he orders the well to be cleaned but finds only antique hair ornaments and a rare, costly mirror. Well aware that mirrors have souls, he has this one polished and places it in a wooden case in a special room. Yayoi, whom he has identified as the mirror maiden, appears to him and explains that she served in ancient courts and was turned into an heirloom and dropped into the well and forgotten. Now that the dragon is gone, she asks one favor—to be presented, as the mirror she is, to the shōgun. She also warns Matsumura to abandon the house. He does so. It is destroyed in a violent storm the next day. When he delivers the mirror, the shōgun rewards him with valuable gifts and also sufficient money to rebuild his shrine.

"The Story of Itō Norisuké" (1905): It is six hundred years ago, in the town of Uji. A handsome but poor samurai named Itō Tatéwaki Norisuké is out walking when a young girl happens by. She permits him to escort her through dark woods to the mysterious home where she is a servant. All is enchantingly beautiful, including slumbrous music. An old matron greets him courteously, says he is the answer to their prayers, and introduces him to Himégemi-Sama, their incredibly beautiful family princess and mistress, who, she adds, saw him in their village and loves him. Although he initially professes his unworthiness, he is told that their marriage seems divinely willed; he succumbs to the princess's charms and agrees. When he is informed that she is the daughter of Shigéhira-Kyō, a famous general and statesman who has been dead for centuries, Itō feels a chill but then only joy, even though he knows that marrying a ghost will make him a ghost as well. Late that evening in their bridal chamber, the princess explains that they first met ages ago, he lived several lives, but she awaited his return. Now, once every 10 years they will be together. She gives him a precious old *suzuri* (ink stone) for remembrance. At dawn Itō returns to his home, resists his mother's suggestion that he marry, and often vainly seeks his wife in the village and woods. Ten years pass. Now mortally ill, he sees his smiling wife, who tells him that they are to meet this night in their new home. He tells his mother about his marriage, shows her his ink stone, and asks that it be buried with him. Experts examine and date it to A.D. 1169, during the time of Emperor Takakura (reigned 1168–1180). Hearn awkwardly interrupts his narrative to interpolate a long description of dark forests of cedars and bamboo. His footnote identifying Shigéhira, however, is a model of academic thoroughness and precision. This is the last dream Hearn translated into English.

"Stranger Than Fiction" (1905): Hearn walks with his friend, a notary, into a West Indian tropical forest. They call on Madame Florin, a planter's Creole widow, whose black servant, looking like a mummified skeleton, greets them, followed by a "callow rabble of chickens." The black servant ushers them into the presence of the old lady, who has sparkling black eyes, pleasant wrinkles, and "argent hair." After rum and sugared lemonade, and business talk, the two men leave. The notary explains that during the slave revolt of 1848 the black servant got drunk and chopped the old lady's husband to pieces with a cutlass, hid out, was found, knelt before her, and begged for—and received—her forgiveness. Eight or nine years ago the fellow was bitten by a deadly fer-de-lance (a venomous pit viper), barely survived, and is now wasting away. The notary says that the killer did not know—with "the mind of a man"—but instinctly *"felt"*—beast that he was—that only the widow would pardon him. Hearn's one-paragraph description of the West Indian forest resembles a mini-travelogue, with sound, colors, and open fragrance vials. Hearn was apparently homesick in 1904 for Martinique. (*See* "Martinique Sketches," Chapter 17, in *Two Years in the French West Indies.*)

"A Letter from Japan" (1904): This pro-Japanese propaganda piece, dated August 1, 1904, from Tokyo, praises the patriotism, courage, endurance, and humor of the Japanese people at the beginning of the Russo-Japanese War (1904–1905). Ordered by the emperor to stay calm, the civilians are avoiding all expressions of anxiety and depression, and they appear to view the struggle as a drama—"interested without being excited." Soldiers and their loved ones exchange photographs as remembrances. Shrines are set up for temporarily or permanently absent combatants. Elaborate floral displays depict war scenes. Excellent lithographs are cranked out, some representing victories that have not yet occurred. Caricatures are printed on towels mocking the ill-placed confidence of Russian soldiers attending the theater at Port Arthur and "never dreaming that the Japanese would dare to strike the first blow." Silks are printed commemorating Japanese battleships. Printed baby dresses feature combat pictures. Shops display war toys. Children play games with cards picturing war vessels and with a tub of water representing Port Arthur; in it they float bits of wood with flags and nails for boats and mines. Soldiers salute little boys, give them models of Russian heads, and promise to bring back real ones from the front. Miniature gardens are decked out with toy soldiers. Dead heroes are celebrated in songs, commemorative gilt-porcelain cups, and doll figures in shop windows. Hearn notes, with a foreign resident's patriotism, that "Old Japan is still able to confer honors worth dying for." In a ringing conclusion he lauds Japan, which, because it has survived earthquakes, tidal waves and floods, and volcanic eruptions, can resist aggressions even more successfully. On the other hand, he excoriates Russia as "a medieval power that, unless vigorously checked, seems destined to absorb Scandinavia and to dominate China."

"Three Popular Ballads" (1896): To introduce this essay, Hearn quotes from a "communication" he published in the *Japan Mail* (June 13, 1891) about his visit, with a tolerant friend, to a village of outcasts near Matsué, inhabited by retired executioners, *yama-no-mono* (slaughterers and hide merchants), junk dealers, and *eta* (defiled pariahs). Hearn observed many sad and a few pleasant aspects of life there, and he paid "a trifle" to hear a few "clear, sweet" songs by some of these so-called Daikoku-mai people. Hearn goes on to explain that later his friend Nishida Sentarō sent him copies of three *yama-no-mono* ballads. Hearn calls them unimaginative, inartistic, crude, and coarse. But, he concedes, they are popular and should therefore interest future scholars of chants and folk music.

In "The Ballad of Shūntoku-Maru," Shūntoku, the good young son of rich Nobuyoshi, lives in Kawachu. When the boy's mother dies, the father remarries. He and his wife have a son named Otowaka-maru. Shūntoku goes to Kyōto to pray and happens to see wealthy Hagiyama's pretty daughter Otohimé; they fall in love. Shūntoku's stepmother wants Otowaka to inherit; so she puts a curse on Shūntoku, and he grows sick and blind. She persuades Nobuyoshi to send him away as a mendicant pilgrim. In a dream his mother tells him about his wicked stepmother and urges him to go to a temple near Kyōto. Otohimé, advised by her good mother, finds him there, comforts him, and fasts and prays. The temple goddess grants her wish: Shūntoku's sight and health are restored, and he and Otohimé go to his home. Nobuyoshi rejoices, but his wife is struck blind and her fingers and toes rot. Her own son leads her to the temple near Kyōto. When they pray for power to curse further, the goddess threatens to send them to hell instead. Although Hearn is apologetic about his translating skills, he renders this ballad in attractively quaint language. For example, Shūntoku fears "I fester to death"; once he is home again with father and girlfriend, "how rejoiced they were."

"The Ballad of Oguri-Hangwan" follows. In it, rich Takakura Dainagon has everything money can buy but lacks a son. He goes to a mountain temple and prays to the god Tamon-Ten. He obtains the soul of one son of a man with eight sons; soon Takakura's wife gives birth to a son, whom when mature the emperor names Oguri-Hangwan Kané-uji. Kané-uji learns that Tamon-Ten gave him to his parents and prays to the god for a wife. Up from a pond comes a serpent transformed into a lovely girl, whom he likes and takes to the emperor's court. A storm comes. Advisers tell the emperor that a serpent caused it and wants that female serpent, his mate, returned. He orders her back and Kané-uji banished to Hitachi. Kané-uji meets Goto Sayémon, an influential merchant, and asks him to provide a bride. Goto says that toward the west lives Yokoyama Chōja, who has had eight sons but only recently a daughter, Teruté-Himé, so wonderful that she has her own house. Kané-uji writes a love letter for her that Sayémon carries to Teruté. He approaches her by giving her guards presents, including "kamoji from Nagasaki." Enthralled by the letter and its princely calligraphy, she writes a cryptic reply. After much confusion she and Kané-uji get together and secretly marry. Her father, Chōja, is incensed but hides his anger and invites Kané-uji to a banquet, after which one of Chōja's sons poisons Kané-uji and his whole retinue. Teruté must also die; so two of Chōja's servants take her out to sea to drown her but, feeling compassionate, stow her in a passing canoe instead. After drifting for seven days, she is rescued by a man who adopts her. But his wife sells her into slavery. She eventually becomes the servant, now called Kohagi, of a pimp in Mino. Meanwhile, Kané-uji, a *gaki-ami* (a shapeless being belonging to the world of the dead, but not dead), is placed on a cart by passing Buddhists who draw the cart to Mino, where Kohagi finds him, although not recognizing him. To earn the gods' favors, she pulls his cart to Otsu and puts a message on his chest, asking him to visit Kohagi in Mino if he recovers. She hopes he can visit the dead and tell her about Kané-uji. Well-wishers restore him to health by means of hot-spring baths. He returns to the emperor, who makes him governor of Mino and other places. Visiting Mino, he asks for Kohagi. They recognize each other and are overjoyed, punish some of the guilty but forgive many, and enjoy a beauteous reunion. It is easy, even exciting, to follow "The Ballad of Oguri-Hangwan," but it is impossible to admire Hearn's craftsmanship here. He uses many Japanese words without translating them, calls his hero by several names, promotes him to "prince" without explanation, inexplicably makes Teruté a princess, calls Chōja "iron-hearted" for little reason, and has Teruté "just[ly]" curse him, forget her "malediction," but punish the actual poisoner.

"The Ballad of O-Shichi, the Daughter of the Yaoya" tells of O-Shichi, whose parents sell vegetables. When their house in Yedo burns, the three find refuge in a temple. The girl meets an acolyte there. The two fall in love, but he deserts her. Evidently to attract his attention, she burns down their rebuilt house. Being 15 years of age, hence an adult, she is executed by burning.

In 1905 *The Romance of the Milky Way and Other Studies and Stories* was issued in England from American sheets; it was later reprinted.

Bibliography: Kunst; Murray.

"ROMANTICISM IN MUSIC" (1878). Editorial. Modern musicologists are studying "the music of savage or barbaric nations" and its "migration" with primitive groups that have migrated. An able music critic is Henry Edward Krehbiel,* a Cincinnati specialist who is now "studying from an ethnological standpoint." He recently presented a concert featuring Chinese musicians, instruments, and music. Savage music has elements of fascinating horror; examples include a Marquesas Islands cannibal song and mystical hymns from the Orient with "invisible magic" in them. More research is needed into musical oddities.

ROUQUETTE, ADRIEN EMMANUEL (1813–1887). Catholic priest and author. Born in New Orleans to French-Creole parents, he associated with Choctaw Indians in St. Tammany Parish north of Lake Pontchartrain, where his mother's family had property. His father committed suicide in 1819 when his wine business failed. Young Rouquette attended the Collège d'Orléans (1821–c. 1824) and then transferred to Transylvania College in Lexington, Kentucky, where he learned English and studied Latin. After his mother died he entered a French school in Mantua, New Jersey (1828), and then emigrated to Nantes, France, where he studied at the Collège Royal. He became a devout practicing Catholic (1833). While living in Paris, he sent samples of his verse to French-language newspapers in Louisiana. After returning to Louisiana in 1837, he studied at a seminary in Plattenville, published a book of verse titled *Les Savanes, poésies américaines* (1841), and was ordained a priest (1845)—the first native one in Louisiana. Although he preached superbly and helped spread the faith in *Le Propagateur Catholique*, a New Orleans weekly, and elsewhere, Rouquette longed to return to St. Tammany and his Choctaw friends. Permitted to do so in 1847, he became their missionary, built chapels and houses near Lake Pontchartrain, lived in a house in Lacombe, and adopted the name Chahta-Ima (meaning "Like a Choctaw"). He gradually became neurotic and somewhat reclusive.

His next published works were *Wild Flowers: Sacred Poetry* (1848), *La Thébaïde en Amerique, ou Apologie de la vie solitaire et contemplative* (1852), and *L'Antoniade, ou la solitude avec Dieu* (1860). These works show his versatility: Whereas his early poetry in French is romantic, his verse in English is weak; both *La Thébaïde*, in prose, and *L'Antoniade*, in verse, are largely devoted to spiritual solitude. During the Civil War, Rouquette was explicitly pro-Union, which enabled him to persuade Admiral David Farragut to permit food and medicine to be shipped to the Choctaws. Rouquette published *La nouvelle Atala* (1879), a sentimental prose-fiction follow-up of *Atala* by François-René de Chateaubriand (1768–1848), whom he had met in France. *A Critical Dialogue between Aboo and Caboo on a New Book; or, A Grandissime Ascension* (1880) is a vicious criticism by Abbé Rouquette (Aboo) of *The Grandissimes* (1880) by George Washington Cable* (Caboo), in which, among other things, he suggests that Cable consorts with the voodoo queen Marie Laveau.* For two years before his death Rouquette was placed in a New Orleans hospital, during which time he was mentally lucid only part of the time.

Hearn met Rouquette in New Orleans in 1877. Rouquette admired Hearn's pieces in the New Orleans *Item* about French literature and Creole folklore. So he published a poem in Creole French in *Le Propagateur Catholique* about inviting "A mo Zami Grek-Anglé, L. H. (To my Greek English Friend, L. H.)" to his Choctaw hut. The first stanza of the 20 in this weird poem begins: "To papa, li sorti péi-Anglé / Mé to mama, li sorti ile la Gréce" (Your father came from England but your mother came from Greece). Instead of meeting in Rouquette's hut, they met in his ascetic room at the New Orleans archbishopric. They became friends despite Hearn's reservations about Catholicism. Hearn favorably reviewed advance sheets of Rouquette's *La nouvelle Atala* (*Item*, February 25, 1879). When *Atala* appeared in book form, Rouquette bound in it a reprint of Hearn's review. In the late 1870s, Hearn wrote to his friend Henry Edward Krehbiel,* a music critic, about Rouquette's interest in Creole songs. Soon, however, Rouquette and Hearn disagreed about religious doctrines (notably chastity), Hearn's seemingly disreputable mode of living, and how to transcribe Creole poetry. Worse, Rouquette's vituperative comments about Cable and his writing in *Aboo and Caboo* incensed Hearn, who extravagantly lauded *The Grandissimes*. This divergence of critical opinions evidently caused a permanent rupture in their relationship. All the same, Hearn continued to admire, and perhaps envy, certain aspects of Rouquette's colorfully unconventional career.

Bibliography: Cott; Blaise C. D'Antoine, *Chahti-Ima and St. Tammany's Choctaws* (Mandeville, La.: St. Tammany Historical Society, 1986); Dagmar Renshaw LeBreton, *Chahta-Ima: The Life of Adrien-Emmanuel Rouquette* (Baton Rouge: Louisiana State University Press, 1947); Tinker; Edward Larocque Tinker, *Creole City: Its Past and Its People* (New York: Longmans, Green, 1953).

"ROUSTABOUT ROWDIES" (1876). Cincinnati news article. Hearn narrates, with objective aplomb, "Domestic Difficulties" among black riverfront workers. Riley, seeking "his 'gal' " Alice, learns she has kept company with other men and beats her up. She won't press charges. Swan married Belle upon her release from prison. When he wouldn't support her, she returned to prostitution. He finds her in Davis's house with Marshall, the fellow who killed Williams a while back. When Swan asks Marshall if he wants Belle, the answer causes Swan to throttle Marshall, who strikes back with a hatchet. Ejected by several men, Swan asks Davis to send Marshall out to be killed. No. Swan breaks down the door. Davis shoots him in the chest. Swan grabs Davis, whose wife takes a rock to Swan's head. Swan is doctored. Davis is arrested.

S

"THE SECRETS OF THE INFINITE" (1879). Editorial. Each time astronomers penetrate to new depths, puzzles farther away taunt them. The same is true of microscopists. Scientists are mocked by "the Infinite . . . with its interminable Enigma." Will they, like the neophyte lifting veil after veil hiding Isis, find, at last, "the eyeless sockets of Death?"

"SELF-SUPPORTING WIVES" (1879). Editorial. Equally misguided are men whose wives demand luxury, idleness, money, and freedom, and men who say that they would not deserve wives if the wives were forced to go out and work. Girls should be taught self-supporting "trades and professions," not least so that they would never be dependent on "drunken or immoral" husbands. Because American wages are falling to European levels, two-income families may soon be necessary. Laudable are Frenchmen whose wives have outside jobs and who are treated by their husbands as friends and comrades, to be "consulted" in troublesome times.

"THE SEXUAL IDEA IN FRENCH LITERATURE" (1881). Editorial. French literature is the most dainty, beautiful, and artistic in the world. Driving it, along with sculpture and painting, is the "electricity" of "[p]assion." French writers expose "the physical . . . mechanism of passion" with the precision of a surgeon. "Northern races" see passion as consequence; "Latins," as motive. In French novels, it is both "motive and . . . consequence." On the other hand, "we [Americans]" feel that worshipping Venus is dangerous. The French historian Jules Michelet (1798–1874) has applied "sexual philosophy to historical enigmas." His writings on insects should inspire tenderness in all of his readers.

Bibliography: Tinker.

SHADOWINGS (1900). A collection of 16 stories and sketches under three headings: "Stories from Strange Books," "Japanese Studies," and "Fantasies." None of the items were published earlier. *Shadowings* and *A Japanese Miscellany* were combined as Volume 10 of *The Writings of Lafcadio Hearn* (16 vols., 1922).

"Stories from Strange Books" has six tales. In a footnote, Hearn identifies the source of each, and he professes displeasure at the inconclusive endings of some of them. "The Reconciliation" concerns a Kyōto samurai who because of poverty divorces his first wife, moves, marries again, and prospers. But he is so unhappy that he sends the second wife away and, haunted by his first wife's sweet speech and smiles, manner, and patience, returns to their old home on the ninth month's tenth day. He finds the lovely wife there, sewing and alone. She accepts his apology, and they lie down and talk until he falls asleep. In the morning he finds her shroud-wrapped corpse beside him. Asking neighbors, he learns she died soon after she was abandoned, on the tenth day of the ninth month. "Reconciliation" was the basis for part of Kobayashi Masaki's 1964 movie *Kwaidan*. Suspense in Hearn's necrophilic piece is diminished by certain giveaway details at the outset.

"The Legend of Fugen-Bosatsu": Shōku Shōnin, a priest, reads about Fugen-Bosatsu, a female Bodhisattva (one approaching Buddhahood). While reading, he falls asleep and dreams; a voice tells him that in order to see Fugen-Bosatsu he must visit a certain courtesan. Going to her residence, he is entranced by her singing. When she looks at him, her brow emits a dazzling light and she is seen to be riding on an elephant. He closes his eyes and continues to see her. He opens his eyes, and she is gone. Sadly, he leaves; but at her gate, she appears and tells him to say nothing of this experience. The moral: A Bodhisattva may use the humblest of mortals, here a courtesan, as a means of an incarnation.

"The Screen-Maiden": Tokkai, a Kyōto student, buys the portrait of a lovely girl painted on a paper-covered screen, takes it home, is bewitched by her unsurpassed beauty, and would give his life to embrace her. When he falls ill, he is visited by an old scholar who tells him that the picture was painted by Hishigawa Kichibei (a seventeenth-century genius) and that the girl's spirit lives in the portrait. If the student gives her a name and fixes all thoughts upon her, she will come to him. Then he must offer her special wine. Thus it happens. They pledge to love one another for seven lifetimes. The original Japanese author ends by saying that such events rarely happen in real life. Hearn's interruptions to discuss problems of translation break the suspense of an otherwise gripping tale.

"The Corpse-Rider": A woman is so outraged at being divorced that she turns ice cold and her heart stops, but she lives on, awaiting a chance at vengeance. When her husband, returning from a journey, is told about his wife, he grows terrified, knows she will tear him to pieces, and seeks advice from an *inyōshi* (expert on the universal male-female principle). He tells the husband to go to his wife's body, sit on her back, hold her hair like bridles, and ride for his life.

Though scared, he does so, and his wife gallops out of their house all night, returning at dawn and then lying still. The *inyōshi* whispers something (not revealed) in her ear. Was Hearn aware of the implications of the sentence in which he describes the wife's final action? It is thus: "Under the man she panted and moaned till the cocks began to crow." Before the woman's second dying, the giddy-up "of her naked feet in the dark," accompanied by "the hiss of her breathing," Hearn presents as "picha-picha, picha-picha."

"The Sympathy of Benten": Hanagaki Baishū, a scholar-poet, is wandering in the gardens of a Kyōto temple built in the eighth century and rebuilt a thousand years later. Near the Goddess Benten's new temple there, Baishū finds a spring. A wind blows a paper ribbon to him. It contains a famous poem concerning "first love," copied in characters so beautiful that he falls in love with the writer, whom he pictures as an adorable young girl. After praying for seven days and nights at Benten's temple, he is accosted by a majestic old man who summons the beautiful poetess. She walks past Baishū into the street. When he follows, she turns and introduces herself as his wife. She proves to be wondrously accomplished. One winter morning while out walking, Baishū is persuaded by a dignified gentleman to visit his guest room and meet his young daughter. The Goddess Benten has told them, he explains, that Baishū will visit them and become her husband. Though married, he agrees to see the daughter, and lo! she is his wife—identical, yet not. The being in his home is "only the soul of his beloved"; the person before him now, "the body." They are wed in her father's house. Hearn concludes that the original tale "breaks off . . . , leaving several matters unexplained." He wonders what the physical girl thought while "her phantom" was married. Did the soul visit the "real bride"? A Japanese friend partially explains: Baishū's "spirit-bride" was created out of the magnificently calligraphed love poem he found in Benten's temple. Hearn presents the potent poem in Japanese only, without a translation. However, he adds a footnote explaining that Japanese scholars can analyze native handwriting and the quality of ink used, describe the writer's "personal carefulness and . . . sense of beauty," and roughly estimate his or her age.

"The Gratitude of the Samébito": Tawaraya Tōtarō lives comfortably in Ōmi but, now age 29, wants to marry a beautiful woman. One day near the famous Long Bridge he sees an all-black, green-eyed *samébito* (shark-man, merman). For misbehaving, he was exiled from the Dragon Palace and is now unemployed and hungry. Moved to pity, Tōtarō takes him home, puts him in his pond, and feeds him tenderly for a year. While visiting a nearby town populated by female pilgrims, Tōtarō sees a lovely girl about 16 years old, instantly falls in love, and learns she is Tamara and is single and can be his wife if he gives her parents a casket containing ten thousand jewels. Home again, Tōtarō longs for the gorgeous Tamara but figures he can never find so many gems, and he falls horribly ill. Serving him is the shark-man, now able to walk about. Tōtarō expresses fear that after he dies no one will feed the shark-man. He adds that perhaps in a previous life he also cared for the shark-man. Hearing this, the shark-man weeps bitterly, and bloody tears hit the floor and become fiery-crimson rubies of great value. Feeling better at once, Tōtarō begins gathering the jewels, explains his amorous ambition and necessary dowry to the shark-man, but is saddened when he does not quite have the requisite ten thousand. The shark-man says he is happy that his master is cured but cannot cry at will, like a hypocritical harlot. He says they should go to the Long Bridge, where the shark-man will think of the Dragon Palace and homesickness may cause more tears. The next day they do so. Sure enough, he cries out enough rubies to make up the total, all of which Tōtarō puts into a casket. Suddenly a palace rises in the sunset. Figuring on an amnesty, the shark-man swims out of sight. Tōtarō pays the red jewels and obtains his bride.

"Japanese Studies" has three essays. "Sémi" (cicadae) begins with the statement that both the ancient Greek poet Anacreon and a Chinese scholar called, by the Japanese, Riku-Un agree that cicadae are honored for their virtue. Hearn quotes a few Greek and Japanese poets about their love for the tiny insect. He discusses eight types of cicadae (spring, mountain, summer, barley-harvest, day-darkening, hot-weather, post-death festival, and autumn), with Japanese names and indications of the different sounds they make. Finally, he presents 38 poems in Japanese (mostly in *hokku* form), with English translations, devoted to cicadae—their sounds, the effects of the sounds on the poet, and the philosophical implications of the cicada life cycle. As for sounds—one buzzes *min—min—min-min-min-minminmin-dzzzzzzz*. As for effect—when one quits singing, fireflies appear and the hour is refreshing. As for philosophy—the cicada's sloughed-off simulacrum resembles "a body consumed by passionate longing." In this essay Hearn displays his considerable erudition.

"Japanese Female Names": *Yobina* (personal names) are given to Japanese girls less for aesthetic reasons (e.g., Ben, meaning "petal") than to indicate moral and mental qualities (e.g., Misao, "wifely fidelity"). Translating is difficult, often impossible (Taka, "falcon," "honorable," "tall"; Ki, with 21 meanings in Hearn's dictionary). Nevertheless, using the publication of a Japanese scholar that listed and discussed the names of about four hundred girls enrolled in a normal school from 1880 to 1895, Hearn selects and lists 164 such names, gives frequency of use, translates, and includes comments in footnotes. The three most popular names: Kan ("forebearing," "patient"); Kō ("filial piety"); and Tsuné ("constant one"). One girl is named Ushi ("ox"), perhaps for zodiacal reasons. Most girls' names are dissyllabic, not counting the honorific *O* prefix (O-Ryō, "generous"). The suffix *ko* sometimes "has the value of a caressing diminutive" (Aiko, "tiny love"). Hearn lists 29 names of virtues and proprieties (O-Ken, "wise"); 83 expressing personal qualities or parental hopes (O-Sai, "talented"); 32 place names (O-Kishi, "beach"); 15 objects and occupations (O-Koto, "harp"); 16 materials (O-Sato, "sugar"); 5 literary names (O-Tusa, "poem"); 23 names related to numbers or birth order (O-Ju-, "ten"; O-Tomé, "stop[!]"); 11 relating to time (O-Sayo, "night"); 15 relating to creatures (O-Tora, "tiger"); 32 relating to flowers, fruits, plants, and trees (O-Také, "bamboo"); and 16 concerning light and color (O-Teru, "shining"; Muraski, "purple"). Among 18 names that are hard to interpret are O-Fuku ("clothing") and O-Toshi ("arrowhead"). Not content with the scholar's report, Hearn consulted 1886–1895 enrollments at a school catering to the daughters of Japanese nobility and lists an additional 149 names, often ending with the sweet-*ko* diminutive (Hosh-ko, "star"). Some of his footnotes are amusing. He laboriously explains that a certain name has little or no meaning; he says that he cannot explain another to those who do not understand the Japanese language; and he contends that "Tatsuro-ko" is probably pronounced as two syllables. Pretty names, like Jewel and Cherry, are given to geishas and prostitutes and therefore are off-limits for respectable baby girls. Hearn says such names "have nothing to do with the present study" because they are "professional appellations only—not yobina." Still, he discusses several of their prefixes and suffixes, signifying "heap," "little," "serve," and "young," and complimentary touches such as "flower-Dragon." In 1889, legislatures were lobbied to stop geishas from trying to "assume real names with . . . even aristocratic yobina." This long essay, with almost innumerable names in Japanese and English, and with careful commentary, was obviously a labor of love for Hearn.

"Old Japanese Songs": One New Year's morning, a friendly poet sent Hearn two gifts. One was cloth for a kimono, of cotton thread and strings of paper containing poetic lines. The other gift was a manuscript collection of Japanese ballads, dancing songs, and love songs. Most contain refrains, and all are different from the poetry Hearn has edited for previous publications. The best are from early dramas, with striking use of repetition and pause. Others have uncompleted phrases, Buddhist allusions, risqué lines, and puns involving numbers. Some songs accompany children's games with bouncing balls. Some have onomatopoetic choruses. Hearn presents most of his examples in Japanese, with English translations (sometimes incomplete) and often extensive commentary. He offers a "true street-ballad," in English only, about a couple fatally in love; he explains that its "irregular measure" has lines of between 12 and 16 syllables. He closes with two Buddhist poems. The "Imayō" measure of the first, perhaps from the twelfth century, alternates 7- and 5-syllable lines and concerns personal salvation. The other, from the sixteenth century, wonders "Who twice shall live his youth?" and implies the answer by wondering if faded flowers bloom again. Hearn's translations in this essay are generally wooden. He enlivens it by comparing a few samples of Japanese poems to French and English verse. A touch of humor comes when a female persona, distressed that her cruel mother-in-law has challenged her to make a skirt out of rock, suggests that the older woman should "twist the fine sand into thread,—Twist it into thread."

"Fantasies" has seven pieces. In "Noctilucae," Hearn describes lights at night against the black sky "all seething with stars." He is "a phosphor-point" between the "burn[ing] red" of "earthly life" and the "ineffable rhythms of azure" generated by "thoughts of supernal being." A voice tells him that by means of his thoughts he creates "Gods." The beauty of this tone poem lies not in any thought but in Hearn's dazzling word-play.

"A Mystery of Crowds": Surface shapes, changing, unchanging, are like people pouring and vibrating through city streets. Laws of movement operate there. To pass, people turn left, turn right. Two yield more often than one does. Few approach and duel eye to eye; more often, one senses whether to give way or not. One who thinks about what step to take is apt to blunder. Hearn suggests that we have inherited the "faculty of intuitive self-direction in a crowd" from animals, birds, fish, even insects. Perhaps they, in turn, have inherited the tendency from "non-sentient substance."

"Gothic Horror": As a child, Hearn was taken to a Gothic church. Its architecture inspired a "ghostly fear." The stony points and arches inspired thoughts of goblins. Growing older, he sought an explanation. Architectural treatises were less helpful than fiction, especially when one writer said Gothic churches resemble hungry animal skeletons, especially their bony points. Why such fear? The answer came to Hearn when in the tropics one morning he noticed an enormous palm. Its "prodigious column" stretched up like a conscious serpent to create "a parasol of emerald feathers" against an electric sky. It seemed to aspire "against Titans" for light, indifferent to beetle-like people in darkness below. Palm trunks in a group suddenly resembled "the pillars of a mighty aisle," and Hearn felt again "the old dark thrill of Gothic horror." The trunks curved up into "prodigious arches" resembling supernaturally exaggerated "vegetal growth." To a child, such a picture is frightening, like a phantom in a dream. This essay is psychic autobiography of an upsetting sort.

"Levitation": While leaning out an upper-story window one sunless, gray day, Hearn's persona falls, feels sick, then wonders, feels joy, floats, touches the pavement with one foot. Up he goes again, feeling superhuman, divine. People stare at him, silently, as he flies through the streets. He concludes that this is a dream but that discovering "this power" is revelatory. He has learned to fly. The next morning, after momentarily thinking of flying again, he realizes that he has discovered nothing. He often dreams of flying. He is convinced he has "a new faculty," which he forgets upon awakening. Gravity is then too real. His dream flights are always at low altitude, with the real world pulling at him. With one exception, other dream flyers he has queried say they also fly low. Why for eons has "humanity . . . thus been flying by night"? In dreams, we feel imponderable, levitated, floating, disembodied, gliding by mere willpower. Do we have an "organic memory of conditions of life more ancient than man"? Or perhaps a normally dormant, "all-permeating Over-Soul, . . . wakens within the brain at rare moments of our sleep-life"?

"Nightmare-Touch": Fear of ghosts results from pains long past and probably begins in intense, vague dreams. What is "the fancy behind the fear"? We are not afraid that ghosts, which are "intangible and imponderable," will devour us, only that they will touch us. This fear is caused by "prenatal experience," stored in us by inheritance, like a child's fear of the dark. Hearn reminisces about

being locked, when he was 5 years old, in a narrow, high room in the dark—
to cure him of being afraid of the dark! If he screamed, he was punished; but
he preferred the punishment to the fear. From his earliest years, he had ugly
dreams of shadowy forms, which were "tangible realities" groping for him.
When he complained of seeing ghosts and was told they did not exist, he knew
they did and concluded that either they saw only him or those denying their
existence were liars. His ghosts wore dark robes, were atrociously deformed,
and could elongate and turn upside-down at will. Only their faces were distinct.
Typically, a dream would begin with a will-quenching heaviness upon him,
while above a yellow glow the ceiling would be black. When trying to escape,
he felt like one wading across the room. He could not cry out. Through his
bolted door a thing would glide, seize him, and toss him toward the ceiling. He
would feel no pain, but "a sort of abominable electricity." Groups sometimes
hurled him about. Hearn's conclusions follow: These shapes come from "experiences of fear in other lives than mine." They are not imagined. They cause
sensations that are massively and deeply thrilling, unlike anything in one who
is awake. When lowly creatures first could think and fear, they must have
dreamed of being hurt by enemies. Creatures higher on the evolutionary scale
could imagine pain and therefore became susceptible to "dream-pain," and later
to "dream-fear." Higher on the scale, we have inherited "the experience of such
feeling." Deep in everyone is a "substratum of ancient animal-terrors," triggering
nightmares. Their touch in the black night stirs memories of race-experiences
eons back. Although most critics regard Hearn's evolutionary theory here as
nonsensical, all readers likely would agree that his account of childish terror is
intensely gripping. He demonstrates his erudition by citing *Traité des exhuma-
tions juridiques . . .* (2 vols., with O. Lesueur, 1831), mainly written by Mathieu
Joseph Bonaventure Orfila (1787–1853), a French professor of medical juris-
prudence and chemistry and the founder of a comparative anatomy museum.

"Readings from a Dream-Book": In "the blind dead of the night," Hearn reads
in a book that is emerging from blackness and illumined by a sourceless light.
Sentences float and disappear. He rearranges eight fragments, each into a nearly
"rational sequence." I. A Wave wants to remain a wave, but the Sea says it
must forever break, without pain, joy, or understanding. II. Each "cosmic par-
ticle" must pass through every possible life experience. III. Millions of years
hence, each of us will be both less and more than we were, our sexes alternating,
though not remembering with a feeling still of having met earlier. IV. Wronging
one who loves mocks the divine. V. Love at first sight by one with an inheritance
from the dead sometimes harms. VI. One should fear death only because one
may be recombined with one's other lives' bad traits. VII. If a dangerous woman
touches a young man, former ghosts in his makeup will cause him to perish.
VIII. When a man tells his former souls he is tired of life, they say they are
too, and they rebuke him for creating what he is, for not listening to their
guidance, for wanting revenge on his enemy. They warn him that "nothingness"
is not the end; then they become worms and eat him.

"In a Pair of Eyes": An adolescent boy sees unique charm in "a certain pair of eyes," looks away in fear, and then is ecstatic upon seeing them again. He asks a friend why they seem divine, is tenderly laughed at, is not embarrassed, but is never enlightened. Those human eyes are more lovely to us than gems, deeper than oceans, because we have "*felt*" an unspeakably marvelous, brief glimpse—not to be revealed again—of the illusory ghost of the "divine itself," by momentarily seeing beyond life's mask into death's night. In this manner, "truth and illusion mingle in the magic of eyes," and all becomes part of "Infinite Memory."

In a letter to Elizabeth Bisland* (January 1900), Hearn described *Shadowings* as a collection of "reveries, and sundry queer stories." Often, the style in which the strange pieces are couched is superior to their frequently eldritch content. *Shadowings*, also issued in England (1900), was often reprinted.

Bibliography: Hirakawa; Kennard; Kunst; Murray.

"SHAPIRA" (1885). Editorial. Charles Clermont-Ganneau (1846–1923), a French Orientalist, exposed the archaeological frauds of M. W. Shapira, who in 1872 offered supposedly genuine Moabite pottery for sale. The objects were grotesque and obscene, with decipherable characters, and therefore seemed authentic. But Shapira's associate, a man named Selim El-Qari, had in fact made them. British authorities were privately tipped off and declined to buy them; so Shapira sold 1,700 pieces to a Berlin museum after selfishly jealous German experts decried Clermont-Ganneau's opinions. When the fakery was fully exposed, Shapira was sued, bribed witnesses and jurors, but was exposed in 1876. In 1883 Shapira offered a supposedly "original manuscript of the Bible" to Berlin experts. Once again, Clermont-Ganneau exposed the fraud, whereupon Shapira committed suicide.

"A SLAUGHTER-HOUSE STORY" (1876). Cincinnati news article. Many ladies visit the Jewish slaughterhouse to drink a glass of freshly spouting bullock blood. It is said that quaffing "the red cream" helps cure consumption, dyspepsia, and other ailments. Some weeks ago a Frenchman came in and drank three glasses, despite being warned by one of the Lowenstein brothers, proprietors, that taking in almost a quart of blood might prove dangerous. Returning 10 days later, the Frenchman said he would not drink so much blood at one time again because doing so previously had made him temporarily blind. Doubting this, Hearn interviewed several physicians. They said it was absurd to think that drinking blood could cause blindness. One doctor did feel that doing so might aggravate an already present kidney disease and thus damage the eyes. Another doubted even this diagnosis. *See* "Haceldama."

"SLOW STARVATION" (1874). Cincinnati news article. Married women and young girls living with their parents augment their income from other sources by making garments. The women sew for 60 to 80 hours a week and receive $2 to $3 a week from clothiers. Hearn first interviews Mrs. ——, who is patiently informative and then sends him to Mrs. S——, who reveals much and sends him to Mrs. C——, who adds a good deal. The jist is that these women rent $85 sewing machines and $100 button-hole machines by the week, must do acceptable work on time or be blackballed, and are paid little, for example, 10 to 40 cents per pair of different kinds of pants (retailing at $8–10), 40 to 80 cents for a winter coat (retailing at up to $10), $2 for a dozen linen coats, and 10 cents for six woolen shirts. Hearn enlivens this horrifying article by means of three devices. First, he portrays himself as having been sent on this assignment because he is "the ugliest local in the office," with a harmless "spectacled visage" resembling "the countenance of an owl." Second, he is still able to catch sweet smiles from several seamstresses, some of whom he describes lovingly. Third, he skillfully reproduces the engaging Irish accent of Mrs. ——. But is he revealing a bias when he goes out of his way to find and list the names of the women's various, employers: Gotterman, Gutterman, Kahn, Nathan, Simmons, Strauss, and Wineman?

" 'SOLITUDE' " (**1886**). Editorial. "Solitude" by Guy de Maupassant (1850–1893) presents "as durable [an] effect on the reader's mind" as a 500-page novel by Émile Zola would have produced. Hearn calls Maupassant's hero an "intellectual hermit," analysis of whom would challenge speculation by Western psychologists and Eastern philosophers alike. The fellow has discovered that no one can understand anyone else. Hearn's conclusion: Those who believe in social evolution may fear that self-isolation, love of individuality, and increased specialized labor will push everyone into "mental desolation impenetrable to all" others and ultimately into a longing for death.

SOME CHINESE GHOSTS (**1887**). A collection of six short stories from Chinese originals, purportedly translations but really unified redactions dealing with love and death. The book takes advantage of then-recent intense interest in matters pertaining to China. In a brief preface Hearn apologizes for the small size of the book, agrees with the comment by Sir Walter Scott in his "Essay on Imitations of the Ancient Ballad" that supernaturalism is treated best when touched on lightly, and cites and praises the work of several Sinologists. Hearn provides notes identifying his sources and also an elaborate glossary of Chinese terms. He dedicates the book to his friend music critic Henry Edward Krehbiel.* A few contemporary reviews called the book obscene and fabricated. An *Atlantic Monthly* reviewer, however, regarded it as "rare" and "delightful" although mannered in style. The book was frequently reprinted, including in England (1907) and by the Modern Library (1927). *See* Appendix for titles of individual stories.

Bibliography: Hirakawa; Kunst; Murray.

"SOME FANCIES ABOUT FANCY" (1881). Editorial. Typically, a great writer produces a masterpiece, then, after an interval, a different sort of masterpiece. Short stories, suggested by facts, are tinged by imagination. Difficult to write, with charm, haunting effects, and power, they are "involuntary parturition of [brief] fancies." Some critics say they have little value. In truth, however, they enrich language and style, nourish thought, and liberate spiritually and socially. Historians and scientists writing "with ornate grace" improve what might otherwise be "dry and bony." Fanciful fiction is preferable to historical novels. Writers whose work is of high quality cannot produce much quantity, the latter being turned out for money. Among many examples Hearn cites are two of special interest. He says that Henri Murger (1822–1861) is known only for his *Scènes de la Vie de Bohème* (1847–1849). This work is known now almost exclusively because Giacomo Puccini based his opera *La Bohème* on it, 15 years after Hearn published this essay. He also mentions Bret Harte here and correctly predicts that Harte would not write anything of high quality in the future.

"SOME FOSSIL ANTHROPOLOGY" (1885). Editorial. Hearn discusses the conclusions of Jean Louis Armand de Quatrefages de Bréau (1810–1892), a French naturalist and ethnologist. In recent publications Quatrefages tentatively supports "the Darwinian hypothesis of descent as . . . the most rational . . . explanation of the origin of species." However, Quatrefages has some reservations based on studies of "fossil man of the tertiary and quaternary epochs," such as their existing alongside certain species of apes, their brain size, their evident religious beliefs, and their often fine physical development. Hearn presciently concludes that "other links may be found."

"SOME GROTESQUE THEORIZING" (1882). Editorial. Recent science fiction writers, emulating astronomers with vivid imaginations, posit worlds where people work and never sleep, observe suns and moons of many colors, have philosophers whose intelligence is in advance of ours, have incredibly developed senses, and can leap prodigiously. Huge worlds may have tiny creatures; tiny worlds (including asteroids), big ones. Why do these fictive worlds have humanlike creatures? Why do they not have intelligent and literate birds, insects, and Houyhnhnms (as in Jonathan Swift)? How about women with blue skin and green hair, living on terrains of chocolate, candy, and ice cream?

"SOME PICTURES OF POVERTY" (1877). Cincinnati news article. In an area called the Barracks, "a locality of . . . picturesque wretchedness," live "the poorest of the poor." They are visited regularly by a city overseer. One rickety lean-to suggests "a medieval . . . haunt of poverty . . . crowd[ed]" close to an old-world cathedral. Hearn accompanies the overseer and observes so many charity cases that their faces and candle-lit possessions blend in his memory: old blacks; fine-featured Indian women; bead-fingering Irishwomen "frozen into apathy," gazing with shadowed eyes and "ghastly tremor." One bony crone, asked how her "old man" is, digs out his "last" letter, dated 1849. Hearn imagines a sequence of "reeling buildings" filled with hopeless people patiently "waiting for the end in loneliness," companioned mainly by memories. The men visit a swollen-limbed old man, bedridden for 16 years and cared for tenderly by one whom Hearn typifies as "the conventional . . . Aged Woman." She regards a noisy, child-beating, drunken woman nearby as "the Divil." Many inmates complain of being robbed by neighbors. Hearn finds "a pretty pathos" in the efforts of some to decorate their hovels with awkwardly whittled pictures. Beside a dying woman's bed a black preacher sings, aiming to offer comfort: "Dese ole bones of mine / Will all come togeder in de morning." Hearn's tone in this heart-rending article combines touching sentiment, humor, and mockery at the monstrous injustice of life.

Bibliography: Cott; Stevenson.

"SOME POSITIVE OPINIONS" (1881). Sketch. This internationally known dancer's face resembles the sinister, ill-featured face in an illustrated edition of Honoré de Balzac's *Peau de Chagrin*, "softened by youth and femininity" but strong, even menacing. The dancer says she likes to arouse hateful men who send her amorous letters, unanswered unless accompanied by presents. Having a juggler's ability to handle fire without getting burned, she lets a few males visit and "smooth me down." Her secret is to make everyone afraid of her. She hopes would-be lovers finally hate her.

"SOME STRANGE EXPERIENCE" (1875). Cincinnati news article. A healthy, attractive, but illiterate "country girl" is a boardinghouse cook. While they sit on the kitchen stairs, she tells Hearn a series of ghostly experiences. In Bracken County, Kentucky, near Dover, an old woman died in a ramshackle farm house and later was heard rocking in her chair. When the girl lived there, she went upstairs one night and was followed by something that moaned and touched her head. Near the place was a henhouse where hens laid eggs supposedly sucked empty by ghosts. A man galloped on the Dover pike toward his home, through a window saw his wife being fondled by a stranger, hanged himself, and began to haunt the region. Near the Minerva tollgate, a man killed a fellow for his money but now flies along the pike in spectral fashion. While employed by a Minerva family, the girl had trouble sleeping one night because a heavy hand kept pulling down her bedclothes. In Lexington, a woman flogged a slave to death and was doomed after her own death to sit crying at her door. In a Cincinnati home where she once worked, the girl saw the ghost of a headless young lady in a mirror. Friends think the girl should become a medium, but she says she wants the dead to leave her alone. Amusingly, Hearn says that he cannot report her stories word for word but then proceeds to reproduce some very vivid talk. He also says that although illiterate the girl "possessed naturally a wonderful wealth of verbal description." True, but one wonders how she picked up such words as "discernible," "enchantment," "hoary," "glutinous," "propagate," and "supposition." The girl, though unnamed, is based on Alethea Foley,* Hearn's wife until Ohio's anti-miscegenation laws declared the marriage null. Hearn was happy to be Foley's ghostwriter here. This 1875 piece shows that Hearn was interested in things spectral and fantastic from a rather early age.

"THE SON OF A ROBBER" (1884). Short story. Bold robbers prey on caravans and then retreat into their mountain fastnesses. So the Persian governors ambush them, capture them, and present them to the king, who orders their execution. A vizier asks the king to spare one especially handsome youth. Though persuaded by others and expressing grave doubts, he does so. The vizier takes the lad to his palace and educates him in weaponry, the arts, and courtly speech. When the king sees him, he still worries. Two years later, the youth while riding encounters some mountain brigands, whose presence kindles all his dormant ferocity. Making a compact with them, he returns to the vizier, kills him and his sons, loots his palace, and escapes to his cohorts. The king hears, laughs bitterly, and says that doing good to the evil is "blameworthy."

"THE SOUL OF THE GREAT BELL" (1887). Ghost story. Every day the great bell of Pe-king is rung. It thunders "Ko-Ngai," then whispers "Hiai." Why? Five hundred years ago the Ming dynasty leader ordered Kouan-Yu to create a great bell of iron, brass, gold, and silver. Twice the metals would not fuse, and Kouan-Yu was warned that he must succeed next time or die. His daughter, Ko-Ngai, consulted an astrologer, who said the metals would wed only if a pure maiden was cast with them. At the foundry she hurled herself into the molten metal despite all restraint. A servant caught only her shoe. The resulting bell was perfect. Its voice is, first, Ko-Ngai's resounding name and, then, her whisper for her lost shoe. Hearn cites his source: P. Dabry de Thiersant's 1877 translation of *Pe-Hiao-Tou-Choue* (A Hundred Examples of Filial Piety); Claude Philibert Dabry de Thierssant (1826–1898) was a distinguished authority on China.

Bibliography: Murray.

"SPRING FEVER FANCIES" (1879). Editorial. Whereas winter induces a "psychological torpor" and a desire to do our duty for material gain, in the spring we "long . . . for other lands and strange places," and the most imaginative of us are especially "cursed, or blessed" thus. In springtime our hearts feel sad, the city walls us in, and we feel homesick like a bird wanting to head north. Have we evolved from birds, to feel this way? Have we inherited these vague longings from our wandering ancestors? The passage just quoted about "long[ing] . . . for . . . strange places" slightly echoes Geoffrey Chaucer's lines in his "General Prologue" to *The Canterbury Tales*: "Thanne longen folk to goon on pilgrimages, / And palmeres for to seken straunge strondes."

"SPRING PHANTOMS" (1881). Sketch. The moon's whisper to sleeping new-borns that they will love everything the moon loves, whether they will ever in actuality see what the moon sees, may be a blessing but more likely a curse. It is surely sad to have visions of never-seen cities of gold or beauteous "phantom bride[s]," especially as we sink into the dreamless sleep of death.

"THE STORY OF AN ORIENTALIST" (1884). Editorial. Hearn praises the wealthy Émile Guimet (1836–1918) for establishing the Musée Guimet. The place contains artifacts of ancient and modern Asian, African, and American religious cults, as well as Oriental ceramics. Perhaps even more valuable is its adjacent library of Oriental manuscripts—a veritable college for translators. Guimet engaged distinguished Brahmin and Buddhist translators to help. A 600-page catalogue lists museum publications. Guimet will donate the museum to France if it is moved from Lyons to Paris. Hearn begins this editorial by saying that the French have criticized the Americans for not expressing sufficient gratitude for the French gift of the Statue of Liberty, but he ends by adding that the French have little warrant for such criticism when they themselves have been slow in accepting Guimet's proffered museum. In 1866 the museum, now called the Musée des Religions, was moved to Paris.

"THE STORY OF A SLAVE" (1876). Cincinnati news article. Admitting that slave stories are numerous, Hearn wants to repeat an especially horrible one that old Henrietta Woods told him yesterday. Born around 1817 in Boone County, Kentucky, she was owned by Moses Tauser, a fairly kind Jew. When she was 14 years old his son sold her, but not her three siblings, to Henry Forsyth in Louisville. Forsyth paid $700, was cruel, and sold her to William Cerrode, a Frenchman, for $700 or $800. The two went to New Orleans. He quarreled with his wife, Jane, and returned to France. Jane hired Henrietta out to people in Louisville and Cincinnati, where after several years of hotel work she fell ill. She went back to Jane and worked in her boardinghouse until Jane manumitted her. Henrietta then worked for Mrs. Boyd, a dentist's mean wife. Mrs. Boyd took her in a darkened carriage past Covington and sold her to three men, one named Jabez Ward, working for Jane Cerrode's mercenary daughter, Josephine White, and her husband. The three men were joined by Bolton, a slave trader. They took Henrietta to various towns and jails, finally to one in Lexington. After a session in court, Bolton went to Covington and got $700 back from the Whites; but Henrietta remained and worked in jail for a year. Ward had her work for his family in Frankfort, where he was in charge of the penitentiary. He shipped her from Lexington to a slave yard near Natchez, Mississippi, where for $1,050 she was purchased by Gerard Brandon, a vicious man with seven cotton plantations and 800 slaves plus their children. In her prime, Henrietta was 6 feet tall and weighed 200 pounds. She witnessed fatal floggings and was flogged herself until she transferred from field work to kitchen work. One over-seer was discharged for killing too many slaves. Another was discharged when he would not whip slaves according to Mrs. Brandon's depraved standards. Henrietta was Brandon's slave for 15 years. When the Civil War began, he decamped for Texas with his 500 best slaves, including Henrietta. After the war, she returned to Natchez with Brandon and worked for him for three years. Without pay from him, she raised chickens and hogs, saved $25, and returned to Cincinnati with her only child, a boy now working in Chicago. In 1873 Henrietta initiated a suit for $25,000 in damages against Jabez Ward. The case is pending.

"THE STORY OF MING-Y" (1887). Ghost story. Why do the trees in a certain place whisper the name Sië-Thao? Five hundred years ago, bright young Ming-Y, the son of Pelou, was hired to tutor nearby rich Tchang's children. While walking to visit his parents one spring day, he sees the house of Sië-Thao, who invites him for dinner. They have wine and soon sing, play chess, compose poetry, and make love. Ming-Y secretly visits her until one day she says they must forever part. She gives him a jade lion and an agate brush-case. Pelou visits Tchang, and the truth of Ming-Y's trysts comes out. He tries to show them Sië-Thao's house, but it has disappeared. Tchang suddenly recalls an ancient verse about peach blossoms over Sië-Thao's tomb. The mystery is solved, and a breeze whispers her name. Ming-Y becomes a talented, learned family man; he keeps the jade and agate pieces but never discloses their origin. Hearn cites his source: the 1877 translation of a story from the thirteenth-century collection *Kim-Kou-Ki-Kuan* by Gustav (Gustaaf, Gustave) Schlegel (1840–1903), a linguist and expert on Chinese geography.

Bibliography: Murray.

"THE STRANGER" (1880). Sketch. A strange, deep-voiced Italian thrills the host and his friends with talk of faraway places, gives the host a Turkish pipe from Constantinople, and leaves for his ship. Smoking the pipe alone now, the host pictures aspects of the East.

***STRAY LEAVES FROM STRANGE LITERATURE* (1884).** A collection of 27 tales from Buddhist, Egyptian, "Esquimau," Finnish, Indian, Moslem, South Pacific, and Talmudic literatures. In his "Explanatory," Hearn explains that this "mosaic of legend and fable" contains his reconstructions of exotic narratives that especially impressed him. In handling them, he augmented on occasion by drawing on collateral material in the same source as the work treated, and he curtailed at times to avoid repeating or to exclude offensive material. He also comments in detail on his several sources and on scholarship thereon. He appends a bibliography. The stories are printed under five rubrics: "Stray Leaves," "Tales Retold from Indian and Buddhist Literature," "Runes from the Kalawala," "Stories of Moslem Lands," and "Traditions Retold from the Talmud." *See* Appendix for individual titles.

"STUDY AND PLAY" (1884). Editorial. Several authorities blame the degeneracy of civilized races on too much present-day comfort, too few hardships, too much coddling of the weak and ill, and too much indoor factory work. With relatively more farmers and other outdoor workers, Americans are relatively better off than Europeans. Students at all levels are confined in rooms with poor ventilation and bad lighting, and they have too little time for exercise. Their bodies, eyes, teeth, lungs, kidneys, and posture consequently suffer, and too many are unfit for military duty. French schools are the most notorious. French observers rightly praise American and British schools for stressing physical exercise. Hearn wrote this at a time when he was vividly remembering his unpleasant year at a French school and before he ever observed the rigors of Japanese schools.

"SUBMARINE GOSSIP" (1882). Editorial. An address by Milne-Edwards on deep-sea life inspires thoughts about fauna and even flora in "the blackness of that liquid night." No sounds, waves, or smells. Only feeling. Some creatures create their own light, which they extinguish when threatened. Some produce color without the benefit of light. Such creatures seem never to have evolved beyond "plesiosaurus and ichthyosaurus" periods. Flora, not rooted in the deepest ocean bottom, can grow hundreds of feet long. Perhaps future scientists will bring up live fauna from "early geologic periods." Where enormous sea plants grow, perhaps there are huge anacondas and pythons. The reference is to the French zoologist Henri Milne-Edwards (1800–1885).

"SUN SPASMS" (1883). Editorial. On June 19, 1883, four huge spots on the sun appeared, united, and split. Eruptions accompany sunspots, which occur in cycles of about 11 years and coincide with wars on earth. Some theorists say wars are due not to solar influences but to "astral or planetary influences." Sunspots predict the sun's eventual death, with "his" light dwindling to "a monstrous blood drop," then a burst of yellow fire. Sunspots cause telegraphic disturbances, weather changes, and earthquakes. Declines in barometric pressure also cause earthquakes. Are we due for a huge war soon? We should regard the sun as creator but also destroyer, the way the ancient worshipful Aryans did. With no evidence whatsoever, Hearn theorizes that stars, pure and white, have no spots.

T

"THE TALE OF A FAN" (1881). Sketch. Hearn praises the delicate pictures of a beautifully colored Japanese fan he found one Wednesday in a streetcar. Its scent provokes elaborate thoughts of the differing odors of women of different complexions. He compares such smells to the fragrances of different blonde and brunette roses. Surely a dark-eyed, olive-skinned young lady lost that fan.

"THE TALE OF THE PORCELAIN-GOD" (1887). Ghost story. Thousands of years ago, "heaven-taught wisdom . . . created" mysteriously beautiful porcelains. The five best types are listed and described, followed by several groups of lesser quality. Here is the legend of Pu, the first master artist. Beginning as a humble Chinese worker, he studies, labors, and is reputed to be alchemist, magician, and astrologer. He gives a glittering vase to the emperor, who commands him to create a vase resembling flesh that, when spoken to, will creep and develop goose bumps. Pu, though fearful to be imitating "the Eternal Moulder," mixes colors, shapes clay, paints, bakes, and prays to "the Spirit of Fire," but he fails 49 times. The Spirit finally tells him to give his life, his indivisible soul, to the process. Pu works with meticulous care, shapes a masterpiece, dismisses his helpers, enters the fire, and embraces the Spirit. When the workers return they find a perfect vase, which, when touched, whispers "Pu." The emperor orders the lamented craftsman to be accorded "godlike honors." Hearn provides beautifully modulated descriptions of the colors, textures, and features of different porcelains. He cites "the good Père d'Entrecolles" as his source but undertakes to correct him and to prefer a French translation of *King-te-chin-thao-lou* (History of the Porcelains of King-te-chin); François Xavier d'Entrecolles (1663–1741), a French Jesuit missionary to China, wrote *La manière dont s'y fait belle porcelaine* (Lyon, 1819).

"THE TANNERY HORROR" (1874). Cincinnati news article. This is the fourth of eight articles about the murder of Herman Schilling on Saturday, November 7, 1874, by Andreas Egner, his son Frederick K. Egner, and their friend George Rufer, in revenge for Schilling's having allegedly seduced Andreas Egner's daughter Julia, age about 15, who died while pregnant. The other articles, in chronological order, are "Violent Cremation," "Killed and Cremated," "It Is Out!," "The Furnace Fiends [1]," "The Furnace Fiends [2]," The Quarter of Shambles," and "The Furnace Horror." After young Frederick K. Egner confessed that his father and Rufer killed Schilling while he watched, the two adults remain silent. Wednesday, November 11: Crowds threaten to lynch them and also to burn Egner's saloon. At his inquest, the coroner assembles a jury, the accused, various witnesses, and the victim's brother. It is learned that Rufer was jailed elsewhere for being a horse thief, is a bigamist, and beat his local wife. Fred stands up completely under cross-examination. Physical evidence is presented. After lunch and more testimony, the jury deliberates for 10 minutes and returns a verdict of guilty against both Egners and Rufer. That same evening the coroner and a reporter persuade Rufer to make and sign a full confession. Confronted with this, Andreas denies all.

"THE TINTED ART" (1884). Editorial. The actress Lily Langtry (1852–1929) rightly insisted on appearing as a tinted statue of Galatea, rather than looking "ghastly white," in *Pygmalion and Galatea*, the 1871 play by William Schwenck Gilbert (1836–1911). She was prompted by seeing the tinted Venus of the 1862 London Exhibition. The ancient Greeks artfully tinted their statues and also painted their temples and public buildings in vivid colors. Perhaps when Christianity came along, its notion of purity, as symbolized by the color white, kept colors off sculpture. Christianity has certainly lessened one's reveling in pleasure, materialism, and sensuality, as the ancient Greeks did. Then, when sculpture "arose again from its pagan tomb," it was wrongly required to display a "spiritual whiteness." Perhaps the tinted Venus has "heralded . . . an esthetic return" to more laudable art standards.

"TO THE FOUNTAIN OF YOUTH" (1911). Revery. May 2–4, 188–, Hearn describes a trip by train to Jacksonville, Florida, then by boat up the Ocklawaha to Juan Ponce de Leon's goal, in sunshine and moonlight. Hearn dreams of floating on a dangerous current, then glides past "a flood of fluid crystal—a river of molten diamond" into a basin in whose depths is an inexplicable "dark gush." The essay combines literary allusions, rhymthic and figurative language (e.g., spring water of "iridescent . . . jewel-fire" and "air-plants nestl[ing] . . . in the arm-pits of . . . cypresses"), and nature worship.

"TORN LETTERS" (1884). Sketch. Hearn describes Gulf Coast sand formations, winds and birds, dead things on beaches, and visitors to a fishing station and the courtesy of its inhabitants. He mentions a "venerable friend" with a romantic past partly in Africa. Hearn describes the fine figure of a firm, lean Basque woman named Marie, of immemorial ancestry, and the swimming prowess of some Creole boys. Hearn wonders why Marie's brother shoots little birds. In happy solitude, Hearn also notes the effect of spirit-like winds on waters. He hints that Marie was his "sweetheart" and remembers her flower-fragrant hair. Once, when he was about to kiss the gray-eyed Marie, he saw a smiling, sphinx-like face intervening. He can still see Marie standing outlined against the sun. "Torn Letters" and "The Post-Office" were preliminary sketches parts of which made their way into *Chita* (1889).

Bibliography: Tinker.

"THE TRADITION OF THE TEA-PLANT" (1887). Ghost story. Centuries ago an ascetic mendicant going from India toward China receives alms from a beautiful woman. He wrongly glances past his fan at her. Despite remembrances of Buddhistic admonitions to avoid thoughts of fleshly pleasures, he cannot forget her jeweled ear, lovely cheek, limpid eyes, "odor of woman," and so on. He questions the old teaching that all forms are painful illusions. Was her golden complexion illusory? Were her alms? Suddenly noisy darkness wafts him to a city of obscenities, to a cathedral-like mountain with carvings of "interplating . . . bodies of women." Then silence. A perfumed crypt by a basin. His lovely temptress is there, caresses him, calls herself his altar, his God. He awakens in darkness, sees stars in a Chinese sky. Penitent now, he cuts off his eyelids. When dawn delights the land, his eyes are normal and where he thought he tossed his eyelids two shrubs are growing with eyelid-shaped leaflets. Naming the plant "TE," he calls it beneficent and formed by "virtuous resolve." Hearn cites as his main source a statement in the *Chinese Recorder* (1871) by Emilii Vasilevich Bretschneider (1833–1901), a botanist with expertise also in Chinese archaeology and history.

Bibliography: Kunst.

"A TRADITION OF TITUS" (1884). Legend. Titus sacks Jerusalem, wraps sacred vessels in the enormous holy veil, and sails back to Rome. When a storm threatens his ship, he challenges the God of the Jews to fight him on land. The storm ceases. Titus no sooner goes ashore than a gnat flies up his nose and into his brain, and it gnaws there for seven years. Titus gets no relief even from the din he orders hammers to make. Ignorant of the Israeli God's power and finally dying, he wants his ashes scattered so the Israeli God cannot resurrect him for judgment. Before his cremation his skull is split, and out comes a big brass-clawed, iron-jawed gnat.

TRANSLATIONS BY HEARN. Hearn knew French well and Spanish slightly. He studied Japanese but admitted that it was virtually impossible for him to learn it well; therefore, several translations alleged to be his were without doubt largely the work of friends. He began translating with the publication in the New Orleans *Item* (1878) of his careful version of "The Mummy's Foot" by Théophile Gautier (1811–1872). During his tenure at the *Item* (1878–1881) and at the New Orleans *Times-Democrat* (1880–1887) he published approximately two hundred translations of foreign pieces, usually short and all but a couple from the French. Most of the originals had appeared in *Le Figaro*, but he found several others in *L'Evénement, Le Nouvelle Revue*, and *Le Voltaire* and a few more in other French periodicals as well. He translated more than 30 short stories by Guy de Maupassant (1850–1893). Hearn and Maupassant may have attended the same school in France (Institution Ecclésiastique, near Yvetot, near Rouen) in the 1860s but if so, not at the same time. Other significant French authors some of whose short works Hearn translated were Charles Baudelaire (1821–1867), François Coppée (1842–1908), Alphonse Daudet (1840–1897), Pierre Loti (1850–1923), Gérard de Nerval (1808–1855), Victorien Sardou (1831–1908), Philippe Auguste Mathias de Villiers de L'Isle-Adam (1838–1889), and Émile Zola (1840–1902). Given his various proclivities, Hearn also translated a few items by Charles Baissac (?–?); author of *Récits Créoles* (1884); Leopold von Sacher-Masoch (1836–1895), a sensational-sex writer; and Ricardo Palma (1833–1919), an anti-Jesuit Peruvian writer. All these writers were Hearn's contemporaries, and most were avant-garde personalities whose nonconformist content and also style, both literary and personal, appealed to Hearn.

His three most extensive translations are of *One of Cleopatra's Nights and Other Fantastic Romances* by Théophile Gautier (1811–1872), translations of two of which he had already published in the *Item* (1878) and which, with four more, appeared in book form in 1882 (republished later); *The Crime of Sylvestre Bonnard* by Anatole France (1844–1924), which was published in 1890; and *The Temptation of St. Anthony* by Gustave Flaubert (1821–1880), Hearn's translation of which was not published until 1910. Hearn has been especially commended not only for the care with which he sought to preserve the nuances, rhythms, and imagery of Gautier and Flaubert when rendering them into subtle English, but also for his success in reproducing the terseness of Maupassant's realism. Hearn revealed his own complex personality by combining a grudging respect for Zola's grim anti-conservatism with an envy of Loti's love of tropical islands and other areas not dominated by whites. In time, Loti became the greatest literary influence on Hearn. When Hearn could not persuade any firm to republish his Gautier translations in book form, he paid $150 to a New York company to do so. It was his first book, and it sold well despite—or because of—reviews critical of its sensuality, and it was reprinted later. Hearn conscientiously translated Anatole France's classic in two weeks; for his work, which in book form came to 281 pages, he received $100, and $15 more for his introduction. Hearn had translated *The Temptation of St. Anthony* by 1882, but no publisher would touch it during his lifetime. When Jerome A. Hart favorably reviewed Hearn's translation of *One of Cleopatra's Nights* in the San Francisco *Argonaut*, Hearn wrote to Hart (December 1882) asking for advice on getting his *Temptation of St. Anthony* translation published, but without positive results. Hearn is said to have finished a translation of Flaubert's *Avatar* by 1885 but, unable to find a publisher, destroyed the manuscript.

Indubitably, Hearn's stint as translator influenced his own style in both obvious and recondite ways. Several of his translations that he saw in print during his lifetime also enjoyed republication later, notably the story "One of Cleopatra's Nights" (reprinted in 1888, 1900, 1906, 1910, 1915, 1927, and 1929) and *The Crime of Sylvestre Bonnard* (reprinted twice in 1890, and again in 1906, 1909, 1914, 1918, 1931, 1937, 1948, and, most successfully, by Modern Library [1917, 1932]). His translation of *The Temptation of St. Anthony* saw posthumous publication (1910 and many times later; e.g., Modern Library [1920]), as did collections of his translations of works by Maupassant (*Saint Anthony and Other Stories*, ed. Albert Mordell [New York: Albert & Charles Boni, 1924]; and *The Adventures of Walter Schnaffs*, ed. Albert Mordell [Tokyo: Hokuseido Press, 1931]). Mordell also edited Hearn's *Stories from Emile Zola* (Tokyo: Hokuseido Press, 1935). Publishers made thousands of dollars on his meticulous translations; Hearn, almost nothing. In numerous letters Hearn discusses French works he would like to translate, the pleasures and difficulties of translating, the spate of poor translations by others, and the hardships, including financial, he faced in obtaining publishers to handle his efforts.

Bibliography: Bisland; Cott; Gould; Hirakawa; Kunst; Régis Michaud, "Lafcadio Hearn et Flaubert," *Revue Germanique* 8 (1912, no. 1): 50–53; Albert Mordell, introduction, *Stories from Pierre Loti*, trans. Lafcadio Hearn (Tokyo: Hokuseido Press, 1933); Murray; Marcel Robert, *Lafcadio Hearn* (2 vols., Tōkyō: Hokuseido Press, 1950–1951); Stevenson; Tinker.

TRANSLATIONS OF WORKS BY HEARN. The first translation of works by Hearn into Japanese began in 1893, when Hearn spoke at the birthday party of a Japanese teacher in Kumamoto, where both men taught. Hearn's words were published in English and also as translated into Japanese. Only after his death did his works begin to be translated extensively. In 1907 a few of his Japanese folksongs, in English, were retranslated. In 1909, 1910, and 1911 extensive selections of his essays, written in English and concerning things Japanese, began to be translated and published. The following began to appear, in whole or in part: *Kwaidan* (1910, 1923, 1925, 1929, 1930), diaries and letters (1920, 1925), insect essays (1921, 1929), travel essays (1921, 1922, 1925, 1930), stories and sketches (1923, 1925, 1926, 1927, 1928), and essays about literature (1924, 1925, 1926, 1929, 1930). The Japanese even issued *Cleopatra No Ichiya* (1921), a book of translations of Hearn's translations of three stories by Théophile Gautier (1811–1872). Meanwhile, between 1926 and 1932 *Koizumi Yakumo Zenshū*

(The Complete Works of Koizumi Yakumo [Lafcadio Hearn]) were being published in 18 volumes, in three versions—Edition de luxe (1926–1928), Popular
Edition (1929–1930), and Students' Edition (1930–1932)—with each edition
totaling 11,622 pages. Many of Hearn's works have also been translated into
Czechoslovakian, Chinese, Danish, Dutch, Finnish, French, German, Hungarian,
Italian, Polish, Russian, Spanish, Swedish, and Yiddish. His international reputation continues to be extremely significant.

"A TROPICAL INTERMEZZO" (1880, 1911). Revery. A Spanish soldier
wanders into a dreamy forest and thinks of Juan Ponce de Leon. Armor doffed,
he swims in a delicious fount, sleeps, then sees a lissome, flower-girdled lady.
Paradisaical viands and perfumed love follow. The lady whispers of eternal life
and warns him not to stray into any shadows. After resisting a brassy trumpet's
call for centuries, he takes his rusted sword and walks off. Now dying, he
narrates his story to a priest who initially warns him to repent, who is told he
will not, and who accepts sight of a satisfied smile on the soldier's dead face.
This charming tale within a tale is framed as a deathbed reminiscence told in
delightfully archaic language (e.g., "ever and anon she bade me well beware").
"A Tropical Intermezzo" is a more polished, more dramatic revision of an 1880
sketch titled "The Fountain of Gold."

TUNISON, JOSEPH SALATHIEL (1849–1916). Journalist and author. Tunison was born near Bucyrus in Crawford County, Ohio. After attending Denison
University, he began a career in journalism. He was on the staff of the Cincinnati
Gazette (1874–1883), the New York *Tribune* (1884–1896), the *Ohio State Journal* (1901–1903), and the *Dayton Daily Journal* (1903–1907). He spent his last
years as a freelance writer in East Liverpool, Ohio. Tunison wrote *The Cincinnati Riot: Its Causes and Results* (1886), *Master Virgil, The Author of the Aeneid
as He Seemed to the Middle Ages: A Series of Studies* (1888), *The Sapphic
Stanza: A Tentative Study in Greek Metrical, Tonal and Dancing Art* (1896),
and *The Graal Problem from Walter Map to Richard Wagner* (1904).

When they were newspapermen together in Cincinnati in the early 1870s,
Hearn and Tunison met. A mutual friend at that time was Henry Edward Krehbiel,* the music critic to whom Hearn often wrote later. When Hearn was in
New York City late in 1889 he stayed with Tunison in his West 10th Street
apartment. Hearn dedicated his 1890 novel *Youma* to Tunison. Once in Japan,
he occasionally wrote to Tunison, to the extent, in July 1892, of inviting him
to accept his assistance in coming to Japan if he had nothing better to do. When
Hearn broke his informal agreement with Henry Mills Alden,* the editor at
Harper & Brothers, Tunison wrote to Alden, whom he knew, to plead for his
friend. Tunison readily admitted that Hearn was eccentric. When Tunison received news of Hearn's death in Japan, he very likely wrote the obituary essay

that appeared in the *Dayton Daily Journal* (September 30, 1904). In it, Hearn was defined as mild and suave in his writings but possessed of a bitter temper.

Bibliography: Bisland; Oscar Lewis, *Hearn and His Biographers: The Record of a Literary Controversy* . . . (San Francisco: Westgate Press, 1930); Murray; Stevenson; J. S. Tunison, "Lafcadio Hearn," *Book Buyer* 13 (May 1896): 209–211.

"THE TWO ARNOLDS" (1883). Editorial. Hearn takes umbrage when Matthew Arnold (1822–1888), a Victorian poet, expressed astonishment during an interview in New York that anyone would think he was the brother of Sir Edwin Arnold* (1832–1904), the British poet and journalist. The latter was the author of *The Light of Asia; or, The Great Renunciation* (1879), a popular poem concerning Buddha's life and teachings that Hearn long admired and praises here. Hearn goes out of his way to criticize Matthew Arnold for vanity and pettiness; places Edwin Arnold's work on Buddhism far above those by others; and calls it "richer and stronger" than anything by Matthew Arnold, whose poetry he labels "colorless." Matthew Arnold, a considerably better poet than Edwin Arnold, lectured in the United States in 1883 and again in 1886.

TWO YEARS IN THE FRENCH WEST INDIES (1890). Travel book. Hearn left New York City in June 1887, visited the Lesser Antilles for three months, returned to New York, and sold "A Midsummer Trip to the Tropics" to Henry Mills Alden,* the editor of *Harper's Magazine*, for $700. In October 1887 Hearn returned to the Caribbean area, commissioned by Alden to submit essays on a regular basis. Hearn intended to stay in Martinique for only a few months but remained until May 1889. Many disputes arose as to the literary merit of later prose pieces Hearn sent to Alden, who published "A Midsummer Trip to the Tropics" (*Harper's New Monthly Magazine*, July, August, September 1888). Alden published four more items by Hearn concerning Martinique between October 1888 and July 1889. That October the two signed a contract for what became *Two Years in the French West Indies*, which included "A Midsummer Trip to the Tropics" and 14 essays under the rubric "Martinique Sketches."

"A Midsummer Trip to the Tropics" (1888) is in 33 untitled, Roman-numbered sections. I. Hearn leaves an East River dock and records his impressions of ship and sea sounds and the varied colors of wave and sky as twilight comes. His essentially sensual nature is hinted at when he notes the "waves . . . patting the flanks of the vessel." II. Between naps on deck he professes an innocent-abroad kind of naivete, discusses shades of blue waters with a passenger from Guadeloupe, and observes weeds in the Sargasso Sea. III. The sea grows ever more blue. IV. The sky on the fourth day is fiercely blue, and the warm winds make Hearn languid. The sea whispers resemble "women telling secrets." V. Trade winds help press the vessel onward. VI. Glorious sunset. Water is blue-black, the bewitching color "in certain Celtic eyes." The Southern

Cross is evident in the heavens that night. VII. Next morning, Hearn catalogues the colors of unfamiliar Caribbean Sea islands while a gorgeous big fly, in shiny black, silver, and green, comes aboard. VIII. On to Frederiksted, displaying Spanish-like architecture, a "wealth of verdure," and a market area including a savagely picturesque piazza, merchants, and compactly built black women shopping. Hearn samples juicy fruits, cigars, and rum, and observes naked male swimmers, including fair-skinned Danish soldiers. He comments on the harmony of black bodies and "Nature's green." IX. On to Basse-Terre, at Saint Kitt's, with commonplace population, nice botanical garden, and distant Nevis mountains. X. They pass Montserrat with its "red town of Plymouth," enjoy a sunset, and continue southward.

XI. They offload the mail at Roseau, on lofty Dominica, its mountain "curved like a hip." Landfall at Martinique, part of "the beautiful volcanic family." A flotilla of naked boys of several complexions rows rhythmically out, to dive like darting fish for shiny coins. The passengers go ashore to quaint, queer, pretty, solid Saint Pierre. Its picturesqueness tempts watercolorists. Cool water rushes everywhere. Rue Victor Hugo is splendid. Dishes are redolent of sugar and garlic. XII. Hearn details the complexions of "the finest mixed race of the West Indies" and the "beautiful audacities of color contrast" of the women's dresses and turbans. Some have gold earrings. On erect heads, others offer, with Creole cries, fruits, medicines, pastries. Hearn inspects stores. La Pelée is coiffed and costumed too. XIII. On to the fountained market, full of oddly named fish (for one, "Bon-Dié-manié-moin"[the Good God handled me]), and many-hued and -shaped vegetables. He mentions the almond taste of fried-alive cabbage-palm worms. He admires trim little children but even more the perfect "symmetry and saliency of [cross-bred male laborers'] muscles." XIV. This section concerns things religious—shrines, statues, carillons, cathedral, and tombs—all invaded by nature's irresistibly green vegetation. XV. Hearn leaves the little city and passes the Savane du Fort to visit the Morne Parnasse, with its Doresque forest. XVI. Hearn quotes his translation of a passage from *Enquête dur le Serpent de la Martinique* (Paris, 1859) by Étienne Rufz de Lavison (1806–1884), with a dramatic image of the dense forests of Martinique as a stormy ocean suddenly struck motionless and green. XVII. Hearn is timid in the awesome forests, in which man is insect-like near fanged plants. Then comes a long exposition of the eight varieties of protectively tinted fer-de-lance vipers, their size, haunts, fecundity, deadly venom, and few enemies. He includes a hypnotic description of how the ordinary cat, motivated by maternal instinct, circles and dispatches its poison-loaded prey. (Later, Hearn repeatedly refers to the fer-de-lance by its scientific name, the Trigonocephalus. *See* "Stranger Than Fiction" in *The Romance of the Milky Way and Other Studies and Stories*.) XVIII. A daylight visit to the "foliage-shrouded" Jardin des Plants, all laced with palms and ravines. Two lakes are there, with artificial little islands lush with imported flowers. Hearn wonders: Did Napoleon's Josephine visit this place in her youth? XIX. This land has lights and colors unknown to northerners. XX. Night does not fall here; it rises. Evenings are splendid; the stars, near; the moon, big, magnetic, muting the woodsy sounds. XXI. The plaza of the wooden Fort-de-France, an hour and a half by steamer from Saint Pierre, is graced by a beautiful marble statue of Josephine, that lovely Creole.

XXII. Overnight by steamer to Barbados; at dawn, a sudden, brief rainstorm. Big-boned blacks, the product of their limestone soil, speak crisp British English. XXIII. On toward British Guiana, the steamer making a phosphorous wake at night. XXIV. The dawn breaks, "foul and opaque," over a "viscous, glaucous sea." XXV. Demerara and Georgetown at last, in memorably radiant light and with palm-bordered avenues. XXVI. The free-standing palms have personalities. The botanical gardens have "idealizations of plants," including gigantic water lilies and snake nuts with fruit like triangle-headed, coiled vipers. XXVII. Demerara has Hindoos, coolie families, brief evenings now, and flaming sunsets. XXVIII. On toward Trinidad, with magnificent sights along the way. XXIX. Next, "a morning of supernal beauty—the sky of a fairy tale—the sea of a love-poem."

XXX. They go ashore at Trinidad through "a great hum of Creole chatter." The city is a mixture of ethnic strains and quaint dwellings. A carriage takes Hearn into a coolie village, with trees, ditches, a temple, and slumbering laborers. At a tattooed Hindoo woman's shop is her little girl, with big-irised eyes like those of birds of prey. Hearn imagines that when mature she will be fought over by men with cutlasses. XXXI. They steam into the harbor of the "senescent city" of Saint George, Grenada, with mouldy, crumbling Spanish architecture, eaten not only by an air seemingly acidic but also by "terribly . . . luxuriant" vegetation, including poisonous manchineel apples. Hearn briefly notes streets, cemetery, closed warehouses, and native talk, which he dismisses as "a baragouin fantastic and unintelligible." XXXII. Next, strangely formed Saint Lucia, with "mountainings . . . [like] broken crystals." Hearn has heard that the curious shadow colors are owing to "inorganic substances floating in the air." They leave the harbor at Castries, take on freight elsewhere, pass the Pitons—"twin peaks . . . like two black breasts"—and anchor at Choiseul, a village of no distinction. Evening in the "vapory gold" of Saint Vincent. With night drawing near, all seems "a geological dream" as one imagines an archipelago borne from a sea primeval. XXXIII. Homeward bound, Hearn avoids summarizing his varied sensory impressions but comments on the diminution of white populations in the islands, the devouring of their heroic and criminal accomplishments, and the inevitable advent of new ethnic conflicts.

"A Midsummer Trip to the Tropics" is often exciting, mainly because of Hearn's gift for varicolored, impressionistic descriptions. It lags, however, because it is choppy and repetitious. Hearn links disparate sections by hints in one section of something to be treated a little later. One example: In section XIII Hearn touches on the fer-de-lance, "whose venom putrefies living tissue," then focuses on the creature in section XVII, which as the middle of this 33-section work is its precise keystone. Further, in XVII he expresses his most profound theme, love (of the cat for its kittens) and natural ferocity leading to death—death, whose smells trail throughout Hearn's entire midsummer trip. His frequent employment of cool clinical diction in describing nature's fatal caresses adds to the horror and is deliberate—Hearn loves to flirt back at nature and seems willing to surrender. Mother Nature is beautiful because she is so deadly.

"Martinique Sketches" follows. Each of its 14 sections is longer than any of the more numerous sections of "A Midsummer Trip to the Trips."

First is "Les Porteuses" (1889). Hearn lovingly limns the tall, graceful, immensely strong female porters at Saint Pierre. Each carries on her head a tray of merchandise—baked goods, fruits, toys, whatever—weighing up to 125 pounds, often for a distance of 40 miles a day, taking more than 12 hours. They go barefoot along splendidly engineered roads, up mountains, delivering goods and returning burdened anew—all for $4 a month. They travel singly or march in pairs in perfect step. They often sing. From bamboo-piped fountains they drink spring water and lace it with medicinal rum or *tafia* (their local rum). They are never molested, although they often carry large sums of money. At day's end strong male arms unload them, and they laugh, sit, and munch dry bread. Hearn delights in their musical names, offering a score or so, including Cyrillia, Fevrette, and especially Ti-Clé. Although with early political correctness he avers that the porters' "clear black skin . . . is beautiful to any but ignorant or prejudiced eyes," he also contrasts them unsparingly to "the population of black Barbados, where the apish grossness of African coast types has been perpetuated unchanged."

"La Grande Anse" (1889) should be of great interest to anthropologists. Hearn goes from Saint Pierre 20 miles by public transportation and horseback to the sleepy "burgh" of Grande Anse (now Lorrain), where he rents an airy room in a wooden house with a view of the Atlantic Ocean beach of volcanic-steel sand. He describes blinding sunrises, roaring trade winds, dangerous coasts, tafia-barrel loading through surf to waiting pirogue, catching huge *tambi* (shellfish) and crawfish, native children at confirmation-day parade, Sunday dances with drums and improvised rhymeless Creole songs (one starting "toutt fois lanmou vini lacase moin" [each time that love comes to my cabin]). The genial host of a colonial estate shows Hearn birds, insects, plants, snakes, and the sugar mill established by Jean Baptiste Labat (1663–1738), a Dominican missionary, called here "the ingenious and terrible Père Labat."

In the punning title "Un Revenant," *revenant* means both "one who returns" (to Martinique) and "ghost." Hearn prepares us for the story of Labat by recounting legends of the disappearance of a ship carrying Missié Bon (Monsieur Bon), mysterious moving yellow lights in the forests, and untrue stories that Labat introduced slavery to the island, was killed by a huge fer-de-lance, haunts the forests to kill such vipers, was gossiped about, and cursed the island. Hearn visits Monsieur ——'s house in sight of fair Pelée and consults Dr. Rufz's authoritative biography of Labat. Extensive details follow. In 1693 this Dominican left a professorship in Nancy, France, to improve the material situation of the Church on Martinique. He built a profitable sugar mill, formulated rules to improve its operation, went to Guadeloupe to aid the French army against the British, traveled throughout the islands and made the use of resources more efficient, built churches and convents and schools, founded cities, after 12 years visited Rome, and was never allowed to return to the Caribbean. Before his death in Paris he wrote *Nouveau Voyage aux Isles de l'Amerique* (1722) in "six pursy little volumes." He reflects, theorizes, admits errors, discusses how to cook parrots, mentions flogging black slaves ("natural child[ren] of the Devil"), offers proofs of "negro sorcery" (rain-making, foretelling the future, making a cane speak, causing white people's hearts to dessicate). Hearn says that the Church lost clout when the slaves were freed and given the vote. He scoffs at ugly native religious icons, laments that a man who flogged a statuette of the Virgin Mary was jailed for life, and concludes that "Christian feeling is almost stifled by ghastly beliefs of African origin." He says that despite disbelieving in ghosts he too has seen the wavering ghost of Labat, who native mothers tell their naughty children will steal them away—"moin ké fai Pé Labatt vini pouend ou!"

"La Guiablesse" is a story of demonic possession. (*Guiablesse* means "female devil.") As a preamble Hearn describes scary, noisy rural nights; records his interview with Adou, a gentle little girl who reluctantly talks about her belief in zombies; and summarizes her mother Théréza's story of a lunatic named Baidaux who suddenly brought home a child who he said was his and who disappeared after shooting up in stature. One cloudless noon while Gabou and Fafa are resting from work, they are stealthily approached by a beautiful woman of "serpentine elegance." She lures Fafa away with a glance—"a blaze of black lightning." He tries unsuccessfully to guess her name. As twilight is falling he accepts her cold hand and is led into the mountains. They take a dark path. Reaching the summit, she asks for a kiss and he plunges two thousand feet to his death in the rocky waters below. This mysterious tale has at least two notable features: Creole dialogue, translated only in part; and a sumptuous painterly depiction of Fafa's final sunset, in which Hearn specifies 13 different hues.

"La Vérette" (1888; title in magazine: "La Vérette and the Carnival in St. Pierre, Martinique") is a jumbled essay on smallpox in Saint Pierre. Hearn combines reporting, footnotes, subjective touches, and partly fictionalized dialogue in English and Creole. Returning in 1887 from other islands during Carnival season, he is lucky to find a room, seeks information from a next-door landlady named Manm-Robert, and sees homeless Yzore and her three tiny children. He observes rival dancing societies, the Sans-souci and the Intrépides, as they improvise satirical songs. Paraders are joined even by those who are deadly sick with disease. Costumes include wiry masks, peaked hats, hoods, and robes mimicking religious orders. A manikin symbolizing the plague is buried in a mock funeral. When a priest approaches, all clamor ceases. Night falls, and a deep-voiced devil figure, accompanied by a 300-boy chorus, chants and claps a rhythmic finale. Hearn describes Yzore's hard life as a seamstress making turbans, pantaloons, and blouses. He offers a mini-documentary on smallpox, tar burned to ward it off, coffins, use of and native skepticism concerning vaccinations. He discusses Yzore's three children's songs and beliefs. Manm-Robert gives him a voodoo charm to protect him from "la vérette." In rapid disorder, Hearn's next topics include the shortage of servants in plague time, a child's dream, plague statistics, survivors' heroism, nocturnal silences, Good Friday solemnity and Holy Saturday funerals, big household spiders, how handsome people are called "bel bois" (beautiful trees), the death of a teenage girl by "la vérette-pouff" (galloping smallpox), the cinnamon-colored race's susceptibility to the disease; outbreaks on American ships; the arrival of typhoid fever; dead Yzore being covered with quick-lime and her carved bed being sold to the *tam-tam-tam* beat of the auction drum, and Manm-Robert's hope that the dead father of Yzore's children will come and claim them.

"Les Blanchisseuses" are the washerwomen of the river. Men ogle the pretty ones, and women watch because they are interested in other women's labors. The stronger and more experienced the woman, the better her position at the edge of a river called the Roxelane. Apprentices, age 12, first learn to soap and wash. The next stages are the "fessé" (lashing cloth against rocks), then folding and more whipping, and bleaching in sunlight. In the evening there is steeping in lye vats, followed by pre-dawn warm-water rinse, river rinse, more bleaching, blueing and starching, and ironing indoors. An able *blanchisseuse*, working 13 hours a day, earns $60 a month. Some work until "maladie-dleau" causes physical decay and death. Under the boiling sun, they can't drink cold water (pleurisy would follow) and rum is too expensive; so they have *mabi* (molasses beer). They don't sing at dawn but raise their strident voices in merry or sarcastic songs in full daylight. Hearn says that half the Creole songs he collected deal with brutal men abandoning girls with babies. The plague stopped the women's singing in the summer of 1887. They watch for evidence of rain over La Montagne Pelée, which causes floods requiring quick action to avoid death by crushing on rocks and drowning. One girl tried to save her laundry and was killed.

"La Pelée," the longest essay in "Martinique Sketches," is a mixed discussion of the tallest (5,115 ft.), most famous, and most dangerous mountain of the more than four hundred on the tiny island. Hearn begins with a scientific description, tells of the peak's dominance regardless of any observer's point of view, reports that almost 30 rivers course down its gently sloping sides, and then compares its shadowy tints to "the landscape colors of a Japanese fan." He dramatically depicts the August 1851 volcanic eruption and the sounds accompanying it. One route to "La Montagne" is by way of Morne Rouge, a village suffering rain 360 days a year. They go more directly by horse-drawn carriage to Morne Saint Martin and up a mountain road. The guide's killing of a fer-de-lance prompts fellow travelers to share anecdotes about the venomous pit viper, fear of which one passenger asserts has hampered scientific research in Martinique's forests. In cane fields are cutlass-wielding laborers, some of whom are fer-de-lanced to death. Next "the grands-bois," with vegetation writhing out of the volcanic soil like ships' rigging. Hearn identifies various hardwood trees, laments their "barbarous destruction" by charcoal-makers, climbs past river sources, discusses succulent fish and murderous mountain-crabs, finds pools and a lake they swim in, and finally arrives at the peak, marked by two crosses at the precipice. He observes a rainstorm below and notes the variously lighted and ridged lesser mountain peaks all about. Everyone is "inspired by the mighty vision and the colossal peace of the heights," which will be there when we are dreamless dust. Hearn has been criticized for trying here to combine personal narrative and geographical data and for conflating beauty, danger, decay, and death.

In " 'Ti Canotié" young Creoles, called *'ti canotié* (little canoe boys), dive from *'ti canot* (little canoes) for coins tossed from ships in Saint Pierre's harbor. The boys construct canoes out of lard or oil boxes or shipping cases, well tarred, and paddle out two in a boat. One afternoon a rich passenger aboard a vessel steaming away lures Maximilien, age 10, and Stéphane, age 11, far from shore by tossing coin after coin, finally one of gold. Diving repeatedly, Stéphane finally brings it up from dangerous depths, with blood coming from his nose and mouth. Out of sight of land now, they paddle but drift into a "devil-current" as darkness falls. A shark fin passes by. After a long night, a baking sun comes up. The boys see the green silhouette of Dominica, the island 40 kilometers north of vaporous Martinique. Palettes lost, they use their hands, but Stéphane grows faint. They capsize, regain cramped seats. Stéphane, delirious, mumbles about his gold coin, complains when Maximilien tries to pray that the Bon-Dié has no eyes, no color, is like the wind. Silence. Another sunset. Warm wind breath. A fish knocks their canoe. Maximilien, stiff and exhausted, sees the bearded Bon-Dié with a lantern. He is lifted under the stars. Unknown words follow. "Poor little devils!" The two boys are lying under electric lights aboard the steamer *Guadeloupe*, and Stéphane is dead.

Hearn introduces "La Fille de Couleur" with a sparkling description of Martinique's women of color—their costumes, jewelry, "gorgeous attire" for religious ceremonies—but soon "gives[s] up all hope of being able to outline the history of Martinique costume." He prefers to touch on the fine physical attributes of young beauties before turning historical, anthropological, and sociological. He theorizes that Martinique's *filles de couleur* have undergone rapid generational changes because the complex consequences of "that strange struggle between nature and interest, between love and law, between prejudice and passion, which forms the evolutionary history of the mixed race" have all been intensified and accelerated by the unique conditions of slavery in a tropical "climate and environment." Hearn's combining of historical research (he cites nine sources) personal observation, personal prejudice, and ingrained pessimism results in a superb essay. He mentions the steady importation of slaves, contrasts the ugliness of certain black types and the attractive physiques of others, summarizes governmental efforts to prevent miscegenation or at least penalize the oft-springing consequences, and dwells on the beauty of *filles de couleur*—diminished by recent economic failures throughout the island. Sympathizing

228 Two Years in the French West Indies

profoundly with pretty girls who are used and abused, he quotes Turiault, a respected Creole authority: "Née de l'amour, la fille-de-couleur vit d'amour, de rires, et d'oublis." He compares their seemingly fragile beauty to that of hot-house plants, which, deprived of careful nurture, grow harder, if they survive, and also "perhaps less comely as well as less helpless." Meanwhile, male mu-lattoes, positioned between blacks and Creole whites, "became an Ishmaelitish clan, inimical to both races, and dreaded of both." Hearn's saddest passage concludes the essay. He says that on the evening of Corpus Christi, paraders stop at "resting-places for the Host" (translated from the Creole "reposouè Bon-Dié"), where altars are decorated with plates, crystals, statuettes, paintings, mod-els of ships, and other curiosities—all loaned by the rich and soon taken back again. Hearn says that the most fortunate resting place for "the mulatress" is also "the Good-God." (Is it too much to infer that to Hearn the *fille de couleur* is almost divine? He did not respect the Catholic Church, but he did worship natural beauty.) This essay is unusually well researched. Hearn cites nine au-thorities, notably Étienne Rufz de Lavison (1806–1884). Jean Turiault (?–?), whom Hearn quotes, wrote *Étude sur le langage créole de la Martinique* (1874).

"Bête-ni-Pie' " (Creole patois for "centipede") begins with an explanation that Saint Pierre lacks mosquitoes found elsewhere on Martinique but has other "dis-agreeable things," including four species of ants, useful (if not hairy), scorpions (offensive because they hide cleverly), and the *mabouya* (an ash-colored lizard). Then come the centipedes, in drains, gutters, and beneath damp fountains. They terrorize those who go barefoot. They are usually 10" to 11" long, and as they age they turn from tinted yellows to black. Their carapaces are iron-tough. Be-cause they like to hide in one's clothing, Hearn warns one to shake out one's pantaloon legs before dressing. He enclosed one for 13 weeks in a dry bottle. When released, it displayed undiminished animosity; so he fed it with live bugs. Centipedes hide in parasols for months at a time. Hens and cats can kill them. Owing to the superstition that dispatching them brings good luck, natives ham-mer them with stones and pans, cursing them as Satan the while. Hearn inter-rupts his anecdotes to relate the etymological evolution of the centipede's name from *bête-anni-pié* to *bête-ni-pié*, meaning "beast all feet" or "beast naked-footed." It horrifies because it is venomous (though but temporarily), of repul-sive form, with movements hypnotically terrifying, and intelligence seemingly calculating, cunning, malevolent: "[I]t is an abominable juggler." Finding one in his coat, Hearn frantically tries to stop it and hit it, even while observing its motions. A servant fatally slaps its head. Trying for some symbolism, Hearn wonders if centipedes may be likened to bigotry and prejudice in our "old black drains of Thought." A friend shows him a plant, with hideous leaves resembling hairy legs, and concealing an "ovoid nut," which looks delicious and if not eaten turns to dust. Hearn uses his experience as a crime-and-horror journalist to make this essay, the shortest Martinique sketch, the most gripping one of all. For chilly prose, try this: The centipede "is a form of absolute repulsiveness—a skeleton-shape half defined:—the suggestion of some old reptile-spine astir, crawling with its fragments of ribs."

"Ma Bonne" is Cyrillia, Hearn's delightful servant. Although unable to read a clock, she punctually brings his mild morning cocktail, a towel for a swim, and whatever he orders from the market. Hearn digresses from Cyrillia to discuss many kinds of foods—rare meats, native flour, fish (dangerous if vividly colorful), "infernal" pimento, and popular native dishes (marsupial, worm, sausage, chicken and rice). He goes on to fritters, vegetables (mainly beans), fruits (bananas, huge oranges, mangoes). The subject of apricots enables him to revert to Cyrillia. She brings him apricots so big he eats only one. Regarding him as skinny, his *bonne* tempts him with syrupy desserts and fears he will "tchoué cò-ou" (kill his body) by violating Martinique superstitions (e.g., washing one's face with soap causes blindness). While they sit on their balcony at night, she delights him with her talk. She wishes she had a ladder to use to climb into God's well-formed clouds, in which she identifies animals and ships. She once saw the moon bravely fight the sun during an eclipse. The sky must be tangible because stars are fastened to it. When he says the stars are suns, she says they are too small and Hearn, anyway, must be a Protestant. Although he denies being either Catholic like her or Protestant, she rejects the statement; he has to have been baptized because he does not see zombies the way "a maudi" (cursed one) does "all the time." This occasions a mini-essay on zombies, details of which Cyrillia only partly supplies. She is kind to dogs and cats but burns the heads off flying beetles. When queried, she merely says, "You do not know Things in this country." She sings with strange rhythms and "tones that are surely African," talks to herself—and answers—but will never tell Hearn about what, and once asks how children in America could possibly learn English. Hearn describes Cyrillia's simply furnished room, with the fragment of a statuette of the Virgin she buys flowers for. She will not let him improve the shrine but asks him to buy a photograph of her faraway daughter. When he manages to obtain one, she weeps before it and wishes it could talk. Hearn closes: "Self-cursèd he who denies the divinity of love! . . . God never repeats his work. No heart-beat is cheap, no gentleness is despicable, no kindness is common." Cryillia is a poignant creation by a master characterizer.

"Pa Combiné, Chè!" begins with Hearn's approval of the word "frisson" to express the shiver of amazed delight one experiences when first responding to the tropics. Then comes renewed praise of the simple natives of Martinique. He gladly adopts their "home habits," including rest after luncheon, and appreciates the delicate concern of servants; he knows but willingly ignores the "less agreeable" side of the "colored population." But when they see a vessel burning in the harbor, they consider it human and lament with genuine tears. Thinking he is managing the difficult task of acclimatizing, the foreigner surrenders to "pleasant languor," to "beatific indolence." He fancies that his knowledge of literature and paintings concerning the tropics prepares him. He believes that walking in the forests will never tire him. But he "must pay tribute of suffering" here. He cannot get used to the humid heat, that weight on the brain, that heightening of nervousness. "[T]his tropical climate" is viciously powerful. Physical and mental energies diminish; will power evaporates; after a while, one realizes one cannot adapt socially, intellectually, or linguistically. The combination of early bedtime and lack of books becomes a torture. How can slim Creole women display such "savage strength" and yet remain lizard-cool to the touch? One now knows why Europeans who come here "produce no sciences, arts, or literature." What seemed bewitching—beauty, light, sounds—becomes distressing. Next comes a sick surrender, followed by gentle nursing by servants, followed by resharpened sensory responses to all natural stimuli. Félicien, Hearn's friend from France, came to Saint Pierre but got sick, spectrally thin, and clammy to the touch, and he was slow in recovering. A magnificent sunset provides the two friends "that ghostly emotion which is the transmitted experience of the race." While they are talking on the fellow's veranda, his thin, half-breed girlfriend glides in and says, "Pa combiné, chè!" (Do not think, dear!), and tells Hearn that he should not let Félicien think, because thinking will keep him from getting well. As she caresses the smiling, doubtful fellow and in a dove-coo voice says, "If thou wouldst love me, do not think," Hearn defines this "weirdly sensuous" woman as golden-fleshed nature luring her wanderer. The moral of this compelling but overwritten essay: Enjoy frissons but fear them, too.

"Yé" begins with Hearn's statement that Creole children tell and retell folk tales. He had some dictated to him, although the process had its limitations. Here is "a free rendering of one." Yé is a lazy, hideously gluttonous negro, with a good wife and many ravenous children. In the woods one day he sees the Devil, who is blind, eating codfish, flour, and pimento. Yé steals mouthful after mouthful but is finally grabbed by the Devil, who jumps on his back and rides him to Yé's home. The Devil squats in a corner and scares Yé and his family all night. At breakfast time the mother loads a table with food, but the Devil puffs all the family into suspended animation, eats everything, then wakes them up, shows them plates full of dirt, and orders them to eat it. Yé climbs Pelée, asks the Bon-Dié for advice, and is told to return without eating anything and say to the Devil "Tam ni pou tam ni bé" not translated, which will cause him to fall dead. But on the way home Yé cannot resist stuffing himself with green fruit, which so sets his teeth on edge that he cannot say anything when he confronts the Devil. The Devil forces everyone to eat more dirt. When Yé consults the Bon-Dié again, Yé's most cunning child hides in his pocket, memorizes the magic phrase, and when they get home bellows it at the Devil, who falls dead. Hearn weakens the story by tacking on two more sections. First, Yé, out hunting, finds the Devil's corpse, shoots it with an arrow, and smells the arrow's stinking point. His nose grows. The Bon-Dié tells him to order some birds to remove their beaks before swimming. Yé replaces his pot-sized nose with the bill of a bird called the *coulivicou*. Second, Hearn explains that blacks, now emancipated in "this enlightened century," continue to have swarms of children but now serve a new Devil, the Devil Tafia (local rum), from whom there is no God to free them. Hearn explicitly adds that abolishing tough but moral patriarchal rule over blacks has made them citizens of the republic. Now they can vote, work, or starve as they wish. So they sin, suffer, and acquire "this new knowledge that stupefies." Hearn never placed much faith in the virtues of democracy.

In "Lys" Hearn bids a tender farewell to Martinique. His local friends shower him with tiny homemade gifts. He depicts the receding island with cinematic, impressionistic touches as his ship, the *Guadeloupe*, heads for New York City. He notices Mademoiselle Lys, whom he dubs Violet Eyes, also aboard; she is a white Creole leaving her native island permanently to become a governess in New York. Pelée turns ghostly. Hearn takes note of island after island as the ship moves from tropical climes to windy, misty, cooler regions. By contrast, New York is an Odin-dominated region of strivers, battlers, laborers, scientists. Hearn pities and prays for poor Lys. In December 1887, Hearn sent Henry Mills Alden,* his editor at Harper & Brothers, a sketch titled "Lys," which Alden bluntly replied was unacceptable. The present "Lys" is a considerably different version.

Hearn dedicated *Two Years in the French West Indies* to Léopold Arnoux, his closest island friend. Arnoux was a notary in Martinique and an amateur scholar. The book is a captivating combination of autobiography, impressionistic sketches, and mini-redactions of history. It has been criticized for its prolixity and point-of-view shifts, but it remains a delightful tour de force in Hearn's varied canon. It was reprinted several times. It was issued in England (1890) and enjoyed a fine illustrated edition (1923).

Bibliography: O. W. Frost, *Young Hearn* (Tokyo: Hokuseido Press, 1958); Kunst; Murray; Stevenson.

u

"AN ULTRA-CANAL TALK" (1880). Sketch. Swindlers persuade an old man to buy worthless "oil" paintings, watercolors, "ceramics," clothes, and furniture. He curses the salesmen, sues, and loses. The narrator, his Creole landlady, says the old man finally died cursing and praying. "Ultra-Canal" refers to the area beyond Canal Street in New Orleans.

"THE UNDYING ONE" (1880). Sketch. The narrator has lived for three thousand years, has enjoyed all pleasures and gained all knowledge, and wants to die. Because there is a power mightier than he, eventually he will. Surely the moon too is tired of its endless circlings.

V

VAN HORNE, SIR WILLIAM CORNELIUS (1843–1915). Railroad executive. Van Horne was born near Joliet, Illinois; quit school at age 14; became a telegraphist for the Illinois Central Railway; and steadily advanced to administrative positions with several midwestern railroad companies. In 1867 he married Lucy Adelina Hurd in Joliet; the couple had a son and a daughter. By 1881 Van Horne had become general manager of the Chicago, Milwaukee, and St. Paul Railroad system. That year the Canadian Pacific Railway, with headquarters in Montreal, named him its general manager to supervise the construction of lines to the West. By 1885 he had completed the project. In 1889 he was appointed president of the company. In 1899 he became chairman of the board, a position he held until 1910. Meanwhile he broadened his activities to include work with iron and steel, life insurance, and educational organizations. He was knighted in 1898. Once the Spanish-American War ended, he began to develop railroads and industries in Cuba. Van Horne collected Oriental pottery and designed two private catalogues of his Japanese holdings; he described each piece and illustrated it with his own full-size watercolor. He read and greatly admired *Some Chinese Ghosts*, Hearn's 1887 book. As president of the Canadian Pacific Railroad Company and Steamship Lines, Van Horne was responsive when William H. Patten, art director of Harper & Brothers, publishers of several of Hearn's later books, approached him in 1889 to help finance the projected trip of Hearn and Harper's distinguished artist Charles Dater Weldon* to Japan to write up and illustrate their experiences there. Persuaded by Patten, Van Horne agreed to provide transportation for both men from Montreal to Vancouver by rail and on to Japan by steamer; he also gave each of them $250 for incidental expenses. In return, Van Horne asked Hearn to write an essay describing his trek overland and across the Pacific, presumably for the benefit of the Canadian Pacific. The result was Hearn's "A Winter Journey to Japan" (*Harper's Magazine*, November 1890). This was his first essay on Japan. Van Horne read it and pronounced it charming. When Hearn was planning a trip back to the United States in 1903, Van Horne promised him a round-up ticket; Hearn was immensely pleased, but the trip never materialized.

Bibliography: Bisland; D'Alton E. Coleman, *Sir William Van Horne (1843–1915): "America's Greatest Gift to Canada!"* (New York: Newcomer Society of England American Branch, 1949); Murray; Stevenson; Tinker.

"VIOLENT CREMATION" (1874). Cincinnati news article. This is the first of eight articles (November 9–16, 1874), about the murder on Saturday, November 7, of Herman (also Hermann) Schilling, age 25, by Andreas Egner, age 42 and a saloon-keeper, his son Frederick K. Egner, age 16, and their friend George Rufer, approximately age 37, in revenge for Schilling's having allegedly seduced Andreas's daughter, Julia Egner, age about 15, who died while seven months pregnant. The other articles, in chronological order, are "Killed and Cremated," "It Is Out!," "The Tannery Horror," "The Furnace Fiends [1]," "The Furnace Fiends [2]," "The Quarter of Shambles," and "The Furnace Horror." Although Hearn says that his account is "divested of unnecessary verbiage," it is long, verbose, and gory. On August 6, 1874, Julia dies; Andreas and Fred attack Schilling with barrel staves, but he escapes. The assailants are convicted of assault and battery, fined, and bonded to keep the peace for a year. On November 7 John Hollerbach, age 16, hears a scuffle near Henry Freiberg's tannery and Schilling shouts to "John" for help. Seeking police unsuccessfully and afraid, Hollerbach goes to bed. The next day, Sunday, November 8, Schilling's body is discovered, cremated in the tannery furnace. The mangled remains are scrutinized by the coroner, Dr. F. F. (also P. F.) Maley, other authorities, a six-man jury, and Hearn, who seems actually to have fingered the charred tissues and bones. The jumbled scene is littered with bloody evidence, including a five-pronged pitchfork. Andreas and Fred are arrested. Rufer, who blamed Schilling for having him discharged by Freiberg, is also arrested. His alibi does not check out, nor do his wife Frederika Rufer's actions lend support to his story. Much transfer evidence permits the conclusion that Andreas and Rufer lay in wait for Schilling; clubbed, fought, and pitchforked him; and stuffed him into the furnace to burn to death. Fred, also there, is merely a suspect. Hollerbach is also locked up, as his story is judged "apocryphal." Incidentally, Dr. Maley, the coroner, is named and figures in 13 or so of these reprinted Cincinnati news articles. Hearn evidently knew him and respected him. Because Hearn was the first reporter on the scene, his "Violent Cremation" was a scoop and was picked up by other papers throughout the United States.

Bibliography: Cott; Jon Christopher Hughes, *The Tanyard Murder: On the Case with Lafcadio Hearn* (Washington, D.C.: University Press of America, 1982); Murray; Stevenson; Tinker.

"A VISION OF THE DEAD CREOLE" (1880). Sketch. A sailor swims ashore and finds the tomb of the woman who 27 years ago so taunted him with her Creole eyes, Egyptian smile, and sinuous body that he killed her. Suddenly she stands before her yawning tomb; her "argentine" voice says she lives on in his tears, agony, and dreams. The imagery of this piece has been criticized for being grossly overdone.

Bibliography: Kunst.

"A VISIT TO NEW ORLEANS" (1879). Sketch. In May, the Devil leaves Chicago, all nicely mortgaged to him, and enters New Orleans, which kept him busy during Reconstruction days. Reports of city reforms are bothering him. He fears that poverty and dirt in the city may be virtuous. He buys local newspapers, but all are virtuous except the *Picayune*. Perhaps he can gain some recruits for his "force below" from police stations. With a Mephistophelean laugh, he notes sin in the auditor's office, the mayor's edict concerning "colored churches," the Board of Health, and the courts. He concludes that New Orleans in 1879 resembles New Orleans in 1866 and, without his assistance, the city is going to hell— where he is heading.

"A VISITOR" (1880). Sketch. A handsome, deep-voiced singer from Spain introduces himself as Juan Guerrero y Marques and asks how to find the consul of a certain South American country, where he intends to seek relatives. A beautiful young woman gives him directions, and their eyes meet briefly. A corner organ plays a chorus from *Faust*. Juan bursts into enchanting song. Then he is gone forever.

"VOICES OF DAWN" (1881). Sketch. Hearn presents several musical cries of street vendors. Two examples: "Straw-BARE-eries!" and "Jap-ans!," the latter sometimes sung as "Chapped hands!" (i.e., "Cheap fans!"). Hearn lacks a second column on which to spread more examples.

"EL VÓMITO" (1881). Sketch. The mother, a grotesque sorceress, has a beautiful, statuesque daughter. Outside their rotting house are sick-smelling flowers and ugly fowls and animals. The physician-narrator, summoned one stormy night, determines that a strange Cuban lying in their house is dying not of fever but of the daughter's infernally humid kisses. She appears and tells the narrator that her mother's will overpowers his science and that he will certify the man died of vomiting. Suddenly she is strangling the narrator in a serpentine embrace and breathing enchantment upon him. Materializing in front of the narrator, the sorceress calls him conscientious and says he has accepted pay to certify as they wish. Hearn's friendship with Marie Laveau,* the New Orleans voodoo queen, and her daughter undoubtedly figure in the background of this sketch.

"VULTUR AURA" (1911). Revery. On June 2, 188–, Hearn describes Fort San Marco, now called Fort Marion, near San Juan de los Pinos, in St. Augustine, Florida. Deserted, lizard- and lover-haunted now, it sports over its sally-port the Arms of Spain, with carved lamb stained as by dripping blood. The majesty of vanished Spain remains. The shadow of a cleansing sun-vulture sweeps across. Hearn eruditely adverts to many a "ghoul of the empyrean" with their time-crunching vision, awaiting future "putrifaction." This melancholy piece echoes much literature of human extinction and heaven's silences.

Bibliography: Kunst.

W

WATKIN, HENRY (c. 1824–1911). English-born printer who had his own shop in Cincinnati. In 1869 Hearn happened to meet Watkin, who took a liking to the friendless lad, hired him as an errand and office boy, fed him, taught him a little typesetting, and let him sleep on a makeshift bed of paper shavings in a back room of his business. During this time Watkin's wife, who never liked—or understood—Hearn much, and Effie, their daughter, lived outside the city; so the two congenial men had ample time to discuss literature, marriage, politics, and religion. Hearn also read avidly in Watkin's library, and the two occasionally crossed the Ohio River into Kentucky to attend revival meetings and lectures concerning spiritualism, all of which they generally ridiculed. Watkin encouraged Hearn to shed lingering fragments of his orthodoxy, pointed him toward other odd jobs, and gave him ample time to read in the Cincinnati public library. Once Hearn became a reporter for the Cincinnati *Enquirer* and then the *Commercial*, Watkin occasionally accompanied him when he was covering stories. Watkin knew early on about Hearn's affair with Alethea Foley,* tried unsuccessfully to persuade him not to marry her, and was their intermediary during their breakup. Once Hearn left Cincinnati for New Orleans in 1877, his wonderful sequence of letters, unfortunately often undated, to "Dad" and "Old Man" (or simply "O. M.") Watkins began. Because of Hearn's love of the works of Edgar Allan Poe, Watkin dubbed him "The Raven." Hearn often signed his letters to Watkin "The Raven," "Kaw," "your son," or "The Prodigal Son," and illustrated them with clever sketches of ravens. When Watkin heard vicious gossip about Hearn's bohemian ways in New Orleans, he sent letters to the *Commercial* editor defending his friend. In the early 1880s Hearn wrote to Watkin about his desire to go to Japan. For five years there evidently was no exchange of letters. Then, before going via New York City to Martinique in 1887, Hearn visited Watkin in Cincinnati for a tearful—and final—reunion. Thereafter the correspondence became thin. Soon after arriving in Japan, Hearn wrote Watkin (April 25, 1890) the first of only four letters sent to him from that country. The letter reads in part thus: "Here I am in the land of dreams,— surrounded by strange Gods. I seem to have known them and loved them before somewhere. . . ." Hearn evidently wrote Watkin a final time in 1894.

Bibliography: Cott; Kennard; *Letters from the Raven: Being the Correspondence of Lafcadio Hearn with Henry Watkin*, ed. Milton Bronner (New York: Brentano's, 1907); Murray; Stevenson.

WELDON, CHARLES DATER (1855–1935). Illustrator and watercolorist. Born in Ohio, he studied art in Cleveland, New York, London, and Paris and exhibited widely in the 1880s and 1890s. He joined the staff of Harper & Brothers, the New York publishers, working under William H. Patten, art director of the firm. When Hearn was in New York in 1889, he and Patten discussed the possibility of Hearn's going to Japan to write about the remote country. Patten admired Hearn's *Two Years in the French West Indies*, which Harper was in process of publishing, and broached the subject of a book by Hearn on Japan to Henry Mills Alden,* Harper's editor. Evidently Patten also suggested that Weldon accompany Hearn and provide illustrations. Although Hearn did not like Weldon when they first met, he suppressed his negative feelings, and the two journeyed to Japan together. Transportation was financed by Sir William Cornelius Van Horne,* president of the Canadian Pacific Railway and Steamship Lines. Evidently on March 6, 1890, Hearn left New York for Montreal. Once in Vancouver, British Columbia, Hearn and Weldon set sail on March 17 for Japan and arrived on April 4. Hearn and Weldon split up almost at once, when Hearn learned that Weldon was being paid more than he was. Weldon did, however, make a charming sketch, from memory, of Hearn that beautifully sums up the man's loneliness as he left New York and began his Japanese odyssey: The sketch is of a slope-shouldered little fellow, seen from behind, in a shabby suit with a floppy old hat and carrying a couple of worn suitcases. Weldon remained in Yokohama at least until 1903, drawing pictures of Japanese children and other Japanese subjects and illustrating books. He died in East Orange, New Jersey.

Bibliography: Frank Luther Mott, *A History of American Magazines 1850–1865* (Cambridge, Mass.: Belknap Press of Harvard University Press, 1967); Murray; Zenobia Ness and Louise Orwig, *Iowa Artists of the First Hundred Years* (Des Moines: Wallace-Homestead, 1939); Stevenson; Tinker.

"WERE THERE COMMUNISTS IN ANTIQUITY?" (1878). Editorial. Disputing a correspondent's attempted proof of "the existence of the tramp nuisance in the Greek Republics," Hearn says that in classical Athens and Sparta "communists could not have existed, neither could tramps have been known." Wandering between tightly knit cities was forbidden. Revolutions of slaves or slave-like classes were not comparable to today's labor disturbances. Wars between Greek aristocrats and the poor came later; with them "[c]ommunism . . . appeared," and riots, savage mayhem, and redistribution of wealth. Succeeding temporarily, communism was then followed by merciless despotism.

WETMORE, MRS. ELIZABETH. *See* Bisland, Elizabeth.

"WHAT IS LIGHT?" (1880). Editorial. We now know that there are fewer elements than we once thought. Likewise, we now know that light, once thought to have heat, light, and chemical rays, has but one ray, which creates different effects depending on what it strikes. Hearn rambles on: Light has no existence or velocity, the retina resembles a photographic plate with "purpurine secreted . . . over it," what we see or hear or taste or smell comprise non-objective impressions. Just as polytheism has given way to monotheism, so science is trying to find the cause of everything in "one . . . mighty force." Perhaps Brahmins, not Christians, are closer to an explanation. When he writes about scientific topics, Hearn often pontificates and includes factual inaccuracies.

"WHEN I WAS A FLOWER" (1880). Sketch. It was a flower, enjoying everything in nature until it was cut and placed in a woman's hair. It and she died together. Its spirit mingles with her grave flowers, as do her blood and breath. Hearn's prose here is delightfully delicate.

"WHY CRABS ARE BOILED ALIVE" (1879). Sketch. In Creole lingo, Hearn explains that crabs are boiled alive because you can't decapitate headless crabs, can't bleed bloodless crabs to death, and so on. Nor can you "stick to dem troo de brain," because they are brainless "same like you."

"WIFE AND MISTRESS" (1874). Cincinnati news article. This article is the third of four articles dealing with the Perkinses, dated October 1–6, 1874. The others are "A Motherly Murder," "The Perkins Tragedy," and "The Perkins Horror." On Wednesday, September 30, 1874, Julia A. Snell Perkins killed her 2-year-old daughter, Clara, and then tried unsuccessfully to kill herself. Facts keep emerging about the Perkins family. Julia learned that her husband, Charles L. Perkins, had a mistress. When the Perkinses moved from Covington to Cincinnati, the "courtesan" followed. The Perkinses were alleged to have argued about Julia's flirtation with a young man the previous summer. But now it is revealed that Joseph Claire, who is a business associate of Perkins and is about 45 years old and long married, was actually Julia's lover as early as the previous spring. Perkins, his suspicions finally aroused, waited in ambush, caught and confronted them, and left the house, promising to return in the morning. Claire was in the house when Perkins and others entered the next morning and found Clara dead, and Julia almost so. Claire has since disappeared. Suddenly Pauline "Susie" Payne introduced herself to Hearn and told him that she was a well-educated Creole with a checkered past, became Perkins's kept woman, and was profoundly in love with him. He wrote to Susie, on the morning of the murder (but not knowing of it), that he had caught his wife and Claire and that she was leaving town. Susie denied ever ringing the Perkins doorbell to ask for Charley. She rambled about her former activities, her mother, her blind stepfather, her income from renting to "respectable boarders," and her hope that Hearn's news article will reflect credit on Perkins, not on herself. Hearn calls her love of Perkins "wild worship." On Friday, October 2, Julia's father arrived from Cleveland and spoke tenderly with her. While he was conferring in the corridor with a nun, Julia got hold of a pair of scissors and opened her already torn throat, but she was saved from death by a nun. Perkins paid for Julia's stay in the hospital but did not visit her there.

"WILLIAM M'DOLE" (1874). Cincinnati news article. On Wednesday night, June 24, 1874, Hearn interviewed William McDole, jailed in Dearborn County, Indiana, and charged with the ghastly murder of Mrs. Bradley and her two daughters. While would-be lynchers milled outside, Hearn took note of McDole, who was tall, well built, seemingly "of an average brain." He declared his innocence and declined the sheriff's offer to summon a preacher on the grounds that his seeming to need one would convince the crowd of his guilt. Hearn was aware that evidence against McDole was only circumstantial. On Thursday morning some clearer-headed men urged the crowd to disperse and await the court's verdict. In Friday's paper Hearn sarcastically concludes thus: "The Law is sacred, aye, and stern. Let it take its course."

"A WOLF'S VENGEANCE" (1872). Cincinnati news article. In some countries butchers, too used to the sight of blood, are not allowed to serve on murder-trial juries. Anyway, William Wolf was an irascible apprentice butcher in a slaughterhouse. Early Monday morning, December 11, 1872, he quarreled with his roommate, Valentine Daum, in their room behind the slaughterhouse, plunged a butcher knife through his heart, went to a saloon for some beer, and escaped—evidently to Kentucky. That afternoon the coroner held an inquest, during which three of Wolf's fellow workers testified against him.

"WOMAN'S INFLUENCE" (1880). Editorial. The French Revolution caused Frenchmen to be skeptical. But Frenchwomen, their hearts unchanged by "the great and bloody upheaval," have retained their ingrained piety. Unlike men, who can be depraved, women—even the worst—are ethical, are optimistic, and have ideals and faith. If today's French Republic, more full of corruption and license than the Empire was, improves, "there will be an *odor di femina* in the transformation."

Y

"Y PORQUE?" (1880). Sketch. When the Spanish lady asks the youth why he will not return to Mexico City, he bursts into tears. He poignantly remembers his beloved, as she lay in death, illuminated by flickering tapers. Hearn equates the dead girl, garbed in white, and "The White Lady," a Mexican mountain "sleeping in . . . [an] eternal winding-sheet . . . of snow."

"YAMARAJA" (1884). Sketch. An aged Brahman priest so laments his comely, learned son's death that he seeks Yamaraja, "the Lord of Death." He is told that Yama, death's kingdom, is on battlefields, in sea storms, and with sensual women. He passes unharmed through deadly jungles to the wisest Brahmans, who scorn his mourning but tell him to proceed to a distant valley near Yama. He finds a radiant city, recites the Mantras, and is admitted by Devas to the palace. Golden doors. Pavement of black marble. Vault of sky-blue. Yamaraja tells the Brahman to go find his son in the eastern garden. But when he embraces his son there, the child says that he does not know him, that parental terms are but transitory, that desires and sorrows are alike illusory. The Brahman departs. The Buddha comforts him by explaining that he was punished for foolishly deluding himself and that wisdom destroys sorrow and thus leads one to "the eternal peace, the eternal rest." The old man will follow the Teacher.

YE GIGLAMPZ. *See Giglampz.*

YOUMA (1890). (Full title: *Youma: The Story of a West-Indian Slave.*) Novel. Hearn begins with an essay on the nature of the Martinique *da*, typically "a Creole negress," the beloved, often pampered slave nanny of a white child. A *da* was often loved more than the child's mother, taught the child the Creole patois, and though illiterate and half "savage" was "physically refined . . . by climate, environment, and . . . mysterious influences." The emancipation of blacks caused the old social structure to disappear. Retired *das* may still be seen in old mansions—proud, courteous, and respected.

Fourteen chapters follow. In Saint Pierre, on the French West Indies island of Martinique, Madame Léonie Peyronnette, a wealthy widow, buys Douceline as a *da* for her daughter Aimée. She and Youma, who is Douceline's daughter and Madame Peyronnette's godchild, become companions of the same age. After Douceline dies, when Youma is almost 5 years old, Madame Peyronnette rears the two girls together. When Aimée's convent education is completed, Youma becomes her servant-companion. At age 18 she is taller than Aimée, is beautiful, and is gorgeously garbed and begemmed by her owner. However, she is never freed—this, for her "moral protection"—and her owner will find her a suitable husband. At age 19 Adélaïde-Hortense-Aimée Peyronnette marries Raoul-Ernest-Louis Desriviéres, age 29. A year later Youma participates in the baptism of their daughter, Lucille-Aimée-Francillette-Marie, called Mayotte. A year after that the fragile Aimée catches cold, develops pleurisy, and dies. The grieving husband leaves Mayotte with Madame Peyronnette, in Youma's care, and spends most of his time at his Anse-Marine plantation nearby. Hearn describes its lush scenery, the labor of the slaves, Madame Peyronnette's annual fête and her inspection of the black children's feet, a 60-foot native canoe, the priest Père Kerambrun's Sunday visits and prayer sessions, and especially the folktales of the elderly blacks. Youma rebukes Mayotte gently for saying she would rather be chocolate like Youma than cream-colored the way she is. Youma tells the child Dame Kélément's folktale of a serpent that could but does not bite a little girl and instead, transformed into a man, returns her to her mother. That night Mayotte, scared by the story, cries out for Youma. When she enters the bedroom, she steps on a serpent and bravely holds it down by her foot while it coils around her thigh. She screams for Gabriel, her master's commandeur of the black workers, to come. He does so, decapitates the snake, and praises Youma's courage, saying, "ou sévè," meaning that she is uncommonly, uncannily courageous. Desriviéres agrees and kisses her on the forehead.

As Youma's fame spreads and she begins to be addressed as Manzell Youma, Gabriel becomes her unspoken suitor, gives her rare fruits, makes a bench for her by the river, and once walks 30 kilometers to purchase gold earrings for her. He and Youma fall in love. But when Gabriel, hat in hand, asks Desriviéres for permission to marry Youma, he is told that this is impossible. Desriviéres, rather amused by it all, dutifully informs Madame Peyronnette in Saint Pierre. Alarmed, she orders Youma to return to the city in three days, without Mayotte. Long-suppressed fires of frustration rise in Youma, but her unaltered sense of responsibility fights back. Simultaneously she images her "Gabou" as "her man of all men, made for her by the Bon-Dié," prays for him to the Virgin, and listens when he tells her they can escape by boat to freedom on the British soil of Dominica—visible "over the sea to the northeast." Her feeling of joy at this prospect of liberty soon gives way to a sense of duty and a remembrance of happy times with Mayotte. Moreover, she promised Aimée never to abandon the child. How could she be false to kind, thoughtful Madame Peyronnette and Desriviéres? Gabriel appears briefly and tells her to meet him at the river. Youma ponders long and hard. Afternoon comes, and while she watches Mayotte at play in the surf, Gabriel approaches and tells her his plans. A family supply vessel has just been launched and will not return in time to follow their taking Desrivières's private boat that night. Youma interrupts to say she cannot go. His terse, sad pleas and criticism of her slave status are all in vain. Liberty means less to her than duty. Saying he will wait, and secretly stirred by "the great wind of Emancipation," he departs. That night Youma dreams that Douceline, her dead mother, takes her by the hand; but Mayotte calls; she and Youma are caught in serpentine tree-roots; Gabriel shouts it is a zombi he cannot cut.

Hearn interrupts the narrative flow to discuss slave unrest in 1848. The 150,000 blacks and half-breeds outnumber the 12,000 whites dangerously. A planter's jailing of a disobedient slave inspires a long-suppressed mob into revolting and shouting "Mort aux blancs!" Black port workers and black farm workers communicate mysteriously, in part by blowing seashells; cutlass stores are raided for weapons; whites gather in big houses and prepare for defensive action.

The Desrivières family holes up in their de Kersaint relatives' big residence, isolated near the Fort. Outside, a male voodoo inflames the black crowd with a potent mixture of serpent grease, crushed wasps, and alcohol. Fugitives within M. de Kersaint's home amuse themselves with anecdotes about the naivete of slaves. When Desrivières tells Youma to take Mayotte to his mother's place, she refuses. Hiding in the darkened house, the whites hear a torrent of insurrectionists begin storming it. When de Kersaint attempts to reason by calling the slaves his sons, a black leader jeers with justifiable sarcasm. Stones shatter windows and shutters. A battering ram breaks down the front door. Some think the French troops will surely come, but they have threatened mutiny if mustered. Kersaint's son shoots the leader and is bayoneted to death. As Desrivières hastens upstairs, he is shotgunned and dies. The house is set afire. Suddenly Youma appears in an upstairs window, with Mayotte, terrified, in her arms. She viciously rebukes the blacks—calling one "Ape"—for turning against their decent and generous masters. Gabriel muscles his way through the crowd, mounts a ladder, and offers rescue. When he refuses to include Mayotte, Youma backs away, says she will go to God with the girl, appears like an image of the Virgin Mary with child, and suddenly falls with the child into the whirling flames. The mob kills some white men seeking to flee. Two others, however, are able to escape. Firemen ignominiously ignore a call by church bells. As numerous fires flicker throughout the city, a cross is seen on a nearby mountain. Elsewhere a ship is bearing news that the Republic has ordered liberty now and universal suffrage soon for Martinique's slaves.

Hearn wrote most of *Youma* while he was living in Martinique (1887–1889) and finished it while living with his Philadelphia friend George Milbry Gould* (1889). Evidently his heroine's self-sacrificial act is based on fact. When in Japan, he wrote to his friend Mitchell McDonald (January 1898) that he had personally seen the ruins of the house in which the prototype of Youma burned to death, refusing the help of blacks and a ladder; further, that one of his favorite historians, Étienne Rufz de Lavison (1806–1884), describes a plantation girl who heroically held a serpent down with her foot. When Youma dreams about her mother, Hearn is recalling his dreams about his own mother and even adds a gratuitous autobiographical touch by saying that Youma's dream includes a "vision of the English island." In February 1890 Henry Mills Alden,* his editor, arranged for Harper & Brothers to pay Hearn $2,000 for serial rights to *Youma* (*Harper's New Monthly Magazine*, January, February, 1890; with one illustration by Howard Pyle [1853–1911]). In book form, *Youma* earned little money. A more realistic novel than *Chita*, it has fewer distracting passages of description and almost no similes or metaphors. Both were obviously built on Hearn's experiences in Martinique, which he expanded on when he wrote *Two Years in the French West Indies* (1890). Connections to its chapters titled "Porteuses," " 'Ti Canotié," and "Yé" can be traced to *Youma*. It is better balanced than *Chita*, the beginning of which is slow and the scenes in which leap as in a movie. The narrative flow of *Youma*, however, also suffers its share of interruptions, as when, for example, Hearn pauses to describe the pretty slaves' dress fashions, island fruits, and subjects of folktales. In addition, its chapters vary awkwardly in length: Chapter XIV, for example, is more than three times as long as Chapter X. Hearn betrays one old-fashioned attitude when he says that "only . . . slaves who had been mothers, who had fulfilled the natural destiny of woman," were permitted to become *das*. *Youma* has been reprinted a few times and was issued in England (1890).

Bibliography: Bisland; Cott; Kunst; Murray; Naoko Sugiyama, "Lafcadio Hearn's *Youma*: Self as Outsider," in Hirakawa, pp. 182–190.

Appendix

Volumes 1 and 2 of *The Writings of Lafcadio Hearn* (16 vols., 1922) contain a potpouri of 108 early essays, sketches, and redacted tales by Hearn. Because there is little unity in the way they were assembled, it seems best to make a separate entry in this "Companion" for each. Their titles, alphabetically arranged below, are placed under the rubrics in which they were published in *The Writings of Lafcadio Hearn*.

Creole Sketches (Vol. 1): "Attention! Azim!," "The Boarder's Reply," "The City of Dreams," "Complaint of Creole Boarding-House-Keeper," "The Creole Character," "A Creole Courtyard," "A Creole Journal," "A Creole Mystery," "Creole Servant Girls," "A Creole Song," "A Creole Type," "The Dawn of the Carnival," "La Douane," "Eleusis," "Furnished Rooms," "The Glamour of New Orleans," "The Grandissimes," "Home," "A Kentucky Colonel Renting Rooms," "Latin and Anglo-Saxon," "Louisiana People Not Gay," "Mexican Coins," "A Mexican's Gratitude," "Old-Fashioned Houses," "The Restless Boarder," "Some Positive Opinions," "A Visit to New Orleans," "Voices of Dawn," "An Ultra-Canal Talk," "A Visitor," "Why Crabs Are Boiled Alive."

Fantastics and Other Fancies (Vol. 2): "Aïda," "All in White," "L'Amour Après la Mort," "Aphrodite and the King's Prisoner," "At the Cemetery," "The Bird and the Girl," "The Black Cupid," "Les Coulisses," "A Dead Love," "The Devil's Carbuncle," "A Dream of Kites," "The Fountain of Gold," "The Ghostly Kiss," "The Gypsy's Story," "Hereditary Memories," "Hiouen-Thsang," " 'His Heart Is Old,' " "The Idyl of a French Snuff-Box," "A Kiss Fantastical," "A Legend," "The Little Red Kitten," "MDCCCLIII," "Metempsychosis," "The Name on the Stone," "The Night of All Saints," "The One Pill-Box," "The Post-Office," "A River Reverie," "Spring Phantoms," "The Stranger," "The Tale of a Fan," "The Undying One," "The Vision of the Dead Creole," "El Vómito," "When I Was a Flower," "Y Porque?"

Leaves from the Diary of an Impressionist (Vol. 1): Under "Floridian Reveries" are "A Name in the Plaza," "To the Fountain of Youth," "A Tropical Intermezzo," "Vultur

Aura." Under "Creole Papers" are "Creole Women in the French West Indies," "Quaint New Orleans and Its Inhabitants." Under "Arabesques" are "Arabian Women," "Rabyah's Last Ride."

Some Chinese Ghosts (Vol. 1): "The Legend of Tchi-Niu," "The Return of Yen-Tchin-King," "The Soul of the Great Bell," "The Story of Ming-Y," "The Tale of the Porcelain-God," "The Tradition of the Tea-Plant."

Stray Leaves from Strange Literature (Vol. 2): Under "Stray Leaves" are "The Bird Wife," "The Book of Thoth," "The Fountain Maiden." Under "Tales from Indian and Buddhist Literature" are "Bakawali," "The Brahman and His Brahmani," "The Corpse-Demon," "The Legend of the Monster Misfortune," "The Lion," "The Lotus of Faith," "The Making of Tilottama," "Natalika," "A Parable Buddhistic," "Pundari," "Yamaraja." Under "Runes from the Kalewala" are "The First Musician," "The Healing of Wainamoinen," "The Magical Words." Under "Stories of Moslem Lands" are "Boutimar, the Dove," "The King's Justice," "A Legend of Love," "The Son of a Robber." Under "Traditions Retold from the Talmud" are "The Dispute of the Halacha," "Esther's Choice," "A Legend of Rabba," "The Mockers," "Rabbi Yochanan Ben Zachai," "A Tradition of Titus."

Bibliography

Amenomori, Nobushige. "Lafcadio Hearn, the Man." *Atlantic Monthly* 96 (July 1905): 510–525.

Asatarō, Miyamori, trans. and ed. *Haiku Poems Ancient and Modern*. Tokyo: Mazuren, 1940.

Aston, W. G. *Shinto (The Way of the Gods)*. 1905. Reprint, Tokyo: Logos, 1968.

Bisland, Elizabeth. *The Life and Letters of Lafcadio Hearn*. 2 vols. Boston and New York: Houghton Mifflin, 1906.

Bloom, Clive, ed. *Gothic Horror: A Reader's Guide from Poe to King and Beyond*. New York: St. Martin's Press, 1998.

Bonner, Thomas, Jr., and Michael P. Dean. "Light in New Orleans: Change in the Writings of Mark Twain, Lafcadio Hearn and Walker Percy." *University of Mississippi Studies in English* 10 (1992): 213–226.

Brooks, Van Wyck. "Lafcadio Hearn in Japan." In *The Confident Years, 1885–1915*, 232–246. New York: E. P. Dutton, 1955.

Clary, William. "Japan: The Warnings and Prophecies of Lafcadio Hearn." *Claremont Oriental Studies* 5 (April 1943): 1–17.

Cott, Jonathan. *Wandering Ghost: The Odyssey of Lafcadio Hearn*. New York: Alfred A. Knopf, 1991.

Cowley, Malcolm. "Lafcadio Hearn." Introduction to *The Selected Writings of Lafcadio Hearn*, edited by Henry Goodman. New York: Citadel Press, 1949.

Davis, Hadland F. *Myths & Legends of Japan*. London: George G. Harrap, 1917.

Dawson, Carl. *Lafcadio Hearn and the Vision of Japan*. Baltimore and London: Johns Hopkins University Press, 1992.

Dorson, Richard M. *Folk Legends of Japan*. Rutland, Vt., and Tokyo: Charles E. Tuttle, 1962.

Frost, O. W. *Young Hearn*. Tokyo: Hokuseido, 1958.

Gould, George M. *Concerning Lafcadio Hearn*. London: T. Fisher Unwin, 1908.

Hayley, Barbara. *Lafcadio Hearn, William Butler Yeats, and Japan*. Gerrards Cross, Bucks: U.K. Colin Smythe, 1988.

Hirakawa, Sukehiro, ed. *Rediscovering Lafcadio Hearn: Japanese Legends, Life & Culture*. Folkestone, Kent, UK: Global Oriental, 1997.

Hulvey-Roberts, Marie, ed. *The Handbook to Gothic Literature*. New York: New York University Press, 1998.

Hylland, Marilyn Gail. "Ghost/Goblins, Dreams, and the Divinity of Art: Three Major Themes of Dimension. A Study of Lafcadio Hearn's Japanese Period." Ph.D. diss., Southern Illinois University, 1972.

Janeira, Armando Martins. *Japanese and Western Literature: A Companion Study*. Rutland, Vt., and Tokyo: Charles E. Tuttle, 1970.

Kirkwood, Kenneth. *Unfamiliar Lafcadio Hearn*. Tokyo: Hokuseido, 1935.

Kleine-Kreutzmann, Alfred. "The Development of the Lafcadio Hearn Collection at the Public Library of Cincinnati and Hamilton County." *Lafcadio Hearn Journal* 1 (Spring 1991): 7–8.

Kunst, Arthur E. *Lafcadio Hearn*. New York: Twayne, 1969.

Lawless, Ray McKinley. *Lafcadio Hearn: Critic of American Life and Letters*. Chicago: University of Chicago Press, 1942.

Lewis, Oscar. *Hearn and His Biographers: A Record of a Literary Controversy . . .* San Francisco: Westgate, 1930.

McNeil, W. K. "Lafcadio Hearn, American Folklorist." *Journal of American Folklore* 91 (October–December 1978): 947–967.

McWilliams, Vera Seeley. *Lafcadio Hearn*. Boston: Houghton Mifflin, 1946.

Metzinger, Sylvia Verdun. "The Development of the Lafcadio Hearn Collection at the Howard-Tilton Memorial Library, Tulane University." *Lafcadio Hearn Journal* 1 (Spring 1991): 5–6.

Mims, Edwin. "The Letters of Lafcadio Hearn." *South Atlantic Quarterly* 10 (April 1911): 149–158.

Miner, Earl, Hiroko Odagiri, and Robert E. Morrell. *The Princeton Companion to Classical Japanese Literature*. Princeton, N.J.: Princeton University Press, 1985.

Monahan, Michael. "Lafcadio Hearn: A French Estimate." *Forum* 49 (March 1913):356–366.

More, Paul Elmer. "Lafcadio Hearn." In *Selected Shelburne Essays*, 25–46. New York: Oxford University Press, 1935.

Murray, Paul. *A Fantastic Journey: The Life and Literature of Lafcadio Hearn*. Ann Arbor: University of Michigan Press, 1993.

Ono, Setsuko. "A Western Image of Japan: What Did the West See through the Eyes of Loti and Hearn?" Ph.D. diss., University of Geneva, 1972.

Parsons, C.O. "Steamboating as Seen by Passengers and River Men: 1875–1884." *Mississippi Quarterly* 24 (Winter 1970–1971): 19–34.

Perkins, P. D., and Iona Perkins. *Lafcadio Hearn: A Bibliography of His Writings*. Introduction by Sanki Ichikawa. 1934. Reprint, New York: Burt Franklin, 1968.

Pulvers, Roger. "Lafcadio Hearn: Interpreter of Two Disparate Worlds." *Japan Times*, January 19, 2000.

Putzar, Edward D. *Japanese Literature: A Historical Outline*. Tucson: University of Arizona Press, 1973.

Quinn, Frederick. *The French Overseas Empire*. Westport, Conn.: Praeger, 2000.

Rexroth, Kenneth. *One Hundred Poems from the Japanese*. New York: New Directions, 1964.

Ronan, Sean G., and Toki Koizumi. *Lafcadio Hearn (Koizumi Yakumo): His Life, Work and Background*. Dublin: Ireland Japan Association, 1991.

Rosenstone, Robert A. *Mirror in the Shrine: American Encounters with Meiji Japan*. Cambridge, Mass.: Harvard University Press, 1988.

Shively, Donald H., ed. *Tradition and Modernization in Japanese Culture*. Princeton, N.J.: Princeton University Press, 1971.

Snell, George. "Poe Redivivus." *Arizona Quarterly* 1 (Summer 1945): 49–57.

Stempel, Daniel. "Lafcadio Hearn: Interpreter of Japan." *American Literature* 20 (March 1948): 1–19.

Stevenson, Elizabeth. *The Grass Lark: A Study of Lafcadio Hearn*. New Brunswick, N.J., and London: Transaction, 1999.

Temple, Jean. *Blue Ghost: A Study of Lafcadio Hearn*. New York: Jonathan Cape, 1931.

Thomas, Edward. *Lafcadio Hearn*. Boston: Houghton Mifflin, 1912.

Tinker, Edward Larocque. *Creole City: Its Past and Its People*. New York: Longmans, Green, 1953.

———. *Lafcadio Hearn's American Days*. New York: Dodd, Mead, 1924.

Today's Japan 4 (January 1959). "Lafcadio Hearn Issue."

Tuttle, Allen Edmond. "Lafcadio Hearn and Herbert Spencer." Ph.D. diss., Northwestern University, 1950.

Webb, Kathleen M. *Lafcadio Hearn and His German Critics: An Examination of His Appeal*. New York: Peter Lang, 1984.

Yu, Beongcheon. *An Ape of Gods: The Art and Thought of Lafcadio Hearn*. Detroit: Wayne State University Press, 1964.

Zenimoto, Kenji. *A General Catalogue of Hearn Collections in Japan and Overseas*. Matsue: Hearn Society, 1991.

Index

About the Author

ROBERT L. GALE is Professor Emeritus of English at the University of Pittsburgh. His most recent books include *An Ambrose Bierce Companion* (2001), *A Dashiell Hammett Companion* (2000), *A Sarah Orne Jewett Companion* (1999), and *An F. Scott Fitzgerald Encyclopedia* (1998), all available from Greenwood Press.